THE COURTS OF THE ITALIAN RENAISSANCE

Sergio Bertelli, Franco Cardini,
Elvira Garbero Zorzi

THE COURTS OF THE ITALIAN RENAISSANCE

contributing authors: Elisa Acanfora, Giuliana Chesne
Dauphiné Griffo, Marcello Fantoni, Ileana Florescu,
Daniela Mignani Galli

Facts On File Publications
New York, New York • Oxford, England

The sections History of a dynasty (page 259) and Some of the ruling families of Renaissance Italy (page 262) are by Caterina Bertelli

Opposite frontispiece: façade of the ducal palace at Mantua (detail)

First published in the United States in 1986
by Facts on File Publications
First published in Italy in 1985 under the title
Le Corti Italiane del Rinascimento
by Arnoldo Mondadori Editore S.p.A., Milan

Translated from the Italian
by Mary Fitton and Geoffrey Culverwell

Library of Congress Cataloging-in-Publication Data

Bertelli, Sergio.
The courts of the Italian Renaissance.

Translation of: Le corti italiane del Rinascimento.
Bibliography: p.
Includes index.
1. Italy—History—15th century. 2. Italy—History—16th century. 3. Italy—Court and courtiers.
I. Cardini, Franco. II. Garbero Zorzi, Elvira.
III. Title
DG537.B4713 1986 945'.05 86-13583
ISBN 0-8160-1540-6

Printed and bound in Italy by Arnoldo Mondadori Editore, Verona

10 9 8 7 6 5 4 3 2 1

Contents

Authors

d.m.g.: Daniela Magnani Galli; e.a.: Elisa Acanfora; e.g.z.: Elvira Garbero Zorzi; f.c.: Franco Cardini; g.c.d.g.: Giuliana Chesne Dauphiné Griffo; i.f.: Ileana Florescu; m.f.: Marcello Fantoni; s.b.: Sergio Bertelli

The Courtly Universe

The Este palace of Schifanoia, the earliest important Renaissance building at Ferrara, was intended for state receptions and amusements. The fresco series in its largest room, the Sala dei Mesi, painted in the second half of the fifteenth century by Francesco Cossa and the Ferrarese school, is one of the most splendid in the secular art of that time. Opposite: a detail from the Triumph of Venus, in the "April" section.

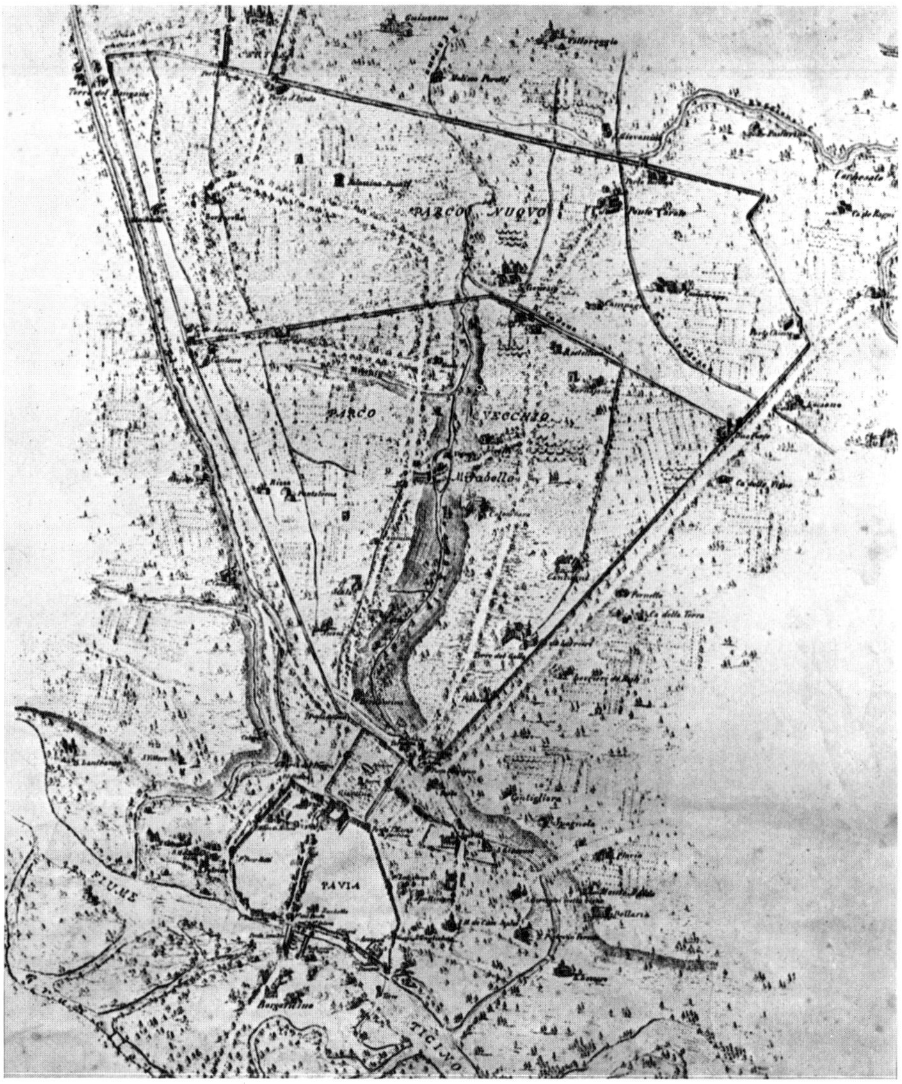

Nineteenth-century map showing the city and environs of Pavia. The Visconti castle was well situated to dominate the town, and to the north of its huge park lay the famous certosa, *or Carthusian monastery, a great complex of religious buildings closely linked with the Visconti and Sforza families.*

The court defined

In his *Iconologia*, published in 1603, Cesare Ripa defined a court as "a company of well-bred men in the service of a distinguished superior." In 1587, however, the lexicographer Tommaso Garzoni da Bagnacavallo, dedicating his *Piazza universale di tutte le professioni del mondo* to Alfonso d'Este, Duke of Ferrara, considered that courts in his time had grown depraved, "the haunt of wicked foxes and the most abject hangers-on, schools of corruption and dens of iniquity." The court, he added, is a princely household where everything is *corto* – curtailed, or in short supply – and transient indeed, "save this unfailing malice and iniquity." The theme recurs in sixteenth- and seventeenth-century works on court life – books such as the famous *Menosprecio del corte* of 1539, by the Spanish bishop Antonio de Guevara – but goes back to the mid fifteenth century at least, and a letter of Aeneas Sylvius Piccolomini to the German humanist Johann Eich, written in 1444 and first printed in 1473, itself based on Lucian's *De mercede conductis potentium familiaribus*.

In his handbook on a Roman court, *Del governo della corte d'un Signore di Roma* (1543), the Florentine grammarian Francesco Priscianese imagines the ideal establishment as numbering "107, with a stable of 40 horses; which I take to be a very fitting number, neither too many nor too few." And, oddly enough, the "family" or household of Cardinal Alessandro Bichi, who died in 1657, is described in Francesco Liberati's *Il perfetto Maestro di casa*, of 1558, as being exactly 109 strong, counting the cardinal, his major-domo, comptroller, master of the household, master of the horse, and the *auditore*, in charge of legal affairs.

These palace employments indicate the main functions of a court of whatever size: internal organization of the palace, administration of revenue, and the application of justice in what were known as "lesser causes" – that is, actions brought between fellow subordinates of the *signore* or between them and outsiders. In other words, there is a nucleus of magistrates and officials – their numbers varying in accordance with the size of the estate and revenues in

Right: entrance to the fourteenth-century Visconti castle at Pavia.
Below, right: inner courtyard, showing the spacious portico, surmounted by an elegant loggia with four-arched windows.
Opposite, below: fresco by an unknown Veronese artist in the guard room of the castle at Avio. This castle, near Verona, is an example of military architecture combined with a medieval princely residence.

question – with whose presence the "company of well-bred men" united in the service of the distinguished lord becomes a court. It is they, supplemented by the staffs of the different offices and chanceries, by servants and bodyguard, who perform the primary and essential duty of any lordship, or government.

The court, in this sense, may be seen as a microcosm of the state, and as carrying out all the chief business of the state. It ranges from the *concistorium* or *consilium* at the highest level, advising the ruler in all his undertakings (first and foremost, in the direction of justice, it acts as a supreme tribunal with membership often including his closest relations, sons or brothers, and his chief vassals), to the various chanceries and departments for finance and administration.

Yet there are aspects in which the court differs from the state. It is, for one thing, the ruler's actual, physical home, where he lives with those who serve and guard him. Since it is a centrifugal structure, revolving about the *dominus*, the ruler's household and its departments must be in his place of residence, and his place of residence distinct from the lands he rules. The palace or castle – *palatium*, *castrum* or *castellum* – is, moreover, not only his residence and seat of administration and justice. It is also the seat of the *curia*, and the abode of functionaries, law-officers, courtiers, pages, servants and soldiers, each with a direct personal link to him, in the still feudal chain. These people are not employed; they receive no salary. They are "bodies" at the lord's disposal and where he lives they serve him, surrounding him as bees surround the queen in a hive.

The center of the whole system is his bedchamber, or *cubiculum*. On the pattern of Weber's "charismatic leader" he exercises power through the court-nucleus, and position in the court hierarchy depends on proximity to the *cubiculum*. Indeed, in some archaic societies, as at the *bamoum*, or royal court of the Cameroons in the eighteenth and nineteenth centuries, the women – and the harem of King Njoya of the Cameroons numbered some 1,200 – the pages and senior officials who saw the king naked (who, in the literal phrase, "surprised the husband of the country") were

immediately in a special category. They were "bodies of the king" in the sense of being his own substance. In medieval Europe, on the other hand, the jurist Accursus, commentating on the laws of Justinian, says that "it is unlawful that anyone who wishes should have access to the prince."

In monogamous societies the presence of a legitimate consort led naturally to duplication of the male side of the organization, and the entire court, governmental departments excepted, was divided into twin branches, male and female. Vespasiano da Bisticci, who sold manuscripts in Florence, relates that Federico da Montefeltro "kept his daughters in a separate part of the house, attended by many noblewomen of respectable age and irreproachable conduct; and to these apartments there was no admittance . . . When he visited his daughters, all those accompanying him were left outside the door." At Ferrara, according to an inventory of 1436, there was even separate accommodation for those of differing age and status, with lodgings reserved for girls, "elderly ladies" and widows. Leon Battista Alberti, in Book v of his treatise *De re aedificatoria*, says that "the apartments of the prince's wife should be separated from those of her husband, save for the innermost, shared room which contains the matrimonial bed," and that there should be bedrooms provided for "married ladies, young girls and guests."

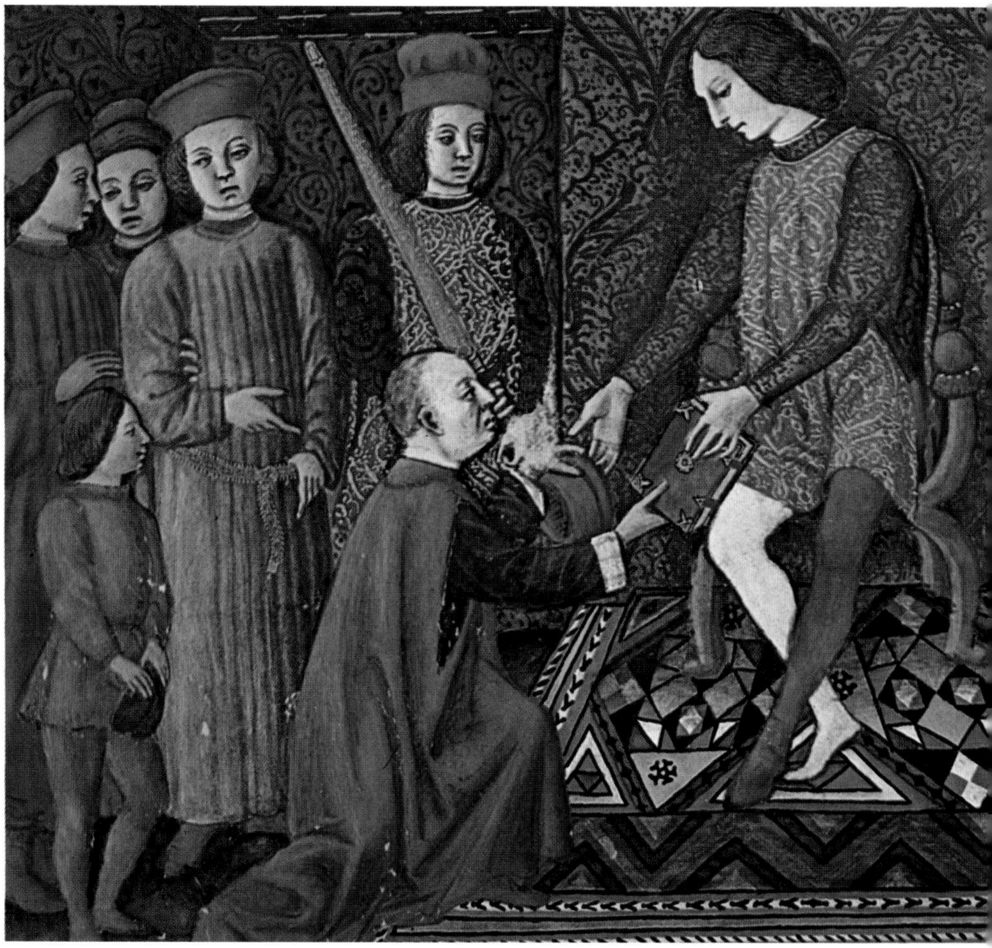

Duke Galeazzo Maria Sforza with members of his court. Illumination from a fifteenth-century manuscript in the Bibliothèque Nationale, Paris.

On the womens' side there was the same direct and personal relationship with the mistress, the *domina*, as that of the men with the *dominus*. At Mantua in 1587 the duke had about him 12 secretaries and counsellors, 6 gentlemen to serve his table, 31 pages, 10 valets and 17 bedchamber attendants; while the duchess had 25 ladies, 7 household officers, 7 grooms and 3 maids. If mistresses of the prince lived at court their situation was clandestine and inferior and they did not enjoy the status they were accorded in societies where polygamy was accepted.

Nevertheless, more than one prince of Renaissance Italy made very public his devotion to a lady not his wife, and first and foremost is Sigismondo Pandolfo Malatesta, Lord of Rimini. In 1445, while married to his second

wife Polissena, a natural daughter of Francesco Sforza, he took as his mistress the poetess Isotta degli Atti, by whom he had several children. He eventually married her, though not until ten years after Polissena's death, in about 1459. In 1450, when he commissioned Alberti and Matteo de' Pasti to alter the thirteenth-century church of San Francesco into a funerary chapel, he thought neither of Polissena nor of his first wife, Ginevra d'Este. It was his love for Isotta he wished to enshrine, sacriligeously requiring a chapel to be dedicated to her, liberally bedecked, on pilaster and balustrade, with their entwined initials.

A few years later frescoes in the Camera d'Oro, or Golden Room, at the castle of Torrechiara offer similar homage from Pier Maria Rossi ("*pater patriae* and founder of Parma's freedom," as he liked to style himself) to Bianca Pellegrini. He had met this lady, wife of Melchiorre d'Arluno, a nobleman from

Caterina Cornaro welcomed at Asolo such distinguished men as Pietro Bembo, who took her court as setting for his Asolani. *Painting by the school of Giorgione.*

Below: a procession at the Este court. Fifteenth-century painting in the Accademia Carrara, Bergamo.

THE SACRED PRECINCT

"The theory of the ruler's divinity," as is explained later (see p. 20), "set the court yet further apart, as a sacred precinct." The first example of such a precinct is the *New Rome* founded by Constantine on the site of the Greek colony of Byzantium. On the shore, within a protecting wall that cut off the triangle of land between the Sea of Marmara and the Golden Horn, the emperor raised palace, forum, senate house, and the earliest Santa Sophia. He enlarged the hippodrome and embellished the ancient acropolis (where the Turks would build Topkapi Sarai). In this imperial quarter (see fig 1: imaginary reconstruction) the rulers of the Eastern Roman Empire established a court etiquette that was handed down to the Western papacy.

From the fourth century until 1420 the Roman curia, save for the periods spent at Viterbo (1266–81) and Avignon (1305–77), occupied the site where once the patrician Plautii Laterani had had their palaces, near the Porta Asinaria. Under Sixtus II, in the fifth century, was built the five-aisled basilica dedicated originally to the Redeemer, later to St John the Baptist and St John the Evangelist: the church which suffered destructions, reconstructions and restorations, is now St John Lateran. A great banqueting hall, the Triclinium, was added by Leo III in the eighth century, and by the ninth century the papal court had grown to a small township (2).

It was in the ninth century that Leo IV built walls to defend the Constantinian basilica of St Peter, on the west bank of the Tiber, where the saint had been crucified and buried; walls enclosing what was later known as the Leonine City. In the mid fifteenth century Nicholas V decided to enlarge the fourteenth century palace of Nicholas III, adjacent to St Peter's; and Innocent VIII, who at the end of the century added the Belvedere as a pleasure-villa, began a long process of building which was to transform the Vatican into a palace-citadel (5).

In such cultural climates as these a court would tend to isolation within the "sacred precinct" carved out of, or raised apart from, its urban

1

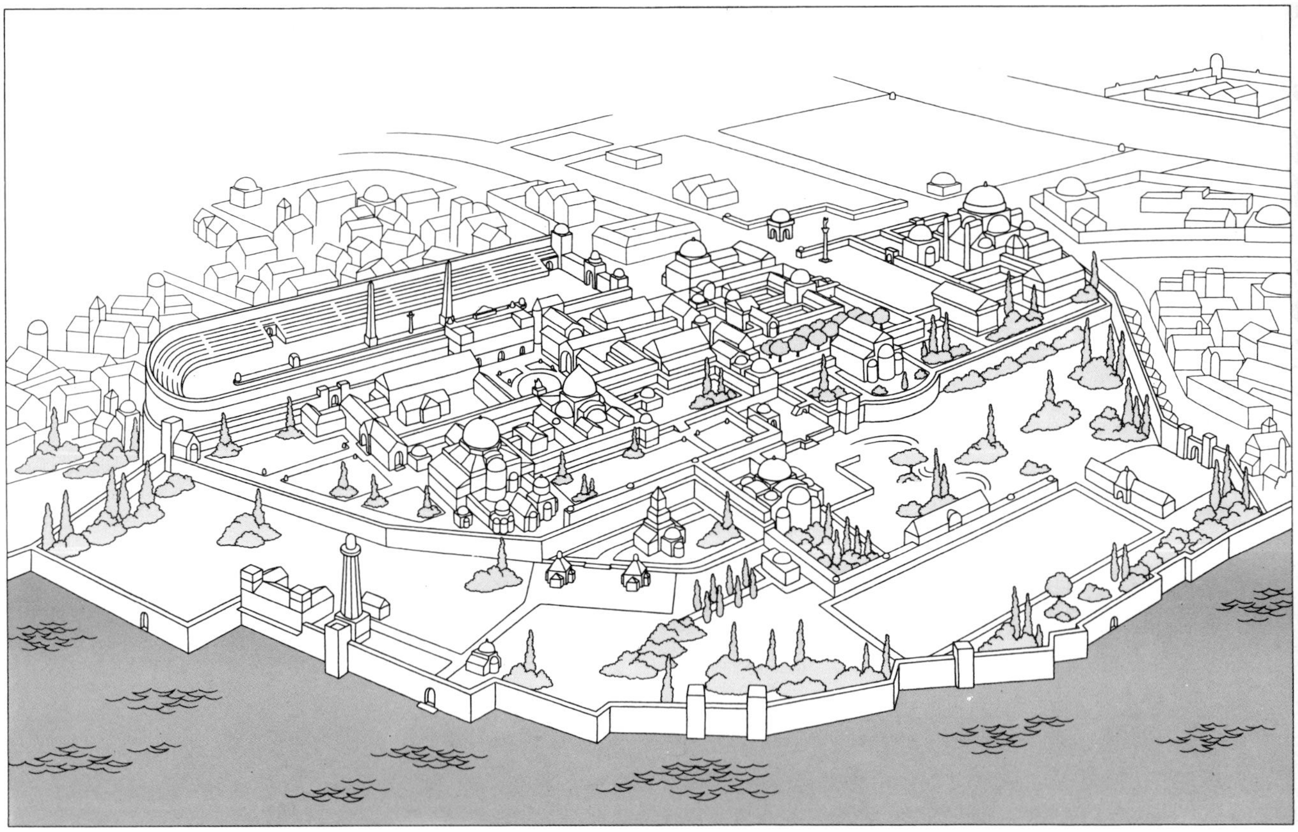

2

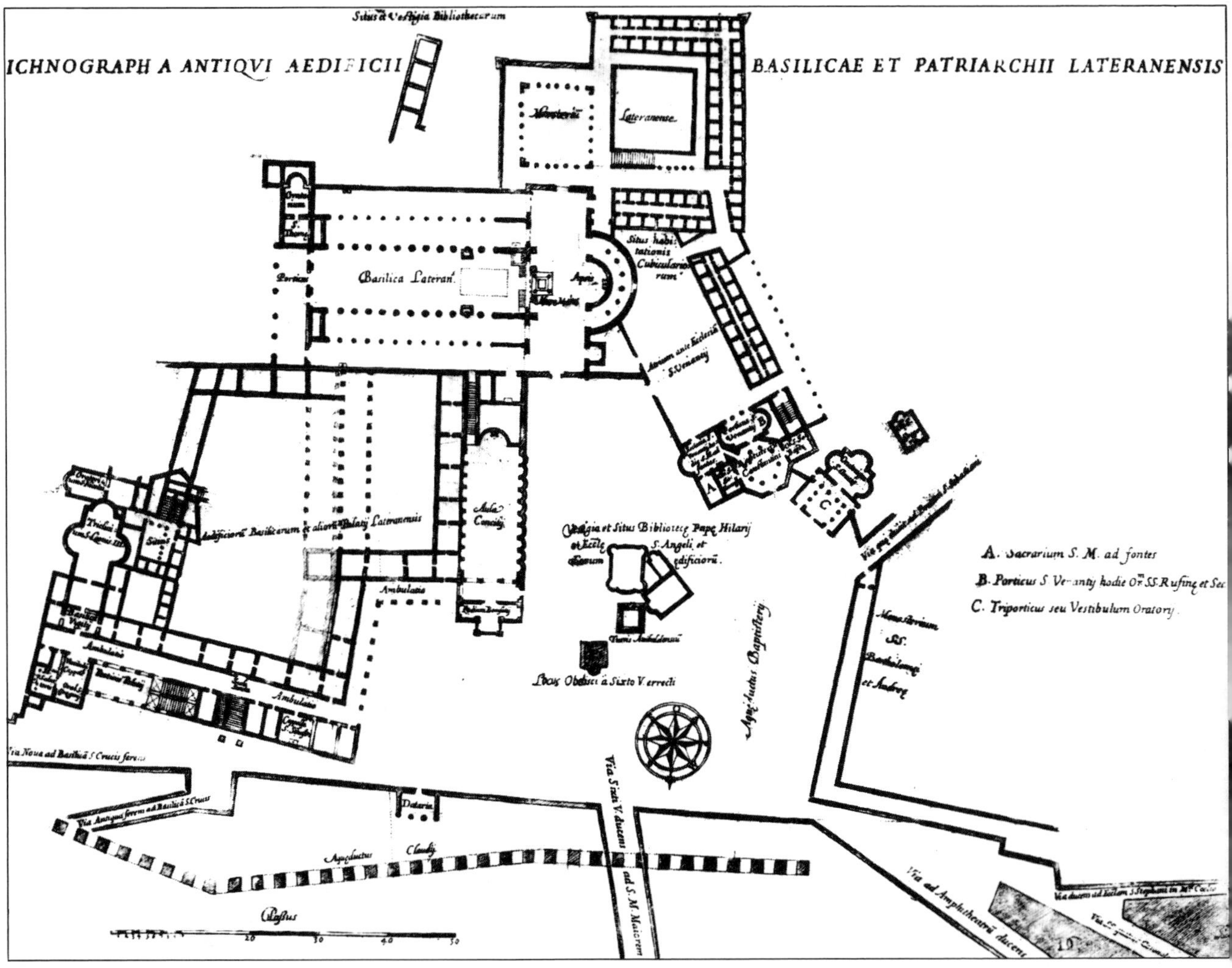

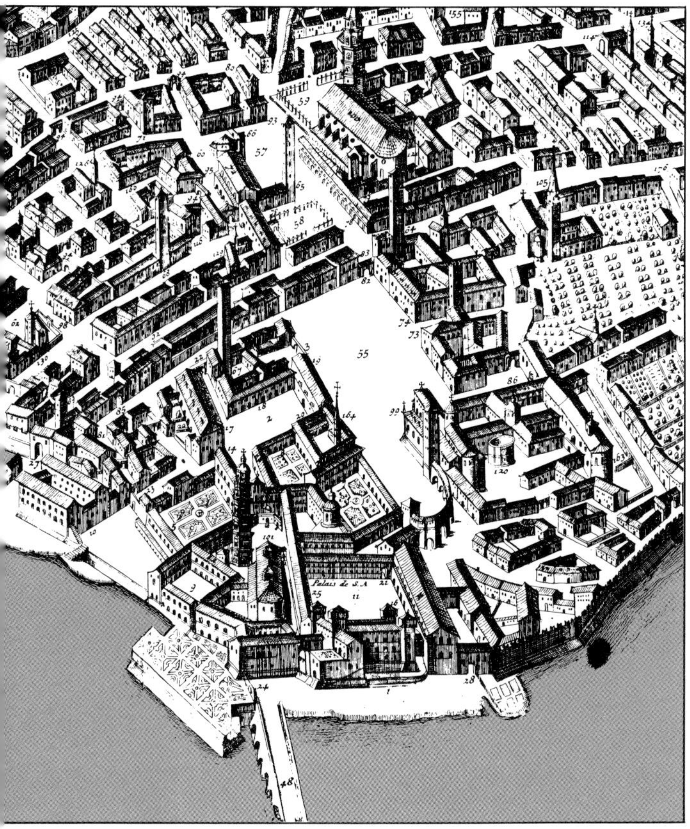

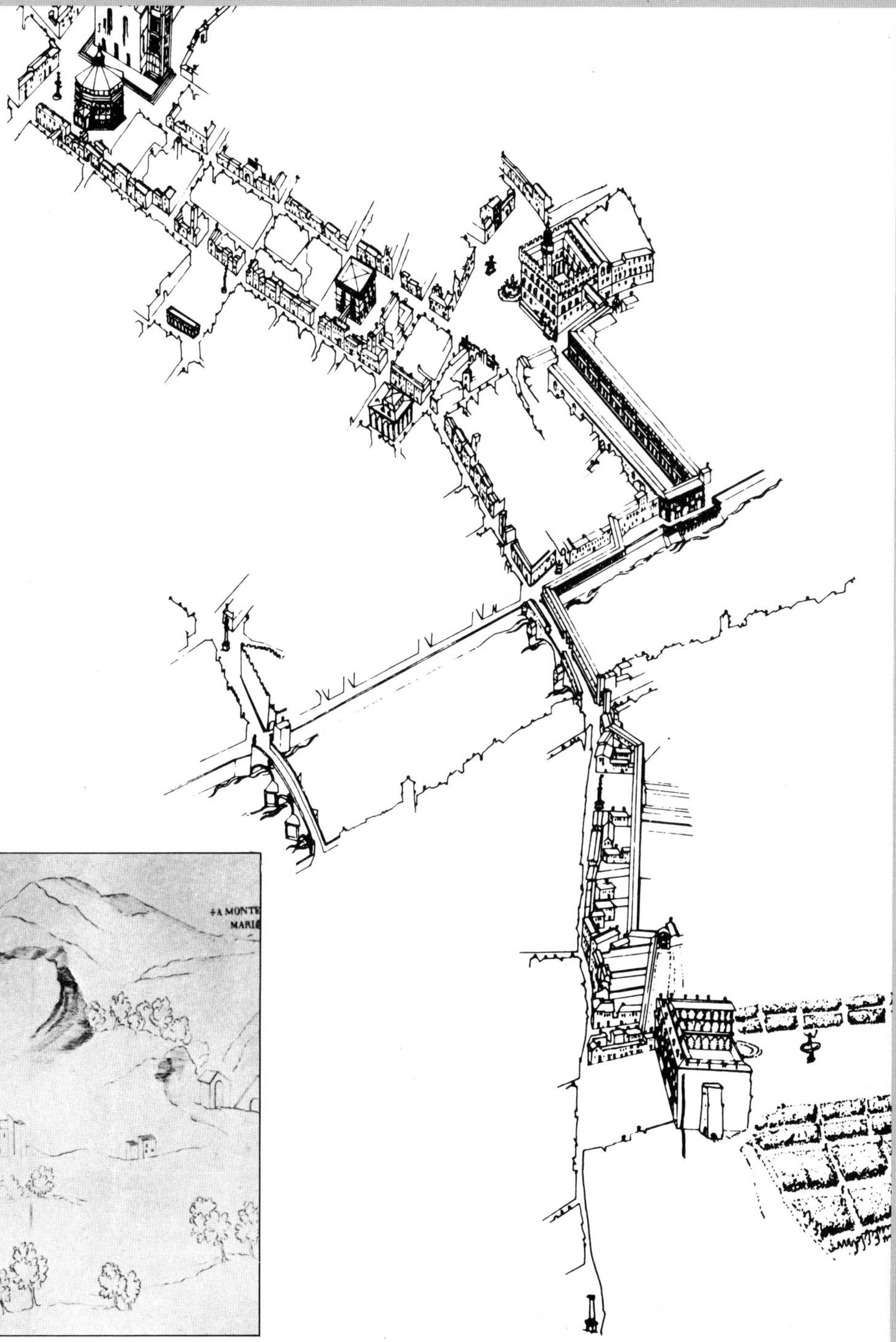

surroundings. The huge Gonzaga fortress in the old plan of Mantua (3) stands by the shallow waters of the river Mincio, as the imperial palaces of Constantinople stood beside the sea. It comprises the ducal palace, or Corte Vecchia, the fourteenth-fifteenth century Castello, and the Corte Nova – 500 rooms in 14,000 square meters of building on a setting of more than twice that area. In Florence Cosimo, first grand duke of Tuscany, adopted the Palazzo della Signoria, traditional seat of government, as his own residence, but when the Uffizi was built between the palace and the river, and the old palace and Uffizi were linked, by Vasari's corridor, to the second grand-ducal residence of the Pitti (designed by Brunelleschi and extended by Ammannati and others), the result was a kind of "sacred precinct" within the town but at the same time separated from it (4). The princes of Savoy followed the same example in Turin, where their palace in one corner of the city was joined, by corridors no longer existent, to Palazzo Madama, as may be seen in Borgonio's view, *Augustae Taurinorum prospectus (6).*

Como, at the Sforza court, fallen passionately in love with her and installed her, not at his own court with the legal *domina*, his wife Antonia Torelli in the castle of San Secondo, but at Torrechiara. (He was also to give her another of his family fortresses, Roccabianca). Antonia was still alive when, in 1462, Torrechiara was readied for habitation and in the *cubiculum* Benedetto Bembo painted a truly pilgrim Bianca seeking her lover in every nook and cranny of his dominions. On the hills and in the plains, from the Val Parma to the Val di Toro, she visits every fief and almost every castle and, finding him at last, knights him and girds him with a sword; they are the room's commanding figures, he in a cuirass, she in a rich robe. These frescoes are among the earliest of the rare depictions of the real lands and castles of a feudal estate. (At Rimini Sigismondo Malatesta, kneeling in a fresco before his patron saint, had exhibited only the castle he lived in, painted in a tondo of the frame). The Camera d'Oro, like the Tempio Malatestiano, is bestrewn with interlaced monograms – here the letters PMB, for Pier Maria and Bianca – as well as with interlaced hearts bearing Rossi's initials, PMR.

Federico Gonzaga was another who, for dynastic reasons, could not marry his mistress Isabella Boschetta. In his Palazzo del Te at Mantua the Psyche frescoes may be interpreted in two ways: as following the *Commentary on Apuleius* of the Bolognese humanist Filippo Beroaldo (1500) which, through the legend, traces the soul's *ascensio* from inanimate matter to immortality; or as the tale of Cupid (Federico), his love for Psyche (Isabella) thwarted by his jealous mother (Isabella d'Este). Giulio Romano's portrayal of Federico, also in the Sala di Psiche, as a naked Triton-Jupiter about to copulate with an Olympia whose features are those of Isabella Boschetta, adds further symbolism, that of the prince as perpetuator of his race.

We should remember that a ruler's natural children were welcomed and reared with the legitimate offspring in most medieval and Renaissance courts, and that there were many requests to the Church for legitimization. Niccolò III of Ferrara had 11 bastard sons and 7 bastard daughters, as well as twins by his second wife Parisina Malatesta and two boys by his third, Ricciarda di Saluzzo. The frequent presence of these illegitimate broods suggests that the ruler saw himself very much as *pater patriae*, and the procreative function may account for the importance of the scepter, among other conveniently vertical symbols of power. In the same context may be understood the ancient feudal *jus primae noctis*, the ritual deflowering of a subject's wife by the ruler, so that the malign influences associated with a woman's blood are deflected to the prince who is, by virtue of his sovereignty, immune.

However, the bastards were not purebred and so could not marry purebred princes and princesses. They had to "marry down," with resultant social decline for either sex. Illegitimate children of pope or emperor could marry only the children of the greatest imperial or papal vassals, as Lucrezia Borgia was married to Alfonso d'Este, or Margaret of Austria to Alessandro de' Medici. Such vassals could marry their own illegitimate children with none but children of their own vassals, and so on down the feudal scale. This explains St Simon's scandalized reaction when Louis XVI "shamelessly" married his bastards to real princes and princesses and mingled the royal blood of France with *la boue infecte du double adultère*.

Alcove of Federico da Montefeltro, Duke of Urbino. The ruler's bedroom, the cubiculum, *was the actual and figurative center of the palace, where his authority was exercised through attendant officials, magistrates, courtiers, pages and soldiers; the degree of physical nearness to the duke's bedroom corresponded to their place in this court hierarchy. Opposite: marquetry figure (Mars or Apollo) from the door of the Sala degli Angeli, leading into the duke's bedroom in the palace of Urbino.*

F
E
C

The courtly culture, drawing largely on pagan mythology, magnified the prince's prestige and invested him with almost sacred qualities. Thus, Andrea Doria had himself portrayed by Bronzino as Neptune, god of the sea. Pinacoteca di Brera, Milan.

For, as the Ferrarese Count Annibale Romei puts it in one of his *Discorsi* of 1586, that on Nobility, "marriage, inessential to procreation . . . is nevertheless required for the making of a nobleman, whose forebears must be of good repute and free from sin. The bastard cannot deny that his parents are stained with the sin of lust, as are all who come together in defiance of the laws of decency . . . He must, therefore, acknowledge that he is not perfectly noble but by that hair's breadth misses true nobility . . . nor will legitimization, though admitting him to riches, make him noble."

The love-affair at court

The custom among the nobility of sending their children to serve lord or lady in some princely household meant, for those children, escape from family control into a very different existence where, living in large groups within the complicated structure of a court, they might also evade the control of their seniors. Their contemporaries were at home, under the watchful gaze of parents, kin and friends – all of whom would be equally involved in the choice of marriage partners for them – while pages and maids-in-waiting had many improved opportunities for acquaintance. Court life was, indeed, their sole taste of freedom before returning to their families, though not a few marriages were arranged at court, under the tutelage of lord and lady. The *Ordini et offitii*, the rule-book of the court of Urbino in 1511 urges the supreme duty of overseeing juvenile morals, "as befits the prince's honour and the trust of those who have confided their children to his service." The master of the pages is never to let a page go anywhere alone. Pages must walk two-and-two and "in case of suspicion are to be followed, in order that they may be reported and punished." From Pavia on 15 September 1514 Isabella d'Este, Marchioness of Mantua, hastens to remind her son of the proprieties. "We have sent the girls to Mantua, and should be pleased if you would visit them now and then. But let the gentlemen you take with you be sober and decent. None of your rogues and rascals, for I don't want them near my girls."

The segregation by sex and age of course included precautions against homosexual practices. The pages at Urbino were not to sleep with the valets. They were to have separate mattresses and sleep alone; "to avoid all occasion of unseemly behaviour."

But neither segregation nor the supervision of elders could prevent meetings and contacts, or the development of attachments which could not have developed elsewhere, or which would have been more easily obstructed. Moreover these boys and girls were brought up in a literary and social climate where chivalric and troubadour tradition positively favoured dalliance. They would know the *Documenti d'amore* of Francesco da Barberino (1309), the tale of Tristan and Isolde, the tragedy of Paolo and Francesca immortalized in the *Divina commedia*; in a famous novella by Bandello they would find another tragedy, that of Parisina Malatesta, married at 13 to the old Marquis Niccolò d'Este and in love with her stepson Ugo. These, certainly, were among the favourites: tales of death and tales of love, set at the court and written primarily for the court to read.

Right: Il giardino delle arti, *or* Allegoria della corte di Isabella, *by Lorenzo Costa. Isabella d'Este, wife of Francesco Gonzaga, marquis of Mantua, was a learned and cultivated woman, who shared the task of government and gathered around her a circle of famous artists and writers – men such as Baldassare Castiglione, Matteo Bandello, Ariosto and Titian. This picture, painted for her* studiolo, *is an obvious allegory of her court. Musée du Louvre, Paris.*
Below: mythological symbolism is also present in Giulio Romano's fresco in the Palazzo del Te at Mantua, showing Federico Gonzaga (Isabella's son) as Jupiter in the guise of a Triton, about to embrace Olympia. Olympia is a portrait of Isabella Boschetti, the mistress whom, for dynastic reasons, he could not marry. The fresco alludes, too, to the prince's love of women and to the princely role of procreation.

A culture apart

The sixteenth-century court, shielded from the outside world, rigidly organized within by rules designed to preserve proper social distances (and to safeguard those between individuals), produced a private culture of its own, for which one needed the right interpretative key. There were many books of hieroglyphs in which this could be sought. Piero Valeriano, dedicating his *Hieroglyphica* to Cosimo de' Medici in 1556, compares these abstruse emblems to the parables of Christ. Both are concealed beneath a veil, "and the vulgar cannot easily penetrate the mysteries." Andrea Alciati's *Emblematum liber* of 1531 was another highly successful work of the same kind.

The recondite significance of the *mysteria* goes back to the humanism of Marsilio Ficino and the discovery and translation of the *Codex hermeticum* in 1463. The loftiest example of this "secret" culture is perhaps the allegory of the Three Graces in Botticelli's *Primavera*, where Amor-Anima, borne on the breath of Zephyr, permeates the earth, to attain the heavens indicated by Mercury *mystagogus* (or Hermes), who opens a path through the clouds with his magical staff. It is a culture which draws lavishly on pagan mythology and on Boccaccio's *De genealogia deorum* for the wide-ranging symbolism that illustrates and cloaks its meanings. The prince himself – Andrea Doria in the guise of Neptune, Federico Gonzaga in that of Triton – can be shown naked and in a godly guise.

In Botticelli's Adoration of the Magi *the entire Medici family is assembled, as upon a Christian Olympus. On the left stands Lorenzo the Magnificent; Cosimo the Elder kneels before the Madonna, and the central figure with his back to us is Piero the Gouty.*

The means of depiction, in a way, "marries" the object depicted. The court projects an image of itself as mysterious and inaccessible; its power is enhanced by this double aim of seeming both very learned and very glorious. The spaces, external and internal, in which the Renaissance court is situated, are the visible measure of its sacred quality; its ideal separateness is accentuated by physical separation from the town in which it stands. Versailles, indeed, was built miles from the city, in a forest, surrounded by great ponds and pools of water – an element difficult to cross – like the moats of the Middle Ages; it could be reached only by the long *allées*, which emphasized how far away it was. And in the squares before the palaces there began to appear equestrian statues – statues of the princes derived from the statue of the philosopher-emperor, Marcus Aurelius. The first was that of Niccolò III at Ferrara. Then, in Verona, the Scaliger tombs bristled with warrior-figures, out in the open spaces of the city.

In state rooms the exploits and "glories" of the princely house would be depicted in vast fresco-cycles. Scaliger portraits in the fourteenth-century hall of the palace in Verona had been mere genealogical records; later fresco-cycles told more, and in greater detail. At Mantua, in the Sala degli Sposi, Mantegna seems to raise a huge painted curtain on the ducal family and leads the spectator into their strenuous, whirling world, where courtiers and attendants come endlessly up the vast staircase.

When, at the Counter-Reformation, the emblem-language once used by the Neoplatonists, with their syncretistic ideas, was adopted by the more orthodox Jesuits, there was still a private, courtly culture. Now, however, its expression was far removed from paganism. The ladies of one of the most bigoted courts in Europe, that of the Medici, were painted by Justus Susterman as so many Mary Magdalenes, and lent their features to an army of female saints; the entire Medici clan is portrayed as the pantheon of a Christian Olympus.

The sense of holy awe was combined with worldly pomp in the coronation ceremony.
Right: fourteenth-century miniature by Anovelo da Imbonate depicting the coronation of Gian Galeazzo Visconti. Biblioteca Ambrosiana, Milan.
Below: Messale Arcimboldi, Coronation of Ludovico il Moro. Library of the Cathedral Chapter, Milan.

A magic environment

The court was an enchanted storehouse for the most precious treasures of its time. Mosaics, frescoes, pictures and tapestries adorned walls and ceilings as in a cathedral. Objects in silver and rock crystal filled cabinets and cupboards. Magical gems and minerals were kept in *studioli*, or small private studies. There were libraries of richly illuminated manuscripts. Huge looking glasses magnified the rooms. The rarest plants grew in pleasaunces like miniature botanical gardens, and water was ingeniously channelled along the most elaborate courses. In menageries exotic beasts amazed the visitor. Magnificence, imagination on the grand scale, and opulence in all things – such were the hallmarks of the court. The man who inhabited a court was not as others were. He was known, to quote Jean-Marie Apostolidès in a recent book on the court of Louis XIV, "by his physical capacity for parading an overplus," in dress, behaviour and appetite for luxury. Byzantium, that apex of courtly and sacred ritual, had the most detailed system of court-costume. There every courtier, whether or not he held official

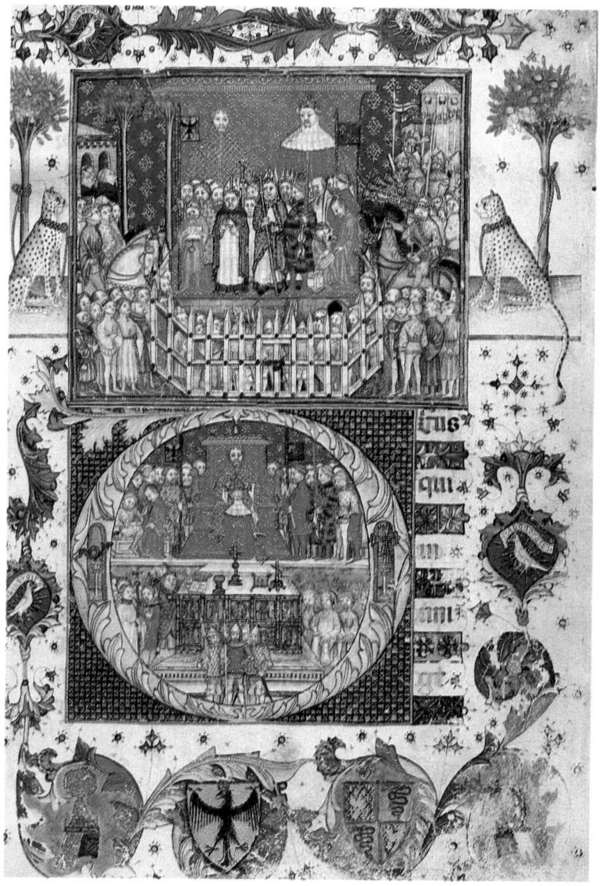

rank, dressed according to his social standing and position in the hierarchy. You could tell that a man belonged to the court by the colour and cut of his tunic, and the ornaments he wore. This was true also of the Carolingian court and the courts of the Renaissance. And at Versailles, which may with reason be considered the last great court of the Renaissance, the system would be revived in all its magnificence.

A closed world

In sociological terms, the court was, as it were, a closed world, its internal relations conditioned by the constant reciprocal contacts of courtiers as they dealt with the world outside – with the city, the wider territory beyond, or with their own kith and kin. Eventually this enclosed society developed its private system of justice, applicable to members only and distinct from that of the state. The *praepositus sacri cubiculi*, *majordomus* or *maestro di casa* – different

Allegory of the good government of Ludovico il Moro. In the left half of the picture, at the top, his patron St Louis is seen blessing the ship of state, while Fortune is glimpsed on the right. Miniature from MS Velin 724. Bibliothèque Nationale, Paris.

names for the Master of the Household – exercised authority as far as the castle gate, or the boundary-walls of the palace and its dependencies. His was the same kind of authority as that exercised by the *consilium ancianorum*, in the days of the communes, over the actual houses occupied by the patriarchal family and its extended kin, but nowhere else in the city. And just as the sway of the head and senior members of the patriarchal family was limited to their peers and younger relations, so the authority of the prince's *maestro di casa* was only over those who lived on the palace premises.

In Renaissance times, as in the Middle Ages, the life in common of a large group of men and women presented endless problems and every court had its *Ordini*, its rules or orders. These strictly regulated the daily life of castle or palace, and kept the social distances. Closed to the outside world, the court was internally open, with interrelations between those of equal or lower rank, and every member of the group in his appointed place. There was thus a definite structure at court, with a cleanly defined code of conduct which sought to maintain order.

Divinity of the prince

The theory of the ruler's divinity set the court yet further apart, as a sacred precinct. The prince did more than govern and administer law. He represented his people before God; his private chapel was the Holy of Holies of the state, and there he prayed for them. He assumed, in short, the functions of a priest.

The notion of Divine Right had existed in the Western Roman Empire, where the emperor was a god, and it developed extensively in Christian Byzantium. There the absolutism of Imperial Rome is mingled with Christianity and the emperor is *Christomimetes*, Christ's image. He becomes the object of a new cult which sees him as the reincarnation of Christ, and God as his collaborator, if not his forerunner. Above the portal of Notre Dame in Paris, the descendants of the kings of Judah are depicted, with Christ appearing as the last in the line of kings – every monarch's ancestor. The monarch sat beneath a canopy or tabernacle, symbolizing the vault of heaven; the torches around him in procession symbolized the light of the sun. But the Byzantine emperor, like the sun, remained

Francesco Sforza seated between Caesar and Hannibal, with the great captains of antiquity. Minature from a fourteenth-century manuscript.

immoveably in the palace which was the heart of his empire. He circulated only in effigy, on coins, seals and medallions. Officials known as silentiaries imposed silence when he appeared in audience-chamber, basilica or consistory. In the palace the *praepositus sacri cubiculi* maintained quiet, as in a sanctuary. As Bishop Paride Grassi writes in his *De ceremoniis cardinalium*, "there can be no sanctity in conversing while holy rites take place." People approached the emperor in a slow rhythm of prayer and adoration. They genuflected before him, kissed his feet or knees. Nobody might look directly at him; one looked sideways when speaking, or at the ground. Patrizi Piccolomini, in a book of papal ceremonial compiled in 1519, says this was to preserve the properly modest demeanour when addressing a superior, while the rules of etiquette at the Cameroon court, the *bamoum*, have another explanation: "if the king perceives that you regard him attentively when he speaks, he may think you do not understand what he is saying." Originally, however, the custom was intended to safeguard the monarch from the effects of the evil eye.

Precise courtly rules also forbade one to "see into" his body, as one easily might when he was drinking. At the *bamoum* the courtiers hid their eyes if he raised a glass to his lips, but at fifteenth-century papal banquets all present fell to their knees when the pontiff drank. This more complicated usage was probably an echo of the similar action during Mass. While the Pope drinks, says Patrizi Piccolomini, *consueverunt omnes astantes, preter episcopos et superioris dignitatis viros, genuflectere*; and he adds, "this custom we have seen in our own times, although we have read of it in no manual of ceremonies."

A hundred years later, at the court of Cardinal Pietro Maria Borghese, who died in 1624, guests would remove their hats when he drank, and receive themselves a similar salute, though only from the cup-bearer. This formality at the cardinal's table, of which we learn from Girolamo Lunadoro, is also mentioned in the *Pratica e scalcheria* (1638) by Antonio Frugoli of Lucca. Whenever "a great prince" drinks, the steward on duty is to "bare his head respectfully, and all the gentlemen at table will do likewise. He is to cover the prince's food with a platter, and when the prince has drunk he will uncover the food, and guests will replace their headgear." The extension of homage from pope and prelates to secular princes and their guests shows that the act of drinking meant more than is suggested by its obvious parallel with the raising of the chalice at Mass.

Although "seeing into" the prince's body might be unallowable, that body was public property, as was his every physical action, however intimate. Pliny the Younger, in his *Panegyricus Nervae Trajano augusto dicto*, denied the prince the right to privacy; he should display his very bedchamber to public knowledge (or *fama*). "Great position requires that he is never alone, or private; not the houses merely, but even the bedchambers of princes are open wide, and all the inner rooms exposed to public knowledge."

At Versailles a meticulous ceremonial governed the *lever du roi*. At eight in the morning Louis XVI was awakened, in his central first-floor room overlooking the *cour royale*, by the *valet-de-chambre* who had slept at the foot of his bed. The pages came in immediately, followed by the grand chamberlain, and then the *entrées* began. The first was that of the king's relations – his children and grandchildren who were *enfants de France*, princes and princesses of the blood – his chief physician, chief surgeon, chief *valet-de-chambre* and chief page. The *grande entrée* was next, with those responsible for the innermost departments of the palace, the *grands officiers de la chambre et de la garderobe*. The *première entrée* followed, consisting of the king's readers, or *lecteurs*, and the *intendant des Menus Plaisirs*. Fourth in order was the *entrée de la chambre*, admitting all other *officiers de la chambre*, with the grand almoner, the ministers and secretaries of state, officers of the guard and marshals of France. The fifth was for court nobles invited by the grand chamberlain, and the sixth and last for the king's remaining sons, the bastards, and their families. In view of the irregular connection this contingent, accompanied by the *surintendant des bâtiments*, or master of the household, arrived by a side-door.

Privacy was impossible even at a royal birth, for witnesses had to attest that the child had not

Public tribute to a mistress was not unusual from a Renaissance prince. The lord of Rimini, Sigismondo Malatesta, immortalized his love for Isotta degli Atti by giving her a chapel in his Tempio Malatestiano with (left) their carved initials intertwined.
Above: the fresco series by Benedetto Bembo in the Camera d'Oro in the castle of Torrechiara depicts the story of Bianca Pellegrini, mistress of Pier Maria Rossi, Lord of Parma; she is shown searching for him through the fiefs and castles of the Tara and Parma valleys. In this last scene she has found her lover, and knights him with a sword.
Opposite: Leonardo da Vinci's Lady with an Ermine, *said to be a portrait of Cecilia Gallerani, mistress of Ludovico il Moro.*

Pictures, looking-glasses, arrases, goldsmiths' work, illuminated books contributed, as did curiosities, plants and exotic animals, to glorify the ruler's image.
Opposite, above: the stately throne room at Urbino, with its two fireplaces and great ceiling-vault adorned with large ornamental rosettes bearing the initials of Federico di Montefeltro. The tapestries were woven in Brussels by the Frenchman Lefebvre to designs by Raphael. The Lion of St Mark on the farther wall is a reminder that duke Guidobaldo, Federico's son, was a condottiere *of the Most Serene Republic.*
Above: medieval scene from a late fifteenth-century tapestry in the palace of Urbino.
Opposite, below: the Tapestry Room in the ducal palace at Mantua, with late eighteenth-century neoclassical decoration.

been substituted. The account by Louise Bourgeois, known as *boursier*, midwife to Queen Marie de' Medicis at the birth of the future Louis XIII, was, when published *chez Henry Ruffin* in Paris, almost a second public performance. "On 27 September at midnight," she relates, "the king said I should be called, for the queen was in pain. When I entered the room he said, 'Are you the midwife?' and I said I was. 'Then come midwife. My wife is ill. See if she is not about to give birth, for she is in great pain.' I saw she was in labour. Then the king said to her, 'My love, you know what I have more than once told you, that the princes of the blood must attend; and I beg you to make up your mind to this, because of your high rank and the rank of your child.' The queen said she had always been resolved to please him. 'I know well, my dear, that you wish whatever I wish,' he said, 'but I know too your timid and modest nature, and I fear the birth may be hard unless you are truly reconciled to their presence. And so, I beg you, do not be in the least ashamed, for this is what must be at the birth of a queen's first child.' The king held her during each contraction as the pains grew worse and asked me at last to tell him when the princes should be summoned, since it was of the utmost importance that they should be there. About one in the morning, seeing how she suffered and fearing they might not arrive in time, he had them sent for. They were the Prince de Conti, the Comte de Soissons and the Duc de Montpensier."

All the ceremonial intrusion on the prince – while he ate, while he slept, when he was being born – was directly connected with his physical sanctity. The sanctity, moreover, spread from his person to the whole territory whose center and sovereign he was – and this in the smallest courts and until a surprisingly late date. Nor was the ceremonial simply an attenuated version of the reverence accorded to the Eastern or Western emperors, or the pope. Up to the middle of the seventeenth century every noble palace had "sanctuary rights," and the very phrase embodies the belief that a ruler's house was sacred.

Courts large and small

"Cosimo, Duke of Florence and Siena, formerly did everything in the grand manner, to match his administration and his government of the state, but has for some time been extremely quiet and retired. He lives not in the accustomed luxury of dukes and princes, but as the head of a leading family. He eats with his wife and children, with no elaborate ceremony. Nor do his children have their own table and other expenses, as is the way at other courts; here there is a single court and one set of household expenses . . . He has stopped feeding and maintaining all comers as he did, save on his rural estates, and occasionally. He used to keep a stable of fine horses at each of his houses; now he merely has such horses as he needs. He used to spend a fortune on hunting; nowadays his hunt is a paltry affair, supplemented by private citizens; to have a good hawk or hound is to be favoured indeed. Finally, he has cut back on any superfluous expenditure and will buy nothing but works of art. This is how his children, who are clever and promising, have been brought up and the lady duchess, a woman of rare gifts who shares his ideas, teaches them to live as he does." Thus the Venetian ambassador, Vincenzo Fedeli, in 1561, noted startling changes at the Florentine court.

Yet the political power of state or ruler had practically nothing to do with the size of a court, which might expand or diminish for reasons quite independent of the needs of the state. It might expand out of all proportion, against the best interests of its subjects, or contract to such an extent as to cause general astonishment, and speculation as to why the prince had turned into a miser.

Federico II, Duke of Mantua and Marquess of Monferrato, had a court of more than 800 persons – too many, in the opinion of the Venetian ambassador Bernardo Navagero. It was also too many in the opinion of his own brother, Cardinal Ercole, who acted as regent on his death in 1540 and reduced the number to 350 "and spent only on necessities; that is, for officers of justice and other ministers." But 50 years later another Venetian envoy, Giovanni da Mulla, describes the Mantuan court with keener admiration than we might expect from one who was presumably conversant with the splendours of the palace of the doges. "The duke lives in a very large and noble palace, fit for any great king. It is richly adorned with many splendid tapestries, some woven in silk, or gold thread. There are antiquities, and many excellent pictures – the galleries are full of them; and so many *loggie*, halls, corridors, courtyards and gardens, some at ground level and some opening out of the apartments, that it is in every way sumptuous and magnificent. The duke occupies one wing, Don Vicenzo his brother another, and yet an almost incredible number of rooms are empty and uninhabited." And still there was the Palazzo del Te for a rest house and summer residence! But Mantua is admittedly the prime example of disproportion of court to state, of splendour and luxury to actual revenue.

The relation of a court to its subject-population is well illustrated by the balance sheet of the Farnese dominion at Parma – "sprung up overnight like a mushroom," in Cardinal Ercole Gonzaga's phrase. Court expenditure rises continually from 12 per cent of the total budget in

COURT STRUCTURE

The court was focused on and arranged around the person of the prince, the proximity of the offices of the various courtiers to his *cubiculum* reflecting the structure of its hierarchy.

His preeminence is vividly emphasized in a miniature (1) of a fifteenth-century codex, showing Francesco Sforza and his wife Bianca Maria Visconti among the dignitaries of their court.) The grades of service, and the interelations between office holders in the *palatium*, were determined by function and occupation, as well as by age, length of service and social standing. It is of course impossible to illustrate diagrammatically every position held at court, and the diagram opposite (5) merely indicates the courtly and/or professional hierarchy. It is based mainly on the *Ordini et uffitii* of Urbino (1511), with some adjustment to emphasize the departments of state administration, of which the *Ordini* tell us little.

Comparison with a later cardinalate court such as that of Cardinal Alessandro Bichi, described in Liberati's *Il perfetto Maestro di casa* of 1658, will make it clear that rôles proliferated, declining from "honours" into *mestieri*, or professions, in a process of subdivision which complicates, but does not change, the model. (The three accompanying tables from Liberati's document list the "family" of 85 "mouths," or *bocche* (2); some items of food consumption (3), and of stable fodder (4).)

The prince was the center of the household, his authority represented by his *mastro di casa*. All eating arrangements were the responsibility of the chief steward, who organized and supervised the prince's meals and, through his subordinate guest and household stewards, those of visitors and "family." The *cameriere maggiore*, in charge of the *cubiculum*, was by reason of his proximity to the master at least partly independent of *mastro di casa* and chief steward. The *Ordini* spell this out: "he cannot be entirely under their authority, because he is constantly with the Prince." The master of the wardrobe enjoys a similar degree of autonomy, entrusted as he is with the *signore's* most valuable possessions in a situation which brings him into frequent contact with other court officials. The same is true of the doctor, who had physical charge of the prince, and of the chaplain who ministered to his soul (and who, through the almoner, managed relations with local ecclesiastics).

State administration may be simplified into three departments: a chancery under a chancery secretary, a department of justice under an *auditore* or magistrate, and a

1

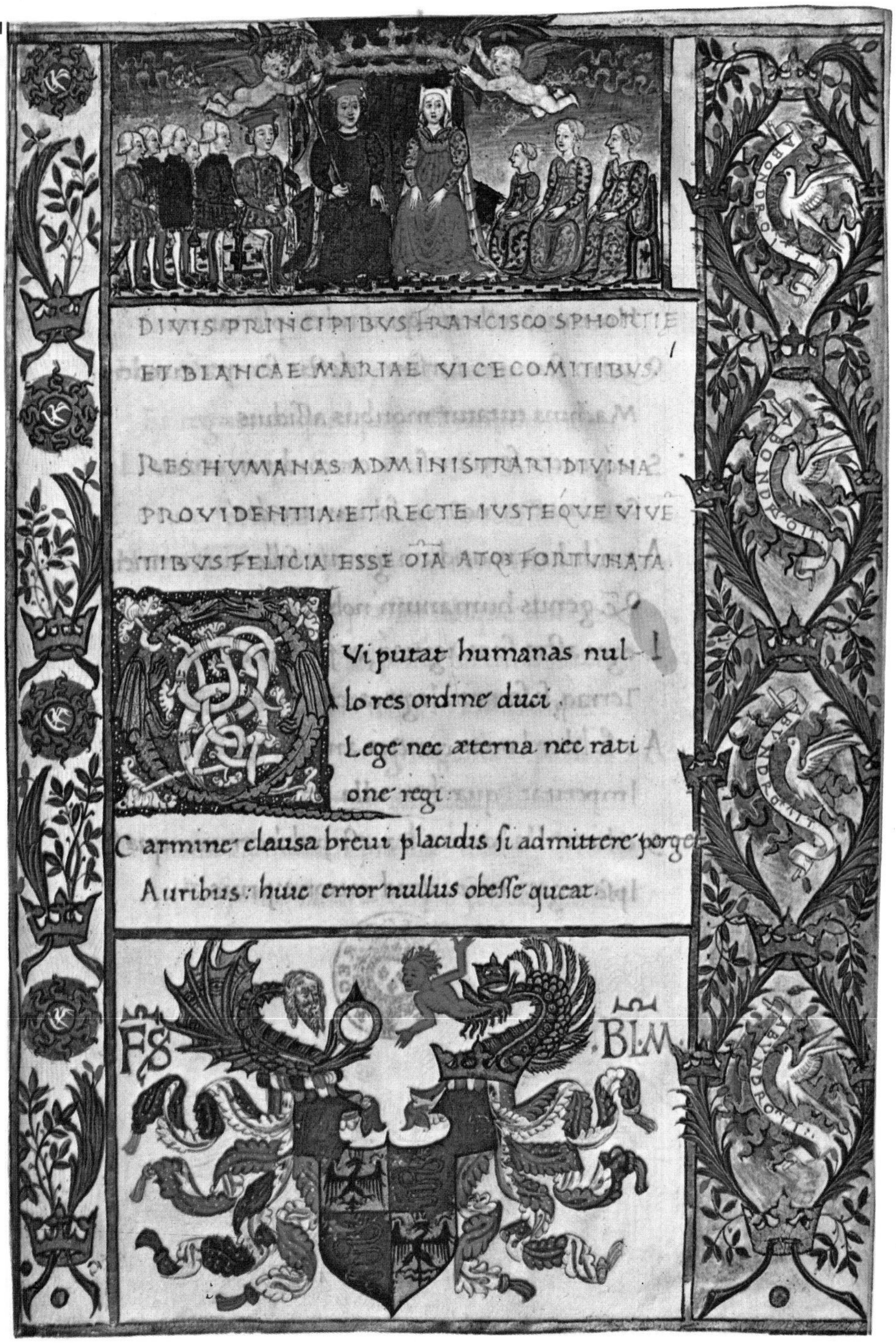

DIVIS PRINCIPIBVS FRANCISCO SPHORTIE
ET BIANCAE MARIAE VICECOMITIBVS
RES HVMANAS ADMINISTRARI DIVINA
PROVIDENTIA ET RECTE IVSTEQVE VIVE
TIBVS FELICIA ESSE OIA ATQ FORTVNATA
Vi putat humanas nul
lo res ordine duci
Lege nec aeterna nec rati
one regi
Carmine clausa brevi placidis si admittere perge
Auribus huic error nullus obesse queat
FS
BLM

2

The court of Cardinal Alessandro Bichi (seventeenth century)

His Eminence	1
Majordomo	1
Superintendant-general	1
Master of the household	1
Master of riding	1
Magistrate	1
Master of the bedchamber	1
Secretary	1
Cupbearer	1
Gentleman of the bedchamber	1
Quartermaster	1
Steward	1
Carver	1
Chaplains	2
Trainbearer	1
Personal page	1
Accountant	1
Doctor	1
Servants of above	17
Valets of the bedchamber	4
Master of the wardrobe	1
Assistant to above	1
Master of the horse	1
Sweeper (private)	1
Butler	1
Bursar	1
Wine steward	1
Provisions dispenser	1
Cellarer	1
Cook (private)	1
Assistant to above	1
Cook (household)	1
Assistant cook (household)	1
Kitchen boy	1
Under-butler	1
Grooms	1
Steward (household dining room *Tinello*)	12
Superintendent of fuel	1
Coachmen	2
Outriders	3
Stableboys	4
Sweeper (general)	1
Porter	1
Muleteer	1
Laundress (private)	1
Laundress (household)	1
Farrier	1
Saddler	1
Total	85

Court of Cardinal Alessandro Bichi
"Mouths" to be fed, and consumption of provisions

3

Mouths	85
Loaves, daily	236
Wine, in measures of 0.45 liters, daily	270
Oil, in measures of 0.51 liters, weekly	34
Monthly budget, in *scudi*	140.10
Daily expenditure for food, in *scudi*	6.4

4

Court of Cardinal Alessandro Bichi **Animal Fodder** daily consumption		measures of fodder	pounds of hay	pounds of straw
horses for use of majordomo	2	6	60	20
horses for use of superintendant-general	2	6	60	20
Corsieri (fast horses)	4	16	120	40
draught horses	13	39	390	130
saddle horses	4	12	120	40
mules for drawing litter and pack-carrying	4	12	120	40
		91	870	290

treasury and financial department under the treasurer-accountant. Each of these chief officials would have the requisite staff, assistants and servants.

The "communicating doors" in the diagram illustrate how the hierarchy worked within the various offices of the palace; they show that there could be access in more than one direction, and thus reflect professional, rather than social, interrelations. We may note, for instance, the relations between almoner, bursar and the actual distributor of charity; or between the latter, his supervisor and the heads of cellar and bakery.

The subordinate courts of the prince's wife and of his heir are not included in the diagram, but their structure was similar, though on a smaller scale and, naturally, without the governmental departments.

5

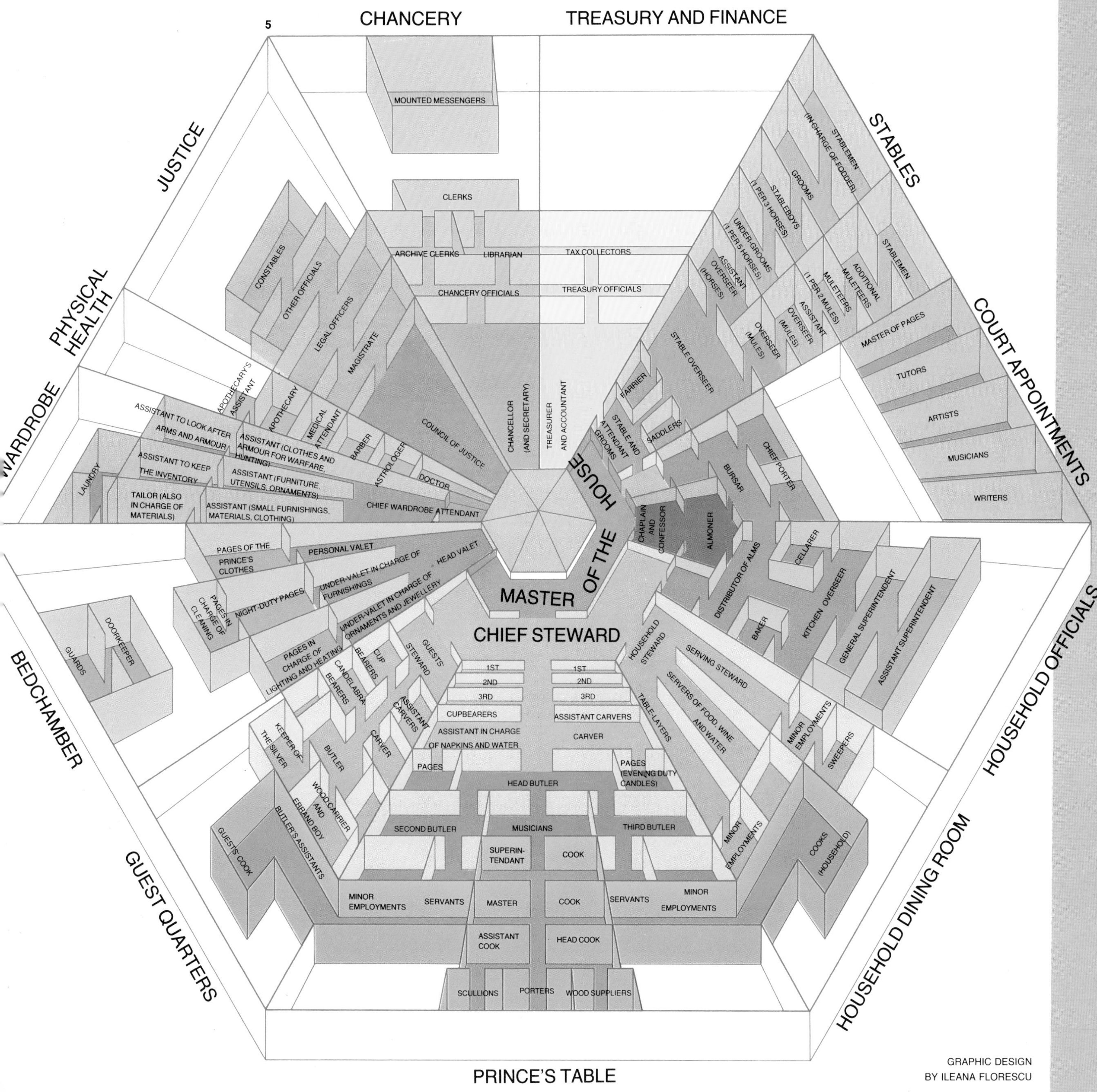

GRAPHIC DESIGN BY ILEANA FLORESCU

Items from the Medici private collections. Above: casket with rock-crystal intaglio panels, by Valerio Belli (1532). Opposite, above: vase with a figure of Hercules, by Michele Mazzafirri. Below: cornelian vase and amphora-shaped jug of lapis lazuli, both from the collection of Lorenzo de' Medici. Museo degli Argenti, Palazzo Pitti, Florence.

1565 to twice as much in 1589; and the Farnese kept what was, in contemporary eyes, a very minor establishment. At the beginning of the seventeenth century Francesco Maria Violardo comments on the modest court made up of "400 horses, a master of the horse, a treasurer, paymaster or under-treasurer, three secretaries, *maestro di casa*, three or four gentlemen-courtiers, eight pages, eight grooms, the musicians, the doctor, eight or ten valets and a captain of the mounted guards; also a steward, cooks and other menials, a painter and three or four counsellors."

The size of the court was not, then, conditioned by the requirements of the state, and the lack of proportion might reflect a ruler's tastes, addictions or a liking for display. Francesco IV, Duke of Mantua, was a dog-lover, and kept 83 dogs. He died in 1612 and by 1617 his brother Fernando, who laid down a cardinalate in order to ensure the succession, had sent the kennel staff packing and engaged instead 21 musicians, thus indicating his own, rather different, preferences. And in France, where Henri III in 1588 reduced the number of those employed in the royal stables from 335 to 170, his successor Henri IV had 619 people working there in 1605.

Since it acted as a government the court did not and indeed could not identify with the state; this divergence would lead to its end – or mummification – setting it on a collision course with the civil society on which it was erected. In this process a main factor was the growth in western Europe in the seventeenth and eighteenth centuries of a new and more complicated mechanism of state, causing in turn the rise of new social classes outside the court and alien from it.

Court employment

Giacomo Colorsi, steward to Cardinal Francesco degli Albizi in the mid seventeenth century, thought of himself as a strategist, deploying his "equipment" as a general his troops. "If, as they say, the man who prepares a banquet has as much to do as he who marshals an army, and is as worthy of praise, then he who serves the tables of the great, and serves them well, may take due pride in his achievements. I have spent not only my best years but nearly all my life in that employment, with no gain but personal satisfaction in a task well done." It was from this long experience with "the great" that he spoke as an authority on his calling.

A report compiled at more or less the same time for the Gonzaga dukes of Nevers on the *Institutioni e regole praticate nella ducal scalcheria di Mantova* (the rules and regulations of the steward's department at Mantua) says that previous dukes had always considered the steward's as the first office at court and "filled it with carefully chosen persons of noble birth; such as, sharing the assumptions and values of their class, would on all occasions, and especially before strangers, display their sovereigns' glory to the world for honour's sake." Other courts, seeing the "particular authority" of the Mantuan steward, "issuing his verbal and written orders" were spurred to emulation.

The larger, richer and more powerful a court the more numerous and diverse were the employments of its "family," the courtiers and servants. Its size was then the reflection of power, its supreme concern the organization of palace life and the allotment of function. This in turn generated new functions and specialized employments. Callings, assignments and appointments were created, modified, rose and

fell in the scale of importance. They could be elevated into occupations for noblemen, and be patterns of excellence; or a new court might bestow them on less experienced people with the sole qualifications of blue blood and poverty.

In 1516 the Florentine Lodovico Alamanni, a friend of Machiavelli, advised the younger Lorenzo de' Medici (grandson of Lorenzo the Magnificent) to reduce the scions of the citizen-patriciate to the status of courtiers. He should "wean" them, "strip off their citizens' gowns" (that is, their republican notions) and "demote them into such courtiers as might be useful to him;" they should be made "secretaries, agents, delegates, ambassadors." Lorenzo, successfully commanding the papal armies against Urbino and becoming, unexpectedly, its duke, had an entire new court to construct which – had he lived long enough – he would have developed into a *signoria* along the lines of his native Florence.

The skills of secretary and ambassador are not acquired overnight, however. For Gasparo Bragaccia of Piacenza, writing a century later for another "new" court, that of the Farnese, ambassadors belong to a true and distinct profession – an opinion which Torquato Tasso, in *Il messagiero* of 1582, and Juan Antonio De Vera in *El embajador*, of 1620, had shared before him. As for secretaries, they are the subject of much sixteenth- and seventeenth-century discussion, inaugurated by Tasso in 1587.

Nor did haste produce the *maestro di casa*, the steward or the carver, all of whose offices were connected with the eating arrangements and had been ennobled by courtly association. "There are many," lamented Antonio Adami in *Il novitiato del maestro di casa*, of 1636, "who desire to be masters before they are pupils and fail in their employments, in the capacity of *maestro di casa* above all, because they have served no apprenticeship and therefore cannot succeed, for it is a calling that demands the whole of a man (*requiret totum hominem*) . . . Not an office for anyone unpractical or inexpert . . ." And Vincenzo Cervio, in his carvers' manual of 1593, inveighed against the sloppiness and lack of pride in their work of those who claim to be carvers but have no proper training. He thinks it a scandal: "I have seen them, often, scum that they are, in Rome, Venice, Bologna and Florence, and almost anywhere you like in Lombardy. Seen them in gentlemen's houses, at family dinners or great banquets when guests are present: the meal is announced, the carver sticks a napkin in his belt for an apron, rolls his sleeves up to his elbows and stands there as if he's spoiling for a fight."

The insistence on professionalism is closely allied to the distinction between roles. The callings of *maestro di casa* and steward, for instance, could overlap and boundaries depended on the size of the court and the scope it offered. "You should know," says Antonio Frugoli, a steward from Lucca, "that in France and Spain the *maestro di casa* acts as steward

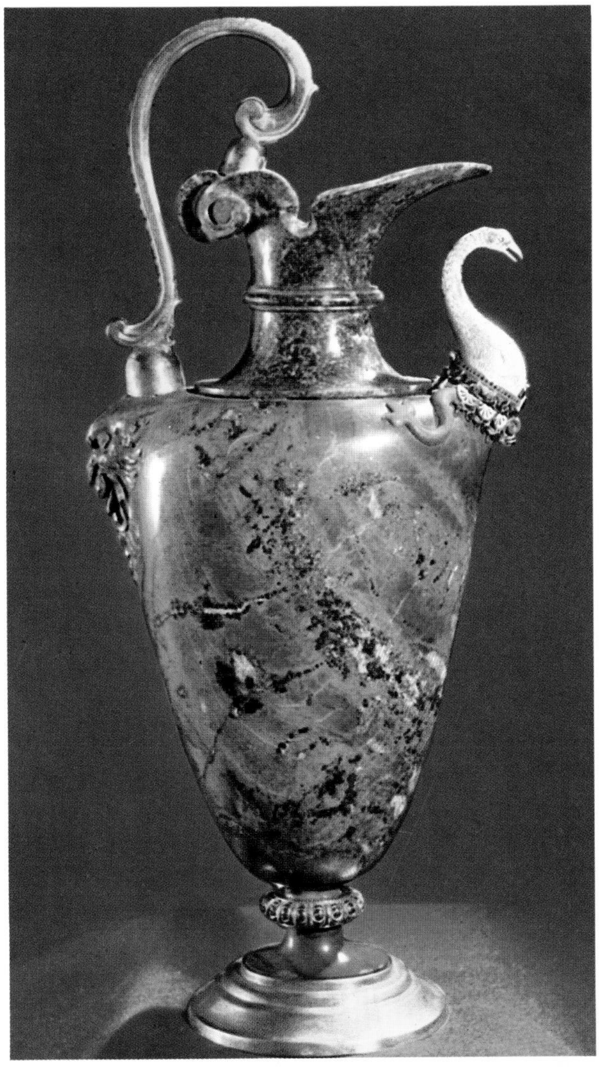

and the two employments are so alike that one man can, if necessary, fulfil both. And in Spain, if they have a steward or *mastro sala* in charge of the pages and of the bearing to table and serving of the food, there is a *maggior d'huomo* to arrange the menus; and in France the *metre d'Utel* is in charge of the kitchen and of organizing the meals, while a gentleman carries the dishes to table. This is a gentleman who is on duty for the week; were he permanent he would be called a steward."

It was thus the repeated performance of some task – in this case the carrying of food to table – which constituted the employment. At the same time, hierarchical distinctions have to be preserved, and tasks are carefully separated. Quite menial tasks might suddenly assume significance and dignity, becoming the province of officials who would have fought tooth and nail to protect them against anyone else. For instance, a dispute on a point of etiquette at Mantua in 1631 touched on the standing of several household dignitaries – the chief majordomo, the *maestro di casa*, the valets and pages of the wardrobe and the head valet. Who, of these, should proffer the duke's napkin when he dined in private? It was the privilege of the head valet, emphasizing that gentleman's all-important nearness to the ducal bedchamber.

This defense of personal territory extended to that of rights and offices acquired by purchase, and continues when the direct lord-to-courtier relationship is replaced by one of employer to salaried employee. To quote again from Adami: "I knew a cook who abstracted his share of everything he handled, as did his assistants, each with his little morsel from the cooking-pots of the gentry." The "right" here was considered to be part and parcel of the job and is wholeheartedly defended by Cervio, who declares that "any carver worthy of the name is entitled, when carving for his master, to a helping of whatever he sends to table; he should tolerate no objections from the *maestro di casa*, nor, I am bold to say, from the *Signore* himself." None of them, cooks, assistant cooks or carvers looked upon these pickings as minor theft. It was "their" meat. They had cooked it, they had carved it: it went with the job. What was, in fact, changing was the relation between the lord and his dependents, and Cervio's remarks seem to belong to an intermediate period. Personal dependents are turning into hired staff, and the old "guild" attitude gives way to the new conception.

Adami, 40 years later than Cervio, bemoans the fact that so many courts in his day were "reduced to paying for everything," with the consequent destruction of the personal master-servant relationship, but still deplores these perks as an "irregularity." Yet his view is not so very different from Cervio's; both wish to uphold the dignity of their callings. The "irregularity," for Adami, springs from a confusion of rôles, the combination of the hitherto distinct responsibilities of *maestro di casa* and steward, and the later's loss of authority over his proper domain, the kitchen. Another 30 years, and the "irregularity" would be downright thieving, while Francesco Liberati, though ignorant of the deep and ancient roots of the custom, condemned the *saccheggio*, or ritual sacking of a cardinal's palace on its master's death. "They are blameworthy who, seeing the chance of personal gain when their lord dies . . . purloin, according to their household positions, the implements and materials of their various charges at the death of him who maintained them." The trainbearers took the two cloaks they wore in the cardinal's chapel. The master of the horse selected a beast from the stables, the master of the wardrobe had the bed the cardinal died in. The clothes, and the bed from the dressing-room, went to the grooms of the chamber; basin, jug and all the shaving equipment to the barber. The cardinal's butler had "all the linen that was in his hands when the master died," the cellarer all the bottled wine. The man who swept the private apartments whisked away lamps, lamp-oil, brooms "and other things appertaining to his duties."

It is as the personal relationship progressively declines into the salaried engagement, and what had been court dignities change into court employments, that professional feelings appear. In 1543 Francesco Priscianese, who wrote *Del governo della corte d'un Signore in Roma*, speaks proudly in the dedication of "my profession;" a generation or two previously a nobleman, entrusted with the same duties, would

Portrait of Galeazzo di Sanvitale, Lord of Fontanellato, near Parma, husband of Paola Gonzaga. The Italian historian Maurizio Fagiolo dell'Arco has contributed to the many explanations of the coin and its number 72, suggesting that the figures 7 and 2 represent, as in the so-called "Hermetic Circle," the Moon and the planet Jupiter. From the recurrent symbols in the frescoes at Fontanellato he also finds that Diana = the Moon = Paola Gonzaga, and Jupiter = the Sun = Galeazzo Sanvitale.

have referred to "the dignity of my charge." Nevertheless, the court exalts the function, thus allowing the holder to present himself as a model for other practitioners. In 1518 Giovanni Rosselli, "not without a modest blush," goes into print with his *Epulario* (*The Eater*, one of the earliest cookery books to be translated into English) on the strength of having been cook to Giovan Paolo Baglioni, lord of Perugia. A century later Vittorio Lancellotti dedicates the *Scalco prattico* to Cardinal Ippolito Aldobrandini, saying that long experience in the household of Ippolito's uncle, Cardinal Pietro, gives him the right to speak for what is by now an acknowledged calling. "I may claim, having spent my life in the office of steward, and always in the service of great lords . . . that I was worthy to serve Your Illustrious Lordship's uncle, the Cardinal Pietro of glorious memory, and afterwards Your Lordship, enjoying many years under the protection of your most excellent House." In his address to the reader he adds: "Many think, as I do, that no one merits the title of steward who has not organized and served the banquets of princes."

In 1658 Giacomo Colorsi's *Scalcharia*, a treatise on stewardship, agrees with him. Colorsi is making what he terms a "public demonstration" of his craft, in the hope that "young people at court may have more profit than I from my experience and reap the harvest I have vainly sought for many years." And in 1668 Francesco Liberati, who was *maestro di casa* to Cardinal Alessandro Bichi, vindicates and ennobles his trade by quoting his "long professional service at the Roman court." It was to a *maestro di casa*, Francesco Cerioli, that the Roman booksellers Battista and Giuseppe Corvo inscribed their reprint of Antonio Adami's *Il novitatio del Maestro di casa*, dated 1 September 1657.

Professionalism, then, was born as offices, once bestowed as feudal honours, passed – when, indeed, they were not actually sold – to men who were neither noble nor patrician. And soon enough it was necessary to be professional, for not everyone was familiar with the skills and procedures of these offices. The compiler of the *Ordini et offitii* of Urbino advises the princes to give audience "two or three times a week without fail to the *maestro di casa*, steward, head accountant and treasurer." Vincenzo Gramigna who was secretary to Cardinal Scipione Cobelluzzi and wrote his manual, *Il segretario* in 1620 from first-hand, practical experience, says that a prince "with any sense" will see that his secretary attends meetings of his council – the *consilium* – for the secretary

The prince was a reserved, almost sacred personage who, outside his court, was revealed to his people in images such as Giambologna's equestrian statue of Cosimo I de' Medici, Grand Duke of Tuscany, which was commissioned by his son the Grand Duke Ferdinando in the Piazza della Signoria in Florence (left); or the statue of Duke Borso d'Este (below), on a column in front of Ferrara cathedral.

alone "holds the keys of the prince's heart." Giovanni Andrea Gilio, in *De le parti morali e civili appartenenti a' Letterati cortigiani* (1574), sets out to demonstrate, "by means of historical examples, ancient and modern," how vital it is for "rich princes" to "favour and support men of letters and fine talents, considering how much honour, fame and glory will accrue to them as a result." The approach is twofold. The new professionals are being taught their jobs; the princely employers are being taught that these jobs are indispensable.

As the medieval court was replaced by the Renaissance one – itself the precursor of the modern state – two professions came to grow in status: that of secretary and that of scholar or man of letters – or, rather, the historian-genealogist. The business of the secretary, the press-agent of his day as it were, was to celebrate and circulate the glories of the family, either through his own writings (as, for instance, those of Giovan Battista Pigna and Tommaso Porcacchi on the house of Este), or by telling artists and sculptors what to paint and carve. (And here we remember the cooperation between Vasari, court-artist of the Medici, and their secretary Vincenzo Borghini). The scholar, with his highly professional assistance, enabled the prince to free himself from reliance on his lesser vassals and members of the patriciate on the various *consilia*. Not infrequently, secretary and court-scholar might be given diplomatic missions, sign of their growing prestige in the household. At Ferrara the secretaries – known as *fattori*, from their distant origins as estate factors, or agents – saw their power increase with the absolute power of the Este dukes. As Guido Astuti has said, in *La formazione dello Stato moderno in Italia*, "The secretaries of state chosen by the princes to be trusted advisers were at first responsible for the general despatch of governmental business, and only later received specific administrative charges. An early instance of such charges is the appointment in the reign of Lodovico il Moro (1494–1500) of four secretaries whose departments were politics, church affairs, justice and finance, the political secretary having the functions and responsibilities of a prime minister." Cosimo I was also to look beyond the patriciate

Detail of the equestrian statue of Bernabò Visconti, by Bonino da Campione. Castello Sforzesco, Milan.

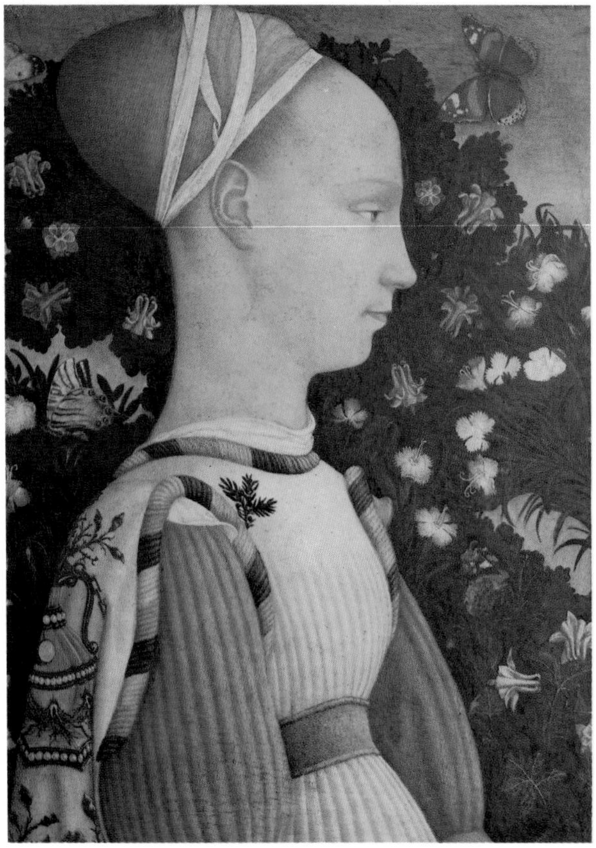

Portraits by Pisanello: Leonello d'Este, who in 1441 became lord of Ferrara, Modena and Rimini (Musée du Louvre, Paris); and (below) an Este princess, possibly his sister Ginevra, wife of Sigismondo Pandolfo Malatesta of Rimini.

for his senior appointees – to men such as Francesco Campana (the original ducal secretary in Florence under Cosimo's predecessor Alessandro), or Jacopo Polverini; while his son Francesco I ran his personal chancery with a secretary and two assistants.

Three kinds of court

From what we have noted so far, we may divide courts into three basic types: those of sovereigns, those of territorial magnates, or *signori*, and those of princes or cardinals. The ruler of a sovereign court acknowledges no superior. A signorial court is that of one who, under a feudal overlord, rules lands of his own, levies taxes, conducts an independent foreign policy and, often, mints his own coinage. A princely court, or the court of a cardinal, exists within a sovereign or signorial state.

For the most part these distinctions are external, for even the smallest court is a microcosm of the same little world, differing in size only from all the other courts. Each, besides evolving its internal hierarchy, codifies its internal relations in a system of etiquette more or less elaborate in proportion to the worldly power of its lord who is, in any case, the arbiter, the tastemaker. Among broadly similar courts we may detect competition. Who can produce the most complex system, whose prince can impose the most intricate behavioural precepts? The best sources of information in this field were ambassadors, musicians, and minstrels, artists and scholars. Then there were marriages between the offspring of distant courts; and there were youthful hostages, constantly deposited by one enemy on another and subjected to very real cultural indoctrination. Much could be learned, too, from the *notitia dignitatum* and books of ceremonial which circulated in manuscript. When a new palace was built every court followed its progress attentively, eager to imitate technical innovations. Thus Francesco Sforza, rebuilding the castle of Porta Giova beyond the north-west gate of Milan, wished to learn what the Spanish architect Guillermo Sagrera was doing at Castel Nuovo in Naples for Alfonso of Aragon in 1455; and Federico Gonzaga commissioned drawings of the palace at Urbino from Matteo da Volterra, "desiring to make this house of ours on the pattern of what has been done there, and which, we hear, is wonderful."

But despite all this emulation the courts were, as we have said, little worlds of their own. They looked inwards, not out. Contrary to what Norbert Elias says in his three-volume work on *The Civilizing Process*, the court dictated neither fashion nor *bon ton* to the rest of the world, but was seen as the sphere in which the laws on how to behave and what to wear actually applied. The world may be said to have modelled its costume and etiquette on those of the court when the court was in decline and thus unable to defend its separate entity; nor could any blending of social groups be thought of in the strongly hierarchical society of medieval or Renaissance Europe, where dress and ornament indicate rank and standing. That change would come, between the later seventeenth and the eighteenth century, with the wider distribution and less open display of power as the social structure grew increasingly political. Until then, in western Europe at least, ceremony, ritual and etiquette had served to set apart and distinguish the court and all its members, both individually and collectively. There was rivalry between different courts which was a political matter, since ceremony, ritual and etiquette all contributed to show how great the ruler was, and placed him on a scale of precedence which was at the same time an accepted scale of values.

The urban patrician class, especially in Italy, where it differed sharply from its equivalent in the Calvinist Low Countries, merits separate discussion. The social patterns of this class, though varying in the Renaissance period, were based, in town *palazzo* and rural villa alike, on an interrelation of groups rather than of individuals. The patricians, in other words, were imitating what we have called the princely courts.

Este family tree, showing Azzo VI, Lord of Ferrara in 1209, and his descendants. From a fifteenth-century illuminated manuscript.

Courtization of the warrior class

If we consider the court as a self-contained unit, and study the structures it evolved and its internal social relations, we will see that there is no obvious unifying and consecutive line of

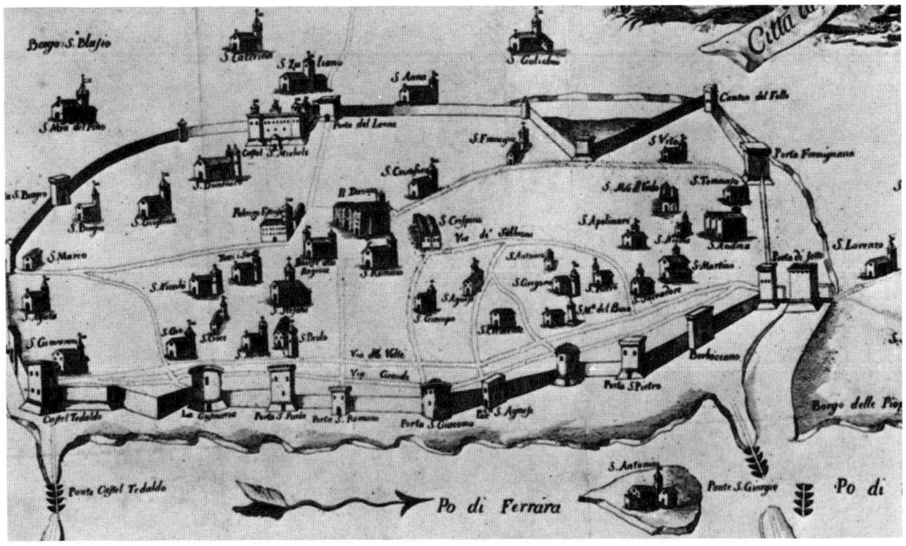

Above: Ferrara and its most important buildings at the end of the fourteenth century. The dominance of the Este family since the late twelfth century was confirmed with the construction of the castle (top left on the map), begun by Bartolino da Novara for Duke Niccolò II in 1385 and completed in the sixteenth century. The university, where the great flowering of Ferrarese humanism began in the early fifteenth century, was founded in 1391.
Below, right: a plan of Milan in the first half of the fifteenth century.

development, and that "civilization" does not stem from the court as such. Norbert Elias, like many before him, has explored the notion of a steady development of courtly custom, linking it to Max Weber's theory that the state, between the barbarous early Middle Ages and the Renaissance, gradually monopolized the use of violence. He sees the process as leading from a vaguely defined period of barbarism, when the warlike instincts of the warrior caste have full play, to an age of *civilité*; and to it he gives the name *Verhöflichung*, or "courtization" of that caste. The "free medieval warrior nobility" used direct violence as its "indispensable weapon" until some prince arose capable of appropriating this weapon to himself, thus making the exercise of force a "public" affair. From that moment on people were torn "between their antagonism to the constrictions imposed on them, their hatred of their dependence and subjection and their nostalgia for the old free rivalries of knighthood on the one hand; and on the other, pride in their own self-control and the new pleasures it brought within their grasp. They had, in short, advanced a step further on the road to civilization."

Yet imperial Byzantium, papal Rome and the Carolingian court at Aix-la-Chapelle can show, from the fourth to the ninth century, the same internal organization and relationships as those of Versailles under Louis XIV – regarded by Norbert Elias as the high-water mark of a "civilizing process" begun with the first institution of a court. Also the same are the social hierarchy and the chain of command, essential gauges of differentiation and distance in any social group and found in every court, medieval or Renaissance.

We are not, of course, dealing with something static. Changes occurred in the 800 years which divide the Carolingian world from the *grand siècle* of Louis XIV. A new attitude to religion affects the ceremonial of sacramental monarchy; the machinery of state is ever more complicated, and traffic in offices begets a new "feudalism" of bureaucrats and administrators, the *noblesse de robe*. It could even be argued that the medieval idea of the king as *imago Christi* lay beneath that of his duality as twin persons, the private and the public man; and in the identification of court with king (the word *cubiculum* denoting the whole palace) lay the fatal seed of the divorce of court from state that corroded princely power. This identification, basic to the thought of jurists in Elizabethan England, is yet more firmly held by monarchical theorists in the seventeenth century, who distinguished between *corpus Reipublicae mysticum* and the person of the king. And that brings us to the downfall of the courts, to be ratified, as it were, by regicides in 1649 and 1793.

The court was an entity, something unique, a product of unrepeatable circumstances, geographico-territorial, or political, or both. At

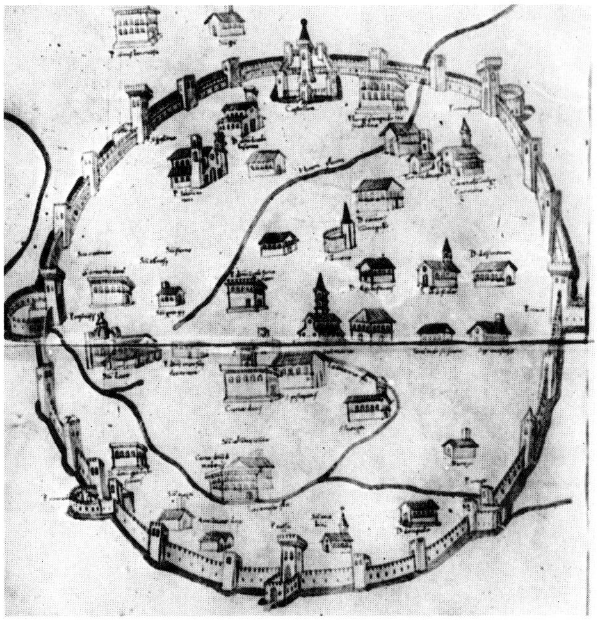

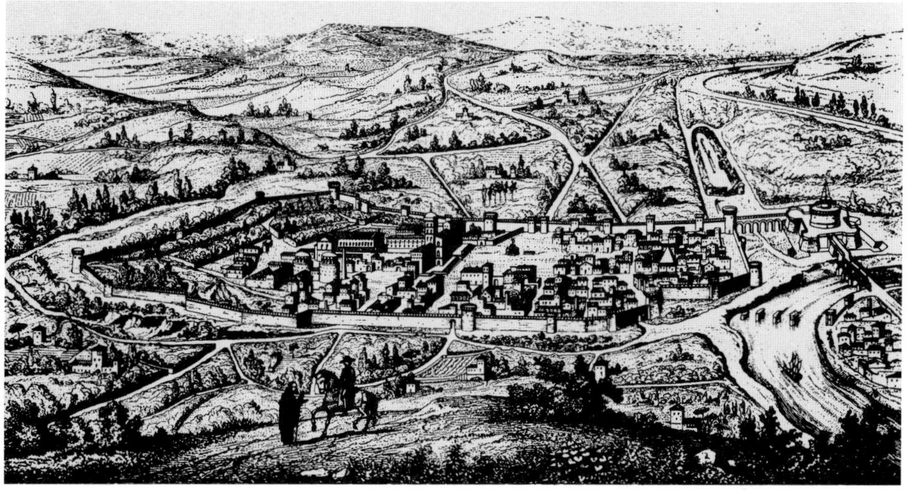

Top: view of Florence in the first half of the sixteenth century.
Above: Rome in the sixteenth century, showing the Leonine walls, the Vatican complex and Castel Sant'Angelo.

Versailles, when the Duc de Lorraine aspired to the enormous distinction of a chair in the Sun King's presence, on the grounds that one was granted him at the imperial court, Louis XIV informed him that "the emperor has one ceremonial, and I another." (A rebuke reported, in a letter of 1 October 1691, by Madame-Charlotte, Princess Palatine, second wife of Louis' brother, the Duc d'Orléans).

It is, then, not easy to trace the evolution of "the court," even if we exclude the courts of non Christian countries. We do better to study the birth, development, expansion and organization of this or that particular court, relating it to contemporary, but not necessarily similar, establishments.

And what finer example could there be of the wide variation of custom, ceremonial and etiquette between court and court in a broad contemporary spectrum than Lucrezia Borgia's wedding? Ferrara in 1502, at the time of her marriage to Duke Alfonso, was the meeting place of several mutually uncomprehending worlds. With the bride were Roman princes and Spanish courtiers. The bridegroom's gentlemen were bred in the manners of Burgundy, whose court had been the pattern in the time of his uncle Borso. There were ladies from Mantua (where fashion and etiquette had a Sforza tinge, adopted from Lombardy), in attendance on his sister Isabella; and ladies from Urbino in attendance on their duchess Elisabetta Gonzaga, who was her sister-in-law.

Soon after the wedding Elisabetta received a letter from the critic Vincenzo Colli. (He was known as Calmeta and before joining the entourage of the bride's brother, Cesare Borgia, had been secretary to another of Alfonso's sisters, Beatrice d'Este, Duchess of Milan, who died in 1497). The letter was full of gossipy comment on the Romans and Spaniards, and Elisabetta's reply is illuminating, not only for the ignorance it reveals of different, though contemporary, worlds, but for the serene assumption that *dominus* and *domina* are *arbitri elegantiarum*. "I have always had, and continue to hold," she says, "the highest opinion of all the Romans and Spaniards who came to Ferrara – their virtues and good manners earned it... I cannot fault the dress of the Roman nobles, nor accuse them of being chilly or reserved: for did they not notice that one of our number was remarkably clever, and nickname her, with one accord, 'the schoolmistress'? . . . You seem much to admire the new hats and the different fashions. Well, some of the ladies would have loved to invent some strange new fashion themselves, but did not, as people already knew about hose *à la* Sforza, and ducal devices in classical-style caps, and they had no wish to displease by imitation . . . From what you say of what went on at the festivities . . . I think you must mean the supper given by the Signora Marchesana (Isabella d'Este) while a comedy was performed. I can only point out that ladies of our standing are and should be free to do what they like and when they like, without being accused of common behaviour . . . As for judging who were the handsomest gentlemen, it is nothing to do with me. Let others decide, who studied them more closely . . ."

Courtly Progression

The river Adige and the castle at Verona. Detail of an early sixteenth-century fresco by Nicola Giolfino in the Franciscan chapel of the church of San Bernardino, Verona.

Above: the Lateran basilica and papal palace, with the statue of Marcus Aurelius in the position it occupied throughout the Middle Ages. Sixteenth-century drawing. On the pattern of imperial Constantinople, the Lateran was a sacred city with its own enclosing walls, set within another, larger city. Below: the papal palace at Viterbo, dating from the curia's brief residence during the thirteenth century.

Princely Italy

In the 1520s, by which time the great monarchies of Europe had become unified states, Niccolò Machiavelli blamed the Church for "our ruin" – that is, the ruin of Italy. Since the days of the Lombards the Church "has held, and keeps the Province divided." Sixty years on, Scipione Ammirato – a canon of Florence though a southerner by birth – points out in rejoinder that the Romans, in his opinion, had enslaved the free peoples of the Peninsula. "Effective and mighty as they were, the Romans brought not glory but destruction to what was beautiful, good and gallant in Italy." Former liberty had been restored at the fall of the Empire, since when the Italian peoples were at peace under the just government of princes of their own.

But it is impossible to regard Italy as a political unity. Or at least, not until her most thoughtful minds, inspired by the unification of France (where Gascony was incorporated in 1453, Burgundy in 1477 and Brittany in 1491) or Spain (with the marriage of Ferdinand of Aragon and Isabella of Castille, and the conquest of Granada in 1491), were pondering the problem of "national" identity. Why should Italy not be a nation, distinct from nations beyond the Alps? Why not a national monarchy? Carlo Sigonio of Modena, a famous teacher of the humanities, wrote a book entitled *De Regno Italia*, but could do no more than make a legend of an unattainable idea. Political life was too fragmented, too many courts rose and fell within the bounds of Italy, for such a proposal to succeed.

Yet even among those tangled courts there were a few general historical-geographical movements, precursors of the Risorgimento and its ensuing unity. Long before the Risorgimento there was a constant, if slow, process of unification. Between the fifteenth and sixteenth century, for instance, lesser feudal lordships are swallowed up by larger states. From the end of the sixteenth to the mid seventeeth century the process continued, consolidated by the establishment of the Papal States in northern and central Italy; and wars of succession at the beginning of the eighteenth century led to a general redistribution of lands and holdings in the Po valley. The south, on the other hand – including the islands of Sicily and Sardinia – was united between the thirteenth and the fourteenth century, and thereafter formed a solid block, unsplintered under a succession of ruling dynasties, Swabian, Angevin, Aragonese or Bourbon, until the Risorgimento. Save for the Angevin period in Naples in the late thirteenth and early fourteenth centuries, and for the passing of Sardinia first to the Hapsburg empire and then to the House of Savoy, the south was chiefly under Spanish influence.

There are, then, three great phases of unification – at the Renaissance, and during the seventeenth and eighteenth centuries – and within them various dynasties rule for considerable spans of time: dynasties whose courts are neither similar, nor of parallel development.

An eastern court

Any study of these long spans of rule must bring us, naturally, to Rome, though we cannot accurately speak of "Papal States" before the Gothic Wars and the Lombard era. The *Constituto Constantini*, which supposedly gave all Italy to the Church in 313, was forged, in fact, in the reign of Charlemagne's father, Pepin the Short. The Church's first territories, nucleus of the Patrimony of St Peter, were lands between Orto and Bomarzo ceded to Pope Zacharias by the Lombard King Liutprand in 741. With the fall of the Lombard kingdom and the confirmatory Donation of Charlemagne, the papal possessions extended over Latium, the duchy of Spoleto and the cities of the Maritime Pentapolis; and in 1115 lands were acquired under the will of Matilda, Countess of Tuscany. It was a fairly small estate even then, and yet, between the sixth and the ninth century, the papal curia had already grown into a large court, its expansion having nothing to do with territorial extent. "The princes of the Church alone," says Machiavelli, "have a state without defending it, have subjects without governing them." (*The Prince,* chapter XI). Ecclesiastical power, or rather, the power of the Roman curia, did indeed flourish within and across every state in Christendom. It was Rome that nominated bishops and abbots, sanctioned the *regulae* of the religious orders, that levied tithes and distributed prebends and benefices. Many fellow-travellers accompanied pious pilgrims on the road to Rome – prelates visiting *ad limina apostolorum*, tithe-collectors, and, very often, litigious holders of prebend or benefice, bent on laying some case before a papal tribunal.

The curia had been lodged since the fourth century in the various palaces built by a Roman patrician family, the Platii Laterani, near the Porta Asinaria. As early as 313 the council convened to combat the heresy of Donatus met "in the house of Fausta," *in domo Faustae*, and the *palatium Juliae* is spoken of, after Constantine's day, as a bishop's residence. These buildings were adapted, and much altered, to the needs of the papal court and partly demolished in the reign of Sixtus III (432–440) to make way for the huge five-aisled basilica, originally dedicated to the Redeemer. The curia was then installed in two palaces, the *interius* and *exterius* (nearer to and further from the church). Oratories – of the Holy Cross, St John the Baptist, St John the Evangelist, and the Dalmatian St Venantius – were in time added to the palace-complex, and Leo III (795–816) raised his magnificent Triclinium, or banqueting-house. By the ninth century the curia was thus a small township, dominated by tall towers and focused on basilica and Triclinium. Only twice did the papal court leave the Lateran, for Viterbo in 1266–81, and Avignon from 1306–77. After each exile it returned, and had been there for nearly a thousand years when it finally removed in 1420. It then transferred to the other side of the Tiber, where much building was in progress, and settled in what was known (from the ninth-century defensive walls which Leo IV had girdled the Constantinian basilica of St Peter) as

The papal palace at Avignon, built between 1334 and 1352 by the first popes of the Avignon "captivity." This removal affected the customs and etiquette of the Roman court, influenced not only by its Provençal counterpart, but by a sequence of no less than seven French pontiffs.

The Vatican, showing the Leonine walls and Castel Sant'Angelo. Detail of a fresco painted in 1580–83 by Antonio Danti in the Galleria delle Carte Geografiche in the Vatican. The curia returned from Avignon, not to the Lateran but to a network of palaces in which pope and cardinals spread their courts throughout the city.

civitas leonina, the Leonine City.

A reminder of the continuity of papal with imperial Rome was the *caballus Constantini*, the equestrian statue of Marcus Aurelius then in the central Lateran piazza and thought to be the emperor Constantine. Yet the early Christian architecture around it, despite inescapable Roman influence, had a strong flavour of the Eastern Empire, and no less did the Roman court reflect Byzantium, to which it was subordinate from the sixth to the eighth century. Of the 24 popes between John IV and Hadrian I – that is, between 640 and 772 – 14 were from Greece, the eastern Mediterranean or regions of Italy under Byzantine rule. It is hardly surprising that even the papal coronation ceremony was modelled on that of Constantinople. Pontiffs since, if not before, Constantine I (708–715) had worn a high conical headdress of white silk, the *camelaucum*, like that of the Eastern Emperor. The Donation of Constantine, an eighth-century Frankish forgery, says that Pope Sylvester was presented with a jewelled gold diadem such as Roman emperors wore: the first and oldest version of the miter that was introduced at the end of the tenth or beginning of the eleventh century. But it seems certain that some kind of coronation ceremonial, based on the Byzantine rite, was practiced in Rome before the papacy had any direct contact with the Franks.

It is interesting to compare the culminating moments of the Byzantine and Roman coronations. At Constantinople the emperor was invested with the tunic-like *divitision* and *tzitzakion* in the *mitatorion*, an area reserved for the imperial family, before entering the basilica itself, with the patriarch, to receive the last ceremonial vestment, the chlamys. By the seventh century an identical *rite de passage*, with investiture and enthronement is found in Rome. From a later book of ceremonial, that of Cardinal Jacopo Caetani, nephew of Boniface VIII, we learn of investiture with the pallium in the chapel of St Gregory. (For Cardinal Stefaneschi, 1261–1308, who also compiled a manual of ceremony, the pallium means more than anything; it is *plenitudo pontificalis officii*). This donning of ceremonial vestments was followed, in Byzantium as in Rome, by a solemn entry into the basilica of the Holy City – Santa Sophia at Constantinople, the Lateran church of the Redeemer in Rome. In Constantinople the patriarch prayed over the crown before placing it on the sovereign's head. In Rome, from the ninth century onwards, the senior cardinal deacon crowned the new pope with the miter and placed the ring on his finger.

After the second stage of the ritual came the no less important *acclamatio*, derived from the election of a Roman *imperator* by the acclamation of his troops. In Constantinople the *demos*, represented by the two main factions of the circus, twice shouted, "Holy, holy, holy! Glory to God in the highest, and on earth peace!" The choir then chanted, "May the great emperor and autocrat (naming him) live for many years!" At this point, according to the *Book of Ceremonies* drawn up by Constantine VII Porphyrogenitus, the newly crowned emperor went into the *mitatorion*, there to receive the ritual homage of the court dignitaries, who in due hierarchical order performed the *proskynesis* (genuflection) and kissed his knees.

The emperor Constantine VII also left on record the royal salutations (*laudes regiae*) at imperial weddings. This acclamation, too, is ritualized, with a chorus of *pollá, pollá, pollá* (literally: many, many, many), answered by the people with, "Many years, many fortunate years!" Again the choir chants, naming the couple, "Many fortunate years to you, o autocrats of the Romans!" and the response is the same.

"Many fortunate years to you, o servants of the Lord!"

"Many years!"

"Many years to you, and may you rule in happiness!" (Literally, have joy in your scepters).

"Many years!"

"Many years to thee (naming the emperor), o Basileus of the Romans!"

"Many years!"

"Many and fortunate years, among the Augusti and the *Porphyrogenitoí*!"

"Many years!"

"And may the Lord and Creator of all things –"

"May the Lord and Creator of all things –" (repeated three times).

"Who has crowned you with His hand,"

"Who has crowned you with His hand" (this is also repeated three times).

"Fill you full of years among the Augusti and the *Porphyrogenitoí*!" (repeated three times).

After these responses the *demos*, divided into its two main circus factions, would hail the imperial pair with wishes for long life and a long reign.

The *laudes* sung at a papal enthronement are clearly the imperial acclamation in a ritualized form. Until Hildebrand of Soana was elected pope as Gregory VII the *populus romanus* was represented by the lay members of the congregation. Gregory was crowned at San Pietro in Vincoli in 1073 and the ceremony, reconstructed by Onofrio Panvinio in the sixteenth century, was attended by "many of both sexes, and of various ranks," together with the clergy. "We have elected a devout man as our shepherd and supreme pontiff," says the reconstructed account, "with the acclamation of the laity." After the acclamation, the chief deacon

Transverse section of the old Constantinian basilica of St Peter. Sixteenth-century copy of a fresco in the Vatican Grottoes. Below: St Peter's Square, c.1588. Fresco in the Sistine Hall, Vatican Library.

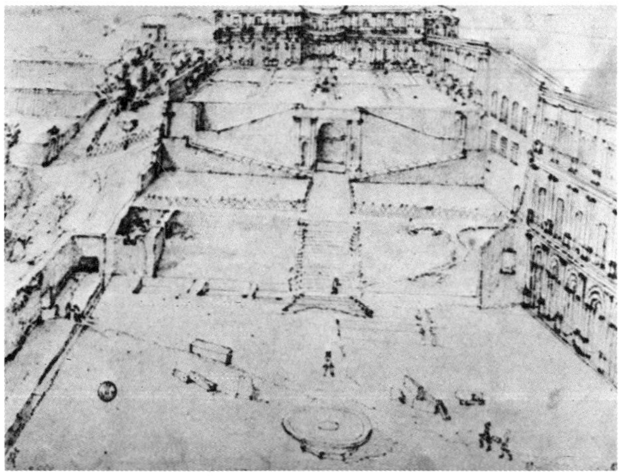

asked the congregation, "*Placet vobis*?" to which they replied "*Placet*" (it pleases us).

"*Vultis eum*?"

"*Volumus*" (we want him).

"*Laudatis eum?*"

"*Laudamus*." (We praise him).

The dialogue completed, "Pope Gregory was acclaimed by all the clergy and people."

But after this coronation that particular ceremony, the *collaudatio*, was discontinued. The autocratic Gregory, who in the *Dictatus papae* summarized his ideas on papal supremacy, could scarcely approve the popular presence at the papal *adventus* and coronation. He must have heard the acclamations of the people on that 28 April 1073 in San Pietro in Vincoli as a diminution, or at least a limitation, of his power. Yet, when he wished to revise the ceremony, in 1080, he could not entirely supress the *acclamatio*. He allotted it instead to the curia, whose legal officials and clerks thenceforth assumed the function of the *demos*. In the new ceremonial – followed, for example, by Gregory x on 27 March 1271 – the pope was invested, prayed at the high altar, then ascended his throne as the cardinal deacons and subdeacons ranged themselves on one side of the altar, the curia officials on the other, and the *laudes* began. The chief deacon "half read, half chanted in a loud voice: *Exaudi Christe* (Hear us, o Christ!). To this the lawyers and clerks replied, "Long life to our lord the pope, by God's will supreme pontiff and universal pope!" Then came the triple *Exaudi Domine* and, also thrice-repeated, *Salvator mundi te illum adiuva* (May the Saviour of the world assist thee). The same invocation was addressed to a long list of saints, and the *laudes* ended with the *Kyrie eleison*.

That the significance of the *acclamatio* was lost and the emphasis now on the divine appointment of an autocratic ruler, does not invalidate the original derivation of the papal *laudes* from those of Byzantium.

There were other resemblances and borrowings. Torches, ciborium, and canopy of state affirm the godlike nature of the pontiff, as they affirmed that of the Basileus at Constantinople who was *Christomimetes* and *Cosmocrator*, the Image of Christ, Omnipotent. When Rome, threatened by the Lombards, sought alliance with the Franks, and Pope Stephen III crowned Pepin the Short of St Denis, he was probably acting as the intermediary between the Carolingian and Byzantine courts, introducing the *laudes regiae* to France.

The connection between Rome and Byzantium is apparent, beyond the ceremonial sphere, in the physical surroundings of the papal court. The very layout of the Lateran complex resembled that of the imperial enclave at Constantinople with the tenth-century walls of Nicephorus Phocas. At Constantinople court life centered on Santa Sophia and the *Chrystotriclinos*; at Rome on the Lateran basilica and the Triclinium of Leo III. The *kouboukleion* of the Eastern Emperor is a sacred and ideal nucleus, whose officials preside over many other departments of the palace. Similarly, the *cubiculum Lateranense* is the heart of the "inner palace," or *palatium interius*, and its *cubicularius*, assisted by a *vicedominus* and such

DEL CARDINALE DI FABIO ALBERGATI GENTILHVOMO BOLOGNESE LIBRI TRE ALL'ILLVSTRISSIMO, E REVERENDISS. SIGNOR D. ODOARDO CARDINAL FARNESE.

IN BOLOGNA Presso gli Heredi di Gio. Rossi

Con licenza de' Superiori.

Frontispiece of Del cardinale *(1591) by Fabio Albergati, a book on the courts of the Roman cardinals and the construction of their palaces.*
Below: part of Rome at the end of the fifteenth century, from the Chronicle *of Hartmannus Schedel, Nuremberg, 1493. In the upper right-hand corner is the Belvedere palace, whose courtyard Bramante began even before the rebuilding of St Peter's.*
Above, left: the Belvedere in the mid sixteenth century. Drawing by Giovanni Antonio Dosio.

Below: Bramante's plan for St Peter's and the Belvedere courtyard. This courtyard has been described as the first open-air theater built since classical times, the first museum, and the first true blending of garden and architecture: a definition confirmed by the illustration (right) in which it is viewed from the northern end during a tournament in 1565.

underlings as the *vestatarius* who looked after the wardrobe, and the *superista* in command of the palace-guard, regulates the day-to-day activity of the whole curia.

In its structure, too, the curia combined Roman and Byzantine elements, as in the *Presbyterium Apostolicae Sedis*. At first the entire Roman clergy sat on the papal council, but membership from the fourth century onwards was restricted to the 25 *presbyteri cardinales* and the deacons of the seven ecclesiastical regions into which Rome had been divided since the third century. It acted until 1170 and was then replaced by the *Consistorium*, composed of cardinals only. Monthly meetings were instituted by Alexander III, but Innocent III, soon afterwards, held them every three weeks. To implement its business the *Consistorium* had a staff of clerks and secretaries whom the documents refer to as *scribae*, *notarii* or *apocrisarii*.

Also based on the Byzantine model were the *Auditorium papae*, or papal court of justice, and the chanceries, each a body of seven senior officials, the *judices*. Of these seven the *primicerius* and *secundicerius* dealt with political affairs, and the *arcarius* with financial; the *sacellarius* was head of the treasury and made disbursements; the *protoscrinarius* had charge of the muniments. (A *scrinium* was the box in which papers were kept, and the clerks were *scrinarii* and *tabelliones*, or "writers"). There was the *primo defensor*, whose functions remain something of a mystery, though he may have been what was later called the *advocatus Ecclesiae*; and lastly the almoner, or *nomenclator*. Whereas the clergy were recruited from the *schola cantorum*, notaries and scribes were

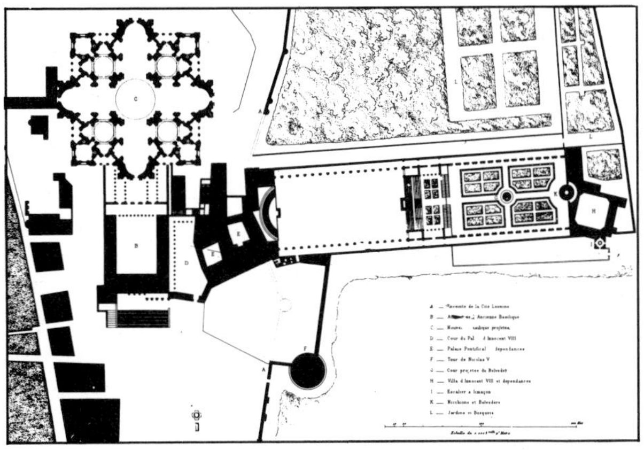

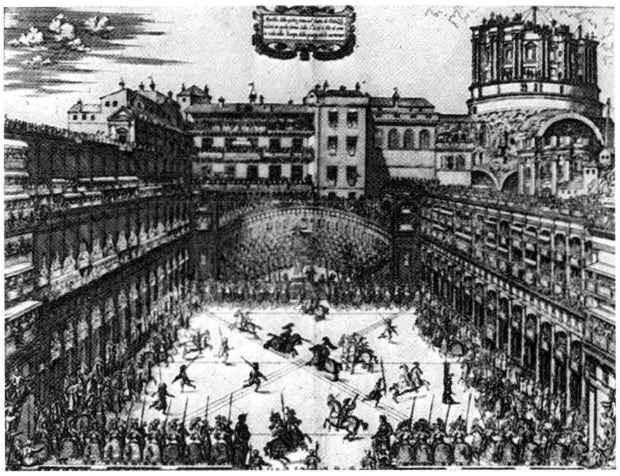

trained for the chanceries in a separate *schola*, much as they would have been in the *tabularii*, or record-offices, of ancient Rome.

Though this curial structure, almost complete between the sixth and ninth century, might be amplified or modified as time went by, the distribution of departmental responsibility and the organization of the pope's *cubiculum* and *palatium* were fundamentally unaltered for hundreds of years. Not until 1588, under Sixtus V, was there any major change. Before that date the structure and ceremonial of the curia were more or less as established in its early Lateran period.

The brief sojourn at Viterbo left no mark on papal custom and etiquette, for the court had not quitted its own cultural milieu. At Avignon, however, this was not so. There the court was influenced by that of Provence and by seven French pontiffs, from Clement V (Bertrand de Got, the first pope of the exile) to Gregory IX (Pierre Roger, who ended it). And during the Great Schism, after the return to Rome, six antipopes, from Clement VII (1378–94) to John XXIII (1410–15), were of the French, or Avignon, persuasion.

The palace at Avignon, built by Pierre Poisson for Benedict XII (1333–42), was still in essence a castle, dominated by the frowning Tour St Jean and centered on a rectangular courtyard. Clement VI (1342–52) extended it, on the plans of Jean de Loubière, adding a second castle and a second courtyard. The Palais Neuf had a huge ground-floor audience chamber, and access from the courtyard to a first-floor tric-

The Sicilian court was the most splendid of the thirteenth century. The school of poetry which flourished around Emperor Frederick II, Stupor Mundi *– a gifted soldier, shrewd politician, generous patron of the arts and himself a poet – was the precursor of the magnificent vernacular poetry that culminated in Dante's* Divine Comedy. *Above: the imperial crown, probably first worn by Otto the Great in 962, recalls two headdresses familiar in the ancient world, the laurel crown and the* imperator's *helmet.*

linium. The south end of this triclinium was fitted with a screen behind which the food was prepared and carved: an indication that there were new notions of what was acceptable, or otherwise, to public view.

Extension

It was not to a resumption of Roman custom pure and simple that the curia came home from the Avignon "captivity" and the fact is obvious under the humanist popes of the fifteenth century, from Nicholas v Parentucelli to Pius II Piccolomini and Paul III Barbo. An urban and patrician culture was giving rise to significant behavioural change and this increasingly affected attitudes to physical space. The ancient accommodation at the Lateran had lain empty for 70 years; it cannot have seemed habitable. But within the Leonine walls was the palace of the Orsini Pope Nicholas III (1277–88). This Nicholas v decided to enlarge and live in as his *cubiculum*: the project, which could not be carried out all at once, is described in detail by the Florentine Giannozzo Manetti in his *Vita Nicolai papae v*. (Manetti, a leading figure in the enterprise, was the friend, and later the opponent, of Cosimo the Elder. His treatise in four books, *De dignitate et excellentia hominis*, is a humanist manifesto).

If the *palatium novum* of Nicholas v remained externally a thirteenth-century fortress, the new interior proportions were those of a palace in Florence. It was perhaps no accident that the erudite architect Leon Battista Alberti was throughout Nicholas's reign a papal inspector of monuments, and devoted these Roman years to the reinterpretation, in the idiom of Vitruvius and according to the harmonic principles advocated by Manetti, of the architecture of imperial Rome.

The aim now was not, however, to make a sacred precinct, as in the palace at Avignon, but to create, for pope and cardinals, an articulated series of palaces. From Castel Sant' Angelo to the Capitoline Hill ran an axial street, the *via papalis*, or Via Papale (of which traces still exist in Via del Governo Vecchio), and eventually there gravitated to and around it the numerous courts of the cardinals. The city was, as it were, invaded by the papal court, and the curia spread itself through a series of monumental palaces. Materially and conceptually, the papal palace extended into the heart of Rome.

By 1450, for example, Cardinal Jean de la Roche Taillé had refurbished a thirteenth-century house there on such a scale that Biondo Flavio compared it, in his *Roma instaurata*, with the papal palace at St Peter's: "the said cardinal has made it so magnificent that there is in Rome nothing finer, from the palace of St Peter downwards." A satellite court was emulating the court from which it sprang. Yet this was only the beginning of an architectural transformation. Cardinal Nardini and Domenico Capranica, prefect of Rome, had their palaces on Via Papale, while, between 1450 and 1470–80, the area from Piazza Navona to the Campo dei Fiori had taken on a new aspect. In Campo dei Fiori itself Aeneas Silvius Piccolomini built a towered palazzo. Cardinal Francesco Condulmer chose his site further towards Pompey's

Theater, and between the Campo and Via Papale Rodrigo Borgia, vice-chancellor of the Holy Roman Church, raised one of the most imposing of the cardinalate palaces. Its only rival (now Palazzo Venezia) was built in 1455–68 by the Venetian Pietro Barbo, whose titular church was San Marco, at the foot of the Capitoline Hill. Near the Santi Apostoli, not far away, were the palaces of Giuliano Della Rovere, of Cardinal Bessarion and – particularly splendid – that of Raffaele Riario, nephew of Sixtus IV.

All this was, in one sense, redistribution: a reorganization of the space to be occupied by the individual dignitaries of the pontifical court and their sovereign. It is to be noted that neither Barbo nor Piccolomini, on election as pope, left his own residence for the Vatican, though that palace had been enlarged by Nicholas V. Not until the reign of the Della Rovere Pope Sixtus IV (1471–84) was anything more done there. His was the ground-floor library, planned by Bartolomeo Platina in 1475; he demolished the *capella magna* of Nicholas III and had it rebuilt (1471–85). The creation of the Belvedere as a villa-retreat by his successor, the Cibo Pope Innocent VIII (1484–92), was the first real step in the construction of a new group of buildings which would make the Vatican such a palace-citadel as the Lateran had been. The cardinals, however, were not attracted to live in it, for by now the court was scattered and they maintained their private courts henceforward as equals of the secular Roman princes.

Frederick's career was meteoric, the achievements of his reign short-lived – a transience hinted at in the miniature (top) from a manuscript of the Carmina Burana, *portraying the emperor on the wheel of fortune. Staatliche Bibliothek, Munich.*
Above: one of Frederick's emblems, the imperial eagle, in a ceiling mosaic in the Palazzo Reale, Palermo; and (right) the sword and sword belt worn by the emperor at his coronation.
Above, right: the crown of his first wife, Constance of Aragon.

So important, and so interesting, were these establishments that in 1510 the lawyer Paolo Cortesi, writing his *De cardinalatu* – a book to match Machiavelli's *The Prince* or Castiglione's *The Courtier* – felt he must have a full chapter, entitled *Qualis esse debeat domus cardinalis*, on what a cardinal's palace should be. Twenty-five rooms, and their uses, are listed. On his ground floor the cardinal required a vestibule, entrance-hall, atrium, portico (referred to as a *compluvium*), quarters for the grooms, guard-room, guest-rooms (*hospitalia cubicula*), library, court-room or *auditorium*, summer bed-rooms and a music room. The mezzanine rooms on the staircase, from which the internal life of

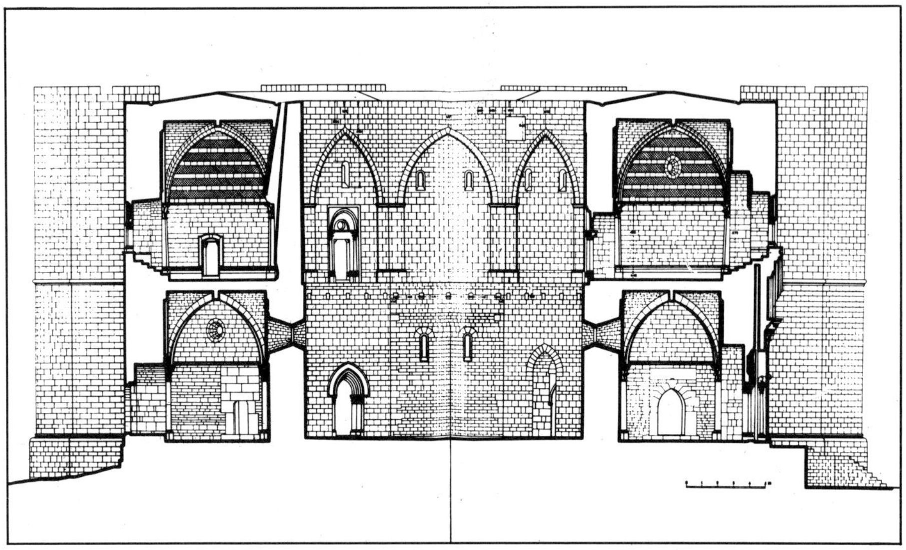

Castel del Monte and (above) elevation, built by Frederick II, for hunting and occasional residence, on a lonely height in the Murge region of Apulia. Opposite, left: top, plan of Castel del Monte; below: two carved stone bosses from vaulting in the castle. Opposite, right: above, courtyard of Castel del Monte; below: rusticated walls of Gioia del Colle, a twelfth-century castle enlarged and embellished by Frederick.

the household could be observed, were for the *maestro di casa* and steward, or *architriclinius*, and included store rooms and pantries. On the *piano nobile* above were the great hall where courtiers spent their day awaiting commands, the chapel, audience-chamber, strong-room (*repositoria argenti*), the collection of antiquities (*cella gemmarum*) and the cardinal's *dormitorium* and study (his *studiolo*, or *cella locubratoria*). Secretaries and clerks were in the north-facing rooms of the same floor, together with the chaplains and other courtiers (*scutiferi*), while servants lodged in the attics under the roof. The audience-chamber is provided with such details as concealed windows and ducts in the walls that allowed one to inspect and overhear one's visitors before proceeding to greet them.

Some 30 years later the subject is taken up, in all its complexity, by Priscianese, with advice on how to conduct a princely Roman household; and in 1591 by Fabio Albergati in *Del Cardinale*, a work in three volumes, dedicated to Odoardo Farnese on his elevation to the purple. A century after *De cardinalatu* the topic flourished in Girolamo Lunadoro's *Lo Stato Presente della Corte di Roma*, and was still a live issue in 1774, when Lunadoro's book was "retouched and expanded" by Francescantonio Zaccaria, who "consecrated" the result to Cardinal Domenico Orsini of Aragon.

From 1510, when Cortesi was writing, to 1774, there had been a vast increase in papal territory. After being practically stable since the acquisition of the Countess Matilda's lands in the twelfth century until the return from Avignon in the fourteenth, the papal territory now incorporated much of central Italy, the Apennine region, Emilia and Romagna. Cesare Borgia's attempt to carve a dukedom for himself, *ducatus Romandiolae*, from the States of the Church in the early years of the sixteenth century led in the end to the reassertion of direct Church rule over the Romagnol lordships, from Pesaro to Forlí and Rimini. Julius II, pope within a year of the death of Cesare's father, Alexander VI, not only deprived the newly raised duke of power and occupied lands he had as yet barely subdued; profiting by the misfortunes of the Baglioni, and ousting the Bentivoglio family, he also strengthened the papal hold on Perugia and Bologna, and seized Ravenna from the Venetians. This policy, aimed at excluding intermediate feudal authority from the States of the Church, continued with the annexation of Ferrara from the Este in 1598.

In the seventeenth century just two territories were wanting (apart from Avignon and Benevento, both far away), to consolidate the domain: the duchy of Urbino and the smaller, but strategically important, Farnese duchy of Castro and Ronciglione. The former was ceded by the last Della Rovere duke, who died in 1631; the latter conquered by force of arms, after two successive wars, in 1649. By then the

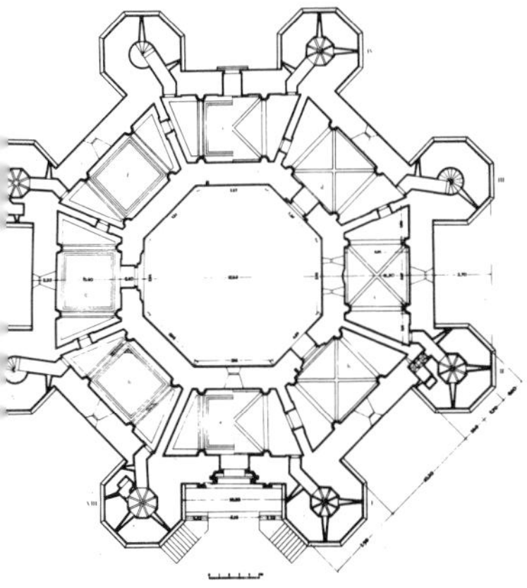

The ground plan of Castel del Monte which resembles the form of the imperial crown.

Papal State – or, more correctly, States – had engulfed everything except Comacchio to the north-east, a fragment of the duchy of Ferrara which the Este still held as an imperial fief. But in 1708 the War of the Spanish Succession afforded a pretext; it was absorbed, and the unification begun by Julius II was complete.

Swabia, Anjou, Catalonia and Castille

Another long territorial occupation was that of southern Italy. The Kingdom of Naples and the Two Sicilies, as it was known from the mid fifteenth century onwards, lasted, within the boundaries by then attained, until the Risorgimento; and yet it is a text-book example of the evolution of different courts, each with its separate development and history, within one realm.

The unification process was set in motion by Roger II, Duke of Salerno, with his coronation in Palermo as King of Sicily, Calabria and Capua in the Christmas of 1130. The Norman palace of Palermo, with its magnificent palatine chapel, conveys, better than anything else that survives from his reign, the atmosphere of that court at the crossroads of three cultures – Greek, Latin and Arab. It was against the Byzantines and the African coast that King Roger and his renegade Greek admiral, George of Antioch, directed their best efforts, but the sole enduring result of expeditions against Djerba in 1135, Tripoli in 1145 and Corfu a year later was the expulsion of the Byzantines from Apulia which, in the fifteenth century, suffered a Turkish invasion from North Africa, and Roger's being able, in due course, to concentrate on the affairs of Italy instead. His grandson, Frederick of Hohenstaufen, was no sooner elected Holy Roman Emperor at Aix-la-Chapelle in 1215 and crowned by the pope in Rome in 1220, than he concentrated on re-establishing the Kingdom of Sicily, fighting on the mainland as his grandfather fought on the Mediterranean.

In a dominion that extended across the straits to Calabria, Apulia and Terra di Lavoro, Palermo was too far from the center of things, and Frederick's constant migrations left the old palace deserted for much of the time. His stays there were brief: from 1222 to 1225, when he

Details from the bas-relief on the triumphal arch at Castel Nuovo, Naples, by Guillermo Sagrera. Left: armed soldiers. Below: Alfonso the Magnanimous. Alfonso of Aragon became king of Naples, replacing the Angevins, in 1443. The triumphal arch (opposite) celebrates his achievements. Between the twelfth century and the unification of Italy in the nineteenth, the southern kingdom knew four courts and the cultures of four different dynasties. The Norman-Swabians, whose culture was Arabic, were followed by the French Angevins; the house of Aragon brought the influence of Spain, the Bourbons that of Catalonia.

was directing a war against the Saracens, and in 1233, when he was subduing a threatened revolt. The Hohenstaufen court was based at Melfi or at his beloved Foggia, *regalis sedes inclita imperialis*, the luxurious palace which chroniclers say was the scene of every delight. "There are choirs making music, dressed in dazzling clothes; some have been knighted, some bear the insignia of their sundry offices. The day is filled with tournaments, every day a festival, and evening bright as day with torches." Yet Frederick's favourite castle was perhaps Castel del Monte, though he had little time for long visits. Of all the castles he built, it tells us most of what his court was like.

Planned as a series of octagons, Castel del Monte has an octagonal inner court and eight octagonal towers, a scheme possibly intended to reproduce the octagonal form of the imperial crown and thus symbolize Frederick's autocratic power. Castel del Monte is the greatest surviving fruit of his genius and in the influences it reflects – Charlemagne's chapel at Aix, San Vitale at Ravenna and the Mosque of Omar at Jerusalem – epitomizes his own many-faceted culture.

His court was, above all, itinerant. When not in one or another of his Apulian castles the emperor travelled, and with him, in a huge moving camp, went the officers of his retinue, his guard, his harem. (He lived like an oriental monarch and was not called "the Baptized Sultan" for nothing). "He had," in the words of Giovanni Villani, the Florentine chronicler, "many concubines, and catamites in Saracen dress." The harem was in attendance at Ravenna in 1231, at Cremona in 1235, at Verona in 1245. It accompanied him to the fortified camp he built while besieging Parma in 1248 – a transient "city" which he named Vittoria and intended to demolish when the town was won. Flavio Biondo, in his *Decadi*, says there were at Vittoria "animals unknown in any theater of Italy since the fall of the Roman Empire: elephants, dromedaries, panthers, lions, leopards, white bears, dogs – of ferocious aspect though extremely timid – and trained birds of prey . . ."

The endless travel did much to cut off the court from officials, chanceries and judicial departments, and these accordingly developed independently. With the Constitutions of Melfi of 1231 (collected in his *Liber Augustalis*), Frederick produced a coordinated legal code for the Norman state, and from the beginning his eye was on Byzantium. The principle of God-given autocratic power is that of the Eastern Empire: and we may remember that at his Roman coronation he had been anointed *episcopus* by Honorius III and, to emphasize his priestly office, was received as a canon of St Peter's.

The machinery of state he also derived from Constantinople. Seven great officers – constable, admiral, chancellor, justiciar, chamberlain, seneschal and protonotary-logothete – presided over seven administrative departments, while the *Magna Curia* was the equivalent of the Byzantine Consistory. This body, the High Court of the realm, though no longer the imperial "family," or household, was composed of judges who were *familiares*, or ministers, appointed by the emperor, and headed by the chief judicial officer. Its authority stemmed from the throne and it administered justice in the seven mainland and two Sicilian provinces of the kingdom. The protonotary-logothete had charge of both state and court finance, which meant that the court lost its financial autonomy. In his capacity as auditor, the logothete

ALFONSVS REGVM PRINCEPS HANC

PHILOSOPHER PRINCE

1

3

Only two Roman equestrian statues were known to the Renaissance: the *caballus Constantini* (1) on the hill of the Lateran, and another, of Septimius Severus, which survived at Pavia and was called the Regisole. In the former the rider sits with right arm outstretched in the gesture of clemency of the *ad locutium*; in the latter the right arm was raised in the victor's gesture, the *adventus*. With neither of these gestures, part of the symbolical vocabulary of Roman power, was Giovanni da Campione acquainted, apparently, when he made the tomb-monument to Bernabo Visconti at Milan in 1357–60, or that of Cansignorio Della Scala (2) at Verona in 1375. In both statues the hands woodenly grip the reins and there is movement in neither horse nor rider.

The earliest reminiscence of classical equestrian statuary is, in fact, a wall-painting: Paolo Uccello's tomb-fresco of the English *condottiere*, John Hawkwood in the north aisle of the Duomo in Florence. The stance of the horse is that of its classical ancestors, although the rider balances the commander's baton on his right thigh in much the same fixed gesture as that by Giovanni da Campione.

Not until Leonello d'Este commissioned a statue of his father Niccolò III was any equestrian monument made in the true classical tradition, set in a public place, and intended as celebration rather than memorial. Leonello's two artists, Antonio Baroncelli, who designed the horse, and Antonio di Cristoforo, completed the model in 1443, although eight years passed before the statue was finally positioned on its pedestal, designed by Leon Battista Alberti. It was, unhappily, destroyed by French revolutionary troops in 1796, as was the Regisole at Pavia, and exists only as a reproduction (3). A contemporary celebratory statue is that by Donatello of the Venetian *condottiere* Gattamelata, erected at Padua in 1447. Two more *condottieri* were similarly honoured: Niccolò da Tolentino, in 1456, with a painted memorial by Andrea del Castagno, close to Hawkwood's in the Duomo in Florence; and Colleoni, whose statue in Venice was cast by Verrocchio in 1488.

Humanist scholars meanwhile had realized that the bronze figure at the Lateran was not Constantine but Marcus Aurelius (1). It was removed to the Capitol in 1538 by order of the Farnese pope Paul III, and placed on a

2

4

pedestal designed by Michelangelo, inscribed "Marcus, adoptive son of Antoninus Pius." Thereafter the ruler is commonly celebrated as a philosopher-prince on horseback.

The first such statue was that of Henri II of France, commissioned by his widow, Catherine de' Medici, from Daniele da Volterra (d. 1566), follower of Michelangelo. The only record is an engraving by Tempesta showing the horse in familiar classical pose and the king turned to the right, raised arm slightly behind him holding a broken lance in allusion to his death in the lists. In Giambologna's statues of the Medici grand dukes Cosimo I (5) and Ferdinando I (6), this lance becomes a baton, resting on the right thigh. The second statue was completed by Pietro Tacca of Carrara, and they were placed in Florence in Piazza della Signoria and Piazza dell'Annunziata respectively in 1603 and 1605. Ferdinando's pedestal is decorated with a relief of bees about their queen and the motto *Maiestate tantum*, "one rule alone" (8).

Two similar designs by Giambologna were for equestrian statues of Henri IV of France (1604) and Philip III of Spain. The Grand Duke Ferdinando commissioned the latter work as a gift to the king in 1606, and it was later cast by Tacca.

5

6

Wishing to depart from the Roman convention, Leonardo da Vinci depicted a galloping horse in the preparatory drawings and in the now lost model for an equestrian statue – never executed – of Francesco Sforza; the design influenced Pietro Tacca who, in 1621, cast a small model for Charles Emanuel of Savoy. The duke, anxious for immortality on a piazza in Turin, had commissioned this model two years earlier, but the statue was never cast. Leonardo's design was later realized, however, in Gian Lorenzo Bernini's Constantine at St Peter's.

The pair of equestrian bronze figures of the Farnese dukes Alessandro (4) and Ranuccio (7) at Piacenza are by Francesco Mochi da Montevarchi and revert to the Roman fashion. Ranuccio's gesture recalls the *adventus* of the lost Regisole of Pavia while Alessandro holds his baton parallel to the body of his mount. Both horses are shown going into a trot. The most marked departure from the classical prototype lies in the flowing lines of the wind-blown mane and tail.

8

supervised the accountants of the *scholae ratiocinii* responsible for provincial affairs, kept the ledgers of the *Magna Curia* and reviewed the expenses of the court. To him were answerable the two *emptores*, appointed every two months, who administered the royal family's privy purse.

This elaborate system, and this cultured court, were to disappear with the downfall of Frederick's son Manfred, victims of the eternal hostility between the papacy and the House of Hohenstaufen. Manfred was killed at the battle of Benevento, Charles I of Anjou was offered the crown of Sicily, and nothing of the old order remained. From 1272 onwards Naples was the capital. Sicily, with Palermo ever more remote from the center, would split away and pass to the crown of Aragon in the War of the Sicilian Vespers (1282–1305).

The barons of Apulia, Calabria, and Terra di Lavoro became, as the people called them, "little kings," *reguli*. In the capital there was no vestige of the former court; Naples lacked even a palace until 1279 when the *palacium de novo* – the *chastiau neuf* or Castel Nuovo – was begun, to be finished in 1282 by the French architect Pierre de Chaulnes. It is doubtful whether Charles of Anjou ever held court there. It was his son Charles II, returned from his Aragonese captivity, who used Castel Nuovo as a palace (adding the boldly experimental *cappella palatina* in 1307) though not as a permanent home. He would remove to Frederick II's Castel Capuano – he spent Easter there in 1294 – and in any case preferred a more modest country retreat he owned beyond the Capua Gate, "where, it is said, St Peter on a journey entered Naples." The New Castle, more fortress than palace, was nevertheless the center of a new district, a veritable "royal mile." From the harbour to Portanuova the princes of the royal house built palaces – Philip of Taranto with his *ospizio tarantino*, Giovanni, Duke of Durazzo with the *ospizio durazzesco* – as did the barons and officers of the court.

And for a second time in the history of the Kingdom the entire regime would vanish. The palace itself was gravely damaged in the turmoil of 1443 that brought the Aragonese to Naples, and there followed a third reconstruction of the state, more drastic than that of the Norman-Swabians or of the Angevins. The great officers,

Left: Naples in 1464, during the reign of Ferrante of Aragon, illegitimate son and successor of Alfonso the Magnanimous. The restored Castel Nuovo dominates the harbour, and the view extends from Castel dell'Ovo on its island to the Carmine. The town's southern walls stretch along the shore, with the hillsides of Pizzofalcone, Sant'Elmo and Capodimonte behind. Strozzi panel, Museo di Capodimonte, Naples. Below, left: schematic engraving of Naples, from the Cosmographia Universa *of Sebastian Münster, 1522. Below, right: Castel Sant'Elmo, above the city of Naples, in a view by Jan van Stinemolen, 1582.*

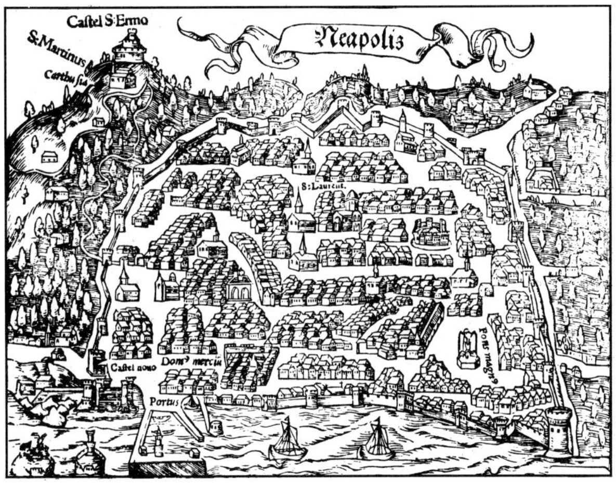

who had become the appanage of feudal barons, were there still, a legacy of Frederick's dispensation, but in 1443 Alfonso I refashioned the state on the Catalan model. His *Sacro Real Consiglio* was a version of the *Consejo Real* of Aragon, a supreme tribunal presided over by the king or someone nominated by him. On it sat the protonotary, who now scrutinized petitions for justice and favours. The royal chancery consisted of a General Treasury and the *Sommaria*, which dealt with administration, economics and finance. The *Gran Corte della Vicaria* applied justice, civil and criminal.

Castel Nuovo was reconstructed by the Spaniard Guillermo Sagrera – only the chapel was standing – and was soon an admired model. Franceso Sforza, planning to rebuild his own palace at Porta Giovia, requested information about it from his ambassador at Naples. By then, in 1455, Castel Nuovo was hung with Flemish tapestries, shipped via Venice and Manfredonia. "King Alfonso daily spends a thousand ducats in his court, as well as what is spent, separately, by messer Piero de Cardona, his *camariero mazore*." The wardrobe department, with its rich stuffs and furs, was patrolled by Indian cats with collars and long leashes of red and yellow silk, keeping the mice at bay.

The court had adopted Catalan customs. It spoke Catalan, not the French of the House of Anjou. The bishops of Seo de Urgel and Valencia were permanently in residence; the Conde de Alife was governor of Castel Nuovo. The king, Alfonso the Magnanimous, was a deeply religious man who took very seriously his rôle of *Christomimetes*. That he thought of himself as a *sacerdos*, a priest, is clear from the short biography by the humanist Vespasiano da Bisticci – though Vespasiano, admittedly, saw him as a bigot and overlooked the true significance of all the praying and the constant attendance at Mass. "He was very fond of Holy Scripture and of quoting saws from the Bible, which he had almost by heart . . . was very good to the poor, and most religious in that he heard three Masses a day, one of them sung, and never missed a day . . . Most diligent in what concerned religious observance. On Holy Thursday he washed the feet of as many poor persons as he himself had years . . . Said his daily breviary, day in, day out . . . nor failed to get up in the middle of the night to say his office . . . kept every vigil fasting . . . and every Friday of the year ate only bread and water."

To square this picture with that of the munificent prince who lived in luxury (though Vespasiano says he rarely chose to wear brocade), owned a wonderful library and surrounded himself, as the emperor Frederick had done, with intellectuals, poets and musicians, we have to realize that the Masses and prayers and Holy Thursday ceremonies were integral and essential to the royal priestly image. And that image we see displayed on the triumphal arch erected, after Alfonso's death, by Francesco Laurana at the entrance to Castel Nuovo.

From the mid fifteenth century, then, Naples had a new court. Or rather, two courts, for soon the heir, Prince Ferrante, with his household occupied Castel Capuano which, like Castel Nuovo, had been altered. And both were humanist courts, patterns for the princes of Italy. Even the disputatious barons were tamed under Aragonese rule. In 1444 Alfonso, on his way to besiege Francesco Sforza in Ancona, received tidings of a revolt by his viceroy in Calabria, Antonio Centellis, Lord of Crotone and Catanzaro. Unhesitatingly the king changed his line of march, came up with his rebellious vassal and carried him prisoner to Naples. He was to set him free, pension him and make him seneschal; but he never restored his estates. Ten years after this Carlo Ruffo, Count of Sinopoli, and Tommaso Caracciolo, Marquis of Gerace were likewise stripped of their feudal possessions and compelled to live at court. The merciful treatment sufficed; the unity of the Kingdom was preserved. But the magnanimous king died in 1458 and 30 years later, after the Conspiracy of Melfi in 1487–88, its disintegration could be prevented only by savage repression. The rift thus opened would cost the Aragonese kings of Naples the support of their barons against Charles VIII of France and Ferdinand the Catholic; although, on the

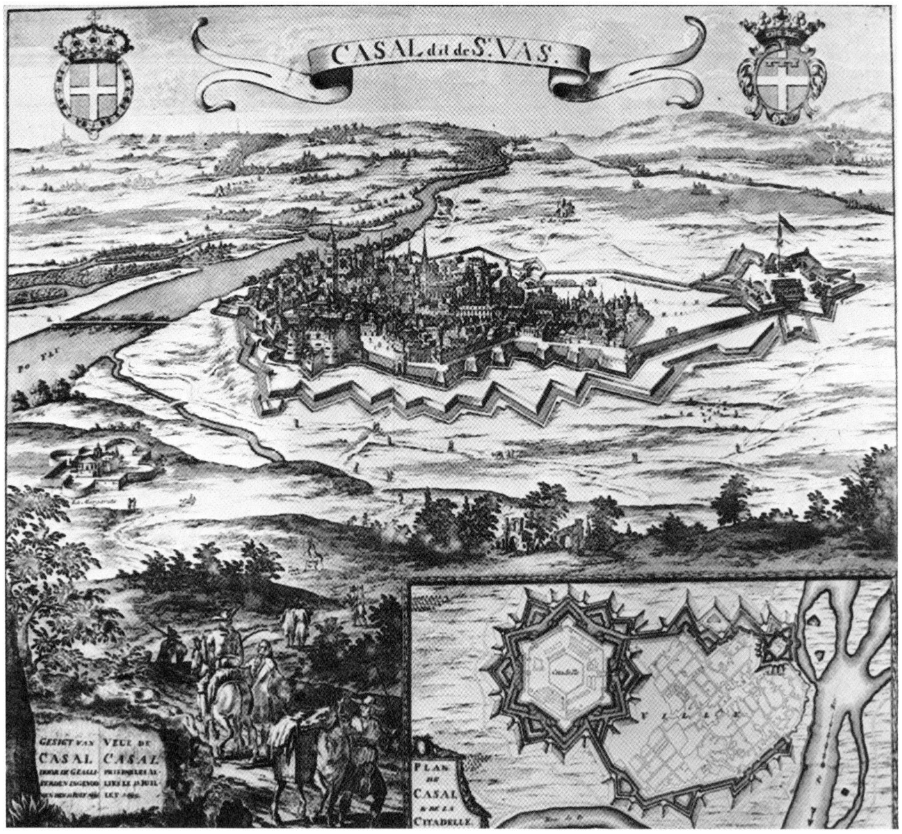

Above: an engraving of Casale in the early seventeenth century. Below: the castle of Moncalieri.

The marquisate of Monferrato dates back to 967, when it was granted by Otto I, as an imperial fief, to Aleramo, founder of the Aleramici family who were to defend it against powerful neighbours, such as the houses of Visconti and Savoy-Achaia and the marquesses of Saluzzo. On the death of the last of the Aleramici in 1305 the state passed to Theodore Paleologus, second son of the Byzantine emperor, whose dynasty reigned in Monferrato for another 200 years. The court in Theodore's time had no fixed residence but lived between the castles of Trini and Moncalieri (opposite, below); it did not settle at Casale until after 1404. Below, right: gateway of Casale dei Paleologi, at Casale Monferrato. (A casale, *sometimes adapted into a villa or hunting lodge, was originally a walled and fortified hamlet built round a courtyard.) When this second dynasty died out, Monferrato was ruled by the Gonzaga of Mantua and, after their extinction, absorbed into the duchy of Savoy, a process completed by 1713. There were thus, over 700 years, abrupt changes of dynasty, with each new court bringing new customs. The local ways, however, were blended with the new, and so preserved.*

other hand, the realm was not fragmented into small feudal enclaves.

Between 1494 and 1502 the southern kingdom lost its court for a third time, though even under a Spanish viceroy it retained its character. It had no court until the arrival of the Bourbons, who ruled until 1860. And so the "long-lasting" court of southern Italy was in fact four courts – the Norman-Swabian with its Arabic and oriental culture and organization, the Angevin, based on French custom, the Aragonese, which was Catalan, and lastly the court of the Bourbons, with the modes and manners of Castille.

Above: the castle of Fénis, started by Aymon de Challant in 1340 and completed by his son Boniface, Marshal of Savoy and governor of Piedmont, in 1410.

From a large to a small scale

A very different example of the rapid and multiple assimilation of cultures is found in the marquisate of Monferrato between the fourteenth and fifteenth century; and here the process takes place not only on a single territory, but under a single dynasty.

Monferrato was a fief of the Holy Roman Empire, and could be inherited in the female line. Its borders were modified more than once, but it lay on either bank of the Po, and at one time or another extended towards Vercelli, into the Canavese, to the region around Alessandrino and the Apennines near Genoa. From the eleventh century it was an appanage of the Aleramici family, who had to defend it against the growing power of communes such as Asti, Vercelli and Alessandrino, as well as stronger neighbours such as the marquesses of Saluzzo and the families of Savoy-Achaia and Visconti.

The most serious threat was in 1305, at the death of Giovanni, last of the Aleramici. Manfredo of Saluzzo, the appointed "guardian" (*gubernator et defensor*) of Monferrato, had every intention of annexing it and opposed its inheritance in the female line. The great vassals and elders of the communes met in a *parlamento* and decided to send emissaries *domine Yolanti serenissime Romeorum imperatrici et filiis suis* – that is, to Violante, sister of the late marquis and wife of Andronicus II Paleologus, emperor of Byzantium, and to the couple's second son, Teodoro. It fell to Teodoro to

continue the family's rule of Monferrato, and the emperor Henry VII invested him with the marquisate in 1310. Meanwhile he landed at Genoa in 1306, a friendless boy of 13. But he found a supporter in the Genoese patrician Opicino Spinola, whose daughter he married, and on 16 November of that year was formally recognized as overlord by the chief vassals and ordinary citizens of Monferrato.

Teodoro was the author of a treatise on military discipline, and to it added some pages of autobiography. They were written in Greek during a stay in his native country from 1326 to 1330, and he himself later translated them into Latin. He tells of the difficult early days, of his first levy of troops, "on the advice of nobles and vassals," and of his going to Constantinople in 1316 for his mother's funeral; and of the homeward voyage (disembarking this time at Venice) when his state was again threatened by its neighbours. He had gone to the East with all his "famiglia," comprising two notaries and other gentlemen whose names we know: Pietro di Riparia, Count of Valperga, Francesco di San Giorgio, Oddone di Ponzone, Brandalisio di Corconato, Giovanni di Montilio, Sozio di Tilio, Giovanni di Romano, Nicolino di San Sebastiano, Guglielmo di Cella, Verulfo di Castiglione, Guercio d'Alfiano, Guglielmo di Santo Stefano, Nicolino Ovarrato, and Perrucono. It was a small household, though a considerable party, and arrived back accompanied by the Byzantine envoy Stephen Siropolous, who speedily convened "vassals, nobles and chief persons, the wise men and the people" *in palatio Clavaxii* (modern Chivasso), to levy more troops for the defense of Monferrato.

The reorganization of the state undertaken soon afterwards, in 1320, had probably been discussed in Constantinople. A council made up of the *familiares* of the marquis, his vassals and high-ranking clergy, was in charge of policy and administration. Justice was confided to a tribunal of noblemen, finance to a committee directed by the collector of revenues, and a notary public headed the marquis's chancery. It was a system based, in all likelihood, on "Roman" – that is, Byzantine – custom, but onto it was grafted a native institution, quite foreign to the autocracy of Byzantium: the *parlamento*. For the interregnum of 1305, when the direct Aleramaci line died out, had given opportunity, and power, to nobles and communes, and taxes and troops could now be raised only with their consent. Thus the governmental traditions of the Eastern Empire met those of the Italian communes under Teodoro's rule in Monferrato.

The court in his day moved about between the castles of Trino and Moncalieri. (When Casale was finally conquered in 1404 it settled there). We have no record of its ceremonial and cannot, therefore, know whether, or to what extent, Teodoro introduced the customs of his boyhood, though he tells us of his continued links with the land of his birth. We may assume, however, that for his immediate descendants those links were weaker. He was 46 when he died at Trino on 21 April 1338. His son Giovanni married a French noblewoman, Cécile, Countess of Comminges (harbinger of yet closer relations with France in years to come); and his grandsons, orphaned as minors, were reared at the court of Otto of Brunswick, in yet another tradition, that of the warrior feudalism of Germany. But these boys died before they had time to influence the court in which they had been born, though not educated. Secondotto, who in 1377 married Violante, daughter of Galeazzo Visconti, was killed in a brawl the following year; and his brother, succeeding him as Giovanni II, was killed in 1381 while attempting, with Otto of Brunswick, to rescue the latter's wife, Giovanna I of Naples, besieged in

Borso d'Este, Duke of Modena, Reggio and Ferrara, patron of the arts, lover of hunting and good company, was responsible for much of the building and decoration of the Palazzo di Schifanoia at Ferrara. Its famous fresco cycle of the Months, by Francesco del Cossa and artists of the Ferrarese school, dates from the latter half of the fifteenth century and is in three horizontal sections. In the lowest are scenes of court life, their central figure that of Borso himself. (Above: the duke with his courtiers, setting out for a hunt in the March section). The central panel consists of the signs of the zodiac and other symbols connected with the various months.
Opposite: a figure from the April section. The upper scenes depict triumphs of the mythological deities presiding, month by month, over mens' labours.

Colorno: detail of the courtyard façade of the ducal palace. Originally a fortress of the Sanseverino family and converted into a luxurious dwelling between the seventeenth and eighteenth century, Colorno was a summer residence of the Farnese, used for spectacular entertainments and shoots in the park.

Castel dell'Ovo.

It is a third brother who imports a new influence. This Teodoro II had been brought up with one of Giangaleazzo's sons, whose foster-brother he was, and lived for 28 years in the Visconti castle of Pavia. He married, first, Argentina Malaspina, then Jeanne de Lorraine, daughter of Robert, Duc de Bar; and after her death Margherita, daughter of Amedeo of Savoy-Achaia. Clearly, after these assorted choices, his court would not readily lose its character as a cultural cross-roads. His son Giacomo married another princess of Savoy, Giovanna, daughter of Amedeo VII, and had two sons, Guglielmo and Bonifacio. Guglielmo was despatched at the age of five to his great-grandfather, who had nominated him heir to the duchy of Bar. But the child's relations in Savoy, unwilling to see the Paleologi of Monferrato thus increase their possessions, kidnapped him en route and held him until the old duke named another successor. Guglielmo's marriage to Marie, daughter of Gaston de Foix, cemented the bond with France; and this was further strengthened two generations later when Guglielmo II, son of Bonifacio, died prematurely and his consort, Anne d'Alençon, became regent of Monferrato from 1518 to 1530. She transplanted the court from the fortress of Casale, built in 1351 when the Paleologi originally conquered it, to an airy, porticoed castle in the town.

The end of the dynasty was in sight, however. Anne's son died in boyhood and an uncle who had been coadjutor, then bishop, of Casale stepped into his place. But the former bishop was too old. After a reign of three years this last marquis died, and the line of Paleologus with him.

Thus, in 200 years, this court, in a region exposed to many cultures, had known the influence of Byzantium, Lombardy and France. But the state of Monferrato itself, which dated back to the eleventh century, did not expire with its second ruling house. Again there was an interregnum, and then in 1536 the emperor Charles V gave it to the Gonzaga of Mantua. Separated territorially and administratively from its court, Monferrato still managed, in one way or another, to retain its unity for almost two more centuries, until after the War of the Spanish Succession, when the Gonzaga were in their turn extinct and the peace treaties of Utrecht (1713) and Rastatt (1714) allotted it to the duchy of Savoy.

A parallel may be drawn between the two feudal states of Naples and Casale-Monferrato for, divided as they were by the length of the peninsula, their experiences were similar. Both knew sudden change from the domination of one court to that of a successor – always with corresponding changes of usage, custom and ceremonial. And all the successive courts followed the same road. They expanded, their own intrinsic characters developed; often they were conditioned by stronger cultural influences. But all of them, though imposed upon strange lands and peoples, preserved their individuality over the centuries, with a blending of local and foreign ways.

Very different were the circumstances of the central city-states of northern Italy; for there the long domination was that of dynastic families sprung from the soil and the people they ruled.

Right, above: the elegant marble doorway at the Palazzo di Schifanoia, designed by Francesco del Cossa. This palace, the oldest parts of which date from the late fourteenth century, was largely rebuilt by Biagio Rossetti in the second half of the fifteenth. Below: a sixteenth-century doorway at Schifanoia.

The city-states

Antonio da Aquila, studying canon law at Padua University towards the end of the fourteenth century, was struck, on reading the *Divina commedia*, by the fact that Dante had consigned tyrannicides to hell. Why, he wished to know, should Lucifer tear Brutus and Cassius to pieces as well as Judas Iscariot? He laid the problem before his celebrated contemporary Coluccio Salutati who, though officially disqualified as a bourgeois of non patrician origins, was both a politician and a holder of government office. After 26 years as chancellor of the Florentine republic Salutati was one of the best-heeded, and most feared, men in the world of politics and diplomacy. As might be expected, his answer, sent to a friend in Padua, Francesco Zabarella, for transmission to the enquiring student, was not a letter but a small treatise. The *Tractatus de tyranno* opens in perfect Ciceronian fashion. "*Coluccius Pyeri cancellarius florentinus salutem dicit magistro Antonio de Aquila studenti in artibus Patavi*" (Coluccio, son of Piero, chancellor of Florence,

to Master Antonio of Aquila, student of arts at Padua, greeting.) But, like all Coluccio's correspondence, the *Tractatus* was meant to be distributed. Nor was it merely the solution of a reasonable query for the Dante reader.

The question of when a prince should be considered a usurper was both practical and vital. As the new century began, Gian Galeazzo Visconti of Milan was trying to unite northern and central Italy into one huge compact state, an enterprise which was to be cut short by his sudden death in 1402. In 1387 he supplanted the Scaligeri in Verona, where they had ruled since 1259. Coluccio could of course point to the recent rise of the Gonzaga in Mantua (which became a marquisate in 1433); or he may well have been thinking of the power of the Este, lords of Ferrara since 1209, who had acquired Modena in 1288 and Reggio in 1289, and whose lands in the Garfagnana bordered on Florentine territory. And there were the lesser lords of the Romagna, where the Malatesta had ruled Rimini since 1312 and the Manfredi ruled Faenza since 1377.

The empire, as Dante conceived it, was no

longer very relevant for the fifteenth-century jurist, since it was no longer the fount of sovereignty. The city-states established between the thirteenth and the fourteenth century had an independence it was impossible to deny. As for the papacy, feudal overlord of Ferrara and the Romagna, when Coluccio wrote the *Tractatus* it was in the throes of the Great Schism, legacy and continuation of the disputes of its lengthy sojourn in Avignon. And Coluccio, chancellor of a republic which was, *de jure*, an imperial fief and which had just emerged from a fiercely fought war in open opposition to Rome, was the first to see that power must be legitimized from other sources.

Some ten years earlier Bartolo da Sassoferrato, also writing a treatise on tyranny, had claimed that the source of power was the people. Obviously he is exaggerating the significance of the *acclamatio* frequently sought by the new ruler of a city-state. ("A city acknowledging no overlord is a city of free people, their power as great as if they ruled the universe"). But for Coluccio, too, the *confirmatio*, or endorsement of power by the feudal superior, pope or emperor, is merely a single, though very necessary, element of signorial authority. He distinguishes "tyrant" of two sorts: those who, having neither *confirmatio* nor *acclamatio*, are usurpers *ex defectu tituli* (of defective title); and those who, while legally entitled to their power, employ it against their subjects and are tyrants *ex parte exercitii*. Looked at like this, many Italian lordships held without *confirmatio* would be difficult to justify, but Coluccio believes that the *confirmatio* may be dispensed with when the fount of sovereignty is a long way off and in its absence a people is in effect deprived of government.

The process by which new rulers came to power is well described in the *Tractatus*. "States torn by civil faction and daily strife may choose a lord in weariness of present evils, and to end the disharmony. Or there may be a popular demonstration, and someone is raised up without debate or choice. Or, if the factions have resorted to arms, the strongest may give the power to one man, and it may be asked whether power thus attained can be legitimate. To which

Above: the great Este castle at Ferrara, begun by Niccolò II in 1385.
Left: drawbridge into the main courtyard.

The castle of Ferrara has been several times enlarged and rearranged. To the original fortified tower were added three others, and after a fire in 1554 the towers received their superstructures and the connecting buildings an extra storey. The castle complex is surrounded by water and entered via drawbridges, once part of the defense system. By the fifteenth century, however, when Este power was secure and the techniques of warfare had changed, the castle was a civil rather than a military base, and became the seat of the court. Right: the moat, and a corner of the fifteenth-century courtyard.

I say that, where a population is its own master, neither having nor recognizing any superior, then the will of the majority is valid; and where a population is subject to a prince, and he confirms the decision, then it is certainly valid. But if the man elected by the people assumes power before receiving confirmation from the overlord, then he is a tyrant, for the popular election has of itself no validity in law. But if a people, acknowledging a prince, is left ungoverned in his absence, then the rule of its elected leader is legitimate, unless expressly forbidden by the prince."

Such circumstances are familiar in Italy early in the fifteenth century, when papal or imperial absence or non exercise of authority, and consequent election of a ruler by the people, are the two main factors in the creation of city-states. But the notion of popular sovereignty, whether argued by Coluccio or Bartolo, could find small favour with the descendents of those who had deployed it, by way of the *acclamatio*, to seize absolute power. In the course of the fifteenth century the princes of Italy tended either to legitimize their power for themselves, or to legalize their existing situation by obtaining superior feudal recognition. Thus Milan became an imperial dukedom from 1395, Mantua a marquisate in 1433, and Modena and Reggio a dukedom in 1452. Urbino and Ferrara become papal dukedoms in 1443 and 1471 respectively.

This was the new situation that Martino Garati, a lawyer from Lodi, tried to formulate in the *Tractatus de princibus* he dedicated to Filippo Maria Visconti. He argues from two basic assumptions: that "the state is indivisible" (Book I, section 19), and that princes "are sent upon earth by Almighty God to reward the good and punish the evil-doer" (Book I, section 97). But just because he sees them as functioning by Divine Right – *legibus soluti*, above the law – Garati willingly accords the rulers bureaucratic assistance. "The prince should have many wise counsellors" (Book I, section 149), and be himself the first among them, *tamquam caput senatus*. Not until 1513, with Machiavelli's better-known book, *De principatibus*, forerunner of *The Prince*, do we find this notion of an intermediate advisory body set aside. By then Cesare Borgia had pursued his meteoric career in the Romagna (and Machiavelli had viewed the corpse of Cesare's governor, Ramiro de Lorqua, neatly cut in two on the piazza at Cesena – a judicial murder for the "satisfaction and amazement" of Ramiro's erstwhile subjects); Louis XII had occupied the Milanese, Ferdinand the Catholic invaded Naples. Observing these "new princes" in "new dominions," Machiavelli sees politics as an autonomous activity and modern conquest as an enterprise undertaken on the sole basis of *virtú*, reliance on one's own action and prowess and a right use made of fortune. The prince should rule directly, and alone.

Yet, unhappily, the princes of central and northern Italy were neither as strong nor as independent as Machiavelli would have wished. Their authority was limited by an existing framework – that of the communes – and by the unfailing vigour of the great patrician families of the towns. When, for instance, Federico da Montefeltro succeeded his brother Oddantonio (slain, with two of his courtiers, by conspirators), the commune imposed numerous conditions. He was not to seek vengeance on the conspirators; he was to continue the appointment of municipal "priors" every two months, with all the exemptions, dispensations and honours of their office as laid down in the statutes, and give them a new official residence, since he and his *magna curia* were in their former headquarters. He might raise no fresh taxes "without debate and popular consent." He was hardly the prince *legibus solutus* Garati and Machiavelli dreamed of.

None of this, however, affects the basic truth that the history of central and northern Italy in the Renaissance is as closely bound up with signorial rule as is that of the south – Naples, Sicily and Sardinia – with monarchy. The attention paid by scholars, in England and America particularly, to the civic humanism of the Florentine and Venetian republics has led us to underestimate, if not to forget, the *homines novi*, the rulers who emerged from the oligarchical communes of the Middle Ages and who – in the fifteenth century at least – looked beyond

The Este palace at Sassuolo near Modena was built by Bartolomeo Avanzini for Francesco I d'Este early in the sixteenth century. Now a military academy, its former splendour is preserved in its façade (above) and interior (left and below). With his passion for building, Borso d'Este had already transformed this originally medieval fortress into a palatial residence by the fifteenth century.

the Alps for their model, to the court of Charles the Bold of Burgundy. How else, if not in this Burgundian context, may we explain the artistic splendour of the great signorial courts – of Milan under the Visconti and the Sforza, Ferrara under the Este, Mantua and Urbino under Gonzaga and Montefeltro?

Burgundy at Ferrara

The Este family had their marquisate as early as the eleventh century. They originated in the region of Treviso, living and fighting their battles alongside the Da Romano, San Bonifacio, Camposampiero and Da Camina families. But they founded a large state that was to be more fortunate, and more lasting, than that of the Della Scala who emerged as *signori* at the same time – in the second half of the thirteenth century, on the downfall of Ezzolina Da Romana and his clan.

The Della Scala rule in Verona was too brief for the establishment of a true court. Nor can we speak of a Carrara court or palace at Padua, nor a Da Polenta court at Ravenna. When the Scaligeri gave Dante shelter in Verona they were scattered in various houses between the river and the Piazza Navona, more in the style of an extended consular family than of a palace-dwelling court. Not until 1364 did Cansignorio begin to build a palace, employing Altichiero to paint its great hall, and it was noteworthy as the first signorial residence in the city. Vasari wrote of it: "There was in this same city of Verona Aldighieri da Zevio, an intimate of the Della Scala lords, who painted, among other things, the great hall of their palace, now that of the *podestà*. He decorated it with the war of Jerusalem taken from Josephus and exhibited much spirit and judgement in the work, dividing the wall-spaces and painting a narrative in each register, with the same ornamental border round it all. Almost at the very top of this border is a row of medallions with lifelike portraits of many famous men of that day, especially members of the della Scala family . . . " Here, predictably, where family deeds and glories publicly shown in a building which fulfilled the functions of the former palace of the commune.

Corner balcony of the Palazzo dei Diamanti in Ferrara, designed by the architect Biagio Rossetti. The palace derives its name from over 12,000 small pointed marble blocks, which create an effect of changing light – accentuated by masterly perspectival use of the stone – on the façade. Begun for Sigismondo d'Este at the end of the fifteenth century and finished in the mid sixteenth, it is the chief building of the Herculean Addition – a new area, carefully planned by Duke Ercole I as an extension of Ferrara and also designed by Rossetti. This was, in effect, the first example of town planning in Europe.

This structure, when Vasari was writing, had been seriously damaged and radically re-arranged after housing Visconti governors and the Venetian *podestà*. But the Scaliger court itself was hardly installed there before it was swept away. Cansignorio's death in 1375 had unleashed a time of troubles. His sons Bartolomeo II and Antonio perforce shared the rule until, on 31 July 1381, Bartolomeo was found murdered near the doors of the patrician Nogarola clan. Antonio's rôle of avenger proved a weakness rather than a strength, for it antagonized the patriciate of Verona, and his subsequent marriage to Samaritana Da Polenta did not mend matters. When in 1385 the Visconti and Gonzaga united to wipe out a dynasty that threatened them both, not even Niccolò II d'Este, husband of Cansignorio's sister Verde, opposed them.

Niccolò d'Este was neither the first nor the last of his house to seek alliance with the other princely families of Italy. Niccolò I had married Beatrice Gonzaga. Niccolò III married Gigliola Da Carrara and, secondly, Parisina Malatesta.

Façade of the Galleria degli Antichi, or Great Corridor, at Sabbioneta. Vespasiano Gonzaga, collaborating actively with his architect, Domenico Giunti, created his small "new Rome" at Sabbioneta on Vitruvian principles – or principles drawn, more directly, from Renaissance commentaries on Vitruvius. The Galleria (1583–4) forms one end of the square in front of it, and was considered a sixteenth-century model of princely building.

The wife of his son Leonello was Margherita Gonzaga; two of his daughters, Ginevra and Lucia, married respectively Sigismondo Pandolfo Malatesta and Carlo Gonzaga. The close network of family and blood relationships among the states of northern Italy undoubtedly helped to create a kind of *koiné*, a language of manners and etiquette common at all levels to the various courts. The Este, furthermore, were kin to many of their vassals and *raccomandati*, or minor landholders in the Po valley. They married their illegitimate children into the families of Correggio, Pio of Carpi, Pico of Mirandola, Boschetti of San Cesario and Uguccioni of Vignola. Such relations with the lesser lords also extended and magnified the procreative function of the prince as *pater patriae*, of which we have already spoken. By and through them he spread himself physically, so to speak, beyond the court, beyond his capital.

Despite their venerable feudal origins, the Este gained signorial power in a civic, not a feudal, context. It was in the office of *podestà*, exercised by Azzo VI in 1196 and again in 1208, that they were established at Ferrara. In the latter year, profiting by this strong position, the marquis was accepted as ruler. (This is the sequence of events that occurred in many other communes.) The document published by the eighteenth-century historian Muratori styles him *gubernator et rector et perpetuus dominus in omnibus negociis providendis, et emendandis, et reformandis ipsius Civitatis ad sue arbitrium voluntatis*." Governor, director and perpetual lord over the conduct of all public affairs, he may "reshape the very state as he wishes."

The real court of Ferrara, however, was instituted by Niccolò III, who reigned from 1393 to 1441, and received its distinctive stamp from his sons Leonello and Borso. Borso succeeded his half-brother in 1450 and in the last year of his life contrived to have the marquisate raised to a dukedom. In a period that marked the high tide of humanism both brothers were humanists, though with eyes most often directed beyond the Alps, to the Burgundy of Charles the Bold.

Leonello's literary circle included the humanist Giovanni Guarino of Verona, who was his tutor; Francesco Arioti, teacher of philosophy at Ferrara university and author of the dramatic fable *Idis*, one of the first humanist texts written to be performed; and Tito Vespasiano Strozzi, poet and lawyer and, in 1497, one of the twelve *savi*, supreme magistracy of the duchy. When Leonello planned a monument to Niccolò III – the first equestrian statue in Italy since the reign of Theodoric – designs were appraised by his personal friend Leon Battista Alberti. To Leonello Antonio Decembrio he dedicated the seven books of his *Politica litteraria*, a work from which we may gather something of the courtly climate of the Este palace, for it introduces the hitherto undiscussed concept of *politia vel expolitio* in the sense of refinement, elegance and polite intercourse, *urbana conversatione*.

Since Niccolò III's day the court had forsaken the medieval palace opposite the cathedral; or, rather, it had expanded into the handsome castle begun by Niccolò II in 1385 (the year the Milanese alliance was threatening Verona). But also in 1385, on the outskirts of the town not far from the church of Santa Maria in Vado, a less defensive building was begun, whose name proclaimed its purpose. This was Schifanoia, (chase-your-cares-away), a palace for intervals of pleasure, entertainment and repose. (Similar names – Belfiore, Belriguardo, Belvedere – were given to their country villas by the Ferrarese nobility.) Single-storeyed, with a large garden behind it, Schifanoia was of modest proportions to start with, but was enlarged by Alberto v between 1458 and 1460. Borso added a magnificent marble portal, probably designed by Francesco Cossa, and an upper floor. Ugo Caleffini's rhymed chronicle mentions the spending of over 30,000 gold ducats. In the huge Sala dei Mesi of the upper floor is a fresco-cycle by Cossa and Cosmè Tura – the best picture-book we have of the Franco-Burgundian fashions of the court of Ferrara in the mid fifteenth century. Here, among gods and goddesses from Boccaccio's *De genealogia deorum* and magical and astrological symbols from the *Codex hermeticum*, Borso is seen dealing justice, riding home from hawking, receiving an embassy or leading a splendid cavalcade.

Yet the luxury we observe in the Schifanoia frescoes, where ladies dress in the Burgundian fashion, their collars and sleeves embroidered with quotations from romances of chivalry, is one thing; the actual living-space, and everyday reality, of the Este palace is another. In March 1436 the apartments of Leonello (not then duke) comprised what was called the *sala bianca*, two bedrooms (a winter and a summer one), a wardrobe room, a guardroom, a room he used as an audience-chamber and eight rooms for his "family" of courtiers, attendants and servants. Furnishings were of the plainest. His "white room" boasted, according to the inventory, one large and one small sideboard-cupboard, or *credenza*; a trestle-table of cypress-wood and one of ash; a perch for a falcon; four candlesticks, two copper bowls and a pair of andirons in the fireplace. The audience-chamber had a table, two benches, a tin-plated candlestick (this was a wall-fixture) and andirons. In the adjoining "little new room," the *camerino novo*, the courtiers who lodged closest to Leonello, Parisino da Bondeno and Giacomo Tosego, shared a trestle-bedstead with no proper sides, under which, during the day, went the *cariola*, or pallet on which their servant slept. They were provided with a painted chest for clothes, a low bench, a small table, and an iron clock, "gilded, with shaft and counterweights, in a fine frame and fit for a gentleman's use." Only one of the sheets was "new and good," though mice had apparently been at it

Above: interior of the Palazzo del Giardino, Sabbioneta. Finished in 1588, this palace was intended as a private summer residence for the prince.
Left: detail of the ceiling in the ducal palace, the first major building completed at Sabbioneta (c.1554–77).

("several holes"). The room of Messer Leonello contained a table, two long benches and a velvet chair studded with brass nails; it had terminals to the arms, and a rosette of gilt brass. The plank-bed was again on trestles, with a mattress, a feather pillow and a dark green satin coverlet edged in black and embroidered with trees and flowers "and five figures, one of them playing the organ." Here, too, is the servant's *cariola*, with coverlet and sheet – one sheet, "old, with a hole in it." Two *bancali* (the draperies often spread over high-backed chests) were embroidered with the Este arms. A tin-plated iron candle-holder was set in the wall, and there were shovel, poker and tongs. Leonello also had a *studiolo*, simple as his summer bedroom, with two benches, a *credenza*, small table, two-branched candlestick and a pair of three-legged stools.

The inventories show that the Este tapestries before Leonello's time were mostly *bancali*, bed-covers and hangings with sacred subjects. A big improvement came when Ercole I (1471–1505) married Eleonora of Aragon, daughter of Ferrante, King of Naples; the bride not only elevated the family's dynastic standing she brought tapestries in her dowry to enrich its collections.

Ercole, succeeding his elder half-brothers Leonello and Borso, had to struggle for his dukedom. In 1476 Leonello's son Niccolò, together with a cousin named Azzo, tried to raise

Fictive hangings are pulled aside to reveal the Gonzaga family in the Painted Room, the Camera degli Sposi, in the ducal palace at Mantua. These frescoes, executed between 1465 and 1474, are a mature masterpiece of Mantegna. To the right of the doorway Cardinal Francesco Gonzaga arrives in Mantua, greeted by his father, Ludovico III. The children in the foreground – sons of the cardinal's brother Federico, who stands on the extreme right – are Francesco, future husband of Isabella d'Este, and Sigismondo, holding the hand of his uncle, the "little bishop," the

hunchback Ludovico. The background figures are traditionally supposed to be those of artists attached to the Gonzaga court, including Alberti and Mantegna.
On the wall above the fire-place the court appears in an interior setting. Ludovico turns to speak to Marsilio Andreasi, his secretary, and with him sits his wife, Barbara of Brandenburg. The others cannot be identified with any certainty, although the pretty girl (detail, far right) may be a marriageable daughter. Right: the frescoed oculus of the ceiling.

PRINCELY CORRESPONDENCE

1

2

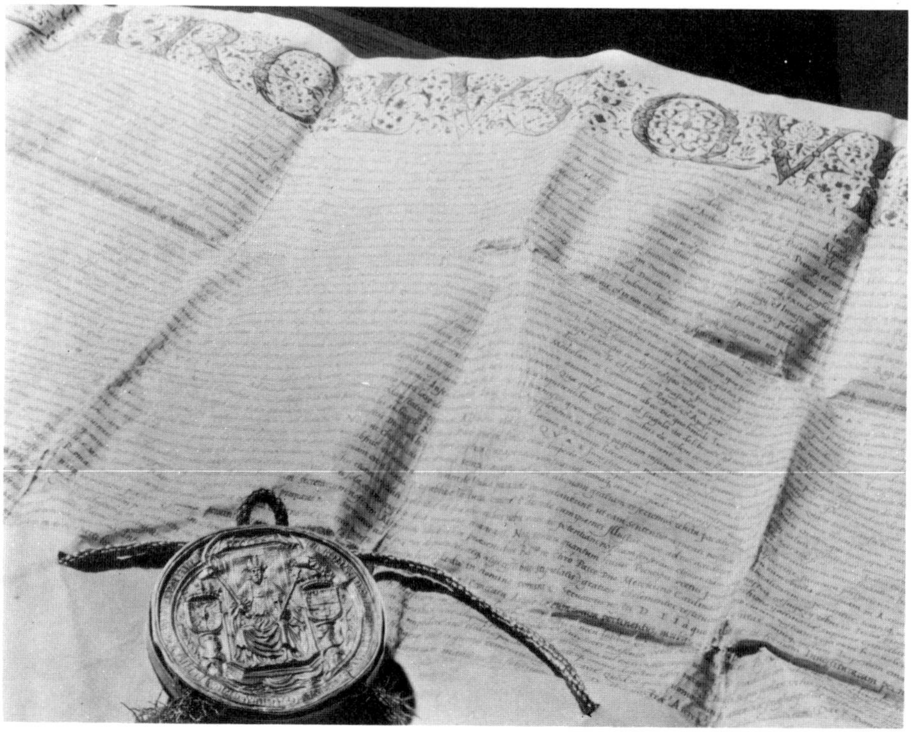

Isabella d'Este, daughter of Duke Ercole of Ferrara, came to Mantua as a bride in 1490 with her trousseau and belongings in thirteen painted chests (*cassoni*); she also brought the artist who had painted them, Ercole de' Roberti. A great lover of the arts, although this love was not without a touch of vanity, she wrote on 13 March 1499 to Ludovico il Moro, who had married her late sister, Beatrice, for his permission to send her portrait to Isabella of Aragon: "I fear I shall be wearying not only Your Highness, but all Italy with my portraits," and in May 1504 reminds Leonardo da Vinci (who had made the famous drawing of her, now in the Louvre, but no painting from it), "When you were here and drew my portrait in charcoal, you promised that you would one day paint it in colours." On 7 April 1520 Paolucci, Alfonso d'Este's agent in Rome, sends word that "Raphael of Urbino was buried today in the Rotonda (the Pantheon), dead of a sharp fever;" and on 16 April Isabella writes sorrowfully to Pico della Mirandola that the death of "messer Raphael" saddened her very much. At the same time, the chancery at Ferrara was requesting the return of a fee paid in advance for a picture commissioned from him.

After the personal, the political correspondence. A Milanese ambassador in Venice relays advice from the Serenissima to her ally Ludovico il Moro: let him make himself agreeable to his troops "so they will not run away when needed;" and let him also "offer some general sign of affection and benevolence to his people, some token that he values their goodwill above their money." Such, in those days, were the tasks of an ambassador (7: the arrival of an embassy. From a Sienese *biccherna*, or wooden document-case painted with a reference-picture, dating from 1498). From Florence on 4 April 1458 the ambassador of Ludovico's father, Duke Francesco, had reported, "when you particularly desire anything, write secretly to Cosimo about whatever it is, and he will do his utmost for you." The envoy wanted his master to realize that Cosimo the Elder was, despite appearances, master of Florence. (Not that the Florentines ever doubted it. "He's rammed his wretched *palle* down everybody's throat," as one citizen put it, alluding to the six *palle*, or balls, of the Medici family arms.)

When Girolamo Riario of Imola and Forlí was assassinated in 1488, those cities appealed for church protection; his widow, Caterina Sforza, turned to Ludovico il Moro whose Milanese troops restored to power her son, Ottaviano, with the approval of Lorenzo de' Medici, who favoured local lordships rather than the extension of ecclesiastical power. As he wrote to his ambassador in Ferrara, "the Church has for some time been much against the barons and *signori*, with never a thought of letting go what it has taken."

Minimum and maximum delivery times in days to or from Venice between 1497 and 1532, according to the records of Marin Sanudo.

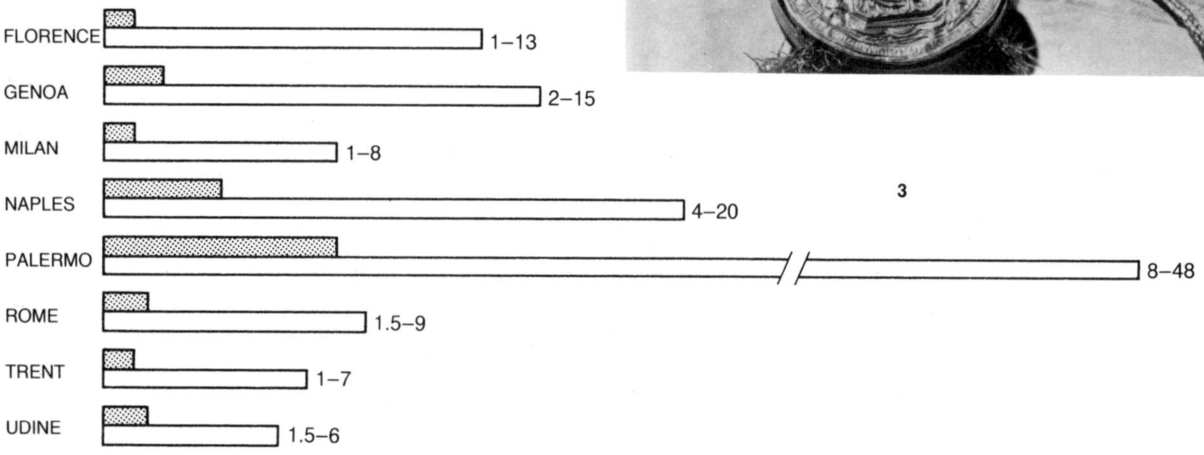

3

Letters written by princes or their secretaries were marked with a seal, which might be of wax, or of more precious stuff for important documents. (1: wax seal of Ludovico il Moro, with the Visconti-Sforza arms. 2: Charles V's golden seal on the diploma, given at Bologna on 2 January 1530, investing Francesco II Sforza with the dukedom of Milan). Recorded in the chanceries, letters were delivered by mounted couriers. (6: a *cavallaro* riding with despatches. From a late fifteenth-century manuscript.)

How long did they take to reach their destinations? "News of the defeat," says Guicciardini in 1512, "was in Rome on 13 April. It was brought by Ottaviano Fregoso, using post-horses from Fossombrone, and greeted by the whole court with the greatest tumult and alarm." He is speaking of the battle of Ravenna where, only two days previously, the French under Gaston de Foix had overcome the papal and Spanish troops of Julius II. Reports did not always travel as fast, however. Between 1497 and 1532 the Venetian diarist Marin Sanudo noted the longest and shortest delivery times from various parts of the country into Venice, and tables have been constructed from approximately 10,000 examples. On these is based the accompanying diagram (3), showing delivery times, in days, from various major towns in Italy.

4

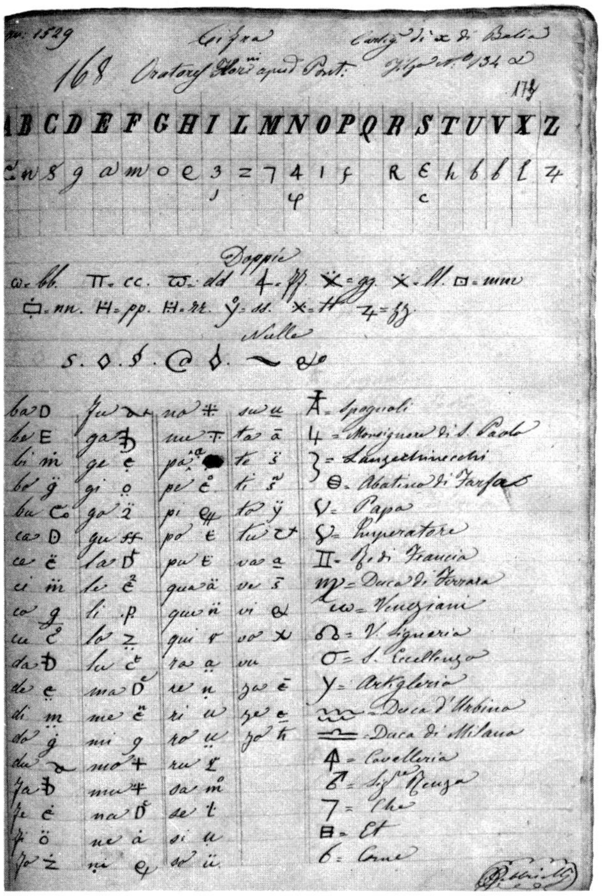

5

The sending of letters was extremely expensive: "There isn't a courier who'll take less than a ducat per packet," laments the Duke of Ferrara's Venetian representative. (quoted by Fernand Braudel); furthermore, a prince's letters could be forged, or read by the wrong person. Guicciardini mentions forgeries. "They say that Galeazzo had received letters, as if from Ludovico Sforza and bearing his seal, with orders to retire to Milan immediately with all his troops, as there was trouble there; no one doubted afterwards that the letters were forged by the Count of Gaiazzo as a stratagem to aid the French victory, and Galeazzo was in the habit of producing them to justify his actions." Here Guicciardini is speaking of Louis XII's incursion of 1499, and the Galeazzo whose withdrawal had left the road open to the French was Galeazzo da San Severino, later to be King Louis's chief equerry. The Count of Gaiazzo was his elder brother, Giovan Francesco da San Severino, "who had a prior and secret agreement with the king of France."

Ciphers were used as a safeguard against unauthorized perusal. Illustrated above are (4) the cipher of the Florentine ambassadors to the papacy in 1529 and (5) the very similar cipher of Niccolò Machiavelli. One – or two-letter groups, and groups of syllables, are represented by other letters or by signs, and some complete words have sign-equivalents.

At court the act of writing must itself be mannerly. Giovanni della Casa, Archbishop of Benevento, exclaims in horror in his guide to good behaviour, *Galeato*, "And what can I say of people who, in company, rise from their desks with pens stuck behind their ears?"

7

the city against him. But, once his position was secure, Ercole abandoned everything to his consort. Duchess Eleonora, said a contemporary, "gave audience and dealt with anything there was to do, ruling and governing entirely." Ferrara was chronically short of money, and "all employments, great and small, in the fortresses or in the communes, were sold to the highest bidder, cash down and for no more than a two-year tenure." During the "salt war," fought to secure the fertile Po delta from Venice, we are told that "the duke of Ferrara paid little heed to his domain, but sang and played his music every day as if he had to . . . and performed incantations and conjurations with a certain messer Carlo Soxena, consulting devils to know what was happening in Italy, and other matters."

The duke, unlike his wife's grandfather Alfonso the Magnanimous, entertained magical rather than religious notions of the next world. He even went so far as to snatch a "living saint" – a nun of Viterbo whom he had transported by mule and hidden in a basket to Ferrara – believing that by her agency he could harness the powers of heaven. She reached his capital on 7 March 1499, and by August two years later he had built a convent, dedicated to St Catherine of Siena, to house his prize.

It is quite consonant with this mixture of magical and religious faith that the duke should join in the ritual upheaval of carnival. At

Epiphany he would go masked through Ferrara, begging food for the poor and meeting with considerable success. His bag in 1473, the first year he adopted the practice, included 1823 capons, 276 large cheeses and 54 assorted calves and heifers, to say nothing of poultry, wine, sweetmeats and waxen torches.

Duke Ercole, who was interested in metallurgy and alchemy, could cast metal and made firearms like an expert. His military skill was demonstrated at the battle of Ravenna, for instead of having the artillery in its usual central position (where, as Machiavelli says, it merely prevented anyone from seeing anything because of the smoke of its guns, and impeded the infantry), he moved it to the sides, and the

The vast and imposing ducal palace at Mantua dates from various periods and contains some 500 rooms and courtyards. Begun by the Bonacolsi, it was enlarged and embellished, from 1328 onwards, by the Gonzaga who succeeded them. The oldest part, the Corte Vecchia, consists of the two late thirteenth-century Bonacolsi palaces known as the Magna Domus. *The Palazzo del Capitano dates from the early fourteenth century and the* Nova Domus, *by Luca Fancelli, from the late fifteenth. The castello di San Giorgio, built by Bartolino da Novara between 1395 and 1406, is a fine rectangular keep which overlooks the lake, as does Giulio Romano's Corte Nuova of 1539.*
On this page, three interior views of the Nova Domus. *Top, left: the Gallery of the Months, with its stucco-work and painted* grottesche, *was begun by Giulio Romano and completed after his death by Giovan Battista Bertani in 1573. Center: the late sixteenth-century Galleria degli Imperatori, or Exhibition Gallery, with busts of Roman emperors in niches. The gallery still contains eighteen wall-cupboards in which were housed the Gonzaga collection of natural history specimens, curiosities and precious objects. Below, left: a detail of the Sala dei Marchesi. This room contains busts of the four Gonzaga marquesses and their consorts, and pieces of allegorical statuary; the fine ceiling was executed in 1579 by Francesco Segala. Opposite, top, right: ceiling of the Sala di Giuditta; center, carved brackets in the Salone degli Arcieri.*

murderous cross-fire thus produced contributed significantly to the action. As a contribution, this was ironical: the man whose court included Matteo Boiardo, arch-poet of chivalry, was doing more than most to bring to an end the time-honoured tactics based on the deployment of heavily armoured men.

And his modernity had other outlets. He was a town planner and responsible for enormous change by inducing his court to emerge from behind the castle-moat and move far into the city, as the Roman court had infiltrated along the *via papalis*. His architect was Biagio Rossetti, who had worked for Duke Borso at Schifanoia, and the new zone, the *Addizione erculea*, or Herculean Addition, was begun in

the summer of 1492. As Bruno Zevi wrote, "if the new, more or less rectangular, street system were to be filled with life and traffic, the old residential districts had to look towards the Addizione." The planning, in other words, must be implemented socially by continuous coming and going between the old and the new quarters. It was a delicate problem, and a heightened one, because of an existing boundary – the street that marked the filled-in channel of the Giovecca stream. All classes, high and low, in being asked to cross it, were being asked to surmount a sort of agoraphobia – the fear experienced by those who, accustomed to cramped and overcrowded streets, are lost and insecure when faced with wider horizons. Rossetti's primary concern, therefore, was to establish a link with the medieval city. By making the castle – i.e. the court – the heart of his new area, he avoided the mistake of building a detached and separate town. Ferrara, old and new, was focused on its castle and traversed by straight, military roads running outwards to the walls, and the court expanded, with its major buildings, along the main axes of the *Addizione*. It built an Arsenal. Giulio d'Este built a palace. There were family palaces of the Giglioli Varano, the Turchi di Bagno, the Prosperi-Sacrati. There was the Diamanti palace. Once again, as had happened in Rome, the court put its indelible mark on the town. The dream of the "ideal city" had come true.

Rome on the Mincio

In August 1509, in a village near Legnano on the Adige, Venetian troops surprised and captured Francesco Gonzaga, fourth marquis of Mantua. It was the following June before he was released, through the pope's intervention and a promise to send his eldest son as a hostage to Rome. The young Federico entered the city in mid August, with what amounted to a miniature court: two *maestri di casa*, Stefano Gadio and Matteo Ippoliti; his doctor Luca Coffani; Domenichino his singing master; his pages and servants. Julius II lodged him in the Belvedere, and he was at once enchanted by the

Roman antiquities of the pope's collection, exhibited in the courts and galleries Bramante had built to connect the villa with the pontifical palace. As Gadio wrote to the prince's mother, Isabella d'Este, on 27 August, her son was living "in the best rooms of this palace, takes his meals in a most beautiful *loggia* – it is well-named Belvedere – [beautiful view] with a prospect of the whole plain. The days are passed in these rooms, and in the gardens with their pines and orange trees, with much pleasure and enjoyment, though he does not neglect his singing and will himself summon the singing master. Also, he repeats his daily office, and will attend to his lessons in the same way . . . His Highness longs to present Your Excellency a Laocoon, and would like to be able to order one (he means a goldsmith's copy), knowing how you would esteem and admire it for the divine and wonderful thing it is . . ."

At barely ten years old Federico was obviously fully aware of his mother's devotion to the art of the ancient world, and as obviously capable of appreciating the Laocoon. Soon he was qualifying as an informed guide to the treasures of Rome. "Today," Gadio reports on 6 September, "he rode to the Capitol, and to view many other antiquities, in excellent company." (This company included the poet Bernardo Accolti, a celebrated eccentric.)

The boy hostage enjoyed a golden captivity, for the old pope was fond of him. Above all, his detention kindled in him a passion for Rome and its ruins, and for classical art. When his gaoler-protector died, and he returned to Mantua on 3 March 1513, his enthusiasm evidently sharpened that of his mother. A year later Isabella, on a state visit to Milan (whose duke, Ercole Massimiliano Sforza, was her nephew) and to Genoa, suddenly decided to journey on to Rome. She arrived there on 18 October 1514, and stayed until 2 February. From Pisa, as she travelled, she wrote to her son, explaining this unexpectedly lengthy absence: "My Federico, I am so ashamed that you, at your age, have seen Rome when I, your mother, have not, that I have decided to go and look. Then I shall have no need to be jealous . . ."

Isabella, fêted and feasted though she was, had neither the money to buy rare pieces nor the effrontery to ask for them as gifts. She simply gazed, and left her heart behind. On 18 March 1515 she writes to her friend Cardinal Bibbiena: "Here I am in Mantua, yearning for Rome. The difference between these tiny rooms and what I knew in Rome! Your Eminence may imagine how strange it seems. I am here in body, with my soul in Rome." And in a fortnight she is looking, for financial help, to Giovanni Gonzaga, her brother-in-law. "Your Highness, knowing I have just been to Rome, where there are antiquities on all sides, perhaps imagines that I came back loaded with them. But when someone shows me a fine and cherished possession I am not brave enough to beg nor even, by the faintest sign, admire it; and so, being over-scrupulous, I returned empty-handed." However, there was now an opportunity to buy marbles, and would he kindly help?

In fact the Mantuan court had for long given concrete expression to a taste for Roman antiquities, and Leon Battista Alberti, foremost disciple of Vitruvius, was its chosen architect for the churches of San Sebastiano in 1452 and Sant' Andrea in 1470–72. Nor did Mantua forget that Publius Vergilius Maro had been born there. Giovan Pietro Arrivabene's poem *Gonzagidos*, Luigi Gonzaga praising the victorious in 1453, was inspired by the *Aeneid*; and the Bolognese Sabadino degli Arienti in his collection of tales, the *Porretane*, refers to another Mantuan poet, Giovan Battista Spagnoli (c. 1448–1516) as "esteemed the rival and, dare one say, the equal, of the divine Maro his countryman." Spagnoli, who was vicar-general of the Carmelites in 1483, saw Rome many years before his princes did so, as the friend of Pomponio Leto and Giovanni Pontano. A fellow-member of Pomponio's *Accademia Romana*, Giovan Battista Fiera (1465–1540) was likewise a fervent admirer of Virgil, as of Spagnoli himself; so much so, indeed, that he had the latter's bust, together with busts of Virgil and the marquis Francesco, placed above a thirteenth-century arch near his house in Mantua. The same love of the Roman spirit must have informed the "academy" assembled by Francesco's wife Isabella d'Este, in palace

Leonis Baptistae Alberti Florentini viri clarissimi Libri De re ædificatoria decẽ. Opus integrũ et absolutũ: diligenterq; recognitum.
Distinctum est autẽ nuper opus ipsum totum / quod antea perula legebatur oratione / per capita / nõnullis e textu reb⁹ insignibus depromptis / et in margine annotatis.
Facta est etiã capitũ ipsorũ nõ inelegans tabula: cũ dictionũ et ipsarũ rerum scitu dignarum quę in margine sunt; indice admodum luculento.

B·R
B·REMBOLT

Venũdantur Parrhisijs In Sole aureo vici sancti Iacobi. Et in intersignio triũ coronarũ / e regione diui Benedicti.

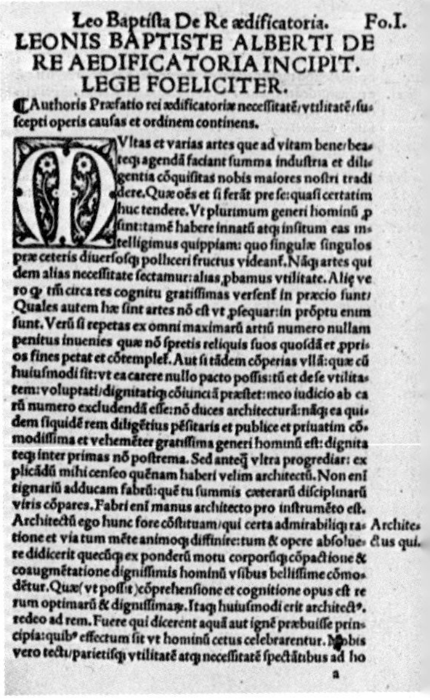

Leo Baptista De Re ædificatoria. Fo.I.
LEONIS BAPTISTE ALBERTI DE RE AEDIFICATORIA INCIPIT. LEGE FOELICITER.

Authoris Præfatio rei ædificatoriæ necessitatẽ / vtilitatẽ / suscepti operis causas et ordinem continens.

MVltas et varias artes que ad vitam bene / beateq; agendã faciant summa industria et diligentia cõquisitas nobis maiores nostri tradidere. Quæ oẽs et si ferãt pre se: quasi certatim huc tendere. Vt plurimum generi hominũ ꝓsint: tamẽ habere innatũ atq; insitum eas intelligimus quippiam: quo singulæ singulos præ ceteris diuersosq; polliceri fructus videanť. Nãq; artes quidem alias necessitate sectamur: alias ꝓbamus vtilitate. Alię vero q; tm̃ circa res cognitu gratissimas versenť in præcio sunt / Quales autem hæ sint artes nõ est vt ꝓsequar: in prõptu enim sunt. Verũ si repetas ex omni maximarũ artiũ numero nullam penitus inuenies quæ nõ spretis reliquis suos quosdã et ꝓprios fines petat et cõtempleť. Aut si tãdem cõperias vllã: quæ cũ huiusmodi sit: vt ea carere nullo pacto possis: tũ et de se vtilitatem: voluptati / dignitatiq; cõiunctã præstet: meo iudicio ab earũ numero excludendã esse: nõ duces architecturã: nãq; ea quidem siquidẽ rem diligẽtius pẽsitaris et publice et priuatim cõmodissima et vehemẽter gratissima generi hominũ est: dignitateq; inter primas nõ postrema. Sed anteq̃ vltra progrediar: explicãdũ mihi censeo quẽnam haberi velim architectũ. Non enĩ tignariũ adducam fabrũ: quẽ tu summis cæterarũ disciplinarũ viris cõpares. Fabri enĩ manus architecto pro instrumẽto est. Architectũ ego hunc fore cõstituam / qui certa admirabiliq; ratione et via tum mẽte animoq; diffinire: tum & opere absoluere didicerit quecũq; ex ponderũ motu corporũq; cõpactione & coaugmẽtatione dignissimis hominũ vsibus bellissime cõmodẽtur. Quæ (vt possit) cõprehensione et cognitione opus est rerum optimarũ & dignissimarũ. Itaq; huiusmodi erit architect⁹. redeo ad rem. Fuere qui dicerent aquã aut ignẽ præbuisse principia: quib⁹ effectum sit vt hominũ cetus celebrarentur. Nobis vero tectũ / parietisq; vtilitatẽ atq; necessitatẽ spectãtibus ad ho

Architectus qui.

a

Frontispiece and first page of De re aedificatoria *by Leon Battista Alberti, a book of architectural theory founded on his study of Vitruvius.*

The Gonzaga passion for classical Rome led to the summoning to Mantua of Alberti, the most faithful contemporary follower of the classical style. His design (1452) for the church of San Sebastiano (right), was carefully carried out by Luca Fancelli. Twenty years later he also designed Sant'Andrea (below, right), an innovatory construction which was built by Fancelli after Alberti's death. The monumental handling of architectural masses looks forward to the style of Bramante.

rooms overlooking the Piazza San Pietro in Mantua. An ornament of this society was Mario Equicola (1470–1525), and any court, says Matteo Bandello in the first book of his *Novelliere*, would be glad of many such, "for he is not only a fount of knowledge, having been educated since his youth in several courts, but a most agreeable companion, clever, witty and, what is more, an excellent conversationalist; one of those people whose pleasant talk never fails to please."

But the chief aim was to make Mantua a second Rome, and it was to Rome, with this end in view, that the young painter Lorenzo Leonbruno was despatched in 1521, to study architectural models for use in the ducal palace. Nine years later Battista Coro went on a similar

errand, and was in Rome when the marchioness Isabella paid her second visit – more extensive than her first and interrupted only by the terrible sack of 1527. She managed during this stay to undertake several archaeological jaunts, not all of them successful. In April 1526, for example, she visited Ostia "to see the ruins and antiquities," as Francesco Gonzaga the ambassador told her son, his cousin Federico (Duke of Mantua since his father's death in 1519). Most unfortunately, the ruins had been reburied on the orders of the bishop of Porto (which was nearby), "to stop people removing all the best marbles, as they have been doing for years: some of the stones being sent here to Rome and the remainder kept, by command of the pope, for the work at St Peter's."

One of Francesco's ambassadorial duties was that of enriching his cousin's collections, and in this he sought the aid of Giulio Romano. "Yesterday I saw the antiquities that Giulio the painter is offering Your Excellency . . . and chose what I judged best from among the objects of a size to be packed on to mules . . . the truth is, the pick of them are so big they would have to go by water . . ."

His mother encouraged the duke in his collector's fever. Taken to see the villa and garden complex, or *vigna*, of Villa Madama on 18 May 1525, she described it to him as "crammed with marvellous antiquities, the sort we have often desired to have in our own houses." And Mantua indeed was changing, profoundly and rapidly, on the pattern approved by mother and son.

Isabella and Federico could have asked no higher praise. Impassioned lovers of the Eternal City, they had created in the Po valley a new model court like that of Urbino. How were they to foresee that imperial troops would repeat in their Mantua the horrors inflicted on Rome in 410 and 1527? But when that time came, in 1630, the Gonzaga dynasty itself had been extinct for three years and more.

HIC AENEAS AFOELICE·V·ANTIPAPA LEGATVS AD FEDERICVM·III·
CAESAREM MISSVS LAVREA CORONA DONATVR ET INTER AMICOS
EIVS AC SECRETARIVS ANNVMERATVR ET PRAEFICITVR·

The Sacred Circle of Mantua

Fresco by Pinturicchio, one of a series on the life of Pius II (Aeneas Silvius Piccolomini) in the Biblioteca Piccolomini in Siena cathedral. The epigraph (bottom) reads: "Here Aeneas, emissary of the antipope Felix V to the emperor Frederick III, receives the laurel crown." This, like Petrarch's, was a poet's crown, for at the Habsburg court Aeneas Silvius was not only ambassador of Felix V (the former Duke Amadeus of Savoy, elected in opposition to Eugenius IV by the Council of Basle in 1439), but a leading exponent of the new humanist culture.

From feudal fortress to palace

Our best evidence for the tremendous importance of architecture in Renaissance culture is, perhaps, the palace, chosen center of the Renaissance court. Externally, in the way it was planned and built, in its visible ornament and relation to the urban scene, the palace was a solid, multiple statement: an affirmation of princely power over the city where it stood, and a source of yet further prestige and glory for the ruler.

As magnet and model the palace attracted subjects and other contemporaries mainly by virtue of its double rôle, public and private. It sheltered the ruler, his assistants, family and courtiers, with their exclusive ways and manners; and to it were drawn craftsmen and peasants from the estates, people who served the prince's wants and pleasures, aspirants for his favour, suitors for his support and protection.

The medieval town-house had been, for the ruling class at any rate, firstly a military stronghold (often shared, as were towers from the eleventh to the thirteenth century, by more than one family); and then a complex of buildings where workshop and other commercial space was also found. But the aristocratic town-house of the Renaissance was more a kind of management-center for the country estates, and evidently independent of the city around it. It was a town within the town, linked to the farmlands that yielded the family income and where the family would build their other houses, or villas. And such villas resembled the town-palaces since the owners clearly wished to enjoy their urban comforts, amid rural advantages and delights, while keeping a close eye on the management of the estates. For banks had crashed in the mid fourteenth century, plague had struck chiefly at the towns, and there was a new appreciation of the countryside. This climate produced the humanists' praise of the rustic life and the evolution of "archaic" literature; here were the ethical and aesthetic roots of the move back – the refeudalization of the countryside.

If we are to understand what a princely palace was – and we may define it as the heart of the court – there are three things to remember. There is the development, from the Middle Ages onwards, of the two great "princely" types of monumental and residential architecture, the feudal fortress (*rocca* in Italian), often dating back to the origins of the family, and the "public" town-palace, traditional symbol of governmental authority. There is the imitation of the prince's abode by ruling-class families in the leading centers of his domain, developing at times into more or less open competition and giving rise to the emergence of many "patrician" courts. (Rome and Venice are exceptions for, officially under the monarchical rule of pope and doge, they were controlled by their cardinalate and senatorial aristocracies.) Thirdly, there is the extension of the town-palace as country villa and the ensuing new relation between town and country, which affects building styles and styles of living.

Between the eleventh and the thirteenth century a nobleman's town house was a modest, or fairly modest, fortified tower. Family and dependents lived there, though not in isolation; they were in touch, often by a system of wooden footbridges, with kith and kin and political sympathizers in other towers. Such connected

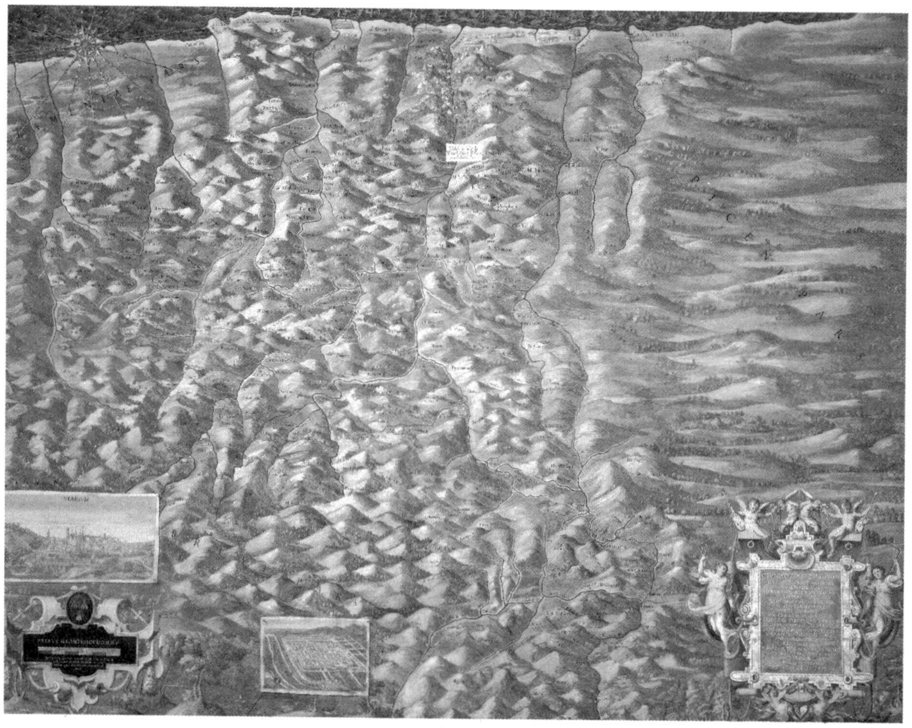

The tiny duchy of Urbino, in a sixteenth-century fresco by Antonio Danti in the Galleria delle Carte Geografiche at the Vatican. The Montefeltro family were established in Urbino by 1155, when Count Antonio was enfeoffed with the city, and after varying fortunes acquired a papal dukedom from Eugenius IV in 1443. The first duke, Oddantonio, was killed in the following year. His legitimized half-brother Federico, who succeeded him, was to make Urbino, clustered round the palace, the most beautiful of Italian Renaissance cities.

A sixteenth-century engraving of Mantua. From the end of the thirteenth century Mantua was ruled by the Bonacolsi family, its first lords and Imperial Vicars from 1311. They were overturned in 1328 in a popular rising engineered by the Gonzaga who then ruled until 1707. The palace, of various periods, lay at the edge of the town itself, as can be seen (bottom, right in illustration) and, unlike Urbino, distinctly aloof from it.

fortresses, forming blocks or *insulae*, were overtopped by the *palazzo pubblico* whose tower, by law, was higher than theirs. Municipal architecture still derived from the feudal and military, as we may see from a glance at the Palazzo Vecchio, seat of the Signoria, or the Bargello, seat of the *podestà*, in Florence. The former, designed by Arnolfo di Cambio, recalls his fortress built for the Guidi family of Poppi.

But in Tuscan communes where feudal lordships had not been established (a partial exception is Arezzo under its Ubertini, then Tarlati, bishops), the urban aristocracy evolved, in the larger towns at least, a building style of its own. Its members were men of mercantile or commercial descent, capable of blending top-storey feudal elements with manifestly bourgeois features on the ground floor; their crenellations might surmount doors wide enough for a warehouse. Florence has examples of such features in the Acciaioli, Davanzati, Bardi and Peruzzi palaces. Palazzo Peruzzi, its foundations among the substructures of the amphitheater of ancient Florentia, follows the curve of the Roman building, with a sequence of projecting doorways echoing that of the Roman exits, or *vomitoria*. (The curving amphitheater dictates, with immense architectural effect, the shape of Piazza Peruzzi itself).

In the fifteenth century fresh ideas were introduced by Michelozzo, Leon Battista Alberti and Benedetto da Maiano, who built, respectively, the Medici palace in Via Larga, and the Rucellai and Strozzi palaces. (These Florentine palaces had loggias, not all of which have survived.) As architects they looked further than feudal and military references. They calculated the harmonic proportions of volume and plane according to the golden section, adopted the square or rectangular ground plan with garden and central courtyard, and favoured the big arched entrance in the middle of the three-storeyed façade. In Florence the typical family palace lost the closed-in, defensive character of previous aristocratic dwellings and was built with a more open prospect, with wide entrance doors, large two-light or mullioned windows and Graeco-Roman-inspired decoration. (Even the heraldic devices conformed to the new style, which was hardly that of their origin.) The architectural repertoire made of the family palace a show-piece, unmistakably a center and a focus, but logically related to, and enhancing, the city around it. The Via Larga and, later, the Via Maggio, in Florence, the Grand Canal of Venice, the Strada Nuova (now Via Garibaldi) in Genoa, the great thoroughfares of sixteenth-century Vicenza, or of Lecce in the baroque period, are so many statements of aristocratic aspiration: the "aristocrats" being political and financial grandees wishing to appear as mainsprings of their city and to claim due admiration from their fellow citizens. The streets themselves became open and extended "courts," while some of the *piazze* were perfect settings for games, celebrations and social encounter. In the larger churches, too, the hierarchical and neighbourhood patterns existing among the families of one district or parish were repeated in the family chapels.

But, at least in northern towns such as Milan, Ferrara and Mantua (the outstanding examples), or in the Po valley, the urban aristocracy was soon relegated to a subordinate position. The process is seen at Urbino, where an early-established signorial domination developed into princely rule; and in Florence, though not until after the Medici assumed princely power in 1530. When this happened a princely court would draw a whole city into its orbit and the city actually derive its character, as a city, from the court.

We should remember that Renaissance writers on architecture, from Alberti to Serlio, Palladio, Pietro Cataneo and Giorgio Vasari, invariably note the social class of the man who gives the commission. The concept of building as an expression of rank persists to the end of the eighteenth century. In the famous *Encyclopédie*, publication of which began in 1750–51, we are roundly told, on the subject of how to build a house, "Style depends, without doubt, on the rank of the person who orders the building." This echoes Cataneo, who in 1554 had introduced a section of his treatise on architecture as "Book IV, wherein are discussed, with various plans, the arrangement of further palaces and houses: from the royal palace to that of the nobleman, the gentleman, and the houses of private persons." In the foreword he elaborates a little. "We are to speak of the high standards necessary in the construction of palaces, houses or other buildings suitable for kings, princes, prelates, noblemen and private persons."

A palace is not always a palace, moreover. Its name may differ with the owner's rank, with its function or its aspect. The *Encyclopédie* states clearly that the word *palais* refers only to a kingly residence. Princes live in "second-grade" palaces, which should be specified as such, and the great town-house of the noble family is correctly termed *grand hôtel*, or simply *hôtel*. In Venice, *palazzi* belong to those with a Doge in the family; any other aristocrats, however lordly, would live in a house that was plain *Ca'* (for *casa*). In this way the strictly limited Venetian ruling class emphasized its rôle and its exclusive character *vis-à-vis* an upper class which, flourish as it might, had to be kept at a distance.

Above: the walls and castellated towers of Soave. Cansignorio, Lord of Verona, enlarged a preexisting castle and built the palace for his governor in the second half of the fourteenth century.
Below, left: The castle at Poppi, built by the Guido counts as a stronghold from which to dominate the Casentino, or upper Arno valley.
Opposite: the superb palace at Urbino, begun by Luciano Laurana for Duke Federico di Montefeltro in the second half of the fifteenth century. The photograph shows the loggie of the western façade between the two soaring torricini, *which are so conspicuous a feature of the city. Even in its exterior aspect, this is clearly a dwelling designed for a prince.*

Wealth was not the sole factor to determine a building's size, beauty and ornament. These elements were governed by a whole range of rank and social condition. Once again, the *Encyclopédie* defines the attributes by which *hôtels* are recognizable as *demeures des grands-seigneurs*. "The beauty of the ornament must suit the owner's birth and station, but be less magnificent than that of a king's palace."

It is Alberti, in *De re aedificatoria*, who is most exact on what a royal or princely palace ought to be. Size is the prime consideration; how many rooms (and they are many), their distribution throughout the wings or buildings and how they are fitted for one purpose or another. The higher up the social scale, the more space each individual is allotted, and the apartments of lord and lady are strikingly different: though connected by corridors and stairs, his are adapted to the cares of state, hers to the cares of motherhood. As for situation, Alberti says, "wise princes have their palace

built outside the city bounds, to be free of continual plebeian interruption . . . for what is the use of power and riches if one cannot have ten minutes' peace?" And indeed we find that in the thirteenth and fourteenth centuries the prince – or the *signore* before him – tends to isolate himself if he dwells in the city. Where the signorial or princely family springs from the feudal nobility – as was the case with the Este at Ferrara, the Gonzaga at Mantua, the Visconti at Milan and Pavia, and the Montefeltro at Urbino – the tendency is yet more marked.

In the fourteenth and fifteenth centuries, however, the palace built or completed by such a family retained features of the feudal *rocca*, but the massive curtain-walls, great towers and donjon-keep, the crenellations, arrow-slits, drawbridge, moat and other military embellishments were no longer really for defense purposes, but more probably deliberate stylistic touches, speaking the language of power to subject citizens. Gradually, in the absence of arrows, for instance, and boiling oil, the arrow-slits serve merely to give an impression of height and elegance to battlemented walls.

Nevertheless it is important to remember that the prince who built his castle in his town did so at the town-limits, with a stretch of the walls in his own defenses and his way open at all times to the countryside beyond. To build further in might well stress his political power, but would also make him more vulnerable; in the event of

Opposite: Laurana's courtyard in the ducal palace, Urbino. Round its four sides Federico's honours and military achievements are recorded in a continuous inscription at first-storey level and over the portico of slim columns beneath. "Federico, Duke of Urbino, Count of Montefeltro and Casteldurante, gonfaloniere *of Holy Church and captain-general of the Italian League, raised this palace from its foundations for his glory and that of his descendants. Engaging constantly in warfare, he conducted six campaigns and, victorious in every combat, extended his dominions. In time of peace his justice and mercy, liberality and faith, equalled and adorned his victories."*

an uprising he would be immediately surrounded. The Visconti stronghold was thus on the edge of Milan, and when Francesco Sforza employed Filarete to rebuild it in 1451 he demanded – for all that he wished his people to see him as living among them – the inclusion of huge walls and high towers. Their message would be clear. Only within were the more peaceful loggias, courtyards and gardens to be found.

Alfonso of Aragon had no sooner conquered Naples, after years of warfare and a protracted siege, than he set about restoring its defenses, and the very next year began work on the damaged Castel Nuovo. Refurbished, but still a stark and soldierly fortress, this became the first home of the Aragonese court. Castel Capuana, brought within the perimeter as the city-walls were extended to the east, was substantially altered, as was the district around it, and here the duke of Calabria, later Alfonso II, held his court. The alterations were on a grand scale, and a vast complex was created, comprising the castle itself, which entirely lost its military complexion, the villa della Duchessa and the former Magdalene convent, with bridges and gardens and private roads by which Alfonso and his court could move from one residence to another.

In the thirteenth century the military feudal fortress was thus still the basic model for the ruler's dwelling, though it underwent extensive modifications, especially on contact with the new aristocratic, secular architecture emanating from Florence. And yet what Sigismondo Malatesta of Rimini built, in the first half of the century, on the site of demolished family properties, obviously harks back to the mode of a hundred years before. The fortified courtyard in front of the castle is gone, but the twin functions, residential and defensive, were certainly present, though distinct.

There was a period (roughly the second half of the thirteenth century in the north and a little later elsewhere in Italy) when the communes were yielding to signorial authority (itself to be superseded by princely rule), and there is something transitional and ambiguous about the actual seats of government. The magistrature of a commune was housed, for its term of

Above: carved door frame between the Sala degli Angeli and the present picture gallery (Galleria Nazionale delle Marche). Federico's palace was not only an architectural masterpiece but a prototype of the Renaissance palace, much studied and copied by contemporary courts. So harmoniously did it blend with the townscape that Urbino was literally redesigned around it, to become what was practically a palace-city in a single architectural unit.

Detail of chimneypiece in the Sala degli Angeli, an antechamber in the ducal apartments at Urbino, so called from this frieze of dancing putti by Domenico Rosselli.

office, in the *palazzo pubblico*, the town hall, complete with a small court of bodyguards, officials, servants, even minstrels. But the lord, the *signore*, did not, on his advent, necessarily move into the same premises. Rather than become identified with the government symbolized by the *palazzo pubblico*, he was more likely, having concentrated power in his own hands, to refurbish his own house to suit his new rôle and stay where he was. Thus Guido "Botticella" Bonacolsi who, in his capacity as captain general, or lord, of Mantua, became overlord of Pinamonte and Bardellone in 1299, freed the *capo di stato* of the obligation to live in the *palazzo communale*, and the custom evolved for a *signore* to hold legal courts in his private house. The *palazzi pubblici* now began to lose their old primacy. When the Gonzaga succeeded the Bonacolsi at Mantua the *palazzo pubblico* there fell into neglect. Luigi II (1369–82) repaired it, though not very thoroughly, for the Gonzaga felt safer in the *rocca* and he was busily engaged on the *castello di Corte*, restoring the castello di San Giorgio and the area round about; it was years later, in 1480, that the new ducal palace, the Nova Domus, was begun within the old Bonacolsi castle.

The work went on for a very long time. The leading Italian artists of the fifteenth and sixteenth centuries decorated this princely citadel, which in form and planning owes more than any other such palace to the previously mentioned theories of Alberti. Mantua was "doubled" into twin cities. The separate regions of prince and citizens adjoined, but did not overlap or mingle. The palace, with its countless rooms, its internal spaces and galleries between the old and new constructions, is the prototype of the Italian palace of the Renaissance. And this is true despite the fact that Urbino was more closely studied and more frequently imitated, both for its architecture and its relation to the urban setting. Urbino under the Montefeltro dukes provides the alternative model. There, new town-building and the intricate organization of the neighbouring territory are alike focused on the *reggia*, the palace. At Mantua the palace is a self-contained citadel; it grows upon and around its own foundations and neither affects nor intrudes into the town, a corner of which it

Below right: the duke's bedroom at Urbino. The Montefeltro eagle over the chimneypiece is by Domenico Rosselli and Francesco di Simone.

occupies. Mantua is the pattern of a city divided, of a palace that is a city within – or, better, adjacent to – a city. Urbino combines palace and city in one great architectural town-scheme.

These two types were not, of course, hard and fast. People did not stick to one or the other when building, but exchanged opinions and ideas. Indeed, we find the Gonzaga marquis Federico I, on 18 March 1481, sending a successful request to the court of Urbino for plans of the ducal palace (erected in 1444, when Federico of Montefeltro succeeded his half-brother Oddantonio, and enlarged by Laurana in 1466–72). "For I desire," wrote the marquis, "to make this house of ours on the pattern of what you have done there; which, we hear, is wonderful."

The Gonzaga and Montefeltro palaces are, then, similar in that each has parts of varying date; and profoundly, almost antithetically, contrasted in their relation of each to Mantua and Urbino respectively.

Federico da Montefeltro had brilliantly resolved the problem as between his own plans, the layout of his city and the existing nucleus of his palace. This lay on a hillside at the southern edge of Urbino, with a ruined *castellare* 150 meters north of it. The duke acquired the intervening land and constructed an enormous palace, several storeys high, incorporating two older houses. He then built the southern façade, where the private apartments overlook the valley from superimposed loggias flanked by the famous *torricini*, a pair of slender towers which, seen from the south-east, pierce the skyline of Urbino. The whole project, a vast complex of articulated buildings to be fitted in with others of medieval date on a very difficult site, demanded careful and subtle balance of the new idiom with what was traditionally acceptable as monumental architecture in a town. The two façades offer an inspired contrast. That facing out to the country, with the chivalric, fairytale reference and vertical emphasis of the soaring *torricini*, seems to belong to a tall medieval fortress; the other, broad and horizontal, faces the town across a wide square and seems trustingly to welcome guest and citizen.

Linking Urbino with Mantua, and both with Naples, is the architect Luciano Laurana. He was apparently in Naples by 1446 and a few years later built, as is fairly certain, the triumphal arch commemorating the entry of Alfonso the Magnanimous. In 1465 he worked on the portico of the castello di San Giorgio at Mantua, possibly to designs by Mantegna, and in 1466 went to Urbino where he remained, in charge of operations at the palace, until 1472. At Mantua, and again at Urbino, he met Alberti. Clearly, the executants of the new ideas on palace building travelled a limited circuit over a short period, and, although they solved a variety of architectural problems in a variety of ways, a central conception unifies their work.

But there was no single solution to the question, answered so brilliantly at Urbino, of how to introduce new building styles into an existing town setting. It would remain open throughout the sixteenth century. One highly original treatment is found at Ferrara, where the "Herculean Addition" was begun in 1492 by Biagio Rossetti for Duke Ercole I. Rossetti was born to do this sort of thing and at Schifanoia had demonstrated his architectonic skill, marrying the innovatory Florentine style with a typically Ferrarese late-fourteenth-century fabric.

Ideas and artists thus circulated from place to place and in doing so, they doubtless forged a common stylistic language, a shared *koinè*. Yet Renaissance Italy was not culturally centralized. Its local cultures were strong, and

DUKE FEDERICO'S STUDIOLO

"He even sent his emissaries to Flanders," writes Vespasiano da Bisticci in his *Vita di Federico d'Urbino*, "to seek out the finest master, whom he brought to Urbino and had him paint many large and most impressive pictures in his *estudio*, of the philosophers and poets, and all the doctors of the Church, both Greek and Latin, rendered with marvellous skill; and he painted His Highness to the life, as to seem that he lacked nothing except the faculty of breathing." This is the tiny, irregularly-shaped *studiolo* behind the first-floor loggia separating the *torricini*, above the Cappella del Perdono and the *tempietto* of the Muses.

Behind the *torricini* façade, "near to nature and the wide, magnificent views," lay what Pasquale Rotondi calls "three very remarkable chapels, dedicated to the Christian godhead, to poetry and the humanities." They were, in his opinion, conceived in one group when this façade, commanding the valley, was built, though decorated after the depature of the Dalmatian-born architect, Luciano Laurana, in 1472.

A poetical description by Antonio da Mercatello (1480) speaks of the "incomparable" *studiolo*, *el studio che di tutti passa il segno*. It communicates, through two small vestibules, with the ducal audience chamber and dressing room, and by a third passage with the loggia.

In a triumph of perspective virtuosity, the four walls of the *studiolo* are covered, to a height of just over two meters, with *trompe-l'oeil* intarsia panelling, giving the impression of a furnished apartment with benches with collapsible seats, strips of classical ornament separating the grilled, feigned cupboards, some of which are shown shut, others half-open, with a profusion of objects to be seen both inside and out: pieces of armour, as if doffed there and then by the duke before settling to his "humane studies," books, the authors' names partly visible – Cicero, Seneca, Vergil, musical instruments, a box of sweetmeats, a caged parrot, a clock with counterweights, an armillary sphere. In three illusionist niches are the Theological Virtues; from a corner, Federico himself appears advancing into the room, bearing a lance point-downwards in sign that he has temporarily abandoned war in favour of peace and scholarship. A landscape is to be seen, in its framework of stately arches, and in front of it, on a *trompe-l'oeil* ledge, a basket of fruit and a squirrel. Among the artists responsible for this world of illusion and symbolism, is mentioned the name of Sandro Botticelli.

In one corner, following the original outline, it has been possible to reveal the three-dimensional effect of a folding seat and lectern (2). The ceiling is of splendid hexagonal coffering; below it the walls, above the intarsia panels are now bare. Their decoration, as reconstructed in the diagram below (4) was of paintings, by Justus of Ghent and Pedro Berruguete, arranged in pairs. They were removed in 1631 by Cardinal Antonio Barberini, and damaged by sawing.

From a document of the period when Urbino passed to the papacy, we learn that "on the death of Francesco Maria Montefeltro della Rovere, last duke of Urbino, when the Apostolic Camera and the Holy See took possession, there were found in some of the smaller rooms portraits of the doctors, sacred and profane, of orators and poets [i.e. the portraits in the *studiolo*]; small pictures of the muses (in the *tempietto*); and pictures in the panelling of the little rooms, fixed and nailed to the walls".

1

2

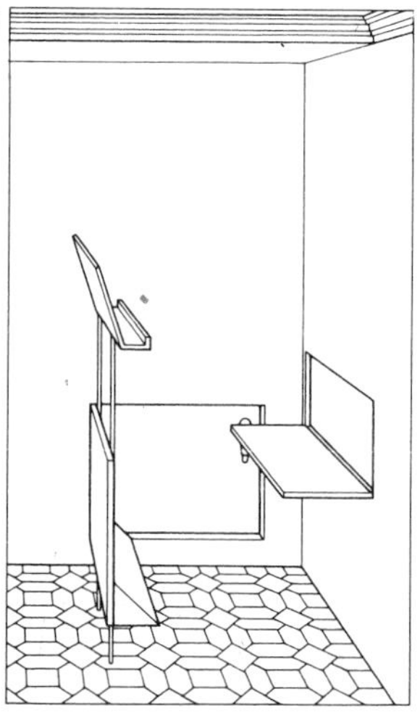

3

The *studiolo* pictures, painted on wooden panels, were for many years in the Barberini collection. Today some are in the Louvre; others, as part of the Galleria Nazionale delle Marche, are again in the palace at Urbino and include the portrait of Duke Federico, absorbed in his reading, with his son Guidobaldo at his knee (5). This picture was originally one of 28 portraits mentioned by Vespasiano da Bisticci which tells us something about the patron's culture and that of his day. These portraits included,

4

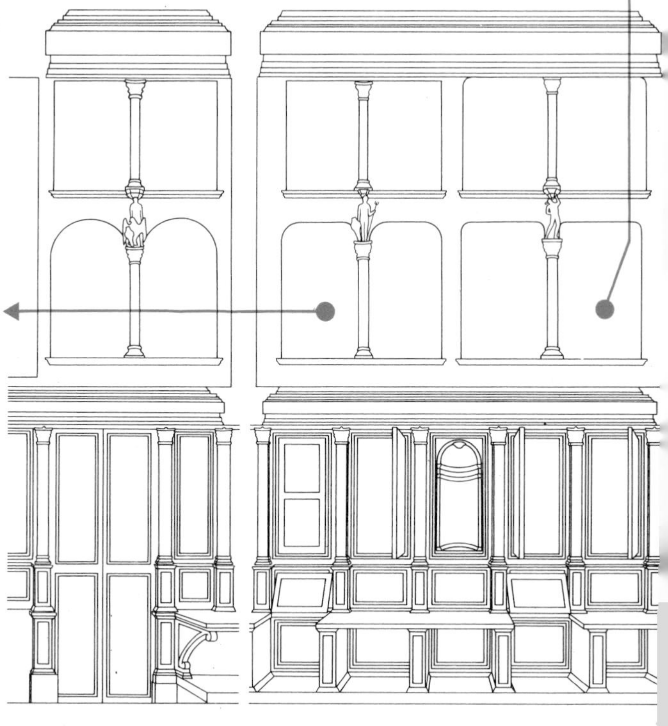

6

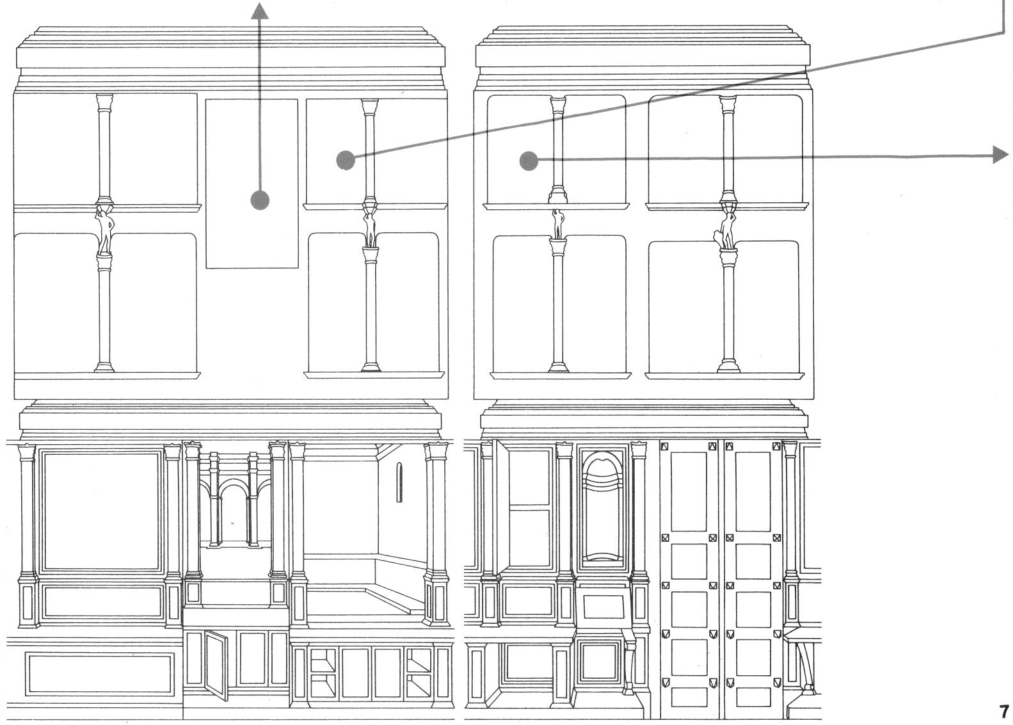

7

from the Bible: Solomon (1) and Moses; from the Classical world: Plato, Aristotle, Homer, Vergil, Cicero, Seneca and Solon (7) (though Anaxagoras was to have occupied Solon's place); from the men of science: Hippocrates, Euclid (6) and Ptolemy, Boethius representing late Latin period; and from Christianity: Albertus Magnus, saints Jerome, Augustine, Ambrose (3), Gregory and Thomas Aquinas. And finally the "moderns:" Dante, Petrarch, Duns Scotus, *doctor subtilis*, and the jurist Bartolo di Sassoferrato, thinker and physician, whose body was dug up and burned by the Inquisition, Pietro d'Abano (substituted in the scheme for Quintus Curtius), the humanist Vittorino da Feltre, Federico's boyhood turor, the humanist popes Sixtus IV and Pius II, and the Greek-born Cardinal Bessarion, champion of the study of Plato and the Greek language in Italy. Latin dedications beneath the portraits, lost when these latter were sawn up in the seventeenth century, are preserved in transcriptions made by the German Schrader in 1592. One ran: *Victorino. Feltrensi. ob. humanitatem. literis. exemploque. traditam. Fred. praeceptori. sanctiss. pos* "To Vittorino da Feltre, teacher, for the humane learning transmitted by letters and example, this is dedicated, in reverence, by Federico."

Above: The studiolo *of the "alchemist grand duke," Francesco I de' Medici, in Palazzo Vecchio, Florence, as restored in 1910. Vasari's decorative ensemble, following suggestions by the learned Vincenzo Borghini, covered the entire, small, elegant room with mythological and allegorical allusions keyed to the ceiling paintings of the Prometheus legend and metaphors of the natural elements. The upper register of paintings, by pupils of Vasari, illustrates the activities of man in relation to the four elements; eight statues of divinities stand two in each corner, their stories told on the cupboard doors below, while historical episodes and subjects drawn from alchemy and divination are on other, similar door panels. The lunettes of the shorter end-walls contain portraits by Bronzino of Cosimo I and his wife Eleonora of Toledo, the first grand-ducal couple to live in the Palazzo Vecchio*

strongly individual. As Paolo Portoghesi says: "Only Bramante's myth of a 'universal architectonic language,' " that expression of the political utopia of Julius II, would lead to the slow impoverishment of local traditions at the height of the sixteenth century. But *differenza*, the creative variety of specifically local values, was a constant aim of the early Renaissance, and even, to a different extent and in a different way, of the Mannerists."

Such individuality helped to preserve regional values and traditions. But it rested on extraneous and undeniable environmental factors of a kind which often posed practical and theoretical difficulties for both patron and builder. In his *Trattato di architettura*, Sebastiano Serlio notes, as occasion arises, the *accidenti*, or crises, to be expected. There will be "oddly shaped sites and irregular dimensions, old things to restore, and things that worked once upon a time to be got going again." His programme is precise. "I shall deal with many locations, and with odd and peculiar shapes, in putting all to rights. I shall demonstrate several methods of regulating a distorted façade so the house looks right and symmetrical . . ." Here is the love of order and regularity, of a symmetry which will confront, but not combat, multiform reality.

One princely house was in every respect unlike any other in Italy: that of the Medici who ruled Florence, then Siena, and then all Tuscany. Their absolutism in the city and state of Florence was no older than the first half of the sixteenth century, by which time the whole of Italy, except the Veneto, acknowledged princely dominion; and among the results of this fact was the extreme newness, by comparison, of their court. The Medici had no signorial or princely forebears to match those of Este, Gonzaga or Montefeltro. They were without feudal tradition, free of allegiance to a monarchical superior; and they continued to live in their Via Larga palace which, since they eschewed the formal trappings of civic authority, remained a private house. Not until 15 May 1540, when he had been for three years the second duke of Florence, would Cosimo I, with his wife Eleonora of Toledo, officially reside in the Palazzo Vecchio. The decision to make this

Right: marquetry panel and (below) doorway from Isabella d'Este's studiolo *at Mantua. Isabella lived all her married life in the palace, and when her husband died in 1519 and she removed from her original suite, the* studiolo *was reconstructed in her new rooms in the Bonacolsi wing.*

his court and family home was meant to confirm and legitimize his personal hold on the city, and yet, paradoxically, the move into the seat of the old Signoria was seen as a return to the constitutional norm. Had not this palace been government headquarters since the birth of the Republic? Only in the days of Cosimo the Elder, from whom Duke Cosimo was indirectly descended, had power been effectively transplanted to the Via Larga. The Medici régime, therefore, appeared to be legitimized in its new abode, though now a family, not a communal magistracy, was installed in that symbolic place of government; and now there was no term of office, and the government was absolute.

The contemporary chronicler Giovan Battista Adriani, had no illusions. Cosimo moved into the Palazzo Vecchio forcibly to proclaim his mastery over the city and to avail himself of better security, military and civil, than he could hope for in Via Larga. "The duke with all his family quitted the Medici house for the palazzo publico, properly the seat of the Signoria and State of Florence, having caused to be altered to his own use rooms previously occupied by the priors, the *gonfaloniere* and various magistrates whose offices were there. And this he did wishing to demonstrate his absolute and arbitrary power, and to discourage those who might cherish the idea – as some had cherished it – that the government of the town could be separated from that of the Medici. The Palazzo Vecchio, as chief center of the state of Florence, had to be guarded in any case, and most of the expense fell upon the Medici; and, as he required a bodyguard, he judged, for this and many other reasons, that he would be at less cost for greater safety, and gain in dignity and authority, by living there. He could govern with more splendour and more security, among obedient citizens and dependants."

What had been the Palazzo de' Priori, housing the priors of the major guilds, was no longer the Palazzo Popolo, seat of the commune. Nor was it the Palazzo della Signoria, seat of an oligarchy. It was a ducal palace. The adaptations and alterations, incomplete when the court arrived, went on for several years. The historian Bernardo Segni, who chronicled Florentine affairs from 1527 to 1555, reports that "the rooms of the municipal authorities were rearranged and reduced with many partition-walls, and the old rooms altered. The stanza della Gabella del Sale, the stanza de' Leoni, the stanza della Mercanzia, all turned upside down so that the duke might live there more conveniently."

Above, and opposite: two compelling, enigmatic pictures, executed by Mantegna for the Marchesa Isabella's studiolo *at Mantua, and now in the Musée du Louvre.* Parnassus *is an allegory of the Gonzaga court, with Mars and Venus (opposite) its presiding deities. Gian Francesco Gonzaga, victor of the battle of Fornovo, is Mars; Venus, goddess of love and – so Plato said – of marriage and the family, is his wife Isabella. Complementary to this scene is (above)* Minerva Hunting the Vices out of the Garden of Virtue. *Minerva, too, is Isabella, and we may deduce that vices are inadmissible to the* studiolo*'s climate of serene contemplation.*

But the transformation of the city into a city-court was barely begun. Throughout the fifteenth century the north-south axis of Florence was increasingly the scene of sharp and sometimes sharply disputed confrontation between official authority – that of the *signoria* of the republic – and the unofficial but real authority of the Medici. The former had its territory from the Palazzo Vecchio to the cathedral and baptistry; the latter radiated outwards from its Michelozzo palace in Via Larga to the church of San Lorenzo, the convent of San Marco and their surrounding districts. After 1540 the Medici sphere extended to the southern quarters and the districts across the Arno as the family found it desirable to draw these areas, too, into their city-court.

The Pitti palace at the foot of the Boboli hill, unfinished when Lucca Pitti ran out of money in 1470, was bought by Duchess Eleonora of Toledo, in 1549. Bartolomeo Ammannati embarked on a vast remodelling programme in 1558, though the great gardens, with the stretch of town wall and the Belvedere fort, were put in hand at the time of the purchase. In 1560–80 the Uffizi palace was started by Vasari, whose designs were later completed by Bernardo Buontalenti and Alfonso Parigi. The Uffizi, built to house the grand-ducal government offices, was joined to the Palazzo Vecchio by a covered gallery above Via della Ninna and connected the ancient seat of government with the Loggia dei Lanzi, on top of which a beautiful *giardino pensile*, or terrace garden, was contrived by Buontalenti for Duke Cosimo's son, Francesco I. The long, elevated and covered gallery from the Uffizi to the Pitti palace was Vasari's conception; it ran above the Ponte Vecchio and the bold plan was executed in five months in 1565. The Pitti by then accommodated the entire court, leaving the magistrature in the Uffizi and plenty of room for ceremonial occasions in the Palazzo Vecchio. Final authority resided there, in the ducal palace, administrative power at the Uffizi, and the Pitti was a "suburban" court residence, distanced from the town. From the town center the ruler could walk to the southern quarter by way of Vasari's raised corridor, isolated from his citizens yet close enough to observe them. He could, in fact, reach the Belvedere without ever quitting the confines of his palace or the Boboli gardens. A kind of parallel city, a Florence of the Medici princes, had been created, while the court imposed itself on the streets and *piazze* of the city, on certain of which it bestowed particular prominence. Thus Via Maggio became as it were a linking "corridor," flanked by the family palaces of courtiers who lived around the Pitti. As for the territory beyond, the Medici villas guaranteed grand-ducal ascendancy. They represented a network of administrative centers – extensions of the court through which the prince could travel the length and breadth of Tuscany.

The prince at home

It is not always easy to tell how palace accommodation was used, for internal arrangements often varied with the demands of hospitality or ceremonial, or even with the seasons. In some cases the carving of a doorway or chimney-piece or the subject matter of wall or ceiling frescoes,

Ceiling of the grotta *in the dowager apartment of Isabella d'Este. Reconstituted, with the* studiolo, *when she moved from her old suite, the* grotta *was used as a music room and for musical gatherings.*

in a palace or villa, give some indication of a room's original purpose or of its purpose at a given date, but little can ever be deduced with certainty from such observations. Only occasionally are facts more certain, when, for instance, apartments were made the private retreat of a consort. Thus Isabella d'Este, as marchioness of Mantua, wife of Gian Francesco II and mother of Federico II, had her rooms in the castello di San Giorgio at Mantua. She personally supervised their adaptation, paying particular attention to the decoration of her little *studiolo* and to what was known, from the *grottesca* stucco-work of its outer courtyard, as her *grotta* beneath it. When her husband died in 1519 she removed to a ground-floor suite in the Corte Vecchia – her "new" apartment – though it was in the old, Bonacolsi, wing. Several rooms were altered and completely renovated, although her cherished *studiolo* was reproduced with its original decorations, as was the *grotta* which, together with her own secret garden, became her private retreat.

At the Palazzo Vecchio in Florence the earliest major reconstruction, in 1540–55, was of the second-floor rooms for Cosimo I's wife Eleonora and her suite; her taste dictated their planning and ornament. Bronzino frescoed the chapel; Ridolfo del Ghirlandaio painted the *camera verde* (the green room) possibly a transitional room or closet; there is a salon, with an exquisite writing desk painted by Cecchino Salviati. Bare walls are masked with gilded leather and tapestries. The sala di Ester has a carved wooden ceiling by Battista Botticelli, tapestries relating the story of Esther, and a decorative scheme planned – quite independently of Vasari, the overall director – by Giovanni Stradano. Depicted in other tapestries are the stories of Penelope and of Dante's "good Gualdrada," and the three ladies – the Biblical heroine, the classical heroine and the heroine of medieval Florence – together offer, as it were, a commentary on queenly rule.

The decorative scheme of Eleonora's apartments tells us much about the culture, religion and ideology of the world she lived in, but unfortunately, not a great deal about how the rooms were actually used.

Carved wooden ceilings, however, and door- and chimney-surrounds generally remained in their original positions and so cast some light on a room's original purpose. Frescoes are even better evidence, for although they could be obliterated or plastered over, no one, at that time, knew how to move them. The same, of course, cannot be said of a whole range of accessories – tapestries, gilded leather, sculptures, furniture and pictures on panel or, later, canvas. These would help to create the atmosphere of a room, but could as readily be taken elsewhere.

Our modern notions of furniture go back no further than the eighteenth and nineteenth centuries. The very word "moveables" shows how they have changed since the Middle Ages and the Renaissance. Until the sixteenth century the scanty and relatively light furniture – tables, chairs, coffers, chests and cupboards – was, literally, moveable. The medieval way, for instance, would be to assemble the dining-table, which was nothing more than wooden planks (*capre*, as they were called) before a meal, and "clear" it afterwards by carrying off planks and trestles, leaving the floor space free. Similarly portable were the chests and coffers and cabinets, the strongboxes and trunks of the Renaissance, including those famous Tuscan cabinets in ebony, ivory and *pietra dura*, with all their little drawers and secret compartments. When the Medici betook themselves to a rural villa, or the Montefeltro princes went in summer to their magnificent Villa Imperiale near Pesaro, with them went the ruler's favourite furniture or pictures. Wherever he was, he could reconstruct his *studiolo* and conduct affairs in comfort surrounded by his most prized possessions.

Much that was medieval persisted in the courts of the Renaissance. From house to house, from one suite of rooms to another, there were the same dislodgements, reflected, more often than one might expect, in a certain indifference to objects and furnishings. There may even be a shortage of such things, disguised in some measure by the magnificence of prized works of art commissioned or collected by the prince, but occasionally revealed by inventories of the humbler effects in daily use. This, however, need not falsify our customary vision – historically verifiable, although owing something to pictorial art – of the *luxe, calme et volupté* of the Renaissance court. In that intellectual climate the display of luxury, the practice of art patronage and art collection, were obviously regarded as activities related, but not secondary, to the exercise of power. They contributed to the image and were considered operational expenses. Some of the inventories assume an almost mesmeric quality as the dazzling details are paraded. "Six pieces of green damask, each five by six *braccia*, handsome enough for our bedroom . . . I desire Your Excellency may let me have his gold-leather hangings for a bedroom . . . fifteen silver plates and fifteen silver *tondi* . . . a silver bowl for the table . . . and as all the goldsmiths are busy for me and my son the duke . . . you can send the orders out to Ferrara." These are only a few of the instructions and requests from Isabella d'Este to the agents, or *procuratori*, of the court when she was equipping her first and second set of apartments.

A taste for sumptuous furnishings, like that for rich clothes, was far more than a matter of fashion and the manifestation of wealth, and the power that accompanied it: an intrinsically valuable and, by contemporary standards, beautiful object represented a tangible manifestation of the sovereign, an expression of his power. The allegorical and metaphorical references in sculpture and painting (whether portraiture or not) all evoke the patron, the man who gave the order. These references may be emblematic and heraldic, or they may be mythological. It is no accident that Cosimo I, Grand Duke of Tuscany, commissioned and collected statues and cameos of Hercules: a hero who had represented the might of imperial Rome was now representing that of Cosimo. It is no wonder that Cosimo responded as he did to Michelangelo's youthful David, the "Florentine hero" who was clearly a Christian symbol since he was a Biblical figure. David as the unarmed victor over the giant Goliath was the personification of the Savonarola-inspired republican defiance of the Empire in 1530. Cosimo's answer was the calm and menacing Perseus of Cellini. Like a hangman, Perseus brandishes Medusa's severed head above the

The giardino segreto *at Mantua. The* studiolo, grotta *and garden were together the private heart of Isabella's apartment, where she received and entertained her erudite friends and which still breathes something of the humanist spirit of the Italian Renaissance courts. She was herself deeply imbued with that spirit, read Latin easily, had a knowledge of the ancient world and its mythology, and was an expert judge of painting and poetry.*

Piazza della Signoria, in view of the population. The locks are self-consuming snakes, a transparent allegory of what republicans called "liberty" and the prince defined, once and for all, as discord. It was a lesson, and a warning. Cosimo-Perseus had decapitated discord in establishing the principate and no one, unless he wished to see the executioners as busy as they were after the last insurrection at Montemurlo in 1537, need think of reintroducing it. The Perseus image rang, too, in proud justification. It justified the House of Medici; the Medici, with their imperial fief and their bourgeois origins, and their fathers who had been bankers to the fathers of their subjects. It justified their scaling of the Olympian heights: as Perseus was begotten by Jove in a shower of gold, so was the ducal power of Cosimo engendered, in showers of gold from the Medici bank, by the emperor Charles v.

Such were the symbols and *Herrschaftszeichen*, the metaphors of power. Such was the jewelled Golden Rose, papal gift to a signally favoured ruler, which was regarded as both honour and talisman. (Pius II gave one to his native Siena in 1429.) And there was the same

Fifteenth-century tarot cards depicting Knighthood and Justice, from a pack painted by Bonifacio Bembo for Cardinal Ascanio Sforza, and now in the Accademia Carrara at Bergamo. The image of the princely courts was much enhanced by the fact that the most famous artists were prepared to employ their talents on what were, ostensibly, minor commissions.

attitude to jewels, whether they belonged to families or to individuals. Wealth and taste were evinced in the careful choice of gems and of design, as was belief in the magical properties attributed to precious stones.

With changing manners and codes of behaviour, more attention is paid to proper ceremonial accommodation. Dining rooms and bedrooms cease to be improvised here and there in the peripatetic medieval fashion, and acquire specially made and permanent furniture. Rooms are larger, hung with tapestries and panelled in wood, with carpets on the floor. Frequently, as in the *studiolo* of Federico di Montefeltro, or Isabella's new apartments at Mantua, they become *trompe l'œil* stage-settings. Bookshelves and drapery were fixed, like scenery, to the walls, and famous fitments, such as Duke Federico's bed at Urbino, had the same "theatrical" character. On chimneypieces the carving is increasingly elaborate, as may be seen in the stucco ornament by Domenico Rosselli, also at Urbino. Articles of furniture, once portable accessories or storage space, took on the lines and aspect of architecture, often enhanced by semi-precious stones or ingenious mechanisms. A notable example in this style is the ebony and ivory "German cabinet" which Duke Leopold of the Tyrol sent to Ferdinando II of Tuscany. Decorated with silver-mounted *pietra dura*, it contains a revolving altar and a clock with a device beneath for striking the hours.

Household articles in particular were more and more sophisticated. The Paduan sculptor Andrea Briosco, known as il Riccio, produced superb lamps, salt-cellars and inkstands, with delicate animal and human figures. There was splendid table-ware – pieces such as the Murano glass goblet with polychrome enamel decoration, now in the Castello Sforzesco at Milan, or the pilgrim-flask with the Sforza and Bentivoglio arms in the Museo Civico in Bologna. There are plates, and huge *taglieri*, or display-platters. There was the celebrated Medici porcelain. (Even the "alchemist" Grand Duke, Francesco I, was involved in experiments to find the secret of true porcelain paste, but the products, blue-painted on a white ground, are of variable quality.) Wonders came from hands of

Women playing with tarot cards. Detail from a fifteenth-century fresco. Scotti-Casanova Collection, Rome.

The Pleasure Garden, with singers and musicians, in a miniature from the De Sphaera *codex, in the Biblioteca Estense, Modena.*

Bernardo Buontalenti, or from the Grand Duke's workshops – amphorae, ewers, lapis lazuli vases with gold mountings. The list of these objects, which combine considerations of use, decoration and display, is almost endless. The salt-cellar in gold and enamel ordered by François I from Benvenuto Cellini in 1543 is a supreme example; Michelangelo himself also designed a salt-cellar, the drawing of which is in the British Museum. No artist was above putting his genius or his talents at the service of a court. The greatest sculptors and bronze-founders cast guns, or were responsible for prodigies of handicraft. Albrecht Dürer, Hans Holbein and Andrea Mantegna painted playing-cards. (Cardinal Ascanio Sforza's tarot pack, by Bonifacio Bembo, is in the Accademia Carrara at Bergamo.)

The art of gem-cutting was perfected in the sixteenth century and the experts, most of them Italian, were in demand at courts all over Europe. The Venetian goldsmith Gian Giacomo Caraglio spent years at the court of Bona of Savoy, Queen of Poland, and Jacopo da Trezzo, from Milan, worked in Spain for Philip II. In Prague Emperor Rudolph II employed another Milanese, Ottavio Miseroni, and Alessandro Masnago. Matteo del Massaro of Verona, active at the French court from 1515 to 1547, contributed to a revival of his art in France and enjoyed an unrivalled reputation for cutting cameos "with the grain."

One of the finest and most admired specimens, now in the Museo degli Argenti in Palazzo Pitti, is by Giovan Antonio de' Rossi, head of a Milanese *bottega* who also worked in Florence, Venice and Rome. It is an onyx cameo with portraits of Cosimo I, the Duchess Eleonora and four of their children. The great Hellenistic model of the art, the Tazza Farnese, in two strata of veined sardonyx, had entered the collection of Lorenzo the Magnificent by 1471 and was owned by the Medici until the death of Duke Alessandro in 1537. Margaret of Austria, his widow, was remarried to Ottavio Farnese and the Tazza, included in her dowry, became Farnese property and has been in the Museo Nazionale in Naples since 1735.

Another much-prized skill was that of engraving rock-crystal. Families such as the Sarac-

Below: two Renaissance gardens, each with a pergola, or arbour. From the Hypnerotomachia Poliphili, *attributed to Francesco Colonna and published in Venice by Aldo Manuzio in 1499.*
Right: Garden of Love in an anonymous fifteenth-century Florentine engraving. The Renaissance garden was a retreat from the world, consecrated to pleasure and the Muses, and heavily charged with meaning and allegory.

chi, Gaffurri and Miseroni practiced the art, as did non Italians from the north – Jonas Falqui, Jacques (or Jacopo) Bilyvert, and Giambologna (Jean de Boulogne, who was a native of Douai). These men made beautiful objects for the grand duke in Florence, one of the most remarkable, though least-known, being a jewelled crown commissioned by Ferdinando I in 1608 as an offering to the miraculous Virgin of Monsummano. His son Cosimo II gave to the shrine a marvellous necklace of gold and precious stones from the workshop of Cosimo Merlini, Odoardo Vallet – the successor of Bilyvert – and Jonas Falqui. The crown is now in the church of Santa Maria della Fonte Nuova at Monsummano, near Pistoia.

The princes of the Church, emulating secular rulers and themselves often of princely birth, were also collectors and patrons of the arts. The Cassetta Farnese in the Capodimonte Museum at Naples was made, between 1548 and 1561, for Cardinal Alessandro Farnese, its panels of rock-crystal engraved after designs by Perin del Vaga. Leo X commissioned the handsome display-dish by Valerio Belli now in the Schatzkammer of the Residenz at Munich; and the same artist's silver-gilt reliquary at the Pitti Palace, decorated with enamels and rock-crystal, was for the other Medici pope, Clement VII.

In Florence the taste for polychrome marbles, *pietra dura* and semi-precious stones was so marked that in 1588 the grand dukes founded the Opificio delle Pietre Dure as a center for mineralogical research. Commissions for this kind of inlay were carried out and artists – Bernardino Poccetti, Ludovico Cardi, known as il Cigoli, and Giacomo Ligozzi – tested their skills there. The Palazzo Pitti was supplied with tables in this intarsia technique when first equipped in the 1570s. The Venetian ambassador Andrea Guffoni, staying there in 1577, speaks in his *Descrizione* of the overwhelming profusion in the new grand-ducal residence – the ornamentation, the furniture and paintings of its 58 rooms, halls and terraces, not to mention the "very good attic bedrooms and stupendous gardens." And this was not the end, "for the palace is only two-thirds finished." Still more interesting are details concerning the meals. The duke and his family "eat always in splendour . . . like kings, from vessels of gold, silver and other precious material . . . and one day the grand duke gave a lavish banquet for the ambassador, where there was not only meat in plenty and abundance, but we were most marvellously served."

As well as precious stones, the Renaissance also loved those objects and substances – animal, vegetable or mineral – that flooded into Europe from distant, newly-discovered lands. These included coral and mother-of-pearl, amber, tortoiseshell and fossilized wood – *naturalia*, and were the subject of endless speculation and mythmaking and affording ample opportunity to experiment with new techniques for the fashioning of new and extraordinary objects. These were raw material for the gifted artists and craftsmen who circulated between the courts of Munich, Prague, Fontainebleau and Florence, ministering to princely taste for the so-called minor arts: a taste expressed, first and foremost, in the rage to collect.

The advent of printing may be said to have had no effect on princely collections save in the library where, until the end of the fifteenth century, illuminated manuscripts had reigned supreme. The noble lord had to have at least one fine Book of Hours, and superbly illuminated Bibles such as the *Bibbia di Borso* with which Borso d'Este celebrated his elevation to a dukedom, are examples of an art whose every

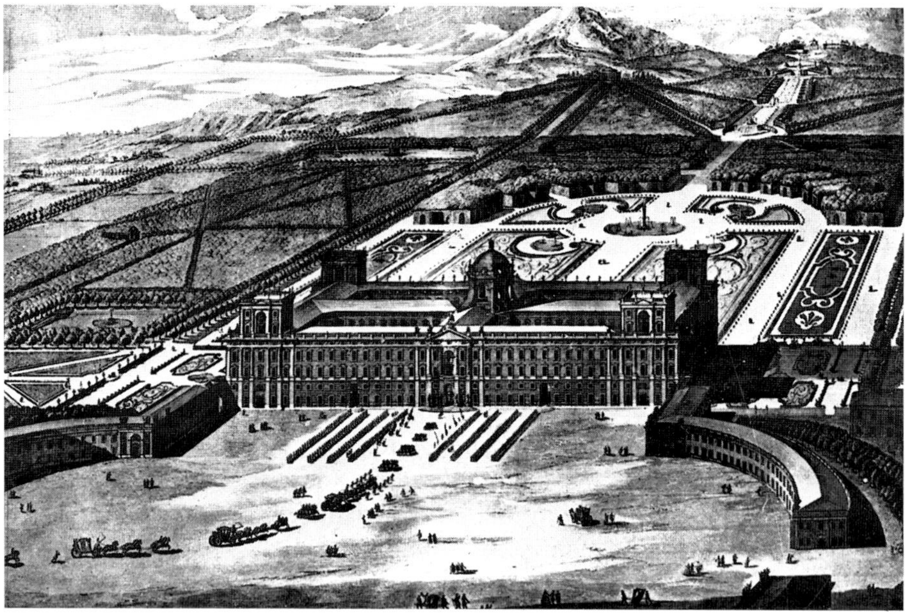

Above: panoramic view of the royal palace of Caserta with its gardens – one of the most magnificent of Italian court complexes. Left: the garden adjoining the palace, in an eighteenth-century print.
Caserta, which the Bourbon King Charles III intended to rival Louis XVI's Versailles, was built by Vanvitelli between 1752 and 1774, and is recognized as his masterpiece. The great park (of some 120 hectares – about 296 acres – and over three kilometers long) was partly altered by his son, Carlo.

product is unique. From Baldassare Castiglione, the "perfect gentleman," we learn that Federico di Montefeltro would admit only manuscripts to his library. Yet the needs and enquiries of science, together with improvements in printing, soon conquered these exclusive preferences, and the printed book came triumphantly to court.

Musical instruments were to be found in plenty, for the court appreciated them, too, as beautiful objects. The Este harp, made at Amiens in 1558 and decorated in 1587 by the Ferrarese master Giulio Marescotti, may be seen in the Galleria Estense at Modena.

Arts, sciences, and marvels

The princely love of luxury thus had many dimensions. It was without doubt a manifestation of power, and of splendour as the symbol of power. But it included the passion for beauty, the obligations, demagogic though they were, of patronage, the demands of scientific curiosity and the mannerist, later baroque, attraction to exaggeration, oddity and the occult. There was all this behind the ample – the sometimes enormous – collections of objects, artistic, scientific or merely "strange;" of actual or supposed freaks, marvels and monsters; of anything that fell under the headings *naturalia* or *artificialia*. And such eclectic ardour demanded in its turn places and spaces of its own in princely palaces.

The art-collection, the treasures and the curiosities were kept in the *Kunstkammer*, the *Schatzkammer* or the *Wunderkammer*: three key-settings, not always, and not necessarily, distinct from one another, which indicate the relation between power, learning and possession at a Renaissance court.

Paolo Cortesi's *De cardinalatu* (1510) includes a chapter on the ideal arrangement of a cardinal's dwelling. On the *piano nobile* he locates chapel, *credenza* or strong-room for the silver, the *cella gemmarum* for the antiquities and the private *studiolo* or *cella lucubratoria*. He points out that a court should theoretically have special rooms, thoughtfully planned in terms of position and suitably decorated for the purposes of study and meditation, and for housing the collections. A library was naturally included among these. Separate libraries had existed much earlier in monasteries where the

problem of how to allot space had been mastered long before being solved in secular building. The decoration of a library, says Julius von Schlosser, was largely traditional and would represent the whole field of knowledge, including theological allegories and the subjects of the trivium and quadrivium. Raphael, who was to paint the sciences, arts and cardinal virtues in the *stanze* at the Vatican, may have been inspired by figures of the liberal arts by Melozzo da Forlí in the ducal library at Urbino.

It is perhaps in the *studiolo*, however, that the cultural interests of a prince, and consequent patronage of the arts, are best and most vividly illustrated. The *cella lucubratoria*, as Cortesi calls it, is the truly intimate and private apartment, usually a sanctum for solitary contemplation.

This character of the *studiolo* probably explains why so many of them have, alas, disappeared; though from surviving examples and a few reliable fifteenth- and sixteenth-century accounts it is possible to trace a certain development. In the fifteenth century the *studiolo* reflects man's concern with the intellect – it is a self-contained *hortus conclusus* ("garden of the soul") embracing culture and memory; by the sixteenth it reflects a more open attitude, containing multiple references to the world beyond and with scenes of nature decorating its walls. The process seems to be a broadening-out, a "secularization" of culture, as natural science weaned the prince away from knowledge embalmed in the written or printed word and towards the concrete, natural universe; or, it may be, the universe he found in his collection of live, or once-live, objects.

As ever, the most reliable evidence is a real instance, and we discover, behind the marquetry panelling of the Camera d'Oro at Torrechiara – that shrine to courtly love, as its frescoes proclaim – a hidden *studiolo* which must have existed before 1463, when it is mentioned by the court poet Gerardo Rustici. There is still a *terra verde* niche, flanked by paired heroes, Samson and Hercules; and on the inner wall are Virgil and Terence, linked by a scroll that bears an allusion to Christ. These are the refinements of literary allegory; the painted figures invite to meditation.

Most of the sculpture on the many fountains and fishponds at Caserta is mythological in subject. The culmination is the grand cascade which plunges from a height of 78 meters into a basin, with marble figures grouped on artificial rocks (detail, above), in poses which illustrate the story of Diana and Actaeon (whom she turned into a stag, to be devoured by his own hounds).

THE LABYRINTH

1

2

3

4

The courtly garden of the Renaissance was, as Franco Cardini says, "dedicated to diversion and intellectual adventure," and one of its features, with more than a hint of initiation and the mystery-religious about it, was the labyrinth. This might be a series of flower beds, as shown in some old prints (8 and 9), or a maze of evergreen hedges, tall and thick, through which one route, and one only, led to a central belvedere. Such was the garden-labyrinth of the eighteenth-century Villa Pisani at Stra.

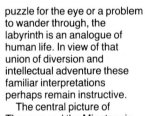

The deception of the labyrinth, concealing an element of uncertainty in what looks like order, lies in its apparent symmetry; yet the all-but-unnoticed irregularities of pattern are in fact all-important, for through them the irregular, unforeseeable path is to be traced. Also, whether a puzzle for the eye or a problem to wander through, the labyrinth is an analogue of human life. In view of that union of diversion and intellectual adventure these familiar interpretations perhaps remain instructive.

5

The central picture of Theseus and the Minotaur in the floor mosaic in the House of the Mosaic Atrium at Pompeii (1) brings us to the mythological origins of the maze. Minos, king of Crete, the story goes, vanquished the Athenians and laid a tribute on them: every nine years they were to send seven youths and seven maidens as victims for the Cretan Minotaur. This monster, with a bull's head and the body of a man, may be related to the bull-headed Phoenician Baal, recipient of human sacrifice, but in the Greek legend is the offspring of Pasiphae, wife of Minos, and a bull.

This animal the king had himself requested of Poseidon for a sacrifice, but when it issued from the sea foam he thought it too splendid for the purpose. He kept it, substituting another on Poseidon's altar, and the god, to punish him, inspired his queen with a passion for the white bull. She bore the monster, which Minos

6

incarcerated in a labyrinth – built by Daedalus – and fed on slaves and criminals or, as in the case of the Athenian tribute, those whom he had conquered.

Etymology supports the identification of the palace at Cnossos with the labyrinth of Daedalus, for "labyrinth" is connected with the Carian word "labrys," an axe, and many of the double-headed Minoan ritual axes have been found on the site. The question, however, may well be more complicated, and the myth continues. The Attic hero Theseus joins the Athenian boys the third time the tribute is due. Assisted by Daedalus and the king's daughter Ariadne, whom Aphrodite has caused to fall in love with him, he enters the labyrinth and slays the Minotaur, his route back to safety marked by the woollen thread Ariadne had provided. She leaves Crete with Theseus and is abandoned by him on the island of Naxos. Daedalus and his son Icarus, imprisoned in the labyrinth, escape by making birds' wings and flying out of it.

The multiple significance of this tale, and the intersection within it of several different myths, are obvious. It seems, even, to convey the sense of human instability or indecision illustrated in the Sala del Labirinto at Mantua, where the proverbial motto, *Forse che si, forse che no* runs through the painted maze on the ceiling (5).

The geometrical patterns can be related to the spiral and meander motifs which preceded and, as it were, paved the way for the labyrinth. The classical meander occurs, as a border, in medieval art – here (6) it is seen in a fresco of the tenth – eleventh century from the collegiate church of Sant'Orso at Aosta – and many medieval gardens contained labyrinthine flower beds.

Sebastiano Serlio (1475–1554), who was born in Bologna and studied Roman antiquities as a pupil of Baldassare Peruzzi, included labyrinth designs in his *Trattato di architettura*. (This was published, in five books, during Serlio's lifetime; one book and part of another were unpublished, and Book Six appeared posthumously). Of the three labyrinths illustrated here, the first (2), in the classical, right-angled pattern, has the feeling, absent from the Mannerist variations (3 and 4), of a unique and magical path.

Our last example (7) is from *I quattro libri dei labirinti*, by L. Pittoni; its flower beds are based on concentric circles and it combines the two main labyrinth-elements of curve and right-angle: the spiral and meander.

8

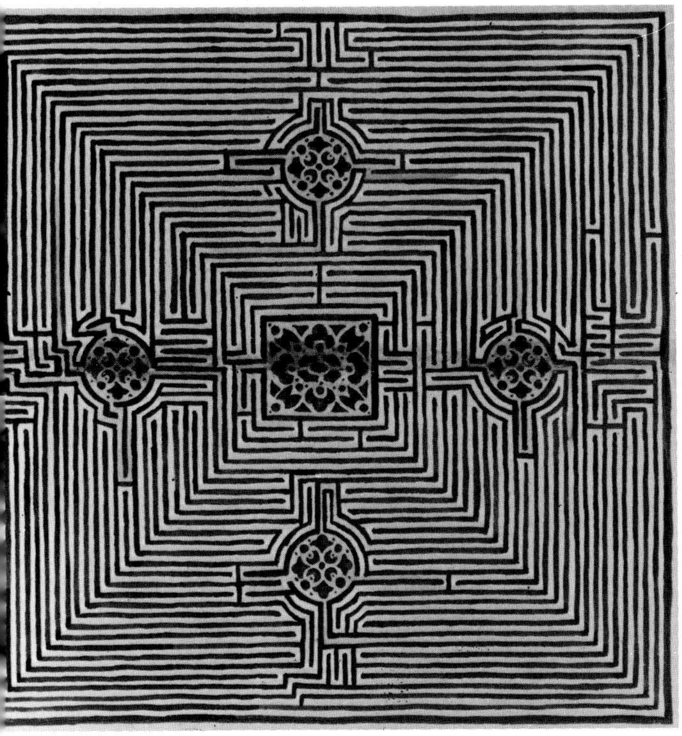

7

9

The orderly and symmetrical villa-garden at Valfonda. Detail of a fresco in Palazzo Giuntini, Florence.
Opposite: Pavilion of Ariadne in the garden of Villa Medici, Rome. Velázquez, c.1630. The villa belonged to Cardinal Leopoldo de' Medici, and the artist had stayed there on his first visit to Rome.

But how was the iconological decoration of a *studiolo* decided on? Can we really believe that the princely proprietor could have suggested what was often a highly symbolical scenario? And is it fair, on the other hand, to dismiss his contribution as no more than a suggestion? A clue to this may be found in a letter from Guarino da Verona to Leonello d'Este of Ferrara, who had asked for advice on the Muses as decorative subject matter for his *studiolo* in the castle of Belfiore. *Praeclara vereque magnifica cogitatio*, is the response; *principe digna inventio*. "Truly magnificent, an idea worthy of a prince;" the very wording limits the excellence of the plan, and the value of the idea. The marquis is culturally unqualified to do much more about it, but has at least laid down an emblematic scheme. (The chequered history of this *studiolo* is, incidentally, well documented. After Leonello's death his half-brother Borso went on with it, Cosmé Tura worked on it, and it was destroyed by fire in 1483).

Federico di Montefeltro's *studiolo* of 1476, evocative and personal, may, fortunately, still be seen at Urbino. It is a small, irregularly shaped room, made to look larger thanks to *trompe-l'œil* panelling. This was designed by Botticelli, Francesco di Giorgio Martini and Bramante (who probably supervised the scheme), and very exactly executed by Baccio Pontelli. There are illusionistic book-cases, doors half-open to reveal, or partly reveal, the books; some of the titles can be made out, even the authors' names. Various objects refer to the passage of time – an hourglass, a dwindling candle, a small brush to sweep the dust away. There are weapons and armour, musical instruments and the duke's emblems. All combine to draw us into the private world of the extraordinary prince, the warrior-intellectual who loved the arts.

Quite different was the *studiolo*, or *camerino*, of Alfonso d'Este at Ferrara. This, as Eugenio Battisti says, was not shut-in but open, through its paintings, "to the Emilian plain and the distant sea." At Mantua, Isabella d'Este's *studiolo* gave on to a little garden whose statuary and decoration are gone, but which may be imagined from Perugino's *Battle of Love and Chastity* in the Louvre, an allegory she commissioned in 1503 on a theme provided by the humanist, Paris de' Ceserari.

We may safely say that the *studiolo* was a kind of indoor *hortus conclusus*, a "garden of the soul" as its often naturalistic decoration was perhaps meant to suggest; "an artificial paradise," in Battisti's phrase, "a substitute for the rural retreat." Then, with the last, most famous example, the *studiolo* of Francesco I in the Palazzo Vecchio, dating from 1570–78, we are, to quote Battisti again, "at the opposite pole," and the whole intention changes. "The room is not only secluded, but totally dark. It suggests not paradise, but artificial night."

Visita interiora terrae rectificando invenies occultum lapidem. ("Visit the interior of the earth by means of right conduct and you will find the secret [*i.e.* the philosopher's] stone"). So ran an alchemists' acrostic, its initial letters spelling "vitriol," by the occultist Basilius Valentinus, compiler of the *Hermetic Museum*. Alchemy inspired a good deal of late Renaissance and mannerist painting. We need only think of Parmigianino and what Vasari calls his "endless flights of imagination," revealed, for instance, in his Actaeon fresco at the Sanvitale castle of Fontanellato (and Giordano Bruno would have interpreted Actaeon as the symbolic "hunter of the divine"), or the unfinished scheme at Santa Maria della Steccata in Parma. Darkness, mystery, night and silence. What Battista says is true: "The daylight Renaissance, the Burkhardtian confidence of man the

wise and dominant, is succeeded by the night-time Renaissance, Shakespearian, clouded with doubt and bitterness, aware of its own limitations."

In 1534 the young historian and Platonist Benedetto Varchi – still republican, but already inclined towards the House of Medici – dedicated to the future Grand Duke Cosimo his *Questione dell' alchimia*, the manuscript of which is in the Biblioteca Nazionale in Florence. He does not believe, he says, that base metal can be transmuted into gold, and yet cannot prove the process is impossible. Gold had, for the Medici, an unfailing fascination and in the sixteenth century they were as likely to think of it in terms of alchemy as, in the

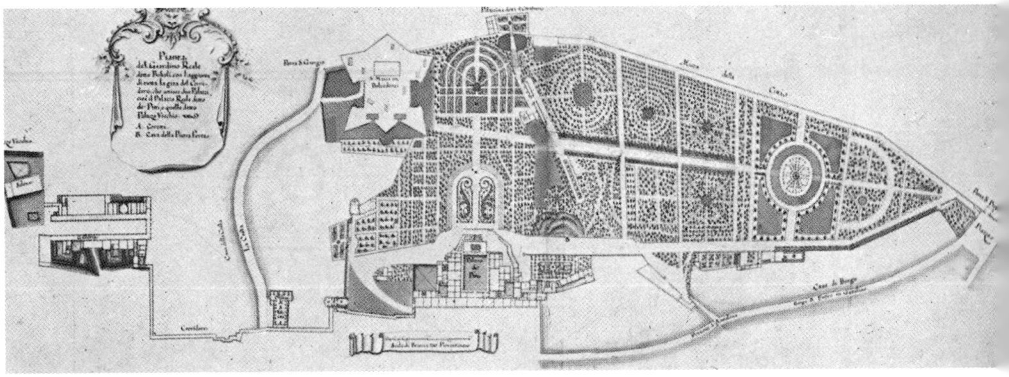

fourteenth and fifteenth, in terms of golden florins flowing to the family bank. When Antonio de' Medici died – a disciple of Paracelsus, devotee of alchemy and natural science – his cherished Casino di San Marco (built by Buontalenti in 1574) was found to be crammed with flasks of oils, with powders, gums, spices and rare plants. He had "*albarelli* full of the fats of various animals," vials of antimony and little boxes of "sublimated substances." Alchemy had certainly claimed a great deal of his attention.

The tiny *studiolo* on the first floor of the Palazzo Vecchio was planned by Francesco I in collaboration with Giorgio Vasari and the erudite philologist and historian Vicenzo Borghini. This minute apartment, once again open to the public after the recent scholarly rearrangement of its contents, was lined with cupboards, their doors disguised as panelling. This was decorated by leading painters with representations of the seasons, and of the sciences and handicrafts that interested the duke – glassblowing, goldsmithing, bronze-founding, mining. Interspersed were mythological and allegorical scenes. The court botanist, Joseph Goedenhuyse, is portrayed in the Alchemy picture, robed as a sage, with the grand duke, an unexpectedly mature assistant, eagerly concocting some liquid over a flame. The cupboards themselves housed, not books, but the wondrous specimens which enthralled the princely naturalist – pearls and coral and fossils, *mirabilia* of every description.

Silence, darkness, secrecy and concentration were as essential for research into the hidden laws of nature, as they were for meditation on

Above: an old plan of the Boboli gardens at the Pitti Palace, Florence. One of the finest of Italian gardens, it covers some five hectares – 12 acres and more – and was a magnificent setting for grand-ducal ceremony, with fountains, statuary and pools and a large amphitheater where spectacular entertaiments were staged. This notable example of the garden conceived as the sphere of man's domination of nature was begun for Eleonora of Toledo in 1550 by Il Tribolo. After his death, the work continued under Ammannati, and then under Buontalenti and Alfonso Parigi il Giovane, to reach completion in the seventeenth century. A particular feature is Buontalenti's grotto, of 1583–88, with the "stalactites" of its façade crowned by the Medici arms (left, center). Of the fountains (detail, left) and jeux d'eaux, *the largest are the* Vivaio di Nettuno *and the Oceanus Fountain at the top of the Viottolone, or cypress walk.*

the soul. Emerging from the suitable dimness of the *cella lucubratoria*, where man investigated the nature of man, the *studiolo* plunged back into the darkness, the *nigredo*, of the alchemist's kitchen, lit by the flare of furnaces.

Was this, then, the end of the radiating light, of Renaissance thought? A retreat, a shadowing-over of the bright faith in man and his abilities – man whose reasoning mind could absorb anything, who could number, measure and weigh whatever existed? Was it, in short, a retreat from the faith of Leon Battista Alberti and Leonardo da Vinci? It may well have been. There is no denying that the image of nature, in art no less than science, darkens in the second half of the sixteenth century. It is hazier, gloomier, more enigmatical, as if branching off to what is monstrous and beyond belief, breaking into abnormality and aberration and the countless forms of the bizarre.

The galleries, collections and museums of the time, though ostensibly in the same tradition, are not the precious accumulations – gems or classical sculpture – made in the preceding century. They serve a purpose other than the mere amassing of fine specimens of classical beauty or the revival of a vanished world. The purpose of the High Renaissance seems rather to be that of losing itself in the unfathomable mystery of nature. Nature mocking, frightful, nocturnal (this was an era of witches' Sabbaths and occult festivals in palace gardens); nature that can juggle with art – and indeed contend with it – and which, in doing so, generates an art whose aim is to reproduce natural forms while distorting and remoulding them. Portraits are composed of leaves, fruit and organic objects; we arrive at the images of Arcimboldo. Art and nature can be transmuted, as base metal into gold.

The first name that springs to mind when we think of museums and collections is that of the archduke Ferdinand of Tyrol, son of the emperor Ferdinand I and nephew of Charles V. No visitor of mark could omit the tour of his collections at Schloss Ambras. Montaigne was among those who went to see the furniture, the *objets d'art* – some of which incorporated tedious tricks and surprises – an immense and renowned armoury and the rich library of

The long, straight Viottolone, the "big path," of the Boboli gardens, lined with laurel, cypress, ilex and statuary.

The "sacred wood," or Park of the Monsters, at Bomarzo in northern Latium was created by Vicino Orsini in the second half of the sixteenth century: a garden-labyrinth based on the idea of a descent into Hell, purification and re-ascent. A particular feature are the gigantic figures, sculptured from a mass of rock such as the Hell-mouth (above), the battling giants (opposite, top) and the seated female figure (below).

ancient manuscripts. Eighteen huge cedarwood cabinets in the *Kunstkammer* contained glass, musical instruments, carved gems, goldsmiths' work, watches and mechanical appliances; *curiosa* and *artificialia*, fossils, spoils of the New World; a fragment of the rope with which Judas hanged himself. It is hardly necessary to stress the resemblance of such collections to the hoards of relics in the Catholic churches, so loudly criticized by Protestants during the Reformation.

Even more amazing were the treasures of the emperor Rudolph II in the Hradčany castle in Prague; and well into the seventeenth century the archduke Leopold of Austria, who then owned Ambras, had a "familiar spirit" in a bottle – expelled, according to the catalogue issued at Vienna in 1720, "from a possessed person." It is there today, in the Kunsthistorisches Museum of Vienna – a black cut-out silhouette in a bottle of what looks like smoked glass. But it could as easily have been at Florence, for the chronicler Bartolomeo Masi notes at the end of the fifteenth century that Lorenzo the Magnificent had a devil imprisoned in a ring, and that when he freed it, on his deathbed in 1492, it flew off, to bring the copper globe from Brunelleschi's cathedral dome crashing to the ground. (As, in fact, it did; and the golden sphere was interpreted as the *palla*, or golden ball, of the Medici coat of arms.)

Every Italian court of the sixteenth and seventeenth centuries had its Ambras or Hradčany. The 1588 inventory of the Casino di San Marco at Florence lists an impressive array of pictures, together with the *Wunderkammer* rarities. In 1589 an inventory of the Medici *tribuna* in the Uffizi emphasizes the pictures and antiquities as well as the inevitable *curiosa*. Artistic and scientific interests were combined in one grand aquisitive fervour, doubtless a luxuriant, esoteric and "secular" version of the old cult of religious relics. And just as there had been a trade in spurious relics, there was a trade in fake "curiosities," or *mirabilia*. Twin basilisks, creatures whose glare could shrivel you to ashes, are preserved to this day in the Natural History Museum at Verona: artifacts constructed from skin and fishbones (skate bones, to be precise). Unicorn-horns also abound;

generally, when not pure fabrications, horns of narwhal. In 1573 Andrea Bacci, later physician to Sixtus v, published a treatise, the *Alicorno*, on the miraculous medical virtues of the beast. It was dedicated to Francesco de' Medici, "to whom the author was indebted for all he knew of unicorns" and without whom the book could not have been written.

But the eclectic, *Wunderkammer* brand of collection was not confined to the closed rooms of a palace. Soon enough it spread beyond them, to invade the garden. Outdoors, artificial features – automata, ingenious fountains, displays of statues and archaeological trophies, "Roman" topiary hedges – met and mingled with the *naturalia*, and each would modify the other.

A garden could itself be a collection. The rarest plants, the loveliest flowers, were grown in the secluded *giardini segreti* or their extension, the *orto botanico*, a horticultural *Wunderkammer* where the prince might study the flora of the world within the boundaries of his neat, geometrical flowerbeds, between his clipped hedges. It was this kind of botanical garden, sacred to the leisure-loving tastes, the *otium*, of his family, that Cosimo I established at San Marco in Florence in 1545, with hothouses and the mineralogical collection nearby. For the grand dukes the whole area between San Marco and the Santissima Annunziata was one huge museum of nature and natural history; and Fra Zenobio Bocchi, a Franciscan in charge of their gardens at the beginning of the seventeenth century, was to provide detailed plans for the *orto botanico* at Mantua.

Art, nature, and scientific experiment together gave rise to the covered-in garden, a shelter for the cultivation of plants requiring extra warmth; the hothouses, and houses for lemon-trees and oranges became important elements in the princely garden, as we may see at the Sanseverino-Farnese palace of Colorno, near Parma. For this garden-palace-museum relation Francesco I found the most original solution. His *giardino segreto* on the roof of the Loggia dei Lanzi was an open-air *studiolo* with a panoramic view of Florence.

But what really links the *studiolo* (for the contemplation of scientific learning and worldly

affairs), the garden (for refreshment and the fusion of *naturalia* with *artificialia*) and the Cabinet of Curiosities with its ancient masterpieces and its strange natural exhibits, was the grotto. Every Renaissance garden had to have one.

Grottoes are associated with mountains. As the secret heart of the mountain the grotto, in myths and metaphors from the Taoist masters to Plato, is a refuge for meditation and moral rebirth. A third-century text on the subject, *De antro Nympharum*, by Porphyry, a disciple of Plotinus, was printed in 1518 and exerted wide and lasting influence. The unlit grotto, or cave, says Porphyry, symbolizes the world and our imperfect understanding. We enter it fearfully, for it is narrow and uneven, and our progress is toilsome. Little by little, however, we can see things. The interior springs to life as light filters in to reveal the most mysterious and exotic beauties of nature – shells, and falling water, gleaming stalactites, and precious stones. The grotto is the natural version of what the prince achieves, with artifice, in the *studiolo*. The *naturalia* of the *studiolo* are "accidents" of nature in apparent rivalry with art, while the grotto continually mimics and travesties art with natural forms. As though nature were artificialized or recreated, shells are set in the patterns of mosaic, the porous rocks have human faces; from rough stones emerge the gods and guardian spirits of the ancients. Nature is imitation, imitation nature. Chief of the animals in the grotto at Castello reigns the fabulous, magical unicorn, symbol, for the alchemists, of Christ and the "philosophical" Mercury.

Earthly paradise and Alcina's isle

Although the Renaissance garden, with its grotto, labyrinth and fountain, and their aura of secret knowledge and mystery, may vary in style from the humanist *orto* in or near a town to the vast park that heralds the age and taste of the Baroque, it is the focus of palace and/or villa life, dedicated to diversion and intellectual adventure.

In the late Middle Ages the garden was often reproduced indoors. If outside there was little more than a courtyard attached to the signorial

The "alchemical" studiolo *of Francesco I is a fitting reflection of the scientific culture of his time. In the latter half of the sixteenth century, in the interregnum between the aftermath of humanist thinking in the fifteenth and the reality of Galilean thought, research into the workings of nature tended to the weird and wonderful, veiled in obscurity, its darkness barely shot through by glints from the alchemist's furnace; ancient themes, beliefs and symbolism from many sources persisted, to be welcomed and adopted by contemporary science, some of whose somber operations are illustrated in the drawings on this and the opposite page, all from libraries in Florence.*
Left, top: an Atenor, *the egg-shaped glass furnace used in the alchemists' search for the philosopher's stone, that imaginary substance whose contact would transmute base metal into gold. The recurring image of the tree as pillar of the universe, magically linking heaven, earth and underworld, is derived from the Biblical Tree of Life and Knowledge. Left: Tree of the Virtues, from a manuscript in the Biblioteca Laurenziana.*
Opposite, top (far right): The "hermetic citadel" within its circles of force (Biblioteca Laurenziana). Hermes, its presiding deity, was messenger of Olympus and god of healing as well as of "hermetic" lore and sciences. His caduceus, or herald's staff, was a powerful image of transformation, of progress through conflict and the union of contrary conceptions.
Opposite, below: alchemical furnaces, from a manuscript in the Biblioteca Nazionale.

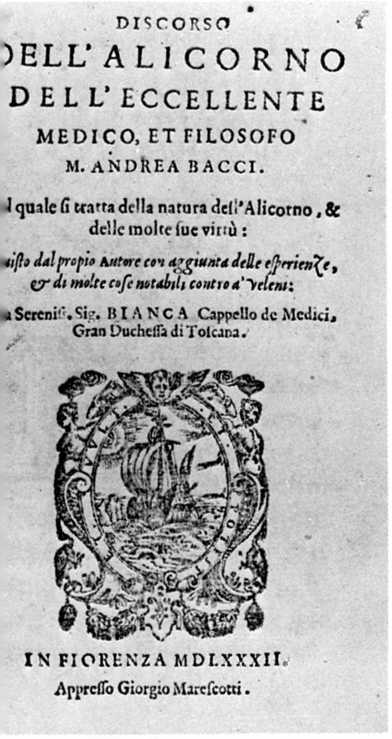
DISCORSO
DELL'ALICORNO
DELL'ECCELLENTE
MEDICO, ET FILOSOFO
M. ANDREA BACCI.
quale si tratta della natura dell'Alicorno, & delle molte sue virtù:
uisto dal propio Autore con aggiunta delle esperienze, & di molte cose notabili contro a' veleni:
Sereniss. Sig. BIANCA Cappello de Medici, Gran Duchessa di Toscana.
IN FIORENZA MDLXXXII.
Appresso Giorgio Marescotti.

Above: frontispiece of the Discorso dell' Alicorno, *by Andrea Bacci, physician to Sixtus V. So-called unicorns' horns, said to have therapeutic properties, were among the most cherished* mirabilia *of the sixteenth century. Intensive research went into finding the elixir of life and eternal youth.*

house or palace, the infinite, illusionistic scenes of fresco-painting would often grace the walls of the rooms inside. Simone Martini painted garden-frescoes in the papal palace at Avignon; Palazzo Davanzati in Florence had its painted *verziere*, and the castle of Torrechiara its *sala del perolato*.

But how should we imagine the late-medieval garden? From what had it evolved, and into what was it developing? One of its models was the monastic *hortus conclusus*, an image of the Earthly Paradise expounded in mystical terms by St Bernard of Clairvaux in his commentary on the *Song of Songs*, and in terms of scientific naturalism in the *De vegetalibus* of Albertus Magnus. Another was the classical notion of the "beautiful place," *locus amoenus*, endowed in Theocritus and Virgil with perpetual spring and immunity from the ravages of time, already introduced as an ideal long before by Homer with Nausicaa's island of Scheria, home of the Phaeacians.

Another Eden, private, privileged, secure, the garden hints at bliss regained, untouched by the fears and cares of the external world, and where ageing and death had no place. The contrast with nature was complete: nature was savage and brutal; in "desert" and forest man walked at the mercy of beast and demon, but the limits of a garden were enchanted. Its magic circle, safe from what is hostile, wintry and untilled, is the *Giardino d'Inverno* of Boccaccio's tale, or the Selfish Giant's "lovely garden" in the fairy-story by Oscar Wilde. And because untamed nature, the perilous waters and the dark wood coincide in medieval symbolism, the enclosed garden and the Happy Island are eventually the same. Similarities are obvious between the island in the *Odyssey* and the Islands of the Blessed which St Brendan – and perhaps Columbus – sailed to find; between the isle of Venus in the *Hypnerotomachia Poliphili* and the garden-isle of the Belvedere palace in the neighbourhood of Ferrara, or the *isolotto* with the Oceanus fountain of the Boboli gardens.

Yet – at least from the fourteenth century onwards – a garden was not thought of as existing solely in opposition or contrast to the surrounding terrain; it also instituted a clearly

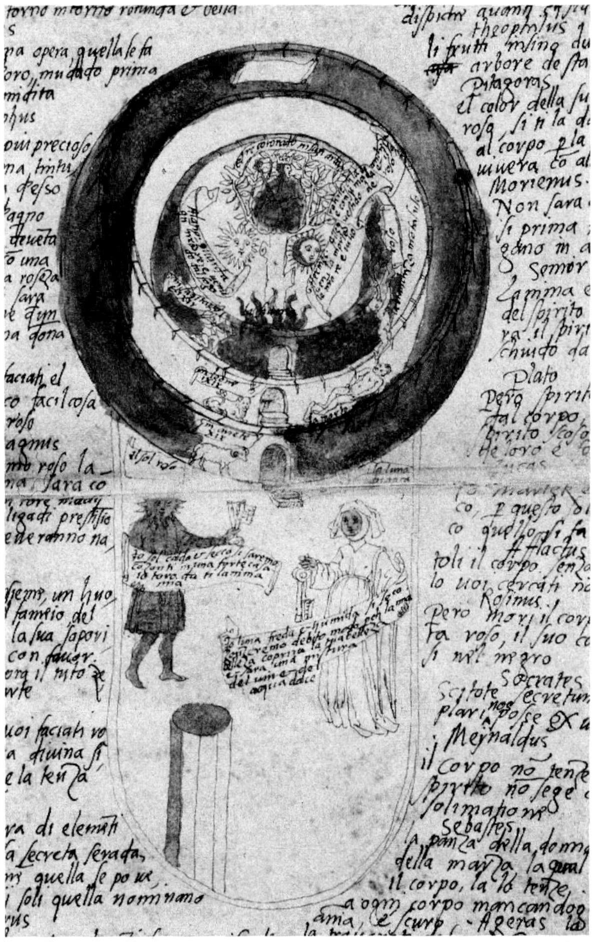

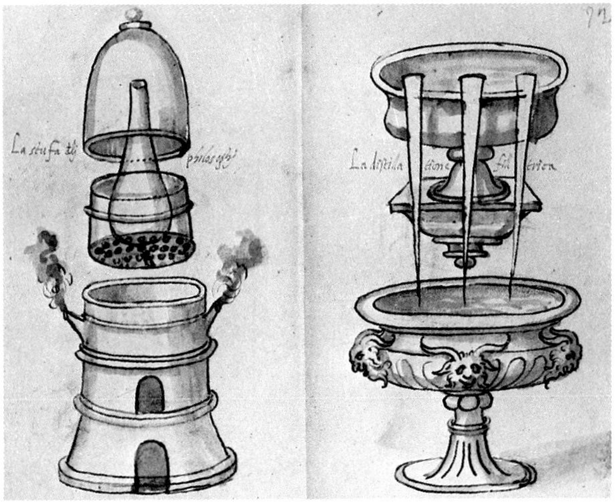

defined link with the urban world beyond.

The medieval city, particularly from the twelfth to the thirteenth century, when the population increased most rapidly, had no green plots larger than a courtyard or a cloister; and although towards the latter half of the twelfth

HERALDRY

When Giangastone de'Medici died childless in 1737, the Grand Duchy of Tuscany passed to the house of Lorraine. But this political union had been anticipated in 1589, when Maria Christina of Lorraine – herself of Medici blood through her mother Claude of France, daughter of Henri II and Catherine de' Medici – married Grand Duke Ferdinando I, a marriage commemorated in the coat of arms (1) in *pietre dure*, Carrara marble and lapis lazuli, made at the Opificio in Florence. Partition-lines divide the coat which has, dexter (left as the reader looks at it), the *palle* of the Medici, and sinister (the observer's right) the arms of Lorraine quartered with the lilies of France, from whose royal house the bride, through her mother, descended. In the fifteenth century the Lorraine title had passed by marriage to René I of Anjou, whose arms were quarterly of six: Hungary, Naples, Jerusalem, Anjou, Bar and Lorraine.

The above bazon, or description, is much simplified; heraldry, the study of arms, is a most complicated discipline. The coat of arms, unknown before the twelfth century, is of debatable, though probably military, origin. First referring to the territorial possessions of monarchs and great vassals, it came in time to be used by lesser feudal lords, by nobles, and even by city-states.

"Herald" and "heraldry" are words derived from the Germanic *hariwald*, a kind of army staff-officer. At a tournament the herald proclaimed aloud, or "blazoned," the arms of those taking part; and as the central shields grew ever more complex, each element having exact historical or symbolic meaning, the business of heraldry was interpretation.

It is concerned with the tinctures (colours, metals, furs) and with the divisions and charges of a shield. Division is by partition-lines and "ordinaries," the latter being bands or strips of colour, the older forms of which are more "honourable" than the newer subordinaries. (The perpendicular pale, and the cross, are honourable ordinaries; the lozenge and stars are charges).

Charges are the multifarious natural, imagined or fantastic objects, figures and creatures that can ornament a shield. Surrounding the shield are crown, helm, crest and mantling, the accessories which together constitute the timbre, or crested helm. The mantling, or lambrequin, represents the piece of coloured material worn at the back of the helmet, over the neck. Later accessories were the mantle and the legend, which might be a *mot* – a motto or war cry.

The metals, conventionalized furs, and colours are basic to heraldry. (3: the second column shows how colours are conveyed in black and white by a system of dots or hatching). One or other of the two metals – gold or silver – should, in expert opinion, appear on every shield, but they may not be superimposed: only for the arms of the king of Jerusalem – argent a cross potent or – was there an exception to this rule. Colours less frequently found are green, purple, orange and murrey (purple-red).

1

2

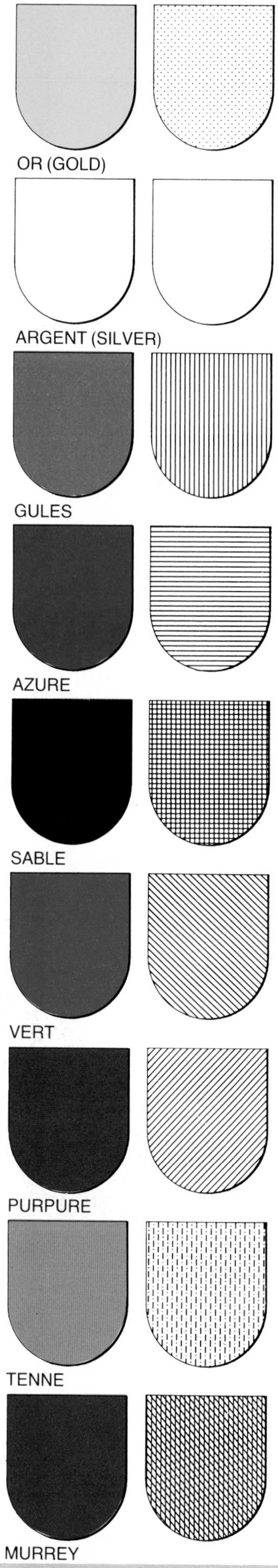

Each metal or colour had its corresponding gemstone, planet or symbol. The sapphire and the planet Jupiter were thus associated with the colour blue, signifying constancy. Echoes of this heraldic colour-symbolism remain in popular lore today – red is for love, blue for devotion, black for mourning, green for hope and liberty. National preferences have also been detected. French heraldry, for instance, favoured blue and gold, the colours of the royal arms of France, while Germany leaned to gold and black.

The two heraldic furs are ermine and vair (4). Ermine may be in gold, or "reversed" from black on white to white on black, and its conventionalization perhaps recalls the animal-tails. Vair, the fur of the Siberian squirrel, lined the cloaks of the nobility, and the patterns of alternating blue and white are those of blue back, and white belly skins.

Ordinaries are made with straight lines, and the various ways of dividing a shield, some of them illustrated here (5), have their correct heraldic names.

The subject of charges, the figures and creatures of heraldry, is practically inexhaustible. Manuals give at least 66 variants of the cross – the "keyed cross" of Pisa among them – while the lion, in 50 or so guises, easily outnumbers other beasts. (There was a French saying that "he who has no arms adopts a lion"). The heraldic eagle was originally Roman, and Charlemagne, after his Roman coronaton, flew it from his palace at Aix-la-Chapelle. It was the Emperor Sigismond, in 1401, who decreed that the imperial eagle should have two heads, in allusion to his double rôle as king of the German lands and king of the Romans. Before this, however, such an eagle had been the emblem of the Eastern Empire, and was to be that of the marquises of Monferrato, dynastic heirs of Byzantium, and of the grand dukes of Muscovy who were its heirs politically.

Churchmen, too, had heraldry and coats of arms, for many prelates were of noble birth. Ecclesiastical rank was indicated by the number and colour of tassels pendant from the hat. Thus (2, left to right): 30 red tassels denote a cardinal, a patriarch has 30, an archbishop 20 green tassels, and a bishop 12.

4

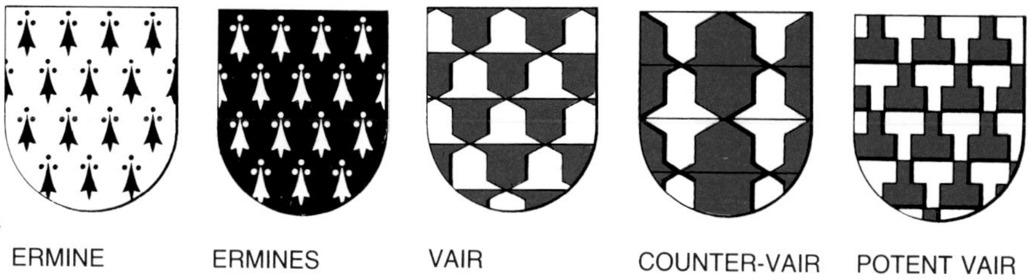

The furs of heraldry. There are also erminois (black spots on a gold field), and its reverse, pean (gold spots on black).

5

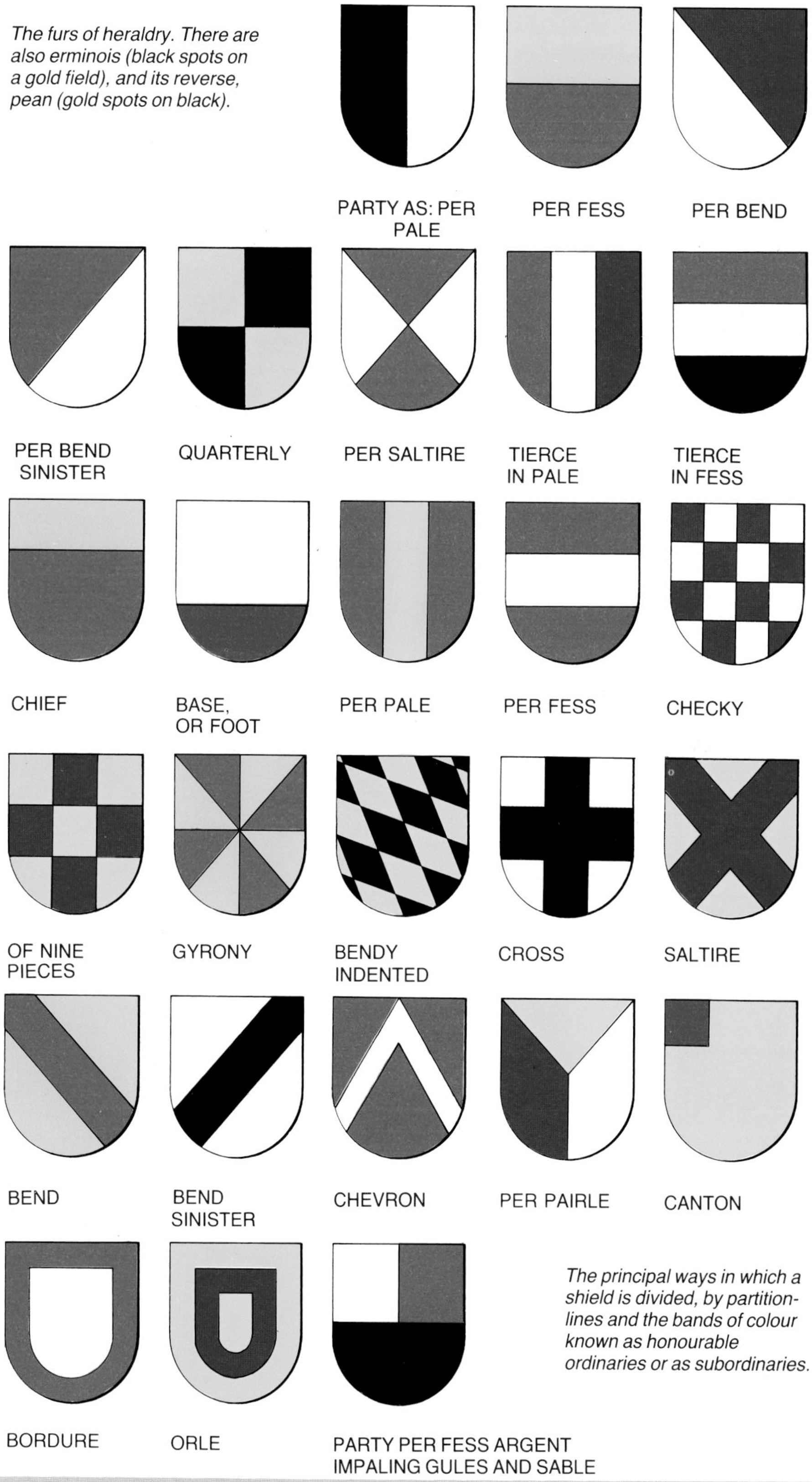

The principal ways in which a shield is divided, by partition-lines and the bands of colour known as honourable ordinaries or as subordinaries.

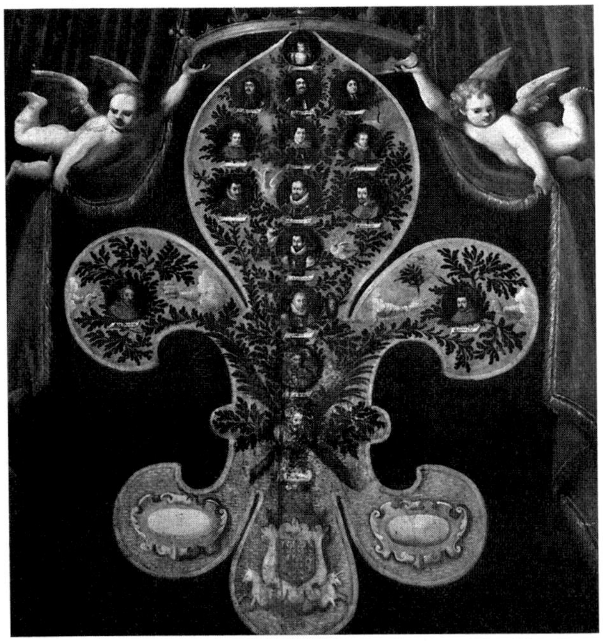

century every major Italian city increased its walled area and gardens were planted just within the new perimeters, the land was soon needed for building more houses.

From the mid fourteenth century onwards, and especially after the Black Death of 1348–50, the situation changed. At a blow populations were reduced by a third, or sometimes half, and this in cities which a few decades previously had increased their bounds by as much as a third. The availabilty of empty and unoccupied property within the walls coincided with the advance of patrician power, the re-feudalization of country districts, and the concentration of wealth in relatively few hands. The great "suburban" gardens resulting from these circumstances were regarded as affirmations of humanist doctrine on the "architectural" control of nature and as redefining the relation of town to country. The garden of a town house was still totally private although one or even two of its highly walled sides might give on to the street. But in the rural or semi-rural house urban dignity and comfort were allied with nature (in the garden of the villa), subdued to the master's taste and framed by further vistas, some cultivated, some not. The palaces and gardens to which the characters in the *Decameron* escape from the threat of the plague are those of a closed and sheltered world, where the city, if needs be, is not too far away, though far enough for the avoidance of its risks and discomforts. While the town, thanks to the increasing number of green areas within the walls, became more rural; the rural territories, in a tightening network of patrician villas, became noticeably altered in aspect and function. At the beginning of the fifteenth century, as Vittorio Franchetti Pardo observed, Florence "was so ringed with castles and villas, with such a wealth of magnificent houses and gardens, as to resemble a castle within a city; for its adjacent territory might have been a city, while the visitor who entered could hardly tell, by the slightest difference in the buildings, that he had left that territory at all."

The gardens described in the *Roman de la Rose*, or by Boccaccio, models of the late-medieval "courtly" garden, would exercise

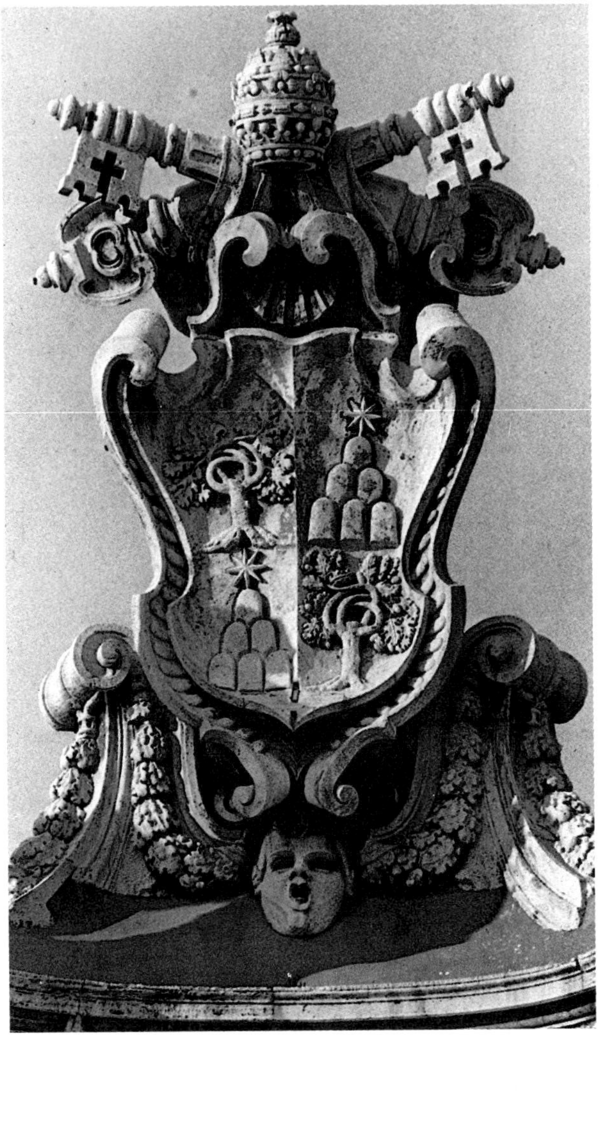

With the great vogue for heraldry at the beginning of the fourteenth century, coats of arms, badges and colours, public and private, appear on palaces, standards, books, furniture, household goods and shields: the distinctive and decorative insignia of a complex and strictly-applied language proclaim private family and public office. Examples are the Farnese lily (left); the stars and mountains of the Chigi, and the Della Rovere oaks (Chigi and Della Rovere are quartered – below, left – in the arms of the Chigi pope, Alexander VII, on Bernini's colonnade at St Peter's) the Barberini bees (below, on the frontispiece of the Tesserae Gentilitiae, *1638); or the viper and* putto *of the Visconti and Sforza families.*
Opposite: arms of Galeazzo Maria Sforza, Duke of Milan, son of Francesco Sforza and Bianca Maria Visconti. From an illuminated manuscript (MS 1856 f 1r), in the Oesterreichische Nationalbibliotek, Vienna.

GZ
MA
DX
MLI
QN
TVS
A BON DROIT
MIT ZAIT

their spell for another hundred years. At the end of the fourteenth century Giovanni da Prato describes such examples in his *Paradiso degli Alberti*, and Sabadino degli Arienti, at Ferrara, was to speak of a *Giardino della Viola*. Fifteenth-century Florence had newer, more disciplined and explicit ideas on the subject, however, paying heed to Leon Battista Alberti and Ficino, with his invitation to the serenities of Neoplatonic *otia* in a groomed and sympathetic landscape, as suitable as any Greek *gymnasion* to quiet philosophical reflection. In Florence the *hortus conclusus* of the Palazzo Medici in Via Larga, Lorenzo's gardens at San Marco, or the Orto Oricellari furnished the requisite green privacy: hidden from prying eyes, as an exclusive club should be, yet near the centers of politics and business, since *otium* did not preclude *negotium*. (There was, on the contrary, mutual modification.) A few miles away the union of utility and loveliness is demonstrated in the gardens of the Medici Villa Careggi, or of Giovanni Rucellai's villa Lo Specchio, "The Mirror," at Quaracchi – the refuge from mundane cares is also a productive, paying estate. But with and in his garden humanist man – the center of the world – moulds nature according to his imagination and desire; he is Adam and the demiurge in a universe of his own design and creation. Thus in the Medici gardens of Careggi and Poggio a Caiano the theme is physical and spiritual refreshment. Sacred to the Muses, poetry – the medicine of the soul – was allied with the physical healing properties of herbs and aromatic plants. (Aware of this, Ficino, who was trained as a doctor, drew inspiration from Careggi for his book, *De vita*.) The plants and flowers of these settings are those of Botticelli's *Primavera*; the Biblical Eden meets the Golden Age in an ultimate synthesis of scripture and pagan myth.

If a harmonious distribution of *orti* in the town, and of villas in the country, made an extended garden-city of Florence and its environs, at Ferrara it was the ruler, acting with the brilliant urban architect Biagio Rossetti, who ordained the palatial gardens of the Herculean Addition. Through them Duke Ercole showed how much of a power-symbol a garden could be, for here the power of government goes beyond the city and beyond the state, to assume a cosmic, universal connotation. In a carefully contrived succession of flowers and foliage spring seems, at the prince's bidding, to endure forever; as in a theater, life and its pleasures are unaffected by the passage of time. It is not surprising that Ariosto bases the enchanted gardens of Alcina and Logistilla in his *Orlando Furioso* on the Este gardens, the *delizie*, which were, without exception, destroyed when the papacy annexed Ferrara at the end of the

Left: green chalcedony seal of Cosimo I, by Domenico di Polo. Above the figure of Hercules, symbol of grand-ducal power, is the Medici crest. Museo degli Argenti, Pitti Palace, Florence.
Left, below: legend of the Visconti viper in a fifteenth-century miniature. The story of how Ottone Visconti acquired this symbol in the First Crusade is told by Giovan Pietro Cagnola, a chronicler in the service of Ludovico il Moro. "These princes and Christian lords being encamped near Jerusalem, a great prince and warrior named Volux, from the other side of Jordan, hearing of Ottone's fame, challenged him, through an interpreter, to combat. Ottone readily accepted, and the sixth day afterwards they met in the field. Ottone bore seven marks cut in his shield as a badge, since he had vanquished seven champions; Volux bore a viper swallowing a flayed man. "At their encounter Ottone unhorsed him with the lance, then with a blow from his mace scattered his brains on the ground. He took the helm of Volux, and all his spoils, carrying them off pro triumpho, *in sign of victory. At his homecoming he dedicated them to God in the cathedral of Milan; and, deliberating, decided that his entire posterity, and not himself alone, should bear the victorious viper as a family badge." Trivulzio Collection, Castello Sforzesco, Milan.*

Right: arms of James, the Bourbon Comte de la Marche, husband of Giovanna II, queen of Naples. From the fifteenth-century codex of St Martha. (Archivio di Stato, Naples). Below: arms of Anjou and of the Church, from a fourteenth-century illuminated manuscript (MS Royal 6 E), in the British Museum, London. The heraldic lily, occurring on the arms of the Capetian kings and of successive French dynasties, is known also as the lily of France, or fleur de lys. Ubiquitous though it is, its origins are unclear.

century. (In 1598 a papal fortress rose on the ruins of Belvedere.)

Otium may consist in serene discussion, leavened with *negotium*, or it may be uninterrupted ease and diversion; through the entire fifteenth century the two facets alternate and mingle in a kind of dialogue. One or other will predominate, depending on the style of garden envisaged, although the prevalence of the one does not exclude the presence of the other. In Rome the *Viridarium* of the Palazzo Venezia was, when begun on a higher level in the 1460s, a magnificent "hanging garden;" at the Vatican Pope Innocent VIII built the Belvedere for his recreation; the gardens of the banker Agostino Chigi at the Villa Farnesina date from 1510 – all purely pleasure-gardens, it would seem and yet they are approximately, and not by accident, contemporary with those resorts of learned "academies," the Florentine Orti Oricellari and the gardens of Caterina Cornaro at Asolo. There, in their havens,, the intellectual societies would debate on politics and love – Ariosto's *armi* and *amori*, the cornerstones of Platonic thought and chivalric vision. Machiavelli set his *Discorsi dell'arte della guerra* in the Oricellari, Pietro Bembo his *Asolani* dialogues of 1504 in Caterina's gardens.

From the end of the fifteenth century onwards the garden is increasingly charged with latent, esoteric symbolism. This emphasis on its character as a "philosophic" reserve owes much to the *Hypnerotomachia Poliphili*, a dream-novel of mystical revelation on the pattern of medieval allegories from Andrea Cappellano to Dante. Written in about 1467, and attributed to a monk named Francesco Colonna, it was published in Venice by Aldo Manuzio in 1499. The broad lines of the story are plain enough. In a series of gardens where art mimics nature, then nature mimics art, Poliphilus, enamoured of the nymph Polia, experiences "the strife of love in a dream." Lost in a wood and wandering in a state of bewilderment, he encounters his guides Logistica (Reason) and Thelemia (Personal Will) in a wonderful garden of glass. With Logistica he enters a second garden, a maze of seven navigable canals whose twists and dangers are those of human life. This initiatory journey brings him to a garden of silk with flowers of gold, and fruit of precious stones. The final goal is the island of Cythera, where, after so much *artificialia*, the sumptuous gardens are "natural;" yet their nature is a subtle

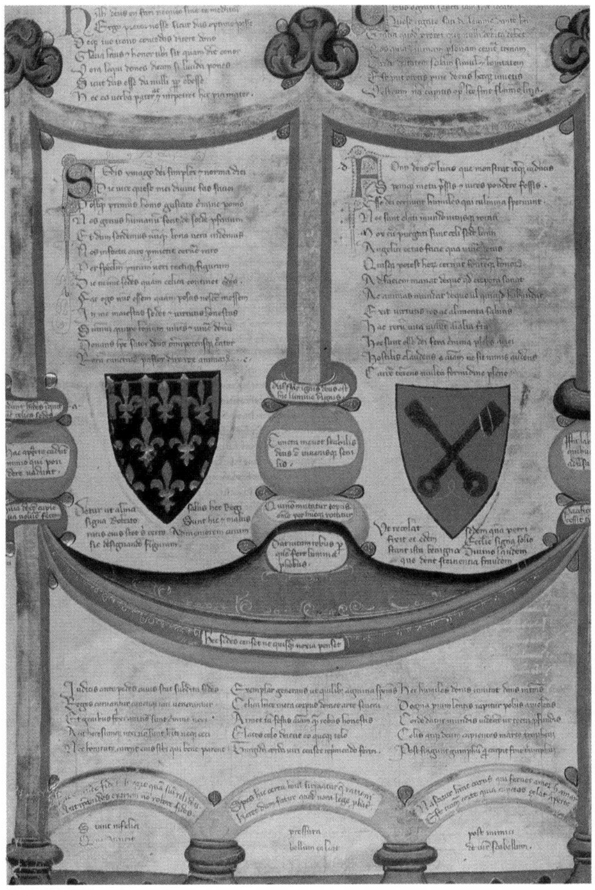

arrangement of woods and lawns and orange- and myrtle-groves around the temple of Venus, the focal point of the entire dream-landscape.

The great sixteenth-century gardens would all illustrate, in varying measure, the same aspirational theme. Gradually, they were invested with various levels of meaning, the design representing an existential allegory, or the evocation of a prince's territorial power; stage scenery, or an allusive "theater of memory."

Three areas, again with many variants, are common to all Renaissance gardens. The *giardino segreto*, descendent of the medieval *hortus conclusus*, was adorned with the choicest plants and sculpture, and would flank the main building used for residence or display. There was a *prato* (lawn) of variable shape around a fountain – the Fountain of Life – as well as a *bosco* (wood). To move from one area to the next is to shift the dialectic relation between art and nature which blurs a little, and becomes less distinct, while that between other parts of the garden gains complexity from stone basins, fountains, fishponds and similar elements – labyrinths, grottoes and mounts, statues (some colossal), and green theaters open to the sky. With its provision for pastime and amusement, its aura of arcane knowledge and spectacular fantasy, each garden offers a different tale to its lord and his guests.

A striving for order and system is discernible in the gardens, as in the arts and sciences, language and political thought, of the High Renaissance. A particular indication of this spirit is the geometrical garden-architecture which, in *ars topiaria* for instance – the clipping and shaping of box-trees and hedges – has learned to force its laws on nature. A new relation, accented by the plants and flowers, the statuary, fountains and grottoes, is imposed on three worlds – the vegetable world, on water, and on the mineral world of cut and carved stone. The rediscovery and reapplication of ancient garden-theory, culled primarily from Vitruvius, points the same way, as does the admiration for Roman models – the gardens of Lucullus, Sallust and Maecenas described by Frontinus, Plutarch and Dio Cassius. Rosario Assunto, the leading modern authority on the "philosophy" of the garden, rightly detects this wish for rule and order as early as in the idealized gardens of Bembo's *Asolani*; while after 1504, and Bramante's alterations at the Belvedere (built by Antonio del Pollaiuolo and Jacopo da Pietrasanta for Pope Innocent VIII), a fashion for garden-geometry was established which would be used by Pirro Ligorio at the Villa d'Este at Tivoli, and by Vignola in the Villa Giulia garden and at Caprarola and in the Orti Farnesiani on the Palatine.

Most Renaissance gardens, however, were not merely for pleasure, or the exhibition of power. Frequently they are to be read as large-scale cryptograms, puzzles devised by patron and designer for the visitor to ponder and solve. The supreme puzzle was at the villa of Cardinal Ippolito d'Este, son of Alfonso I of Ferrara and Lucrezia Borgia. The Tivoli hillside had been excavated and the Aniene river diverted to create an enormous garden, with innumerable fountains; and the subject was the legend of Hercules torn between vice and virtue.

Opposite: Knight in a Landscape, *by Vittore Carpaccio. The young knight has been identified as Francesco Maria della Rovere (1490–1538), heir to the duchy of Urbino and a* condottiere *in Venetian service. An ermine at the bottom left-hand corner, with the motto* malo mori quam foedari – *Better Death than Dishonour – indicates his membership of the Neapolitan Order of the Ermine (an animal said to prefer death to the soiling of its white fur, the symbol of purity).*

Left: crests and imprese *of Gian Galeazzo Visconti, from the Cremosano codex, in the Archivio di Stato, Milan.*

MALO MORI
QVAM
FOEDARI

the peace, progress and well-being attained under Cosimo's wise and moderate rule.

The territory-garden equation is no flight of fancy. Was Italy not the "garden" of the Holy Roman Empire? Emanuele Tesauro (1592–1675) mentions a Piedmontese tournament for which, early in the sixteenth century, a town square, symbol of Piedmont itself, had been converted into a flower-garden – further evidence of the connection between signorial power, disposition of territory, the enclosed space of a garden and the production of spectacle.

The connection is also perfectly illustrated by the splendid complex of the Boboli gardens in Florence whose history begins, as we know, when Duchess Eleonora bought the land, together with the Pitti palace, in 1549. After the death of Il Tribolo, her first architect, Ammanati took over, working chiefly on the courtyard, and was followed by Buontalenti. As well as the *cortile*, the gardens have two other sizeable "stages" – the amphitheater and that combination of *teatro marittimo* and *naumachia*, the *Isolotto*, with Giambologna's Oceanus fountain. The fountain in Piazza Pre-

The fullest and most lucid exposition of territorial power – power conceived, above all, as ownership – is in the glorious Medicean gardens of the sixteenth century – Castello, Boboli or Pratolino. The grand duke Francesco I commissioned 14 lunettes of the family villas from Justus Utens in 1599; the pictures, destined for the villa at Artimino, are beautifully exact, and provide a highly detailed record of the gardens, most of which, alas, are either gone, or have been radically changed from their original layout.

In the garden at Castello, reorganized in 1537 by Francesco's father, Cosimo I, on his accession, it is possible to descry a definite allegory of Florence – figuring as Venus and Spring – and of the Medici domain of Tuscany. There is both symbolism and naturalism, with a wild cypress-plantation at the highest spot to represent the Apennines, further personified in a bronze statue by Ammanati; each grotto, each figure and fountain (all recorded by Vasari) carries its precise geographical and political reference to

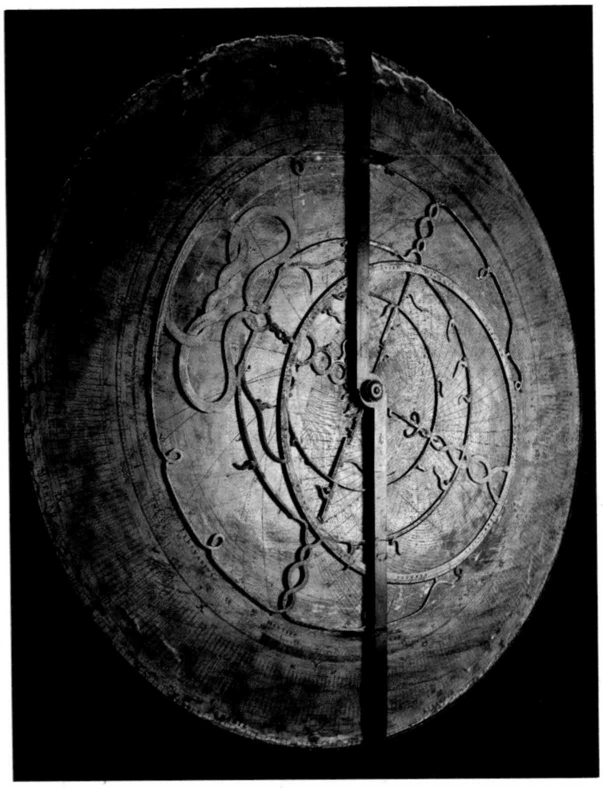

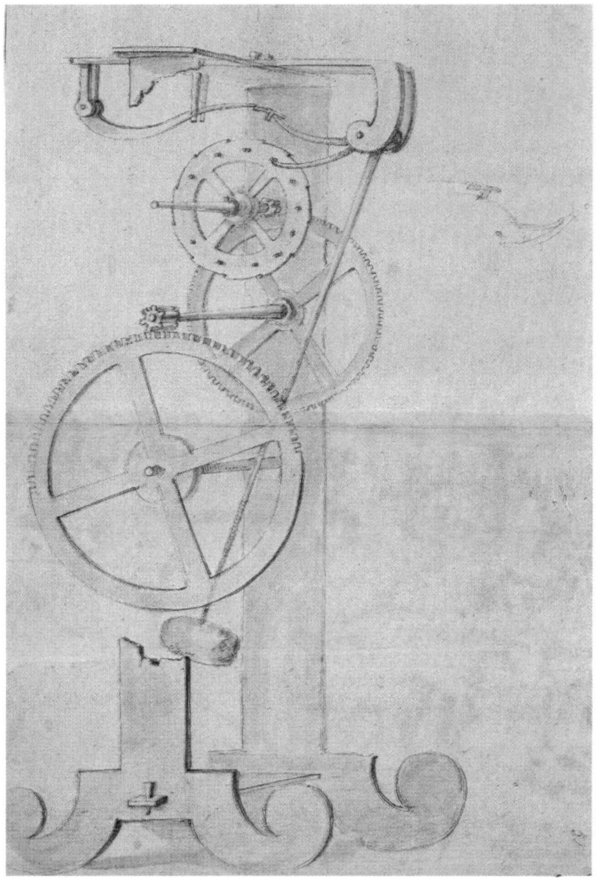

Opposite, top: an intarsia panel depicting astronomical instruments from the studiolo *at Urbino, evidence of the enthusiasm of Renaissance courts for astronomy, even before Galileo introduced Copernican thought to Italy. With Cosimo II and Ferdinando III, the Medici, patrons of art and scholarship in the fifteenth century, extended their patronage to science, and to Galileo and his teaching, in particular. The latter's return from Venice to Florence in 1610 was the outcome of an exchange of correspondence in which he agreed to name his discovery of the satellites of Jupiter, the* Sidera Medicea. *As such they appeared in his book,* Siderus Nuncius (The Starry Messenger), *a propaganda coup of the first magnitude, of which we may be sure, Cosimo took full advantage.*
Opposite, below: astrolabe, once Galileo's, now in the Museo della Scienza, Florence.
Above, left: solar clock in the form of a regular dodecahedron, with painted decoration, made in 1587 by the cosmographer and cartographer Stefano Buonsignori. It comes from the Medici collection, and is now in the Museo della Scienza, Florence.
Above, right: study of a mechanical clock, by Galileo Galilei. Biblioteca Nazionale, Florence.

toria, Palermo (made for the Florentine garden of Luigi di Toledo) already owes something to the Roman "marine theater," as does the Fontana dei Mori in the grounds of the Villa Lante at Bagnaia; while the *naumachia* had influenced a possible *circo acquatico* planned for Tivoli. The planning and laying out of the Boboli gardens was a slow process, however, and the walls of the amphitheater were not finished until 1630.

Pratolino was more coherent and organic by comparison. It was the garden as *studiolo*, a museum of *mirabilia*, product of the gloomy but perceptive taste of Francesco I. Little of the vast scheme remains today save the giant statue, again by Giambologna and again personifying the Apennines, which critics have, not unreasonably, associated with Arcimboldo's bizarre paintings. Human and natural forms, sculpted in stone, combined in this garden, where both the grotto and the mountain and its hermetic counterpart, were incorporated. The vanished grottoes of Pratolino housed automata derived from the sketches and theorems of Heron of Alexandria and there was, as Batista sadly reminds us, an open-air antique sculpture-gallery. "The fountains," he says, "one of them a towering specimen in white *tufa*, gleaming like mother-of-pearl, could have been a mineralogical museum."

Not every garden restates as vigorously the theme of the arcane, but Pratolino set a fashion which grew more marked towards the end of the sixteenth century. It was then, and especially with the publication in Amsterdam in 1583 of the treatise *Hortorum viridariorum*, by J. de Vries, that the labyrinth – a motif which seems to haunt the European imagination from ancient to medieval times – evolved into an essential garden feature. Labyrinthine flower-beds existed in antiquity and in the Middle Ages, but by now the garden-labyrinths were of box. An early example of box-hedging was the *dedalus* constructed for Louise of Savoy, mother of François I, in 1523, while several labyrinth-designs are included in Sebastiano

THE EMBLEM AS PERSONAL DEVICE

The emblem and the art of portraiture emerge almost at the same time in fifteenth-century Italy, as signs of a new era and a new concern with individuality. The portrait, evolving from an earlier tradition, for which the sitter was primarily the member of a group – family, order or confraternity – now concentrated on him as an individual. In like manner the emblem became the individual's private "sign" and declaration of intent, and which would be seen as a challenge issued to the world at large.

First and foremost the challenge was that of sheer obscurity, for an emblem was not, or not generally, comprehensible unless the owner chose to make it so; the key to its symbolical meaning was wholly or partly hidden.

It consisted, originally, of a design and motto. The design could be simple or a composition of themes, human figures, animals, objects of every kind, fantastic or mythical beings as in Alciati's

2

Emblemata (8). The motto might be in Italian, Latin or Greek, even Hebrew; or in some "compound" script or tongue. An emblem is at once a symbol, riddle or proverb, a maxim or an epigram.

And, just as the culture of the Christian West had the basic symbolic elements of the Word and the Written Word, or Scripture, so the emblem is directed at the faculties of sight and hearing. It is written to be read (and thus, first of all, to be listened to); it is something to be thought about and interpreted (and thus, to begin with, looked at and read). It is an existential message, a philosophical argument, to be unravelled.

3

Behind the language of heraldry is the theologic symbolism of the bestiaries and herbals of the Middle Ages, in the case of the emblem, it is the abstruse Neoplatonism of fifteenth-century Florence, its doctrines founded chiefly on resurrected Alexandrian texts of later Roman times. The Renaissance emblem was seen as a form of Egyptian hieroglyphic, a "rebus"; and there is a close and more than casual relationship, aesthetic and typological, between emblems and specifically "magical" characters found on seals and amulets.

But because the main influence, beneath the philosophy and magic, was the culture of chivalry and the knightly quest, the emblem became the *impresa*, or personal device, proclaiming knightly purpose. And since the code of chivalry had so strong an erotic element, the emblem-*impresa* is inspired less and less by military matters (as in the medal of Giovanni de' Medici, son of Cosimo I (2–3, obverse and reverse)), and more and more by love. The favourite feudal-military themes of conquest and fidelity, are also those of chivalrous romance.

The language of heraldry, though complicated under the impact of the emblem-cult in the fifteenth and sixteenth centuries, was stereotyped. By comparison, that of the emblem itself is not only extraordinarily rich but highly capricious and given to making its own rules. It drew on philosophy, religion, mythology – in Alciati's Icarus, for example (8) – on history, technology and actual personal events. When consisting of a thoroughly disparate collection of items it was impenetrable unless the necessary secrets were acquired. The emblem, with a "body" or graphic design and a "soul" or motto to complete and explain it, had indeed an aura of esoteric collusion, a hint of the secret society.

Paolo Giovio wanted it to be

1

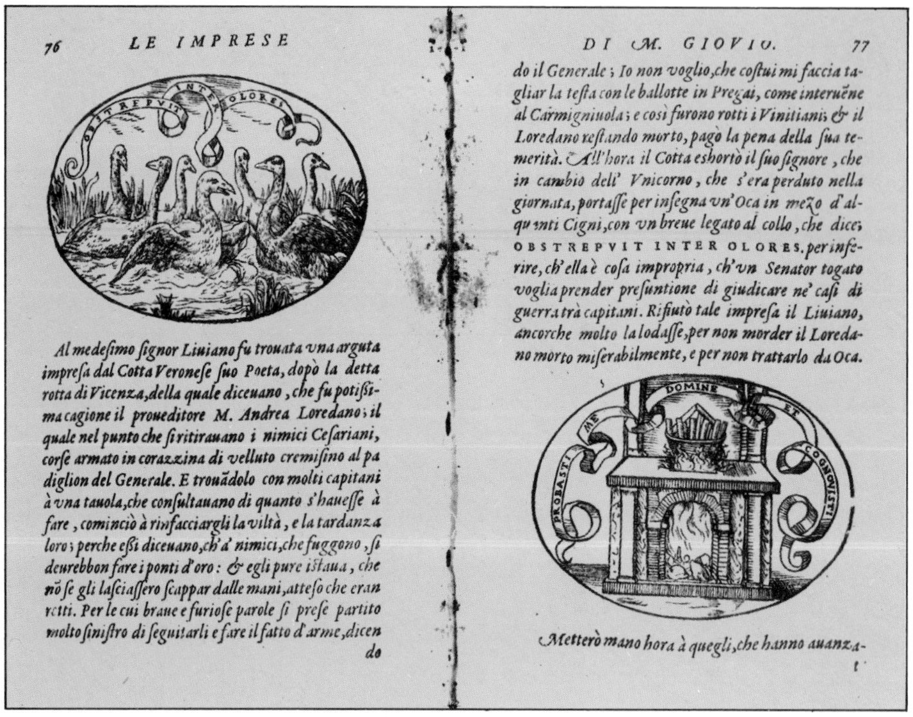

76 LE IMPRESE

Al medesimo signor Liuiano fu trouata vna arguta impresa dal Cotta Veronese suo Poeta, dopò la detta rotta di Vicenza, della quale diceuano, che fu potissima cagione il proueditore M. Andrea Loredano; il quale nel punto che si ritirauano i nimici Cesariani, corse armato in corazzina di velluto cremisino al padiglion del Generale. E trouãdolo con molti capitani à vna tauola, che consultauano di quanto s'hauesse à fare, cominciò à rinfacciargli la viltà, e la tardanza loro; perche essi diceuano, ch'a' nimici, che fuggono, si deurebbon fare i ponti d'oro: & egli pure istaua, che nõ se gli lasciassero scappar dalle mani, atteso che eran rotti. Per le cui braue e furiose parole si prese partito molto sinistro di seguitarli e fare il fatto d'arme, dicendo

DI M. GIOVIO. 77

do il Generale; Io non voglio, che costui mi faccia tagliar la testa con le ballotte in Pregai, come interuẽne al Carmigniuola; e così furono rotti i Vinitiani; & il Loredano restando morto, pagò la pena della sua temerità. All'hora il Cotta eshortò il suo signore, che in cambio deli' Vnicorno, che s'era perduto nella giornata, portasse per insegna vn' Oca in mezo d'alquanti Cigni, con vn breue legato al collo, che dice; OBSTREPVIT INTER OLORES. per inferire, ch'ella è cosa impropria, ch'vn Senator togato voglia prender presuntione di giudicare ne' casi di guerra trà capitani. Rifiutò tale impresa il Liuiano, ancorche molto la lodasse, per non morder il Loredano morto miserabilmente, e per non trattarlo da Oca.

Metterò mano hora à quegli, che hanno auanza-

as simple as possible, to be easily understood, but not too banal as to be plain to all and sundry; it should be harmonious, pleasant to the eye and without human figures. These recommendations, illustrated (1 and 6) in pages from his *Dialogo delle imprese*, were, however, counsels of perfection. They were in conflict with a fashion which tended to obscurity and a monstrous over-indulgence in symbolism; symbolism which, in fact, strove to frustrate and misguide any who, without assistance, tried to decipher messages not addressed to them. Nor need people bother with the meaning. The aim of the emblem is to spell out wonder, the "marvellous" (which accounts for its apotheosis in the Baroque period). It is not the meaning of

4

5

6

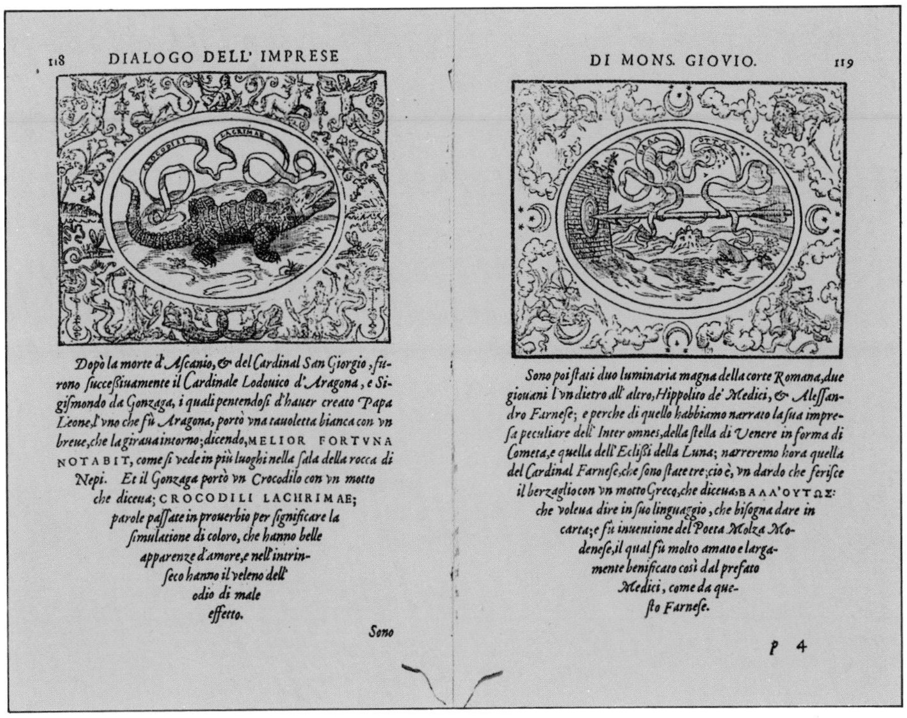

118 DIALOGO DELL' IMPRESE

Dopò la morte d'Ascanio, & del Cardinal San Giorgio, furono successiuamente il Cardinale Lodouico d'Aragona, e Sigismondo da Gonzaga, i quali pentendosi d'hauer creato Papa Leone, l'vno che fù Aragona, portò vna tauoletta bianca con vn breue, che la giraua intorno; dicendo, MELIOR FORTVNA NOTABIT, come si vede in più luoghi nella sala della rocca di Nepi. Et il Gonzaga portò vn Crocodilo con vn motto che diceua; CROCODILI LACHRIMAE; parole passate in prouerbio per significare la simulatione di coloro, che hanno belle apparenze d'amore, e nell'intrinseco hanno il veleno dell'odio di male effetto.

Sono

DI MONS. GIOVIO. 119

Sono poi stati duo luminaria magna della corte Romana, due giouani l'vn dietro all'altro, Hippolito de' Medici, & Alessandro Farnese; e perche di quello habbiamo narrato la sua impresa peculiare dell' Inter omnes, della stella di Venere in forma di Cometa, e quella dell'Eclissi della Luna; narreremo hora quella del Cardinal Farnese, che sono state tre; cio è, vn dardo che ferisce il berzaglio con vn motto Greco, che diceua, ΒΑΛΛ'ΟΥΤΩΣ: che voleua dire in suo linguaggio, che bisogna dare in carta; e fù inuentione del Poeta Molza Modenese, il qual fù molto amato e largamente benificato così dal prefato Medici, come da questo Farnese.

p 4

7

8

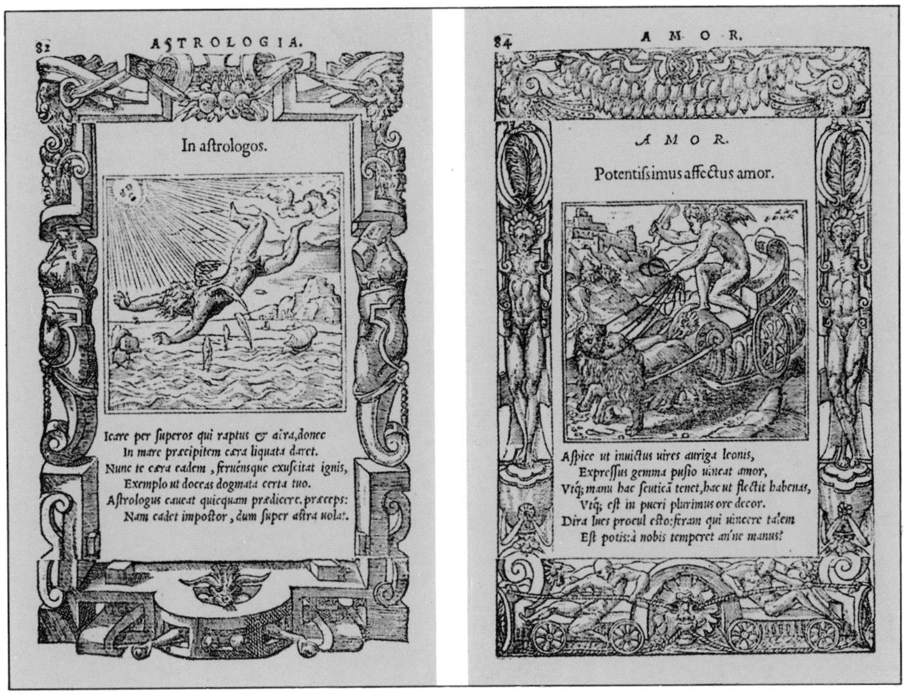

82 ASTROLOGIA.

In astrologos.

Icare per superos qui raptus & aëra, donec
In mare præcipitem cæra liquata daret.
Nunc te cæra eadem, feruénsque exuscitat ignis,
Exemplo ut doceas dogmata certa tuo.
Astrologus caueat quicquam prædicere, præceps:
Nam cadet impostor, dum super astra uolat.

84 AMOR.

AMOR.

Potentissimus affectus amor.

Aspice ut inuictus uires auriga leonis,
Expressus gemma pusio uincat amor,
Vtq; manu hac scuticã tenet, hac ut flectit habenas,
Vtq; est in pueri plurimus ore decor.
Dira lues procul esto: feram qui uincere talem
Est potis: à nobis temperet an'ne manus?

the emblem itself which matters; its fame resides in the personage of the one who bears it. It is a personal seal, the mark of ownership, possession and belonging.

The composition of emblems thus became an art in itself. Following his fancy, a prince in the fifteenth and sixteenth centuries might choose the dog, "Fidelity" (4: Gonzaga emblem in Castello San Giorgio, Mantua); or the elephant, for "Strength" or "Continence" (5: medallion with profile of Sigismondo Malatesta, supported by elephants, in the Tempio Malatestiano, Rimini). It might be a letter of the alphabet, initial, perhaps, of the owner's name or nickname. The dark-complexioned Ludovico Sforza was known as Il Moro, and the M is seen in his portrait by Boltraffio (7) in the Trivulzio Collection, in Castello Sforzesco, Milan. But, in time, the emblem was swamped by meaning. Its constituent figures and objects, colours and wording, are forced into the most involved and far-fetched of echoes and relationships. Borne away on the mysterious currents of alchemy, it was overtaken by the occult, and vanishes. What conceivably began as the mere declaration that so-and-so would conquer such-and-such a land or lady was, by the end of the Renaissance, a cosmic communication. The intentions announced were now on a universal scale, the programme was one of universal perfectability, and Baroque art took it over. In the seventeenth century, poetry and opera, villas, palaces and fountains, were to be, in reality, one colossal emblem.

Pollaiolo's tomb for Sixtus IV ("the first true pope-king," as Gregorovius called him), was constructed in 1493 and is now near the Treasury in St Peter's. The reliefs, personifications of the Cardinal and Theological Virtues and of the Liberal Arts, accurately subsume late-medieval thought on human knowledge and divine revelation. The Liberal Arts were studied in two groups, the trivium and quadrivium, Astronomy and Music (above) being included in the latter.

Serlio's *Cinque libri d'architettura*.

Most alarming of esoteric labyrinths is the Park of the Monsters at Bomarzo, a garden-tour that goes beyond the grave, into the depths of Hell and culminates, as in the *Hypnerotomachia Poliphili*, in a purifying ascent. The visitor-initiate wanders among stone monsters which speak through, or are explained by, emblematic inscriptions; the inspiration for the garden clearly lies in the *Hypnerotomachia* and Neoplatonist writings of Porphyry and Iamblichus.

The Renaissance garden, indispensable adjunct of a court that is itself the abode of marvel and deception, follows a significant course of development – from Careggi and Poggio a Caiano, their severe Neoplatonic symbolism approved by Ficino; to the pleasant retreat of the Orti Oricellari, devoted to Platonic debate on how men should be governed; from the idealized nature and debates on love at Asolo, and finally to fear and trembling, orphic rites and "mystical death." Compare once again the Orti Oricellari with Bomarzo: not, however, the sunlit Oricellari, so tranquilly concerned with the establishment and strengthening of civic liberty, but the secret, black and midnight scene of an "evening of magic" offered by Bianca Cappello to Francesco I and other illustrious guests in 1570. The gardens, lit only by the sinister flare of torches, are redolent of witchcraft. The "rites," as recounted for us in a novella by Celio Malispini, are a joke: the guests, having duly fallen into a ditch and traversed a subterranean tunnel, are presented with a sumptuous feast in a loggia lit by golden lamps. As at Bomarzo, they have trodden the path from Avernus to Elysium, from terror to delight. The garden is again a theater of catharsis.

Heraldry to emblem

The taste, or mania, for heraldry reached Italy in the first half of the fourteenth century. In his *Inferno* Dante condemns the dishonoured arms of usurers; in the *Paradiso* he speaks of the radiant heavenly signs in Mars, Jupiter and Saturn – the cross, eagle and ladder – and puts into the mouth of his ancestor Cacciaguida a panegyric on the aristocracy of Florence, each clan identified by its arms.

From this period popes, emperors and kings, communes and guilds, town-districts and popular magistracies, as well as private families, all displayed their colours and badges on shields, flags, clothing, chimney-pieces, column-capitals, hangings and household goods. The ubiquitous coat of arms appeared on tomb-slabs which paved the churches in carved stone or glazed tiles, they would adorn the family chapel and the walls of the Palazzo Pubblico, where *podestà* and captain of the people commemorated their years of office, as was their right and duty. Every jousting session or tournament was prefaced by the elaborate recital of heraldic qualifications (heraldry is indeed the science of armorial bearings), and detail as elaborate also weighed down chivalric poetry and romance. Writers of novelle took a different view and were inclined to mock those worst-bitten by the frenzy – predictably the *nouveaux riches* of the day and "nobles" whose nobility was by purchase rather than by birth.

It is probable that heraldry was developed to provide family cognizances and clearer identification on the battlefield: colours and emblems were originally very simple, with none of their later, near-hermetic, allusiveness. By the mid fourteenth century, however, there was a growing and intricate heraldic "grammar," with both moral and political implications; and the noble science, "increasingly important," as F. Cusin says, "in the development of oligarchical consciousness in Italy," increasingly demanded an organization and laws of its own. It was a lawyer who supplied them – Bartolo da Sassoferrato, whose treatise *De insignis et armis* dates from 1356.

The attitude of humanists towards heraldry was ambivalent. Humanism stood for the philological approach to antiquity, whereas the communicative and highly decorative code in which heraldry by now held its recognized position, needed permanently to adapt itself to the new, classicizing aesthetic values. The symbols and metaphors of classicism stemmed, however, from the specialist, "triumphal" vocabulary of Rome; how, then, were the "barbaric" elements – the bar, the fess, the pale, crosses, partition-lines and beasts, strangely stylized in Gothic fashion – to harmonize with military ornaments and eagles (*phalerae* and *victrices aquilae*) or with tablets carved in ancient style, laurel-crowns and ceremonial fillets? And how, without clashing, could triangular or mandorla-shaped shields keep company with the features of classical architecture?

The problem appeared to be one of style only, and after an eclectic and undecided phase, spanning the fourteenth and fifteenth centuries, solutions were gradually found. The charge, abstracted from a shield, might be freely applied, like a seal, to objects and architecture; or it could be redesigned in the modern – *i.e.* antique – idiom. For example, the eagle of the Holy Roman Empire became that of a legionary standard. Shield shapes were revised or redesigned, befitting the classical context; there were oval and hexagonal shields, and octagonal shields based on the horse- or ox-head motif, the *bucranium*. Insignia borrowed from them, even without their heraldic colours, were perfect tokens of state or family power, serving much the same purpose on effigy or monument

Botticelli's allegorical fresco of the Liberal Arts. In a sacred grove a youth is introduced to the seven Arts, presided over by Philosophy, who sits above them. Logic is seen with her symbol, the scorpion (also symbol of heresy, and Rhetoric), and at Philosophy's left hand are Geometry with a set square over her shoulder, Astronomy and Music, who plays a small portable organ. The figure introducing the young man is probably Grammar, since that study is the key to higher learning. Musée du Louvre, Paris.

Left: triumphal procession; an illustration from the Hypnerotomachia Poliphili, *attributed to Francesco Colonna (late fifteenth century).*

as a martyr's attributes in religious art. The Farnese lilies, Della Rovere oaks, the Medici balls, Barberini bees or Chigi stars and mountains acted as both embellishment and proprietor's stamp on palace, villa and architectural friezes.

But the question was only apparently stylistic. Linked as it was with lineage, birth and the acceptance of loyalties, heraldry was bound, at the Renaissance, to surpass the collective glorification of the dynasty to glorify the individual; the result was the recondite language of the emblem, the highly personal heraldry that expressed the bearer's aspirations, his power-through-erudition. Not by accident did the emblem and the "heroic" individual portrait share an almost contemporary popularity.

The new, heroic and individualistic notions of the world created ever more complicated heraldic insignia. Heralds busied themselves with imagining the coats of arms of Adam, Moses and Hector, and a whole fantasy-science sprang up around the adventure-epics and the cult of the "paladins" of antiquity. With the invention of gunpowder, however, shields and helmets, encumbered with their flamboyant, monstrous crests, were less and less serviceable to the warrior in action.

The earliest individual move towards heraldry may have been verbal, or rather written, for as early as 1332 knights at a tournament wore such mottoes as "I am Aeneas, fighting for Lavinia." Thus the personal emblem was introduced – generally an animal or object chosen for its covert relevance to a specific resolve or exploit of the wearer. A knight might wear an emblem in evidence of a vow, or until a particular feat had been performed or goal achieved. The custom was deeply rooted in religious practice: antecedants of the emblem are oaths of pilgrimage, the cockle-shell and palm-branch, and even certain marks of infamy, such as the badges of the "closed" confraternity.

The most widespread type of emblem, adopted from France during the reigns of Charles VIII and Louis XII, and which became the rage in Italy, was the *impresa*, or personal "device" (from the French word *devise*, in the sense of aim or resolution). Petrarch is said to have fabricated Gian Galeazzo Visconti's device of the turtledove on a rayed sun, which was later adopted by the Sforzas. A device contained both body – its graphic design – and soul. The soul found expression in the recondite motto, often abstruse and requiring further elucidation. Many of the princes of Italy adopted one or several of these emblems, with their accompanying mottoes. The Este of Ferrara had an eagle, with the words, *Proxima soli*; the Farnese and Gonzaga chose Mount Olympus, and so on and so forth. Quite often the *imprese*, like symbols in alchemy, were bizarre, meaningless, or even vulgar; they might be partnerships of ordinary, humble articles, or grotesque juxtapositions of objects or animals, to be read as a rebus.

Society was not totally unprepared for emblems, however. In 1419 a Florentine priest, Christoforo Buondelmonti, on a manuscript-hunt in Greece, acquired on the island of Andros a codex of the *Hieroglyphica* by the second- or fourth-century Alexandrian, Horapollo. Horapollo interpreted ancient Egyptian hieroglyphics, according to an erroneous theory accepted by Apuleius, Plutarch and Plotinus, as a cryptographical system used to conceal sacred truths from the eyes of the non adept. Studied by Ficino and Alberti, the *Hieroglyphica* were fundamental to the symbol-language of the *Hypnerotomachia Poliphili*, as to the western passion for ancient Egypt which endured, with all its mystagogical trappings, into the eighteenth century and beyond. The book was published by Aldo Manuzio in 1505, and was consulted by all who wrote on emblems thereafter. It influences the *Emblemata* of 1531, an enquiry into and analysis of the subject by Andrea Alciato; it influences Paolo Giovio's detailed study of the emblem-concept, *Imprese militari e amorose*, or 1555. Tasso's contribution is the dialogue *Il conte overo de l'imprese*; for him the purpose of the device is "adornment" or, more precisely, "the revelation of what is accomplished or intended."

The title of Giovio's book leaves no room for doubt. We are fairly and squarely at court, among knights and ladies, and *eros* will determine the device: this is the realm of *armi* and *amori*, Mars and Venus, the heroic and the erotic. The emblem, he says, is *motto e disegno* of battle and of love. In *Il Rota overo dell'imprese* Scipione Ammirato was to see it as "knightly philosophy;" a philosophy couched in secret language, precursor of the hermetic "chivalry" that would be embodied in the Rosicrucian doctrines and nourish masonic symbolism.

Not surprisingly, the language of the emblem has elements in common with that of alchemy, and both are strongly affected by technology, of which there is no trace in heraldry. While heraldry is related to the old Gothic and feudal imagery (although often admitting new words for *armes parlantes*, or canting arms), the emblem includes images of tools, machines and ordinary everyday objects.

And in its wake armed might and princely power abandoned their antiquated accouterments and ceased to ignore technology. The sword remained the weapon of chivalry, but cannon and shell were no longer regarded as abominable contraptions. They were considered instead *ultima ragione regis*, the final kingly argument. The roar and explosion of the bombard joins the thunderclaps and bolts of Jupiter. Roberto Valturio illustrated a manual on warfare with cannon in the form of dragons and monsters; military architects planned forts with the outlines of mighty eagles, or of tortoises, to strew a prince's territory with giant emblems and cyclopean devices, like an endless Bomarzo.

Occasionally a device might be adopted in proud celebration of some personal triumph over adversity, or destiny, or the stars themselves. Capricorn had been in the ascendant, not at the birth of Grand Duke Cosimo I of Tuscany, but when he survived the threat of Montemurlo; after Montemurlo he preferred this sign to any of his emblems, including the tortoise-and-the-sail. Thus the grand duke chose Capricorn, the constellation of the Golden Age, zodiacal sign of Augustus and of Jesus Christ, although it had not, in the first place, chosen him.

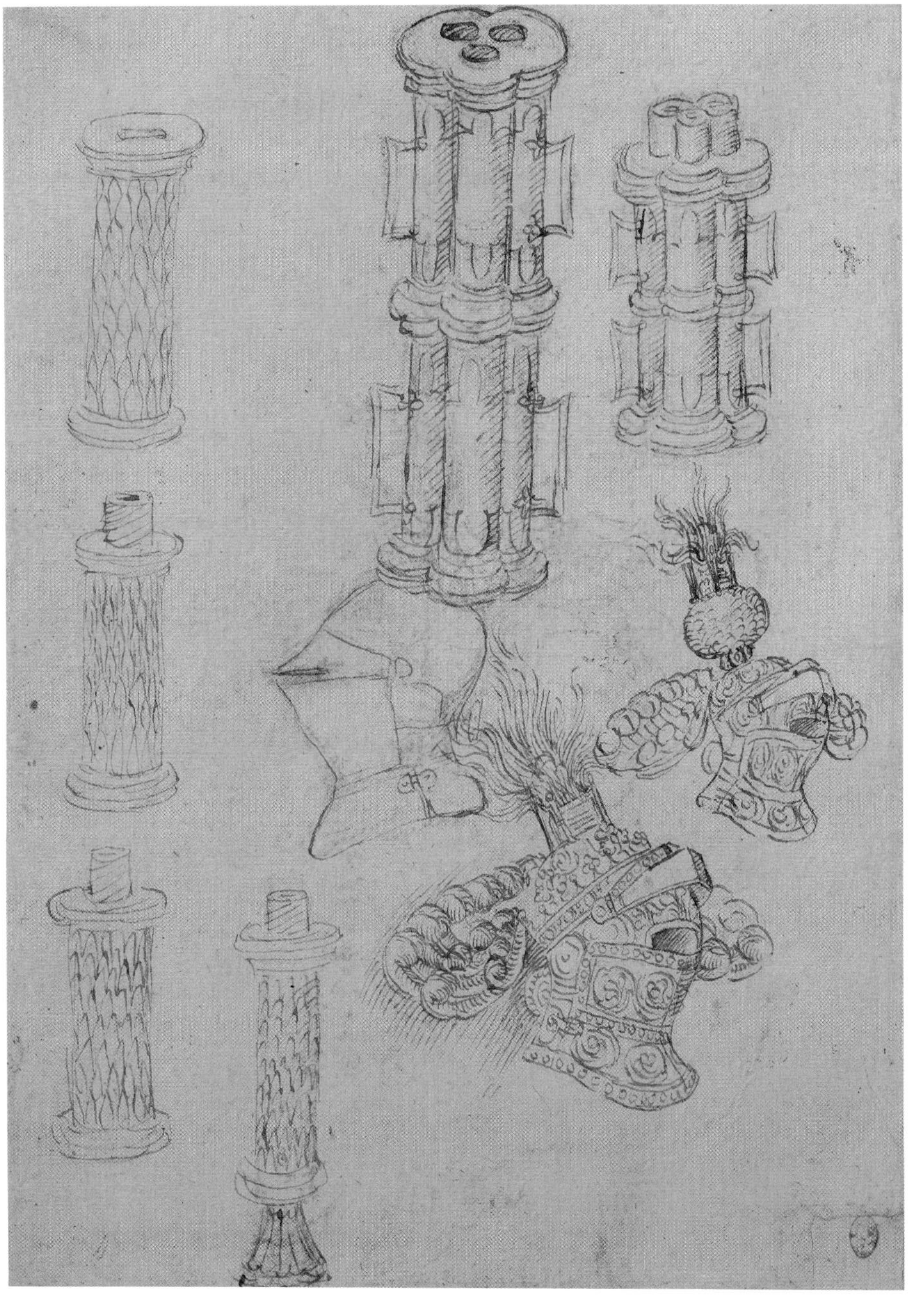

Above: a mixture of drawings by Pisanello with two designs for tournament helmets. Plumed and crested, these helmets, with their decorative elements derived from mythology, recall the vogue for emblems in the Renaissance courts of fifteenth-century Italy. Musée du Louvre, Paris.

Court Spectacle

The carousel at Palazzo Barberini, Rome, in honour of Queen Christina of Sweden. Painting by Filippo Gagliardi and Filippo Lauri; seventeenth century. Rome, Museo di Roma.

Private and public aspects

The form of a Renaissance court spectacle was determined by location rather than by any other single element; it basically depended, therefore, on whether the celebration was held in public or in private. The public street provided the setting for religious and ceremonial processions and for horse racing, the town square for jousting, tournaments, ceremonial hunts and suchlike. The *sacre rappresentazioni*, or religious interludes, might take place in church – which was at once public and private – or on the *parvis* outside. The private and exclusive entertainments of feasting, dancing and watching plays, took place in palace rooms.

Any investigation of Renaissance spectacle must begin with a study of the "scenic" space – in the sense of social space – which involves the very fabric of the city, with all its ideological, social and utopian implications. The fifteenth-century town, still recognizably medieval, was kinetic space where, in order to be acquainted with and to appreciate it, one went on foot. The winding streets provided a unifying and continuous route in which the breaks and pauses of crossroads and the wide-open squares imposed their own rhythm and direction on processions, and whose architecture formed the backdrop for diverse spectacles.

Popular festivity was often closely linked with court diplomacy, since some of the celebrations to welcome a distinguished foreigner, an honoured guest, or the prince's bride on her state entry for example, were public and the procession, flowing through the streets, would unite participants and audience. Lookers-on and looked-at were equally involved. Everyone was aware of his rôle, and of the social divisions obtaining in the town.

For private entertainments there were settings within the palace: the courtyard for tournaments and jousting, the great hall for banquets, plays or dancing, or on occasions the courtyard might accommodate the banquet, or the hall the joust, and either could be flooded for a naumachia or mimic sea fight. In fifteenth-century Florence noble weddings might spread onto nearby streets and squares, as when

The church provided the first "theater space," though neither built nor designed for the purpose. Annunciation plays were given in the Florentine churches of the Santissima Annunziata and San Felice in Piazza to celebrate the Ecumenical Council of 1439. Some of the congegni *which produced the complicated scenic effects are illustrated here, reconstructed from detailed contemporary accounts.*

Lorenzo the Magnificent's sister Nannina married Bernardo Rucellai in 1466 and a dais for the banquet and dancing filled the street from the family palace to the Loggia de' Rucellai, along what is now Via della Vigna Nuova. The scene, as described by the bridegroom's father, cannot have differed much from that depicted on the Adimari dowry chest, now in the Accademia, Florence. "An open-air festival, on a rostrum with sumptuous hangings and tapestries, benches and seats, and deep blue awnings for protection against the sun, decorated with garlands . . . and many other adornments, chief among them a *credenza* laden with vessels of wrought silver, . . . and on the rostrum dancing and merriment, and the serving of luncheon and supper."

None of this seems to have been lost on Giovanni II Bentivoglio, Lord of Bologna, who put on a similar display for the wedding of his eldest son Annibale to Lucrezia d'Este in 1487, also celebrated in the square before his palace, with seats for the public, a wooden "castle" as the centerpiece, and an awning run on ropes from his roof (not, however, to fend off sunshine, but the rigours of winter). Part of the festivities was a public game of *palla*, or volleyball, but before the spirited contest began, the spectators were treated to a lively debate between Prudence and Fortune.

The backdrop of a Renaissance spectacle was a cinematic riot of rich stuffs and carpets draped from the windows of houses and palaces alike, of fine baize hangings, triumphal arches and garlanded streets, while tapestries, frescoes, pictures and cloths of gold and silver embellished the rooms and courtyards of the princely host. At his command his city and his house had been transformed; and this new look, ephemeral, liberating and carefully suited to the matter in hand, made of the one a humanistic dream of the Ideal City, of the other a dwelling, the evidence of whose wealth and magnificence could not fail to enhance it's master's political power and prestige.

The theater of faith

A "theatrical space" is not necessarily a space or building intended and designed for spectacle. It may be a space or building occasionally, and increasingly, used for the celebration of memorable events; the earliest theater in this respect, is, of course, the church, where the regular or exceptional *sacra rappresentazione* was shared by all the townspeople. Such an occasion could mark the court's reception for the ruler's bride, or the honour paid to an important guest, at the same time boosting the prince's pride to be able to show the visiting ambassadors, *signori* and foreign dignitaries how wisely and well his good government managed to reconcile the trappings of passing fancy with the more eternal verities.

*Opposite: machines (*congegni*) used for the* Annunciation *at San Felice in Piazza. Top, left: the revolving cupola, or hemisphere, where twelve angel singers stood, and (right) the mandorla in which hovered the boy playing Gabriel. Bottom: a model of the rope apparatus by which Gabriel approached the Virgin's "house" in the Santissima Annunziata play.*
Above: angels round the lantern of the Portinari Chapel in Sant'Eustorgio, Milan (built by Michelozzo and Averulino in 1462) give some idea of the kind of effect achieved in the sacra rappresentazione. *Left: the type of capstan used to manipulate the* congegni.

In the first half of the fifteenth century the *sacra rappresentazione* was growing away from its medieval predecessor, the *ludus*, or church play. Onto the scriptural content were grafted story-telling elements, ordinary secular incidents to allure the faithful, while, in a related bid to stimulate a waning interest in church rites, innovations were gradually added to the dramatic content. Temporary platforms on which "sets" could be erected alternated between the church interior and the church square and the staging effects appear more elaborate and eye-catching in an attempt to satisfy the imagination of an ever-growing public. These settings, deliberately chosen for their proximity to the fresco-cycles on church walls, revived the old idea of the *biblia pauperum*, bible of the poor, of the frescoes, but now more vividly brought to life with music, song and verse.

In Florence, however, where the cultural climate favoured technical experiment, Filippo Brunelleschi was responsible for enormous strides in the mechanics of the *sacra rappresentazione*. It was only to be expected of the greatest architect then active in the culture-bed of the Renaissance, the begetter of its major architectural innovations. He came well-equipped to apply his revolutionary notions of carpentry, construction, perspective, even clockwork, to the making of *ingegni*, i.e. machines, for mobile and altogether startling stage effects. The organization of the sacred interludes was dictated by mechanisms of this kind until the coming of the Baroque theater introduced new astonishments at the end of the sixteenth century. But it was Brunelleschi's innovation to have restored the *sacra rappresentazione* solely to the church interior, centering the action in the nave and dome.

Students of theatrical history have to thank the Ecumenical Council held in Florence in 1439 (under discussion was the reunion of the two Churches, Orthodox and Roman) for the sole surviving description of the *ingegni* installed that year for *sacre rappresentazioni* in two of the conventual churches – the Annunciation play at the Santissima Annunziata, and the equally spectacular Ascension at the Carmine. The Russian bishop Abraham of Suzdal was a fascinated and altogether stunned spectator of both spectacles and it is to him we owe the descriptions of the marvellous *ingegni* that were used. A third *ingegno*, for the feast of the Annunciation at San Felice in Piazza, is reported in Vasari's *Life* of Brunelleschi. These three mechanisms repay closer attention as the prototypes of later examples by followers of Brunelleschi or craftsmen from his workshop, for spectacles, both sacred and profane, in other Italian cities, among them Leonardo da Vinci's *Festa del Paradiso* at the Castello Sforzesco in Milan in 1490, a *coup de théâtre* of the utmost splendour and éclat.

The *ingegno* in the Santissima Annunziata at Florence took up the length of the nave. Above the main door was a revolving construction of concentric circles representing the star-spangled heavens, providing a background to the figures of God and his angels. At the other end appeared the Virgin and the prophets. The boy

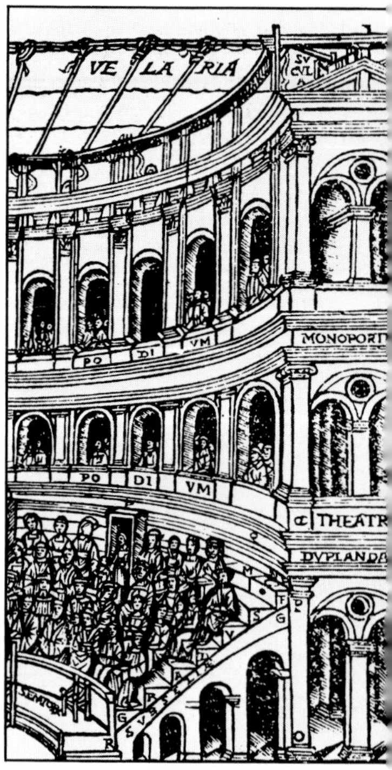

Above: the classical Roman theater as illustrated by the Milanese Cesare Cesariano in his 1521 edition of the treatise De architectura, *by Vitruvius.*
Left: frontispiece to the Comedies *of Terence, published in Venice in 1497. This is our earliest record of what the humanists thought a theater should look like. The tiered seating recalls that of classical times, and the simple "cabins" of the settings are like the* mansiones *of medieval pageants.*

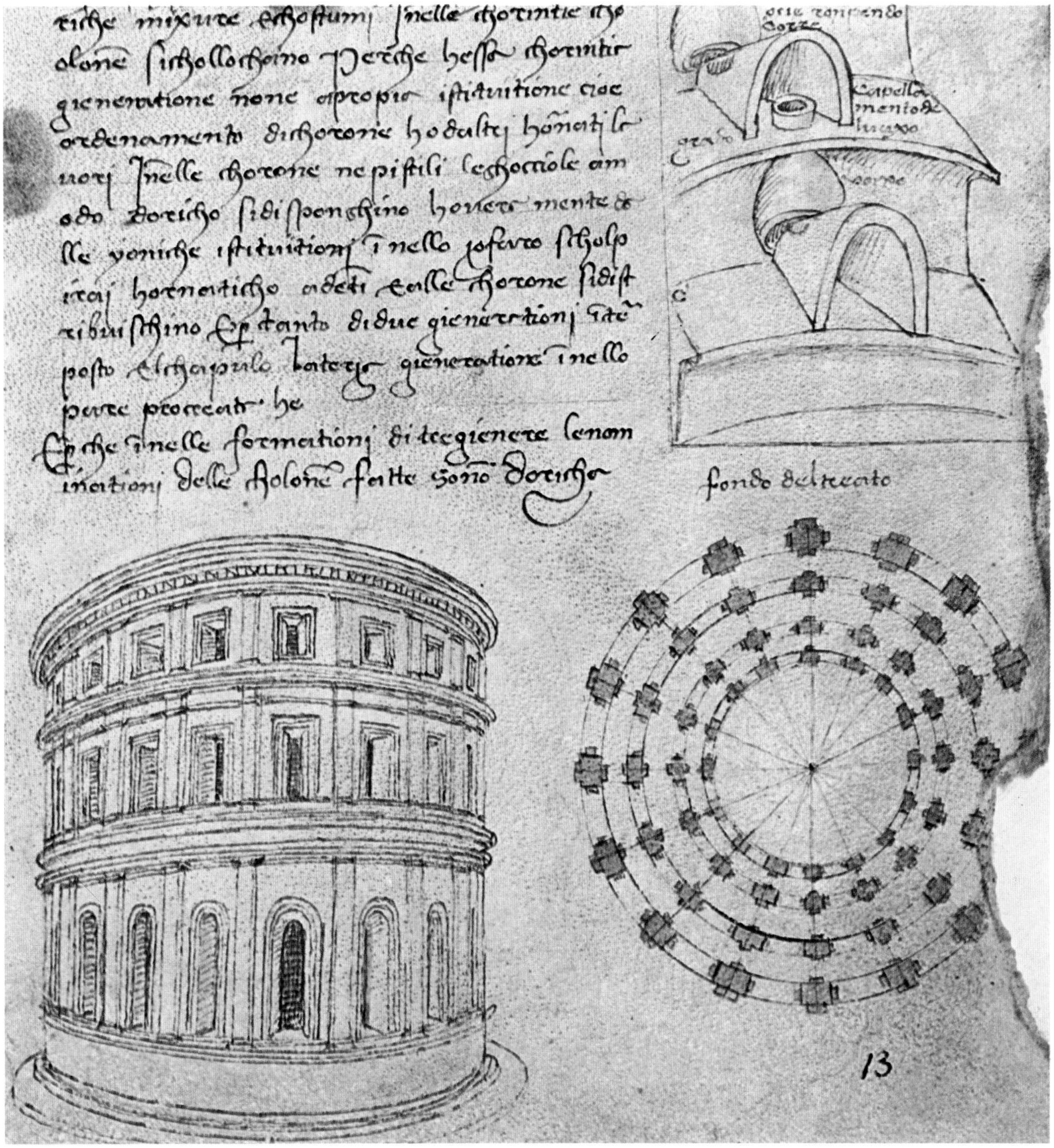

Plan and exterior of a Roman theater in a drawing by Francesco di Giorgio Martini in the Biblioteca Laurenziana, Florence. The artist is more interested in the technical and constructional aspects of the theater as architecture, and less attentive than Cesariano to scenery and staging.

playing Gabriel was wafted aloft on hempen ropes from one end of the nave to the other. Following the Archangel's announcement to Mary, artificial fire ran the length of the nave on parallel ropes. (This symbolism of the Holy Ghost as issuing from the Father and the Son alluded to a point in the Creed under discussion by the Council.) The whole spectacle was enacted in three-dimensional space, in front of, behind and above the heads of the congregation as if they themselves were a part of the whole breathtaking experience.

At the church of the Carmine three scenes were enacted in front view of the congregation. One was of the city of Jerusalem with the Mount of Olives in the background. Christ, the Virgin and the Apostles were seen leaving the city. On a suspended platform above appeared the heavens with God and the angels. The Ascent into Heaven was achieved by means of

PALACE AND CITY: THREE EXAMPLES

When Count Oddantonio da Montefeltro, lord of Urbino, was murdered in 1444, he was succeeded by his twenty-two-year-old, illegitimate half-brother Federico.

Federico was a gifted, and a lucky, professional soldier who tripled his territory in 30 years, wrung papal recognition from Sixtus IV, and received the title of duke in 1474. Urbino itself was a small township crowded into a narrow valley between two hills, that on the west crowned by a fortress built by the Spanish cardinal Albornoz in the fourteenth century.

The ducal palace now stands on the steep and craggy eastern hill, where Federico bought the land, and a few small medieval houses standing there, between the old Montefeltro family palace at its southern end and a fortified *castellare* further north.

The palace on this difficult site was built, facing the mountains, by Luciano Laurana, with its "beautiful colonnaded courtyard with fine rooms above," as described by Antonio da Mercatello in 1480; the façade facing onto the piazza is L-shaped, while the side looking towards the valley, due to the difficult terrain, is built at an oblique angle. "A glorious abode in an expensive situation," wrote Raphael's father Giovanni Santi, in his rhymed chronicle, "and enough to make one tremble at the undertaking."

Architecturally, it is the valley-facing façade, the loggie flanked by the two soaring towers, which sets the seal on this magnificent urban panorama.

The Mercatale, laid out in the valley by Francesco di Giorgio Martini, is in perfect "landscape" relation to the palace above, and so the pattern for the future Urbino was laid. A mid eighteenth-century engraving (5) shows the dominating position of the palace in relation to the town itself, shown with its sixteenth-century walls in (4). Figure 7 shows a plan of part of the ducal palace, while figure 6 shows its location within a setting of other important buildings and older parts of the town.

Describing the palace interior and gardens, Antonio da Mercatello speaks of "250 rooms, arranged with much ingenuity, 660 doors and windows; rooms and salons and loggiaed courtyards; there are 40 perfect fireplaces that never smoke; anterooms, lofty halls, convenient stabling and kitchens, storehouses for wine, grain and flour . . . and I should add that there is in the palace a beautiful garden with fountains, all sorts of herbs and jasmine, and a gardener to water it . . ."

The creator of Pienza, Aeneas Silvius Piccolomini, entering the Church at the age of 40, rose to be pope (Pius II) by the time he was 53. In 1459 he summoned the princes of Christendom to Mantua, to plan a crusade against the Turks, and on his way from Rome, with Leon Battista Alberti in his suite, stayed at his birthplace, Corsignano, on the north-eastern slopes of Valdorcia. It was then that he thought of rebuilding the little town, to be renamed Pienza, as an occasional residence for himself and his court. The architect chosen to carry out the pope's and Alberti's ideas was Bernardo Gambarelli, known as il Rossellino, who came from Settignano near Florence.

Rossellino picked his site for the cathedral and the Palazzo Piccolomini about halfway along the main artery, and Pius persuaded some of his cardinals – Ammannati, Rodrigo Borgia, Jouffroy and Gonzaga – to raise palaces there. Besides a new look to the palazzo pubblico, on the same square, behind it a marketplace was created, out of sight of the noble and official center. At the northeastern edge of the town twelve identical two-storey houses were constructed for the poor and destitute.

Pienza, retired and peaceful, bears some reflection of what the Renaissance conscience meant by the "ideal city." (2, an early nineteenth-century lithograph; 1, present-day plan). It is an organic and harmonious whole, and its fifteenth-century additions blend with the medieval fabric in a way that was then – but would be no longer – possible. Most remarkable of all is the piazza, trapezoidal (a design to be followed by Michelangelo for his Capitoline piazza in Rome), with divergent sides –

1

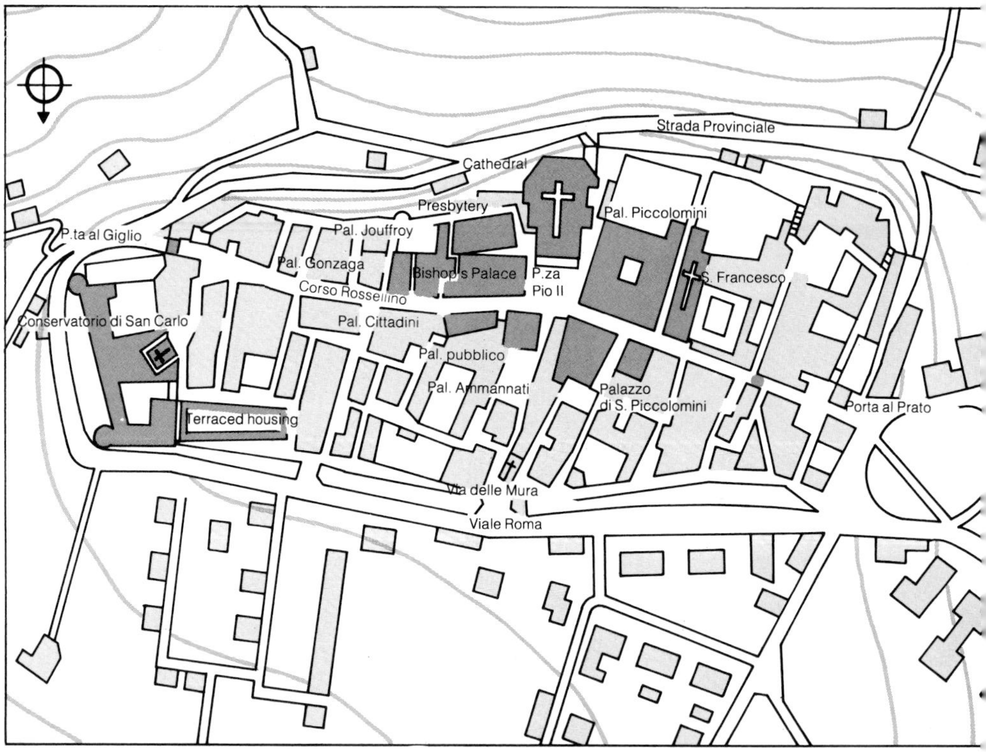

2

3

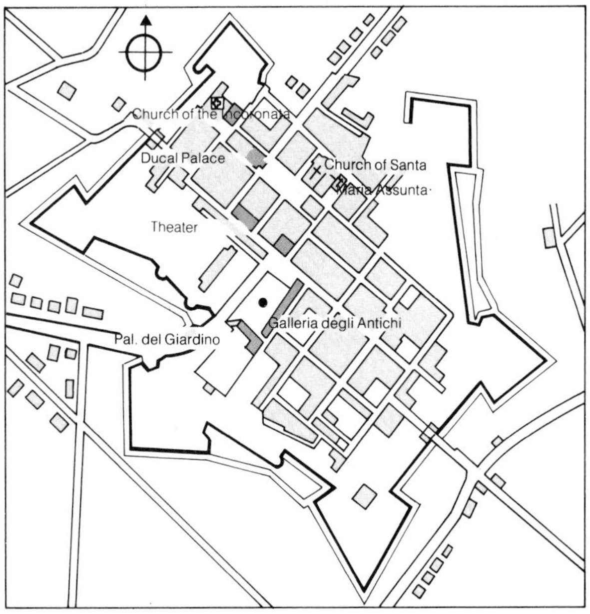

4

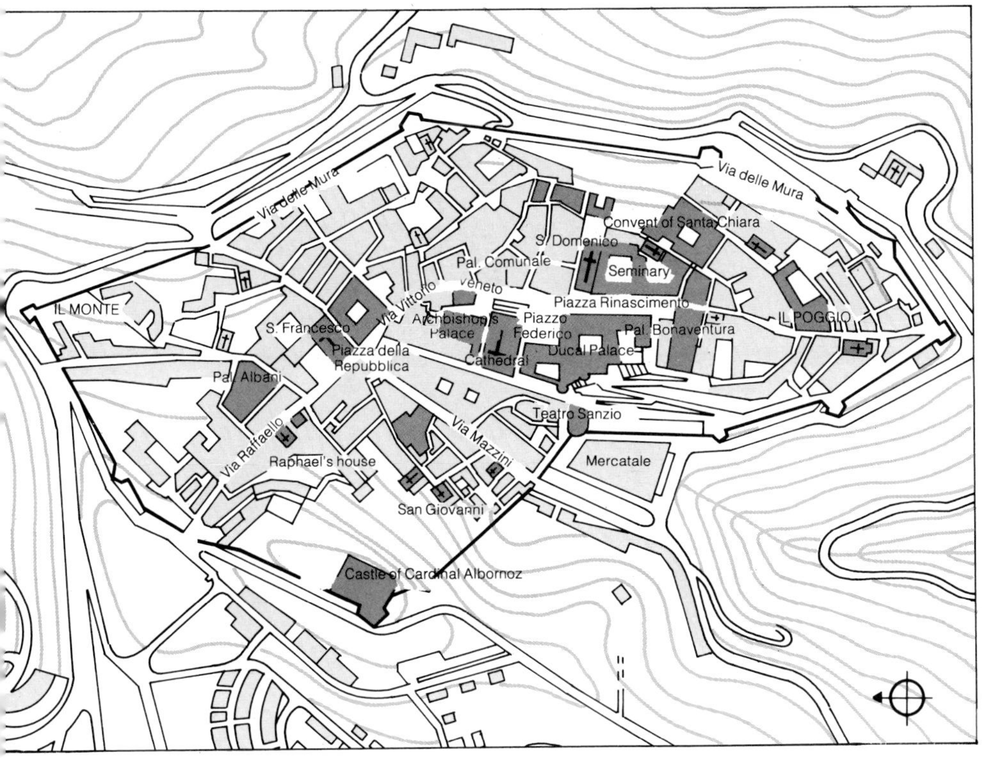

that of Palazzo Piccolomini to the right of the cathedral and of the episcopal palace (once Cardinal Rodrigo Borgia's) to the left; and between the cathedral and Palazzo Piccolomini, a *longue-vue* of the multicoloured landscape of the valley beyond.

Sabbioneta, our third example, was the village, not far from the Po river, southwest of Mantua, where Vespasiano Gonzaga set up his small state when granted lands of his own by Charles V in 1541. Vespasiano was a soldier and an engineer, whom Charles's son, Philip II of Spain, made a grandee of the first class. His personal device was a muzzled dog, with the motto *In libertà mi godo* – In liberty is my delight.

In 1576, in his forties, he settled at Sabbioneta and modelled it into his private "ideal city." The fortified walls were laid out in a rough hexagon; the street planning rectangular (3); church (1581) and ducal palace (1568) were on the piazza; and behind the palace was the octagonal parish church of the Incoronata (1588), where the duke is buried. Scamozzi built his Teatro Olimpico (1590) between the Piazza Ducale, and the adjacent Piazza d'Armi, which has a Roman column in the middle. Situated along two sides of the Piazza d'Armi is the Palazzo del Giardino (1584), once a summer palace, *luogo di delizie*, of the court, which contains the long *corridor grande* where the ducal antiquities were kept. (These had been acquired by Vespasiano's father, Luigi Gonzaga – known as Rodomonte after Ariosto's vehement warrior at the sack of Rome in 1527).

Sabbioneta was, for a brief time, a cultural center (" the Little Athens"), with its library and academy, its mint and an important press where Hebrew books were printed.

Vespasiano died in 1591; two wives had predeceased him, and not, rumour said, from natural causes. His third wife Margherita, like himself, was a Gonzaga. The family, therefore, disputed the succession of Isabella, Princess of Stigliano, his daughter by his second wife. As a result of their quarrelling, the ideal township fell into decline and soon lost its soul.

5

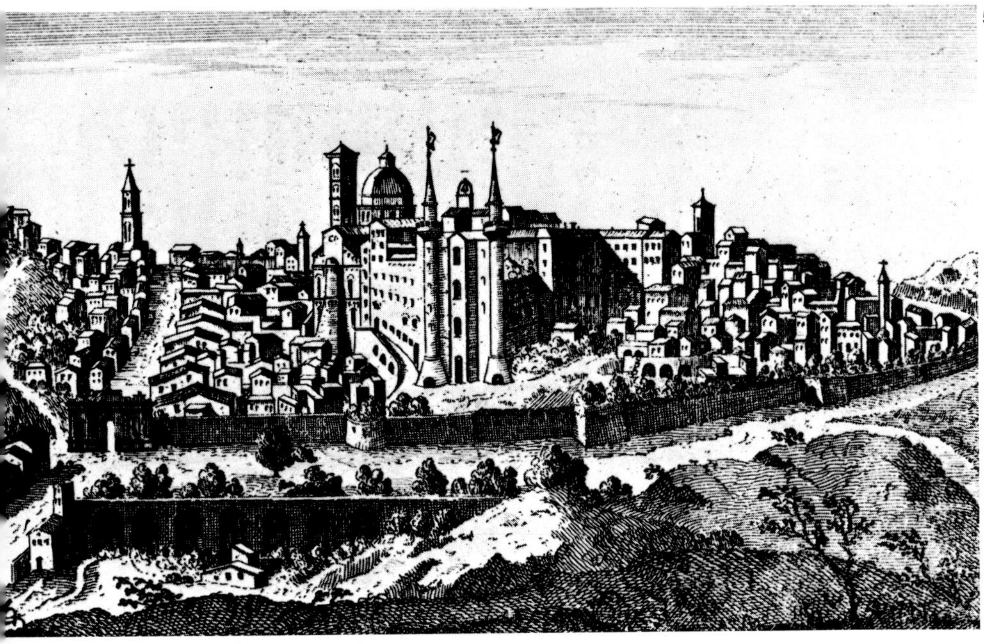

6

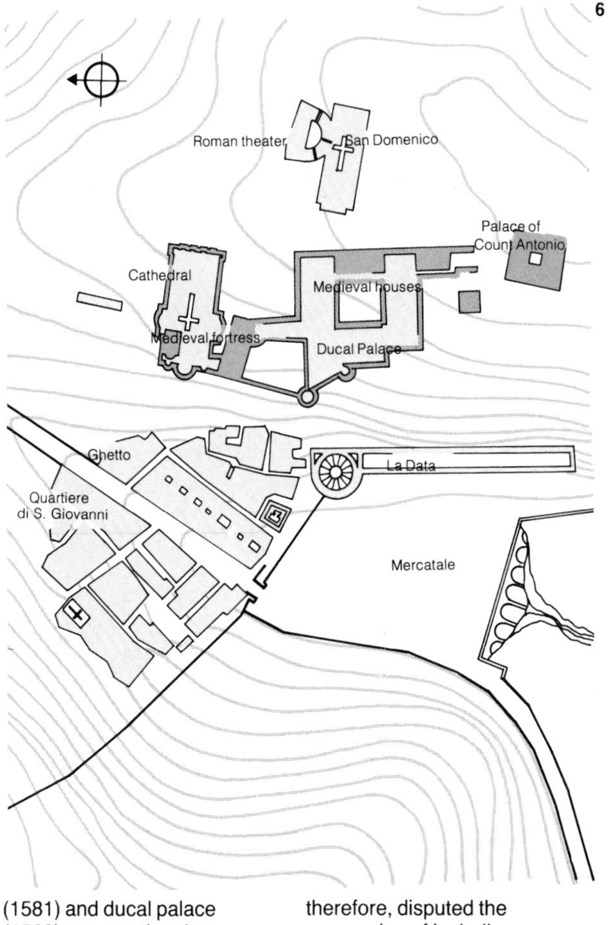

Urbino: first floor of the ducal palace.

7

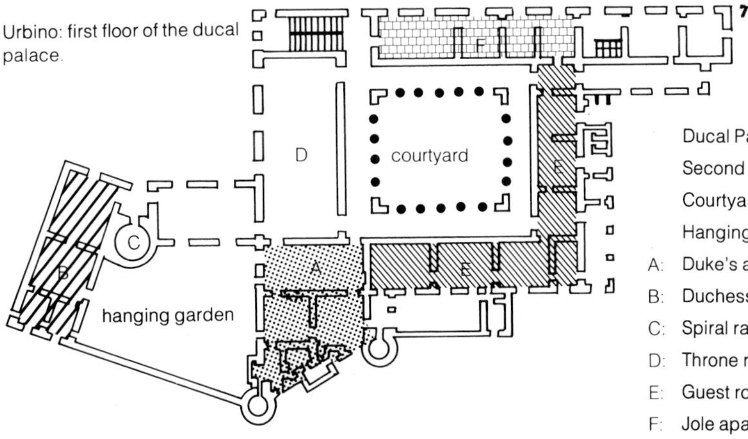

Ducal Palace of Urbino
Second floor plan
Courtyard
Hanging garden
A: Duke's apartment
B: Duchess' apartment
C: Spiral ramp in form of tower
D: Throne room
E: Guest rooms
F: Jole apartment

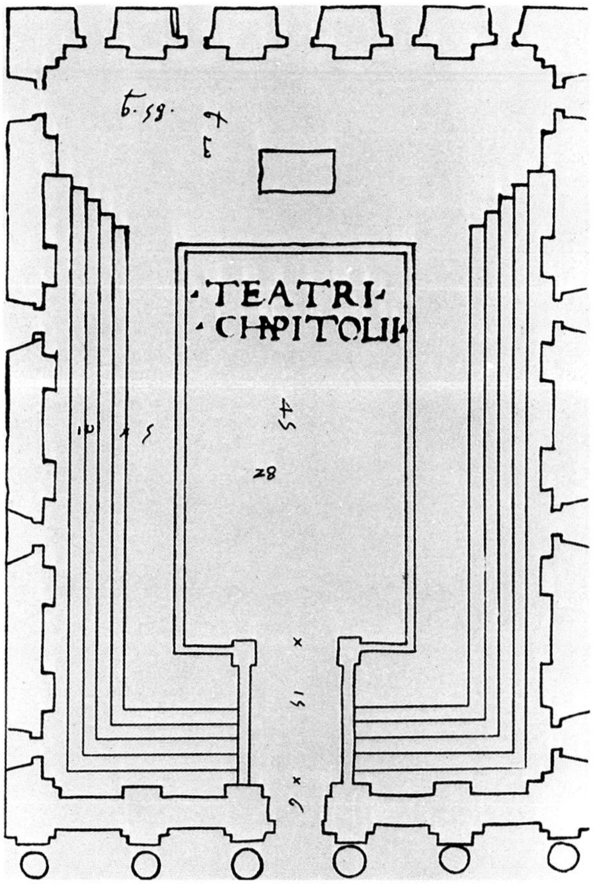

ropes, from the rear of the Mount of Olives. Winches on the hanging platform hauled the actor aloft and simultaneously lowered a cloud bearing two angel escorts. A sudden darkness concealed his passage from the *ingegno* to the gates of heaven and he was next seen, where the Creed dictated he should be, at the right hand of God the Father.

For the Annunciation play at the small church of San Felice in Piazza the mechanism functioned, as it were, telescopically, in vertical space. Action in the tiny church focused on a revolving wooden half-dome, or hemisphere, hung centrally between two roof beams over the single aisle. On it rode and sang 12 small boys attired as angels and from it hung a second *ingegno*, the *"mazzo,"* so called, with eight more, younger, boys. From the *mazzo* an illuminated mandorla, in which stood a slightly older Archangel Gabriel, descended to ground level. (The assorted and theatrically effective heights of these children served to demonstrate the newly discovered science of perspective). Having reenacted the Annunciation scene with the Virgin Mary, Gabriel reentered the mandorla and the whole thing went into reverse. Hidden winches in the hemisphere hoisted the mandorla into the *mazzo*, and the *mazzo* to the empyrean. Heaven's gates clanged to with thunderous noise as wooden shutters slammed across the base of the hemisphere, bringing the spectacle to an end.

In the cupola of the Cappella Portinari in Sant'Eustorgio in Milan there may be a hint of what the congregation saw in that small Florentine church. The chapel was commissioned in 1462 by a Florentine banker from Michelozzo and Averulino – both Tuscan, and each both a sculptor and an architect, as was Brunelleschi. The vaulted drum, and the frieze of dancing plaster angels recalled Brunelleschi's arrangements for the San Felice Annunciation.

Some of the *ingegni* were developed from known devices; the Archangel Gabriel used what was essentially a tightrope-walker's apparatus. Others were quite new, and all were frequently employed at a variety of feasts and spectacles, with Florentine workmen, famously skilled technicians, engaged to operate them. When at Reggio Emilia in 1453 St Peter and two angels swooped down from the top of the church, bearing a laurel-crown to place on the

In 1513 Giuliano and Lorenzo de' Medici received the citizenship of Rome, and the temporary theater erected for the celebrations on the Capitoline Hill was a great step forward in playhouse design (see plan, left). The reconstruction by Francesco Bruschi (opposite, top) shows tiered seats along the sides and the walls hung with pictures. An overhead awning resembled the velarium *of an ancient Roman theater.*

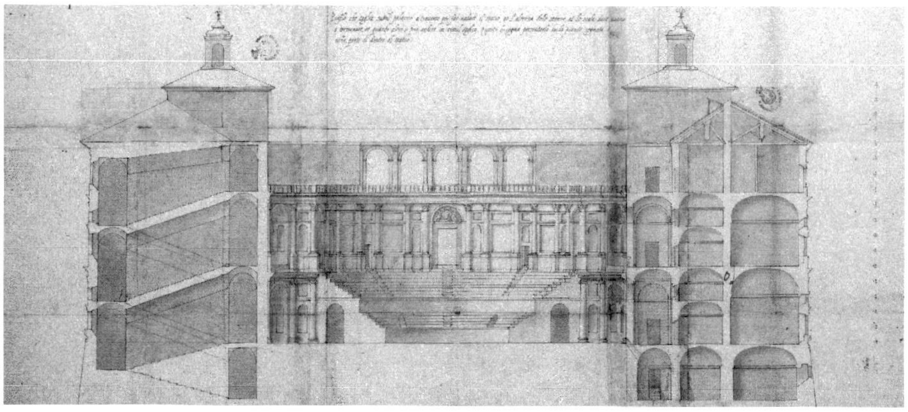

Above: plan for a permanent open-air theater in the gardens of the Farnese palace at Piacenza. Drawing (1558) in the Archivio di Stato, Parma.

brow of Duke Borso d'Este, on his state entry into the city, the feat was engineered by Niccolò Baroncelli, a Florentine professional at the Este court.

In 1475 "several Florentines" assembled a Resurrection drama for Galeazzo Sforza in Milan. He may have had in mind the *sacra rappresentazione* seen in Florence a few years before, as he demanded similar machinery, and a flight into heaven as the climax. For the wedding of Duke Guidobaldo da Montefeltro and Elisabetta Gonzaga in 1488 a *Life of St John the Baptist* was played out in the square of Casteldurante (the modern Urbania). From a rock representing Paradise, we are told, "came three descents of cloud-borne angels on a rope. One paused in midair to proclaim the festival and two were deposited on the stage to talk with Zacharias."

The concentric, rotating circles of the *Primum Mobile* and the nine spheres occur in many *sacre rappresentazioni* and in 1549 were even erected in the streets of Antwerp – again by Florentine workmen – for a *tableau vivant* of Paradise at the state entry of the future Philip II.

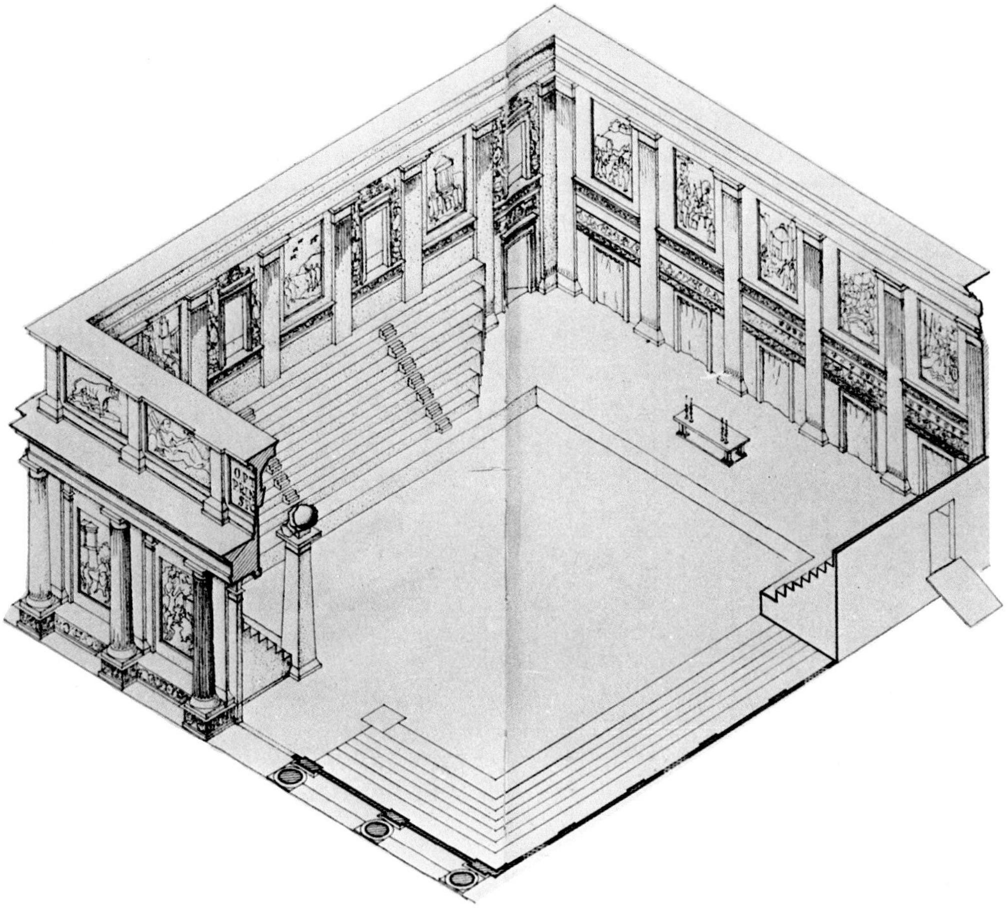

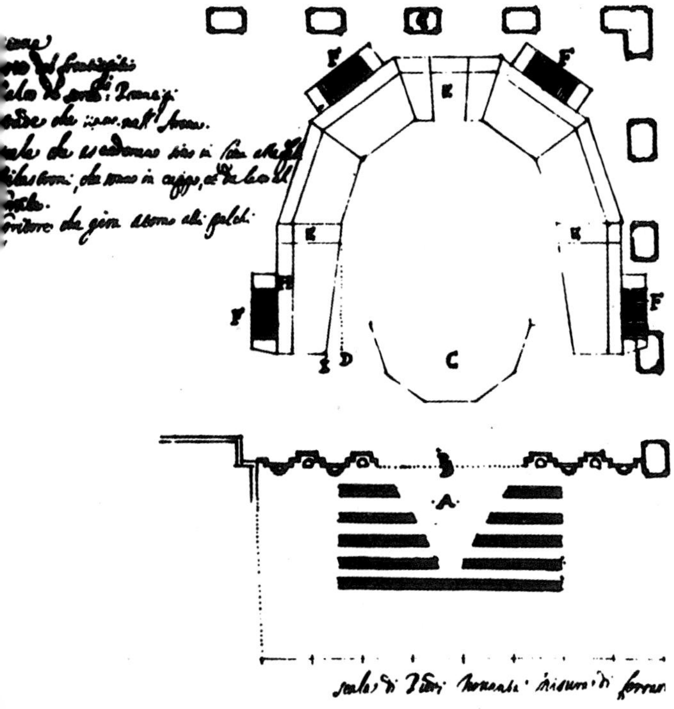

When Odoardo Farnese married Margherita de' Medici in 1628 a theater was built in the courtyard of San Pietro Martire at Parma. The design (left), by Francesco Guitti, is yet another landmark in the very slow development of theater design. Ferrara, Biblioteca Civica.

The half-dome, with its lights and heavenly or zodiacal signs, was adopted as well for non religious spectacle. In 1490 the Milanese chroniclers Tanci and Tristano Calco speak of "a hemisphere of iron hoops" at Ludovico il Moro's *Festa del Paradiso*, "the seven gyrating planets being men in the shape and garb of the planets as the poets tell of them." The guests were amazed and enchanted, "and the festival was called Il Paradiso from the wondrous Paradise contrived by the great art and cunning of Maestro Lionardo Vinci, the Florentine."

In 1487 we hear from the diarist Bernardino Zambotti of the *ingegno* for Jupiter in the *Amphytrion* of Plautus at Ferrara: "a heaven in the palace courtyard, built high up in a corner by the clock-tower, with lamps shining like stars through perforations in a covering of thin black material; and little boys, dressed in white, as the planets."

These spectacles, then, relied heavily on the complex machines that allowed the staging of

The courtyard was a perfect setting for Renaissance festivals. In 1579 Ammannati's courtyard at Palazzo Pitti was transformed into a tournament ground beneath a canvas ceiling. Ten years later it became an improvised lake for a naumachia organized by Buontalenti, when spectators occupied, not only the tiers of seats beneath the porticoes, but the windows and balconies above. Contemporary engraving by Orazio Scarabelli.

sacre rappresentazioni in the upper reaches of the dome, and nave, and which would become standard stage equipment of the Renaissance and Baroque theater.

"...under a ceiling draped in cerulean blue"

Theater as an exclusively court phenomenon is a sixteenth-century development, yet we have evidence of its origins a hundred years previously.

By the 1450's erudite debate on the Vitruvian theater and how to reconstruct it had raised the question of specific architectural space for plays and spectacles. But while learned humanist coteries in many Italian cities engaged in heated discussions over ambiguous passages in Vitruvius, the practical achievement remained a dream. Not until the late sixteenth century did it come to realization (and then in a non courtly milieu) when Palladio, who had illustrated Daniele Barbaro's edition of Vitruvius, designed the Teatro Olimpico at Vicenza.

Yet, earlier in the century, when Vitruvian scholarship was at its height, architects in Rome and Naples were already turning palace courtyards into permanent, theater sites. Towards the end of the century, before ever Bramante, Raphael and Giuliano da Sangallo had embarked on a similar project for the courtyard of the Belvedere. Giuliano da Maiano built a theater-courtyard at the villa of Poggio Reale, near Naples, with tiered seats (no longer in existence) and porticoes. The project, keenly supported by the Medici Pope Leo X, to include an antique theater in the Villa Madama at Rome was the result of Raphael's collaboration with Fabio Calvo, the antiquarian, topographer and translator of Vitruvius.

Following similar lines, though the site was a public square and not a private courtyard, was the temporary theater erected on the Capitoline Hill in 1513, celebrating the conferment of Roman citizenship on Giuliano and Lorenzo de' Medici. The spectators were protected by an awning, a distant recollection of the *velarium* as seen in the reliefs from the classic monuments of ancient Rome then being copied so assiduously by architects and scholars; there were straight rows of seats at the sides and pictures on the walls. The pattern was to be repeated, and marks a definite milestone – a point of continual reference – in the very slow and complicated evolution of what we today think of as a theater.

But the court spectacle took place, to begin with, in the palace courtyard, great hall or garden; that is, in an already available area, not a theater as such, though from time to time adapted for such a purpose. Of these areas the courtyard most easily accommodated any type of Renaissance revel – feast, play, tilt or tourney, a naumachia or the reception of a guest. A little alteration, and the court had acting-space for the figurative and glorious activities that were part of its cultural image.

The Este and Medici palaces witnessed some of the earliest courtyard spectacles, with Ferrara to the fore in the fifteenth century. Duke Borso d'Este had attended religious and secular festivities with the townsfolk – processions, outdoor *sacre rappresentazioni*, palio races through the streets. But for the Carnival of 1486 Duke Ercole I, as though to inaugurate better days after an anxious period of famine and scarcity, turned the old courtyard of the palace into a theater and had the *Menaechmi* of Plautus given in the vernacular. Again, the following year, the courtyard was turned once more into a temporary theater for performances of Niccolò da Correggio's *Cefalo* and the

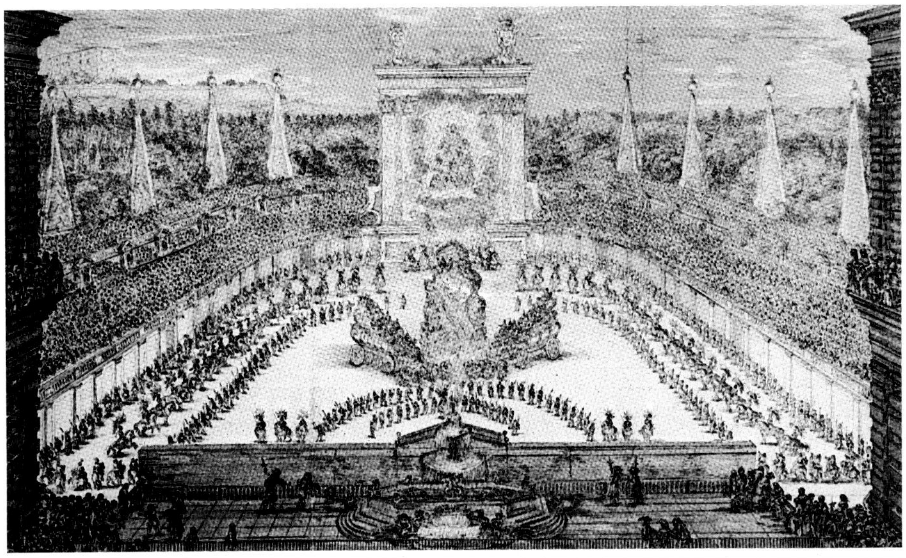

The naumachia for the wedding of Francesco Gonzaga and Margherita of Savoy in 1608, was held on a real lake at Mantua; the engraving (top) is by Paolo Fabbri.
A carousel, or equestrian ballet, was part of the celebrations when Grand Duke Cosimo III married Marguerite Louise of Orléans in 1661. The engraving (above), by Stefano Della Bella, shows the figurations of the ballet round "Mount Atlas" in the amphitheater of the Boboli Gardens.

Amphytrion of Plautus.

Ferrarese diarists, especially Bernardino Zambotti, have left some details of the accommodation arrangements for these spectacles. In 1486 the stage, for example, backed onto the long southern wall, and tiers of wooden seating were "near the Palace Chapel" on the north side. Across the intervening free space the chief actor sailed onto the stage in a ship – a converted wine vat from the ducal cellars. In 1487 an awning stretched overhead, the stage was on one of the short sides, and the tiered seating below the loggia where the duchess sat. There is no evidence that this seating was anything but the time-honoured medieval *gradinata*; and since no decoration of the walls is mentioned we must assume they were bare and not, as for later entertainments, adorned with tapestry and hangings.

Theatrical transformations went on apace at Ferrara. For the wedding of the last duke, Alfonso, to Barbara of Austria in 1565, the court put on what was its favourite pastime, a jousting tournament in the courtyard cum garden of the palace, with a *mise-en-scène* of customary grandeur (previous tournaments had featured the battles of *Castello di Gorgoferusa* and *Monte Feronia*), only this time scene changes were introduced throughout the action to the surprise and wonderment of everyone present.

On two occasions, the garden courtyard of the Medici palace in Florence was converted into a "theater." In 1533, when Charles V's daughter Margaret married Alessandro de' Medici, it was transformed into the archetypal *hortus conclusus* of medieval and Renaissance image: the walled garden with flowers, a tree, a fountain; an Earthly Paradise, *locus ille locorum*, the "place of places," symbol of privacy, to which the elect might withdraw to cultivate their virtues in seclusion.

On the second occasion, in 1539, for the wedding of Cosimo I and Eleonora of Toledo, the courtyard was converted into a sumptuous apartment by Bastiano di Sangallo and the young Giorgio Vasari. On the interior walls hung large pictures, illustrating the glories of the Medici, echoing the theme of Mantegna's *Trionfi* at Mantua, and "under a ceiling draped

The Teatro Medici, in what had been the great hall of the magistrature in the Uffizi, was twice decorated by Buontalenti, in 1586 and 1589. The sketch (left, upper) may be for one of these schemes. Opposite: a recent reconstruction, by the architect C. Lisi, showing the scheme of 1589.

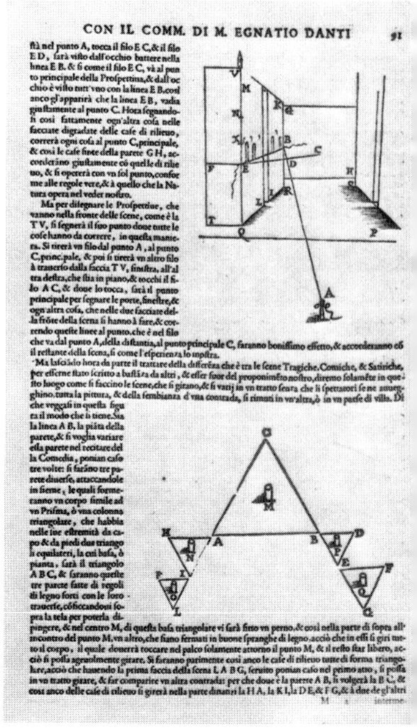

CON IL COMM. DI M. EGNATIO DANTI 91

ſtà nel punto A, tocca il filo E C,& il filo E D, ſarà viſto dall'occhio battere nella linea E B. & ſi come il filo E C, và al punto principale della Proſpettiua,& dall'occhio è viſto tutt'vno con la linea E B.coſi anco gl'apparirà che la linea E B, vada giuſtamente al punto C. Hora ſegnandoſi coſi fattamente ogn'altra coſa nelle facciate digradate delle caſe di rilieuo, correrà ogni coſa al punto C,principale, & coſi le caſe finte della parete G H, accorderãno giuſtamente cõ quelle di rilieuo, & ſi opererà con vn ſol punto,conforme alle regole vere,& à quello che la Natura opera nel veder noſtro.

Ma per diſegnare le Proſpettiue, che vanno nella fronte delle ſcene, come è la T V, ſi ſegnerà il ſuo punto doue tutte le coſe hanno da correre, in queſta maniera. Si tirerà vn filo dal punto A, al punto C,principale, & poi ſi tirerà vn altro filo à trauerſo dalla faccia T V, ſiniſtra, all'altra deſtra,che ſtia in piano,& tocchi il filo A C, & doue lo tocca, ſarà il punto principale per ſegnare le porte,fineſtre,& ogn'altra coſa, che nelle due facciate della frõte della ſcena ſi hanno à fare,& correndo queſte linee al punto.che è nel filo che va dal punto A,della diſtantia,al punto principale C, faranno boniſſimo effetto,& accorderanno cõ il reſtante della ſcena,ſi come l'eſperienza lo inpſtra.

Ma laſciãdo hora da parte il trattare della differẽza che è tra le ſcene Tragiche,Comiche, & Satiriche, per eſſerne ſtato ſcritto a baſtãza da altri, & eſſer fuor del propoñimẽto noſtro,diremo ſolamẽte in queſto luogo come ſi faccino le ſcene,che ſi girano,& ſi varij in vn tratto ſenza che li ſpettatori ſe ne auueghino.tutta la pittura, & della ſembianza d'vna contrada, ſi rimuti in vn'altra,ò in vn paeſe di villa. Di che veggaſi in queſta figura il modo che ſi tiene.Sia la linea A B, la piãta della parete,& ſi voglia variare eſſa parete nel recitare della Comedia, ponian caſo tre volte: ſi farãno tre parete diuerſe, attaccandole in ſieme, le quali formeranno vn corpo ſimile ad vn Priſma, ò vna colonna triangolare, che habbia nelle ſue eſtremità da capo & da piedi due triangoli equilateri, la cui baſa, ò pianta, ſarà il triangolo A B C, & ſaranno queſte tre parete fatte di regoli di legno forti con le loro trauerſe, cõficcandoui ſopra la tela per poterla dipingere, & nel centro M, di queſta baſa triangolare vi ſarà fitto vn perno.& coſi nella parte di ſopra all'incontro del punto M, vn altro,che ſiano fermati in buone ſpranghe di legno.acciò che in eſſi ſi giri tutto il corpo, il quale douerrà toccare nel palco ſolamente attorno il punto M, & il reſto ſtar libero, acciò ſi poſſa agruolmente girare. Si faranno parimente coſi anco le caſe di rilieuo tutte di forma triangolare,acciò che hauendo la prima faccia della ſcena L A B G, ſeruito ponian caſo nel primo atto, ſi poſſa in vn tratto girare, & far comparire vn altra contrada: per che doue è la parete A B, ſi volgerà la B C, & coſi anco delle caſe di rilieuo ſi girerà nella parte dinanzi la H A, la K I, la D E,& F G,& à due de gl'altri

M interme-

Bottom, left: another reconstruction, by Ferdinando Galli, with Buontalenti's 1589 arrangement, and his setting for the second of six intermezzi given during La Pellegrina, *a comedy by Girolamo Bargagli. Above: diagrams of periaktoi – revolving machines for the rapid change of scenery – drawn for Vignola's* Trattato della Prospettiva *by the sixteenth-century architect and mathematician, the Dominican friar Egnazio Danti.*

Above: stage-sketch by Raphael. Gabinetto delle stampe, Uffizi.
Right: Sebastiano Serlio's designs for (top to bottom) comic, tragic and pastoral settings. These settings, from his Secondo libro di prospettiva *(1545) were type models for scenic artists in the sixteenth century.*

in cerulean blue," (intensifying the illusion of seclusion) were suspended a throng of amorous Cupids with bows and arrows. Each Cupid – or so we learn from the historian Pier Francesco Giambullari – had a small light in his hand to illuminate the tiers where the women sat on the longer sides. (Men were on benches in the center.)

The play was *Il Commodo* by Antonio Landi, interspersed with interludes of allegory and music. From a special pavilion the duke and his court gazed across at a stage-prospect of Pisa. Regulated by a truly astounding *ingegno*, the sun rose, shone and sank according to the hour in the plot (humanist playwrights, we remember, adhered to the dramatic unity of time).

Transformation was again the order of the day at the Pitti, newest of the Medici palaces, for the wedding of Francesco I and Bianca Cappello in 1579. On this occasion the courtyard had become a luxurious tournament-ground where "hostile" forces, separated by a barrier (hence the title of the event, *La Sbarra*) jousted with bated lances. But *La Sbarra* was less a contest than an ultra-Mannerist display of the most diverse elements – joust, carousel, combat and pageants of allegory and myth. It was punctuated by literary readings, choruses and madrigals. Spectators watched from seated accommodation in the side porticoes and numerous lamps hung from the galleries and from an artificial sky, lighting up the scene below.

Ten years later, when Grand Duke Ferdinando I married Christina of Lorraine, the same courtyard was flooded for a naumachia. The mock sea fight, of European tradition, with carts camouflaged as ships, was new to Florence; but at the Pitti few innovations were introduced, save that Bernardo Buontalenti, who was in charge, seated the spectators at the windows and on the balconies as well as under the porticoes.

More radical by far was the decision by the Grand Duke Ferdinando II to celebrate his wedding to Vittoria Della Rovere in 1637 with the performance of a *favola cantata* or musical play in the open air, unprecedented for a work of this type. The libretto, aptly entitled *Le*

nozze degli Dei (Wedding of the Gods), was by the abbot Giovan Carlo Coppola, the staging by Alfonso Parigi, whose father Giulio designed theater apparatus for almost every spectacle in Florence in the first decades of the seventeenth century.

Parigi drew upon a technical repertoire going back nearly a hundred years, to the courtyard of the old Medici palace in Via Larga. He situated a huge proscenium arch against the Boboli garden wall, with seating in the central courtyard space, while a dais for the bridal pair and guests of honour communicated with the private ducal apartments. (This plan, common to court theaters, persists in the modern theater, with private access to the boxes and an anteroom behind the royal box.) The remainder of the onlookers sat in a tiered crescent, or at the windows and behind balustrades. Decoratively and architecturally, what Parigi did clearly suggests the Baroque, operatic theater as it was developing in other towns of Italy; a theater, not for a restricted court audience, but for a wider, paying public.

At Florence, then, the idea of the separate theater evolved by way of synthesis and integration. Served by artists who were to father the imaginative, fantastic local school of Mannerism, the Medici court outstripped its rivals; the Florentine ideal of a theater was the accepted model and standard of comparison.

Above: engraving from the Itinerarium Italiae *(1628) of Joseph Furttenbach, an architect and stage designer who here combines Florentine reminiscence with stage scenery.*

"... to deck the hall where we shall be feasting"

During the sixteenth century theatricals came in from the courtyard to a room or hall of the palace. And though the quadrangle, with its semicircle of seats, had been exactly what Vitruvius recommended – four equilateral triangles, base and height respectively giving stage-length and auditorium-depth, and which could be inscribed in a circle – it was the rectangular hall with seats in an elongated horseshoe, which set a pattern little modified until the beginning of the eighteenth century.

In the hall the prince, with his courtiers and guest of honour, had a dais or box in the middle of the floor, and his was the viewpoint chosen

"Tragic Setting," by BaldassarePeruzzi. Siena, Istituto di Belle Arti.
The perspectival scenery of the period might be imaginary, or of real places: the design (opposite) by Baldassare Lanci for Giovanbattista Cini's La vedova *(1569) depicts the Piazza della Signoria in Florence.*

for descriptions of the spectacle, since on him converged the perspective sight-lines of the backdrop. The decorative theme would embrace the whole room, ceiling, walls and stage. Often the signs of the zodiac shed benevolent influence from above. Painted greenery, as in Leonardo's fresco of ilex leaves for the sala delle Asse in the Castello Sforzesco at Milan, entwined with natural wreaths and festoons to evoke a garden.

On the walls glowed hangings and gorgeous tapestries. The Trojan War series woven for the Duke of Mantua was so immediately famous that Francesco Gonzaga begged it for his wedding to Isabella d'Este in 1490; "to deck the hall where we shall be feasting," as he wrote to Guidobaldo da Montefeltro, requesting the loan. Or there would be enormous pictures, pleasing mementoes of family achievement – family *condottieri* at their dashing exploits, or the capture of subject cities. The heroes of antiquity, with the attributes of demigods, appeared in meaningful allegory. (Six of Mantegna's *Triumphs of Caesar* were on display – and never to better political purpose – at the Mantuan carnival of 1501.) Emblematic mottoes ran the length of the room at ceiling level, others in letters or words picked out by well-placed candelabra, candles and torches. Thus, for Cardinal Bibbiena's play, *La Calandria*, at Urbino in 1513, the motto DELICIAE POPULI was a well publicized feature of the decorations. But a never failing target of attention was a platform, giving access to two doors for the entrance and exits of actors and technicians; for these were the magicians who made it all possible.

At Milan Leonardo prepared his great stage machines for the festivals of the Sforza – a succession of dance, theatrical illusion, allegorical and mythological wonderlands created by technology. The tradition of the medieval *ingegni* (revived by Brunelleschi towards the end of the fifteenth century) still held good: mountains moved, the heavens spun, and acrobats flew through the air. But in his *Festa del Paradiso* of 1490, the like of which for splendour and brilliance surpassed anything ever seen before, the Florentine master, peopling the stage with mythological divinities and

zodiacal figures, linking the allegorical, the astrological and the sacred, further enhanced the mystery and magic by the device of a "cloth of satin," precursor of the modern drop curtain, which concealed everything before dropping to reveal the wondrous spectacle.

The by now inevitable play was the most eagerly anticipated of entertainents at any major court festival. The mise-en-scène of the Renaissance theater demanded an ever-increasing sophistication in the treatment of background scenery, a mixture of the real and the imaginary. Gone was the simple, frontal, medieval conception of stagecraft, the scenery was of cities, part real, part imaginary, ever more varied. As the taste for perspective grew, the stage effects became more pronounced, requiring the painted buildings to be aligned with the stage diagonals.

The historian Ludovico Zorzi has suggested (1985) that the "Ideal City" – an image pursued in the abstract by utopians and practically, as the city-state, by politicians – is here being transferred to the sphere of make-believe. Having no place in the real world, it enters that of the theater, as scenery. In the earliest perspective scene-drawings (urban backcloths for Latin comedies), the city is a collection of buildings symbolizing Rome. Rome had been The City of medieval iconography: Rome personifying Italy in Cimabue's fresco at Assisi; Rome of the pilgrims' guidebooks, the *Mirabilia Urbis*; Rome on commemorative medals. For scene-designers, from Peruzzi in a pioneer sketch preserved in the Uffizi, to Bastiano da Sangallo and, later, Vasari and Baldassare Lanci, it was the Ideal City still.

The Roman experience of these first great theater artists resulted in a reciprocating influence and what might be called master-pupil relationships. Peruzzi, for instance, bequeathed plans and drawings to Serlio, who had studied with him in Rome, and on them Serlio based the second book of his *Architettura* on the theater, published at Paris in 1545. In the same way, Florence is a link between Bastiano da Sangallo, Giorgio Vasari and Bernardo Buontalenti.

It was thanks to the architectonic innovations of these artist-engineers that the rest of Europe

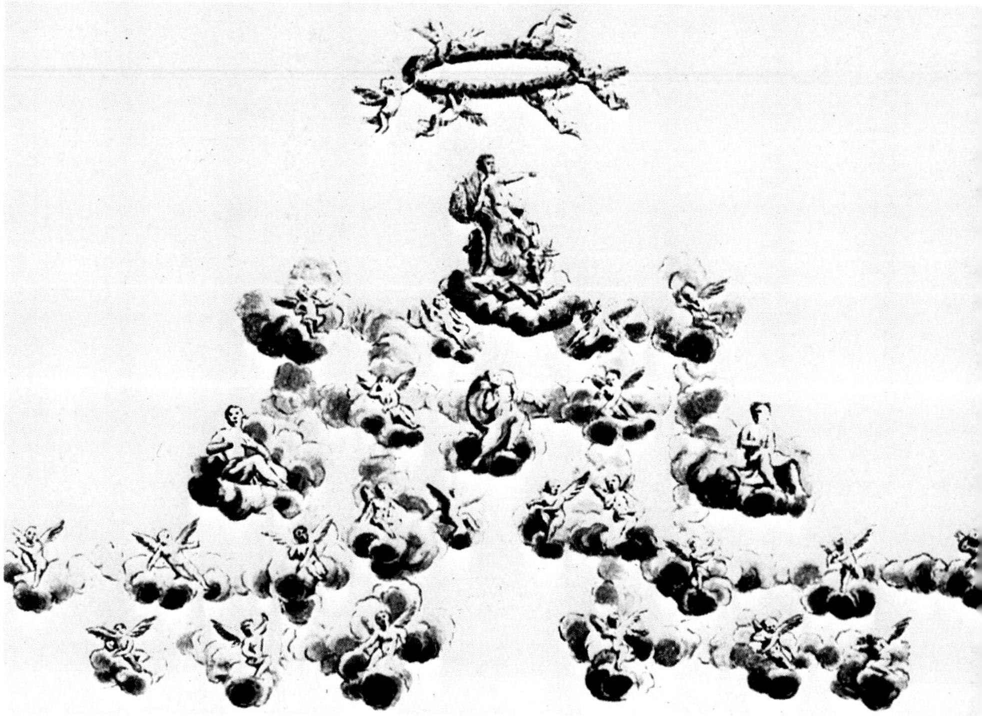

came to accept the *scena fissa*, or permanent set which evolved, in step with stylistic and technical advances, in more than one Italian center during the early sixteenth century: it was known simply as "Italian scenery."

"The scene was of a very handsome city, with streets, palaces, churches, towers, actual street-entrances, and everything *in relief*" – our italics – "the more so because of the excellent painting and masterly perspective." Thus Castiglione writes to his friend Ludovico Canossa of the stage design for *La Calandria* at Urbino in 1513. In a prologue the author, Cardinal Bernardo Dovizi da Bibbiena, had said in so many words, "what you see is Rome, and here Rome is small enough . . . to fit into this town of yours." The *Calandria* at Urbino, with its scenery, is another milestone for scholars, marking the birth of the Italian theater; as Voltaire agreed, it can be seen as "modern Italy's first play."

A literary and social event of the utmost importance, it was important too for its perspective "in relief," the "excellent painting" of Girolamo Genga adding to the three-dimensional effect. His setting surpassed both the *picturatae scenae faciem* mentioned by Sulpicius Verulanus in his dedication to Raffaele Riario of the first printed edition of Vitruvius,

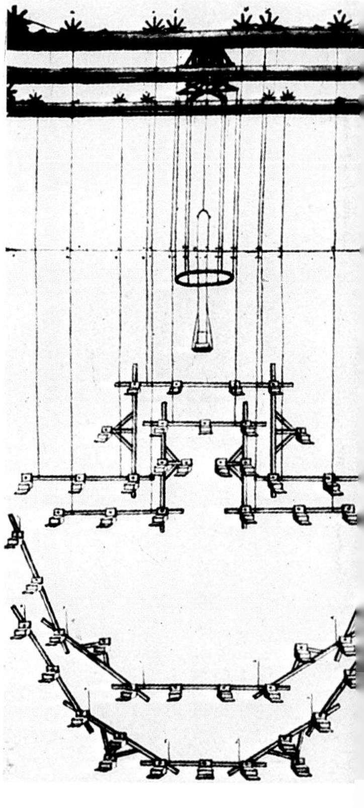

The Ferrarese engineer-architect and poet, Francesco Guitti, came to Parma in 1627 to prepare the stage macchine *and settings for the wedding celebrations of Odoardo Farnese and Margherita de' Medici. A* Tournament of Mercury and Mars *was presented, with music by Monteverdi, at the court theater, and a series of drawings shows some of the mechanisms that produced enthralling and wondrous effects.*

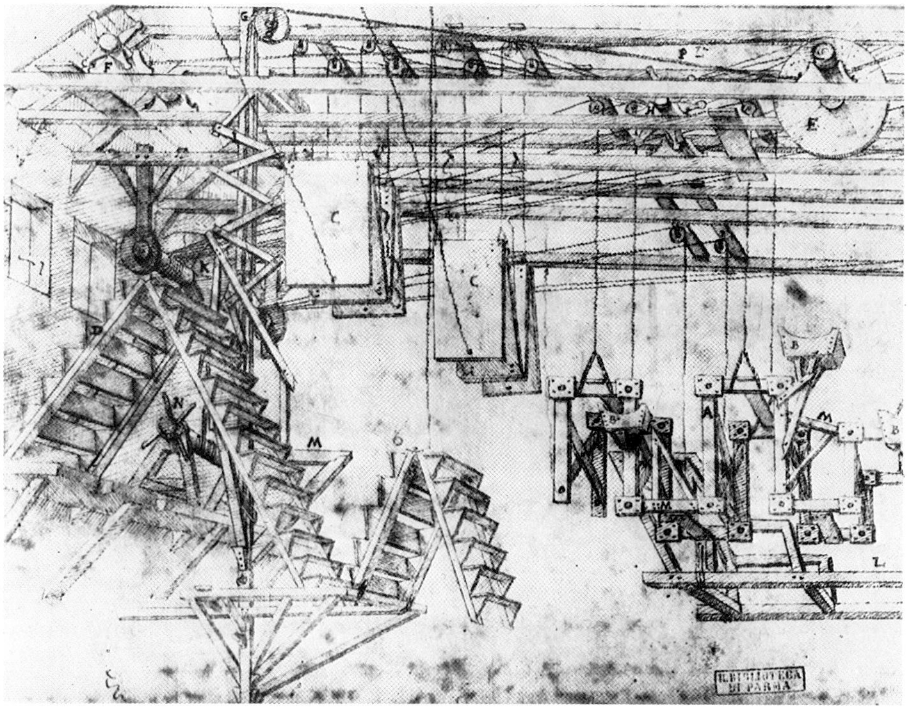

and the perspective backcloth for Ariosto's *Cassaria* painted by Pellegrino da Udine at Ferrara in 1508. It must have been nearer to Raphael's design for Ariosto's *I Suppositi* in Rome (a drawing for which is in the Uffizi,) or Baldassare Peruzzi's for later performances of *La Calandria*. Vasari, the first to put Baldassare's designs into practice, thought them "marvellous" and "the source of what has been done in our own day."

At the wedding of Francesco de' Medici and Joanna of Austria in 1565, and again when the Archduke Charles, her brother, visited Florence in 1569, it was Vasari who prepared the Salone dei Cinquecento in the Palazzo Vecchio for the usual play. The *gradinate* at the sides, "as in an antique theater," were made, like modern units, in sections, and the scenery had all the up-to-date features – an architrave connecting two lateral framing columns, a street-scene in perspective, *periaktoi* (rotating machines working, perhaps, as a cyclorama) and lighting refracted and multiplied by coloured water in chandeliers and crystal bowls. (This had been Leonardo's method, and would be popular for many years.)

With modern technical progress and a growing demand for drama, every court saw the

Opposite, top: a sketch for the "Entrance of Venus," with (bottom) a working diagram. Note the folding supports for the seats of the goddess's attendants, the support for her chariot, the coronal over her head, and the powerful winch that moved it all.
Left: machinery for the "Entry of the Attendants of Mars and Venus." Above: machinery installed over the stage of the theater at Parma.

STATE ENTRY INTO FLORENCE OF THE ARCHDUCHESS MARIA MAGDALENA, BRIDE OF COSIMO II

In 1608, a year before the death of the Grand Duke Ferdinando I, his son Cosimo married the Habsburg archduchess Maria Magdalena. The bride's father was the Archduke Charles of Austria and Styria, her brother the future Emperor Ferdinand II. Twenty-one when she came to Florence, she was to bear her husband eight children and, outliving him by 16 years, would rule, bigotted and autocratic, as co-regent with her mother-in-law, Christina of Lorraine. The splendour of her state entry is recorded in the print (2) executed by Matteo Greuter for the Marchese di Campiglia, *'Maggior Duomo maggiore* of His Most Serene Highness the Grand Duke of Tuscany."

There were five triumphal arches on the route from the city gates to Palazzo Pitti. Maria Magdalena was received by the grand duke at the Porta al Prato, where "His Highness, with the most reverend bishop of Fiesole, placed the crown on her head" (5). On the first arch, in Borgo Ognissanti, "the noble city, *Firenze Fiorenza*, rejoiced, with the rivers of Danube and Arno, at her advent." An arch at the Medici church of San Lorenzo displayed "pictures and statues" of Habsburg emperors related to the Medici by marriage, and figures of the bridal couple. "The arch erected at the Paglia was adorned with pictures and statues of the dukes of Bavaria, maternal kin to the Most Serene Lady." Finally, the last two arches were reserved for the glorification of Cosimo's equally illustrious genealogy. First, in

1

3

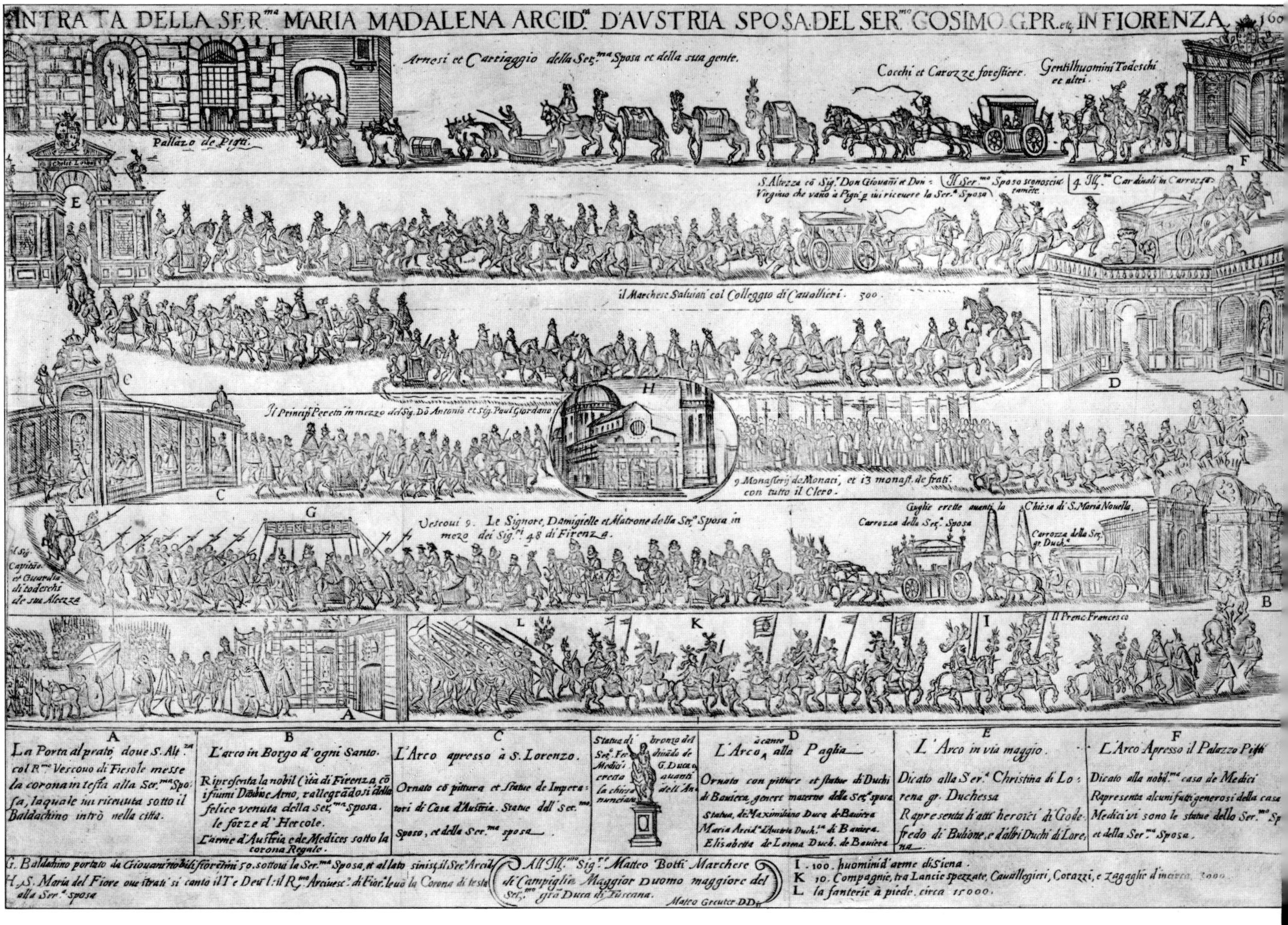

2

compliment to the Most Serene Grand Duchess Christina, his mother, the arch in Via Maggio (1) showed the ancestral deeds of Godfrey de Bouillon, the crusader who conquered Jerusalem, "and of other Dukes of Lorraine;" and on the final arch, at Palazzo Pitti, were "sundry liberalities" of the Most Noble House of Medici. Two square-based obelisks, or *guglie*, were

erected in front of the church of Santa Maria Novella, and all these short-lived structures, with their perishable wax, clay or *papier-mâché* images, were, naturally, executed by the best artists that could be found. (Did not the young Michelangelo – or so it was said – model a statue in snow for the Medici of his day?)

The ceremonial entry had its practical aspect. As at any great marriage, the lady was being removed, with suite and possessions, to a new and distant home, and so the convoy included "the goods and baggage of the Most Serene bride and her people." Yoked oxen hauled trunks on sledges, mules with nodding plumes bore laden pack-saddles, These were, records the same Matteo Greuter, "coaches and foreign carriages with German gentlemen, with four illustrious Cardinals and, on horseback, His Most Serene Highness, the bridegroom, incognito."

There was a halt at the cathedral for the singing of the Te Deum. The archbishop took the crown from Maria Magdalena's head and, emerging, she mounted a horse for the remainder of the journey (4). The baldacchino above her was borne by young Florentine nobles, her German guard and its captain preceded her, and immediately behind were nine bishops, the ladies

4

5

6 of her household, and 48 gentlemen of Florence. Immediately behind them (6) was her empty coach (drawn by four horses) and, also empty, that of the Grand Duchess of Tuscany (drawn by a pair). The clergy, secular and regular, were present without exception – nine monasteries of monks, thirteen of friars, with their banners (3); and the nobility followed up, a band of knights, under the Marchese Salviati, attending the grand duke's carriage as he went to meet the bride. There was a large body of troops: 100 mounted knights from Siena (7), with cuirasses and crested helms, and pennons on their

7 lances; "ten companies of lancers, light horse, cuirassiers and spearmen," and some 15,000 foot soldiers.

Maria Magdalena's procession is a concrete example of the court parade as civic pageant, The *rappresentazione*, the whole ceremonial programme and setting with which the city fathers in the fifteenth and sixteenth centuries greeted the distinguished visitor, or their lord on his accession, or his bride on her arrival, still hinges on the life of the court.

need for a permanent playhouse; and provisional Renaissance staging in the great hall culminates, in the 1580's, in three glorious but dissimilar theaters, each with a different cultural background – the Teatro Olimpico at Vicenza, the Teatro Olimpico at Sabbioneta, and the Teatro Mediceo in Florence.

Court entertainment, we should not forget, also comprised private entertainment – less solemn, less magnificent, than the official festivity addressed to purely political ends, and requiring no "official" space. Courtiers in private indulged in the elegant pastimes and amusements consummately portrayed in Castiglione's *Il Cortegiano*. They enjoyed short verse interludes, eclogues and pastorals; they adored dancing, and could consult authorities on the subject from Domenico da Piacenza and Guglielmo Ebreo in the fifteenth century to Marco Fabrizio Caroso, author of *Il Ballarino* in the sixteenth century.

Then there were the Zanni, or *Comice dell' Arte*, companies of professional comedians privately engaged. Scarcely a day goes by but they are mentioned by the diarists of the later sixteenth century, acting in the private apartments of a palace with a minimum of props and scenery, or in hired rooms. The prince himself would go to see them, sitting, where possible, behind a grille where he and his friends could savour, unobserved, the lewd gestures and pungent impromptu dialogue of the "intimate" comedy, for which there was no written text.

The Zanni are heard of in town after town of Italy from the 1550's onwards. Famous troupes, such as the Comici Gelosi, led by Francesco and Isabella Andreini, were at times permitted to play at the big court theaters, when they received valuable tokens from the prince, over and above what he paid them. Actresses received costly dress materials, the men gold chains. An exceptionally pleased and generous sovereign might bestow gold medals with his arms stamped on them, signs of signal favour, and favourable testimonials which could be produced anywhere when contracts were negotiated.

Often the prince in person was patron, employer and manager of a company. The Gon-

In 1569, a naumachia in honour of the Archduke Charles of Austria was given in the moat at Ferrara, near the Montagnola. Its theme was the Isola Beata, *and the Marchese Bentivoglio, an expert in hydraulics, collaborated with the painter-architect Pirro Ligorio on machinery for the spectacular transformations. Above: one of Ligorio's drawings of this festival (Ferrara, Biblioteca Civica). Opposite:* The Contest of the Four Seasons, *an equestrian ballet in the courtyard of the ducal palace at Modena in 1652. Contemporary engraving by Stefano Della Bella.*

Costume design by Vasari, or one of his associates, for the Buffalo event in Florence in 1566 for the wedding of the hereditary prince Francesco. These masquerades were held in Piazza Santa Croce – the public space most often used for civic celebrations – and preceded by a procession of chariots and people in costume through the city streets.

zaga, for example, may claim to be the first impresarios; certainly Duke Vincenzo qualifies. From their substantial correspondence with fellow-rulers, and the letters that poured in from actors, it is evident that Mantua in the sixteenth century was the Mecca of the Commedia dell'Arte, not only in Italy, but in Europe as a whole.

The prince at the theater

With the ever-widening ramifications of dramatic entertainment, the permanent theater which as we have seen had already made its appearance in arcaded courtyards, gathered momentum by leaps and bounds. And – a further advantage – the *apparati* or stage props, hitherto designed for at most a few nights' entertainment could, of course, be stored away, and deployed again and again.

Yet progress towards a settled court theater should be seen in context, for theaters, of various dates and styles, were already built in towns under non princely rule. A loggia-version of the Roman *frons scaena* was designed by Giovan Maria Falconetto in Alvise Cornaro's garden at Padua in 1524; finished in 1585, to Andrea Palladio's plans, was the Teatro Olimpico for the Accademia at Vicenza. The court meanwhile, certainly until the second half of the century, was content with the refurbishing, temporary though sumptuous, of a space in the palace.

Theater settings were for special exhibition; theater decoration was put on, like a suit of clothes, for ceremony. To have a permanent theater was to restate claims to wealth and dominance. The prince who possessed one intended to inspire, in other princes, awe and admiration and to augment his fame in the world.

In the earliest examples, with their synthesis of previous "theater spaces," the most significant changes were, as before, in the stage itself; and Ferrara, Modena and Mantua were first in the field.

Little is recorded of the theater built at Ferrara to Ariosto's specifications, save that his *Lena* and *Cassari* were acted, as was a play in

The Judgement of Paris by Michelangelo Buonarroti il Giovane, Michelangelo's nephew, was presented at the theater in the Uffizi on 25 October 1608, for the wedding of Cosimo de' Medici. Incorporated as fourth intermezzo was an episode by Giovan Battista Strozzi, its subject the arrival of Amerigo Vespucci in the West Indies. The poet and dramatist Ottaviano Rinuccini, describing the entertainment, says that after the landing there appeared a cloud which opened to reveal the Almighty, seated on a globe and flanked by Fame and Glory. To one side were Apollo and the Nine Muses; on the other an historical collection of poets who sang a chorus in the navigator's honour. The cloud continued to move, the rock began to sink into the waves; everything vanished and the scene changed to Mount Ida, where shepherds performed the fourth act of the play. The etching is of Giulio Parigi's setting for the intermezzo.

the Paduan dialect by Angelo Boelco (or "Ruzzante", as he was known, after his peasant soldier-hero). It burned down in 1532, and the loss is said to have sent Ariosto to an early grave. In 1551 the theater in the riding school at Mantua (built by Giovan Battista Bertani, pupil of Giulio Romano), was also damaged by fire – inevitably the constant peril for these wooden structures – but it was both repaired and improved.

It may appear strange to find a permanent court theater installed in a location like a riding school. But the great hall is left to its own functions and instead is chosen an adequate vacant space: disused manège, ball court or granary. The former names were preserved in the Teatro della Cavallerizza at Mantua, the Teatro della Spelta (a kind of wheat) at Modena and the Teatro della sala del Ballone at Reggio Emilia, though this last was not, properly speaking, a court theater. It was, however, patronized by the Este court on visits to the town and details in the official *descrizione*, printed soon after its inauguration in 1568, help in the descriptive details of other, contemporary theaters. Stage and auditorium were conceived as one, with no dividing arch or stage framework. The realms of fact and fancy merged as one, as did actors and the audience; and above them both, to emphasize the unity, stretched the familiar, azure blue artificial sky.

For the most part the permanent court theater still harked back to the porticoed courtyard given over to a single performance, and three of this type are still extant, fascinating and, perhaps, strange to modern eyes: the Teatro Olimpico at Sabbioneta, the Teatro Farnese at Parma, and the superb Olimpico at Vicenza (though the latter, finished, as we have noted, to Palladio's plans after his death, was not for a court, but an Academy, and so falls outside the scope of this book). Of others we have very full descriptions, and there has recently been an architect's reconstruction of the Teatro Medico in the Uffizi.

In 1588 Vincenzo Scamozzi, having completed his theatrical apprenticeship by adding the perspective stage-set at Vicenza, built the Teatro Olimpico at Sabbioneta. This miniature town was the attempt of Vespasiano Gonzaga, who died in 1591, to achieve, in Mannerist idiom, that hundred-year-old dream of the humanists, the rationally-ordered Ideal City; and since, in humanist theory, the seats of religious and civil power were to be spatially related and in harmony with the neighbouring architecture, the theater of Sabbioneta is near the church and palace, new and independent.

In it the genius of Scamozzi brings together every contributory element of the permanent theater, yet with intimations that this small Gonzaga state was a shade behind the times. Heeding the past rather than the present, it remains in essence a courtyard, three sides of which are treated as palace façades. Loggie, balustrades and perspective, fresco views of Rome on the walls, foster the illusion. His auditorium is in classical tiers, with a peristyle of wood and painted stucco. The stage is slightly raked, and there is no proscenium arch; the perspective and painting of the scenery were a composite derivation from the tragic, comic and satiric settings in the treatise of his beloved master, Serlio. On the architrave of the peristyle are gods and heroes, repeating the perennial theme of praise for the princely ruler. The spectators were apparently in a roofed courtyard, looking into a piazza and a street-perspective; above, as in the theater of Reggio Emilia,

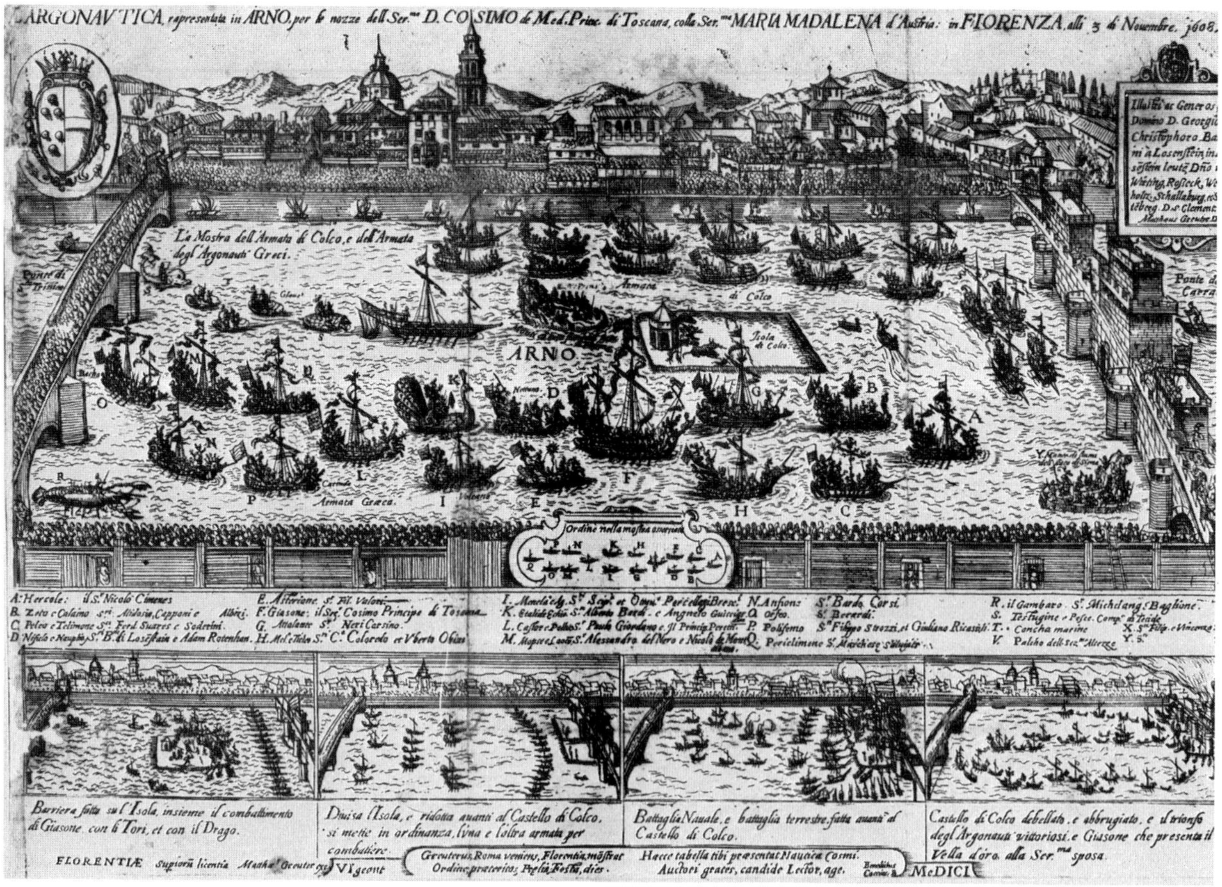

The Argonautica *on 3 November 1608, part of the wedding celebrations for Cosimo de' Medici. It was held on the Arno, between the Santa Trinità and Carraia bridges, its theme the battle of Jason with the inhabitants of Colchis for the Golden Fleece. Preliminary designs were by Jacopo Ligozzi, Ludovico Cogoli and the versatile Giulio Parigi (who, as architect and theater artist, with an official position at court, exercised enormous influence on Florentine taste, especially through the plays and spectacles at the Teatro Medici.) The fantastic ensemble is recorded in Matteo Greuter's engraving (left).*

was the hanging sky-ceiling, the *cielo finto di rovesci*.

Sad to say, this beautiful theater had a less than remarkable stage history. It was used briefly, and always by Commedia dell'Arte troupes, better accustomed to treading improvised boards in palace halls or rented rooms, *stanzoni di soldo*. (In Florence Buontalenti was even then busy building quarters for them – the "Baldracca", named after a street of ill-fame behind the Uffizi and the Teatro Mediceo itself.)

The decisive step towards the permanent Teatro Mediceo had been taken when a large rectangular space was designated in the Uffizi, within easy reach of Palazzo della Signoria, as the site for a theater. The project antedates 1574, the year of Vasari's death, since this theater area is shown on his plans, with such practical minutiae as the slope of the auditorium. ("So that people in front should not impede the view of those behind," wrote Giovan Antonio Rossi in his *descrizione*). Bernardo Buontalenti, Vasari's collaborator in many plays and spectacles, was entrusted by the grand duke with the completion of the decor and technical equipment.

There were two distinct decorative programmes. One, for the marriage of the grand duke's half-sister in 1586, suggested a wooded garden, half natural, half counterfeit, with live birds and real fruit in the trees and self-propelling mechanical small creatures. This was the "naturalism," neither true science nor illusion, peculiar to the atmosphere surrounding Francesco I, of which the architect Buontalenti was the most subtle and sympathetic interpreter.

For the disposition of 1589, unaltered thereafter, Buontalenti retained the horseshoe form of six ascending rows of seating, but substituted for his woodland scheme an architectural decor agreeable to the tastes and cultural preferences of the new grand duke. On the first evening of the festivities in celebration of the wedding of Ferdinando and Christina of Lorraine, scenery

Above: the ship of the Argonaut Asterion, protected by Jupiter Tonans, in an engraving by Remigio Cantagallina.

and walls were masked, when the audience arrived, in neutral-coloured drapery which, having concentrated everybody's attention, was gradually withdrawn. In niches along the walls, between the arches of a colonnade through which were glimpsed illusionistic distances, stood large statues on tall pedestals. Once they would have been of demigods and heroes, but it was enough, these days, for the duke to contemplate his political ascendancy in the city of Florence on the stage. The new personifications had a fresher significance and were, indeed, more intellectually stimulating: Old and New Comedy, Invention, Beauty, Eloquence, Painting and their subordinates, lined the theater from doors to stage.

The wood of walls and seating was convincingly painted in imitation of the rare marbles and many-coloured *pietre dure* of Florentine mosaic, to look solid and enduring. For here, as at Sabbioneta, the spectator was supposed to feel that he sat in an airy porticoed quadrangle, facing the world of fantasy conjured up before him. Among fictive precious marbles and bright, gilded reliefs, beguiled by the allegory of sculpture and the music of the *intermezzi* (those predecessors of opera), he could share, enraptured, in the glorious cultural supremacy of the Florentine court.

The Teatro Farnese at Parma, for all its progressive seventeenth-century style, has echoes of the architectural traditions of Vicenza, Sabbioneta and the Teatro Mediceo. It was begun by Giovan Battista Aleotti in the *salle d'armes* of the Palazzo della Pilotta in 1618, and opened ten years later. The horseshoe of tiered seats is crowned by two rows of distinguished Serlian, or "Venetian," arches and is of exceptional length – nearly 90 meters. This redoubles the area available for the play and adds a dimension to the action, which could spill over into the horseshoe from the stage. Two triumphal arches, separating stage and auditorium and emphasizing the entire composition, were references, within the theater space, to the urban space outdoors, as if symbolically echoing the public homage of the streets.

The most tremendous and extravagant stage effects, well-suited to the exhibitionist pomp and splendour of a seventeenth-century court, were produced here by the most complicated machines. Beyond the new-style proscenium arch each magnificent "miraculous" change was more elaborate than the last. The whole spectacular Baroque theater stems from Aleotti's revolutionary stage space at Parma; and Baroque spectacle was moving from the privileged and restricted milieu of the court to the modern, public theaters then developing in Italy.

But at court, within the palace, the permanent theater had proved to be yet another jealously-reserved corner, to be protected and defended. Admission was strictly by invitation and the properly-bidden guest had to show his ticket – often a porcelain disc with the ruler's arms on it – or be identified by gentlemen, if not by the ruler himself, at the entrance. An astonished visitor from Urbino wrote in 1586 that he had seen "His Highness in person (the Grand Duke Francesco I) at the doors for hours on end, letting people in and ensuring they were comfortable. And, heaven knows, he could have spared himself the trouble, for these Florentines are ill-tempered and ill-mannered beyond belief." Entrances to the square in front of the palace were even patrolled by a mounted guard, to ward off any potential intruder who might get in and desecrate the precincts, or threaten the security of those within, we are told by the same visitor.

That night in 1586, when *L'Amico Fido*, by Count Giovanni Bardi, was given at the Teatro Mediceo for the wedding of Francesco's half-sister Virginia, the grand duke delayed the play, says the diarist Francesco Settimani, by going through the offices of the town magistrature "beneath the theatre" – which was on the second storey of the east wing. "The rooms, the cabinets, shelves, boxes, writing desks and everything else were unlocked and examined, as he thought explosives could have been planted there to blow up the theater during the performance . . . Having seen it all, he had the doors secured again and returned to his seat;

Below, and opposite: three examples from a large and extremely well-documented collection of stage and costume designs by Giorgio Vasari and his collaborators for The Genealogy of the Gods, *a masquerade held in Florence on 21 February 1566 for the marriage of Francesco de' Medici and Joanna of Austria. There were 265 performers and 21 elaborately decorated cars or chariots.*

and soon the play could start."

The Medici court, politically and culturally dominant in the sixteenth century, was also unrivalled in the art of court spectacle. Its fêtes and lavish celebrations were the most admired and, naturally, the most copied, in respect of which an unequalled amount of literary and iconographical evidence remains – enough to furnish a comprehensive survey of Renaissance theater and entertainment. Modes of festivities elaborated by other courts became, in Mannerist Florence, vehicles of the boldest stylistic and aesthetic innovation, unimaginably subtle and elegant. It is impossible to overestimate the importance of Florence and the magnificence of the Florentine tradition in Italian theater history.

A general picture of the fêtes, and not those of Florence alone, may be gathered from the printed *descrizioni*. The *descrizione*, something between a report and a learned essay, was commissioned by the princely host (for whom its circulation had immediate political value), and offered rich detail for the reader. Considerably inflated in the telling, any happening that touched the life of the court – parade or solemn entry, feast or funeral – was officially divulged to other courts. These descriptions were to be, in a way, manuals and guidebooks for those who, whether courtiers or not, founded associations, clubs, and academies, dedicated to the theater. Everywhere in the seventeenth century the "lower" model tends to prevail over the "higher" – in this case the popular over the court theater. And yet, while the process is apparent in architecture and scenography, the image of the higher, court theater suffers no real diminution.

In that century, what had been sovereign dominions lost political and economic independence and the intellectual and social climate changed; the theater, naturally, changed as well. There was less and less need for the private theater and it was *melodramma*, with its mingling of spectacle and emotion, that reconciled the response of the one and the many. *Melodramma*, the dramatic union of music and poetry, is the last product of the courtly culture and with it theater, as a public institution, enters a new chapter of its history.

A design by Alessandro Allori (also for The Genealogy of the Gods*) of the Chariot of Heaven. Drawing in black pencil and wash. Florence, Biblioteca Moreniana.*

Theater of prince and people

On street, piazza and sometimes river, the city, in its public spaces, was the scene of popular spectacle that involved all ranks of society, as originators or onlookers. Palio races, religious or secular processions, jousts, masques, football games, stone-throwing contests or tournaments, the festive occasion, especially when decreed and supervised by the court, was a mixture of the popular and the learned, uproar and refinement, spontaneity and calculated grandeur, which the prince of a city-state could exploit very profitably. His presence exalted the proceedings which in turn mesmerized the visitor. And this combination of mass-junketing and diplomacy, with all the trappings of a fairy tale, and crammed with erudition (thus replicating the thought and aspirations of the governing class), was either a regular, recurring extravaganza – for Carnival, or the local saint's-day – or some nonrepeatable, particular celebration.

The palio, with its prize, an actual "palio" – a banner or length of rich material – was a medieval inheritance in several Italian towns. As a rule it was a horse or donkey race, and if an Este duke competed he entered his Barbery steeds. The Este passion for horseflesh made the St George's Day palio at Ferrara the most competitive of fifteenth-century festivals; the more so when other famous studs, such as that of the Gonzaga, were contending. Bloodstock earned a large proportion of the state revenue; the race was a perfect shop window, especially when it attracted the best from other famous studs, and victory did wonders for the court image. It was victory or nothing on the day; in the case of runners-up it was a sucking-pig for second place, a cockerel for third.

There were also "joke" palios – one is depicted in the Schifanoia frescoes – where the jockeys were small boys on donkeys, or perched high on Barbery horses; or – it was that sort of sadistic joke, – they might be naked Jews, or prostitutes. In Duke Borso's reign banners awarded for the minor events would be in the Este colours – white for the donkey races, red for the male riders, green for women. Ferrara was in holiday array as seen in Cossa's fresco, while official decoration, costumes and settings were in the hands of Sagramoro, Cosmé, Tura and similar artists.

Under Lorenzo the Magnificent the sumptuous processions, jousts and masquerades in Florence were inspired by the Republic's notions of civic pomp and ceremony and, stunning as the costumes were, spectacle was the thing. Tradition, retailed by Vasari and Antonio Grazzini (the playright "Il Lasca"), has it that Lorenzo himself invented the masquerade: parades of allegorical floats through the city's streets to the accompaniment of carnival songs. From the 1450s onwards the St John's Day processions, which took place on 24 June, feast day of the city's patron saint, had been a kind

Vincenzo Scamozzi was to realize the humanist dream of a theater in its own right. His court theater at Sabbioneta – that complete "ideal city" of the late sixteenth century – was rectangular, with tiered wooden seating and a colonnaded loggia surmounted by twelve statues of classical divinities (opposite). The original permanent scene was destroyed in the nineteenth century, and there were, originally, separate entrances to the auditorium for the ducal family, gentlemen and ladies.

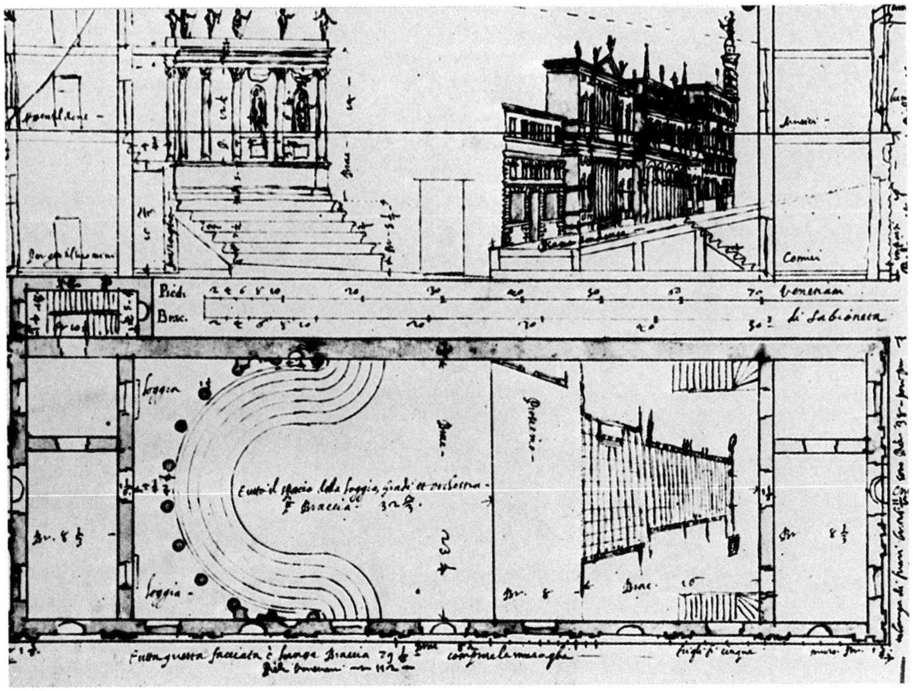

Above: a plan of the theater, drawn by the architect, and sent by letter to Vespasiano Gonzaga, duke of Sabbioneta.

The statues on the colonnade at Sabbioneta both flattered the prince and suited the antiquarian taste of an audience which liked to feel it was in a classical theater. Yet by this time the eternal symbolic praise of the ruler at feast and festival was beginning to seem incongruous and excessive. For instance, one notes the change of tone in a letter, written in 1592, soon after this theater was built, by Baldassare Castiglione il Giovane to Duke Vincenzo Gonzaga about the decoration of the theater at Mantua: "I should tell Your Highness what the artists have decided . . . of the 14 figures, the 12 on the wall are to be portraits of our 12 Princes . . .
I myself turned down the idea of the Twelve Caesars, whom one finds everywhere . . . As for the two canvases, figures of Mantua and of Virgil may be executed later, and thus we shall keep to our own local glories."

of ambulatory theater, with ingenious constructions depicting episodes from the Old and New Testaments. Lorenzo supplemented these *edifici* with the triumphal cars, or *trionfi*, that were the pride of court pageantry. It was at his suggestion that the *compania* of the Star organized its Triumph of the Consul Aemilius Paulus in 1491, a procession of fifteen floats; and this, Vasari said, was the best of the *galanterie* to which the artist Francesco Granacci "so greatly contributed."

For jousting, another medieval exercise, contestants rode to the piazza by a prescribed public route. The objectives varied, and the game might be riding at the ring, riding at the quintain (the figure of a Saracen, or a tilting-post), or the charge *all'incontro*, between two horsemen. It fed two appetites – the love of splendour with the preliminary cavalcade, and the sporting instinct. Leonardo da Vinci ("the marvellous creator, arbiter of elegance and, above all, of entrancing spectacle," as Giovio calls him) created a jousting tourney as the culminating festivity at Milan for the double wedding that took place in 1491 of the future Duke Ludovico il Moro to Beatrice d'Este and of Duke Alfonso I d'Este to Ludovico's niece, Anna Sforza.

This *giostra-torneo*, in the square before the Castello, was as successful as Leonardo's *Festa del Paradiso* of the previous year. The victor, Count Galeazzo Sanseverino, and his suite were

"savages" in fantastic garments adorned with feathers and gold, riding horses bedecked as fabulous monsters, in shining coloured scales. The bystanders saw them as outlandish and rather alien beings, who were both primitive and barbaric: Scythians, probably, or Tartars from the East.

In Florence in the second half of the sixteenth century authority still felt that a popular feast assisted its own celebrations. Thus the wedding of the Hereditary Prince Francesco coincided with the Carnival of 1565–6 and court spectacles intermingled with the traditional carnival *giostra* and hunt. One of the most spectacular was the cavalcade through the streets of the city, with masquerades of allegorical characters on floats, representing the Genealogy of the Gods. Costumes, by the court artists Giorgio Vasari and Alessandro Allori, were in the late-Mannerist Florentine style – that imaginative, bizarre and slightly decadent taste of whose sophistication we have ample pictorial evidence.

At this period, too, the *giostra* had a new setting at Mantua, Ferrara and Modena as some of the attributes of palace entertainment – the huge mechanisms, symbolic fabrications and complicated scenery of plays and intermezzi – are found in the public domain. Changes over a few decades clearly indicate the pre-Baroque appreciation of near miracle and enchantment, and the seating plan laid out in the piazza foreshadows that of the modern theater with its rows of boxes. With all the stage impedimenta involved, every square inch of the piazza was obviously valuable and elevated galleries proved less intrusive and more capacious than the old cumbersome seating arrangements.

As early as 1561 Mantua raised "four wonderful large constructions" of wood and canvas in the piazza di San Pietro for the wedding of Duke Guglielmo. In his *Descrizione*, Arrivabene names them as the Palace of Love, the Hell of Hate, the House of Apprehension and the Hostel of Hope, for "the four passions by which the love god sways and manipulates lovers' hearts;" they were very impressive structures, "such masterpieces that even after the tournament people crowded to inspect them."

One of the Gonzaga emblems was Olympus,

This page and opposite: costume designs by Leonardo da Vinci for the Festa del Paradiso *given by Ludovico il Moro on 13 January 1490 – in belated celebration of the marriage of his nephew Gian Galeazzo and Isabella of Aragon – in the castle at Milan.*

and there is an engraving, of 1622, with an Olympus in the middle of this same piazza, spitting fireworks, a reminder that seventeenth-century audiences loved the final burst of pyrotechnics, with flames consuming scenery and fitments.

For years towns with waterways had used them for miscellaneous entertainments – anything from fireworks to political, musical and dramatic displays. In 1569 Ferrara honoured the visiting Archduke Charles of Austria with a naumachia on the theme of the *Isola beata*, in the city moat, near the Montagnola. This spectacle included incredible transformations – as of the island into a garden, for example – the mechanism for which, to be seen in a contemporary drawing, was by the Marchese Cornelio Bentivoglio, an expert in hydraulics, and the painter-architect Pirro Ligorio, who designed the setting.

In the early years of the seventeenth century in Mantua – years when Monteverdi's *Orfeo* and *Arianna* were lavishly staged in the ducal theater – the wedding of Francesco Gonzaga in 1608 provided the populace with a spectacle on the Lago di Mezzo of "a fleet of ships, and an attack on a castle full of fireworks." The castle, we learn from Federico Follino's *descrizione*, was on a fictive island. Fought over by Turkish and Christian fleets, it fell, not unexpectedly, to the Christians. Grand Duke Ferdinand of Tuscany was so struck with the skill and ingenuity of the hydraulic engineer responsible, Gabriele Bertazzolo (expert besides in stagecraft and pyrotechnics), that he snapped him up to collaborate with Giulio Parigi on a sea fight in Florence later that year – the *Argonautica* for the wedding of the heir, Prince Cosimo, to Maria Magdalena of Austria. On a November evening of the same year, 1608, battle was joined on the Arno for the Golden Fleece between the inhabitants of Colchis and the Argonauts, with the bridegroom as Jason. The designer had risen to the challenge with a flotilla of fantastic barges, at whose helms, as though to assure Ferdinando that his domain was nothing less than Olympus on earth, were the gods themselves.

Ludovico had himself suggested to Leonardo and the poet Bernardo Bellincioni the theme of the Festa del Paradiso – *the exaltation of the beauty and virtues of the bride by Jupiter who, descending to earth, endows her with the Three Graces and the Seven Virtues.*

The Triumph of Love; *ivory carving. Florence, Bargello Museum.*
Opposite: triumphal car of Massimiliano Sforza, from a miniature by Giovanni Pietro di Girago in a late fifteenth-century MS of the Grammatica *of Aelius Donatus. Milan, Biblioteca Trivulziana.*

The state entry

The idea of exhibition and performance is implicit in the ceremonies and decorations with which city fathers, in the fifteenth and sixteenth centuries, greeted the distinguished visitor, their lord on his succession or his bride on her arrival. The public festivities, in Italy as elsewhere in Europe, would include the solemn entry, the joust, the tournament, the attack on a symbolical fortress, and, now and again, a *sacra rappresentazione*.

The official welcome was a spectacle put on for a definite occasion by those of a definite social class. The entire population could happily watch, but had nothing to do with the arrangements. This public pageant was a necessary political instrument of the newly emergent state and, in some external aspects, a secular version of the religious procession whose origins it shares. It, too, takes to the streets, pauses at improvised stages to see mimed or recited episodes, and its wardrobe is breathtaking. There is a prelude *extra moenia* – outside the walls – where delegations meet the guest and his attendants. The keys are proffered, the town symbolically yielded; and when the cavalcade disappears into the palace the public programme is over and court festivities begin.

Characteristic features of the state entry were the triumphal arch, *tableaux vivants* and allegorical chariots. The latter, pulled by concealed draught animals or propelled by internal windlasses, had a tiered upper structure on which the participants acted out their rôles.

There are many descriptions of mimes and declamations prepared for the welcome guest. At Reggio Emilia in 1453, for example, when Borso d'Este received the dukedom of Modena from the Holy Roman Emperor, the town accorded him a state entry, emphasizing its congratulations with the unprecedented descent of St Peter bearing a laurel crown, and with a series of arresting mechanical *tours de force* along the route.

These dizzy flights and sudden visions, which could have been powered by Brunelleschi's *ingegni* in the churches of Florence, were contrived, as we have said, by a Florentine technician at the Ferrarese court. The procession

itself was awe-inspiring: every person in it as richly clad as could be, with gold thread and jewelled embroidery – pearls for preference – glittering in sun or torchlight. (Processional apparel was made, to the prince's liking, by tailors who comprehended the nuances of fashion and the etiquette of ceremonial colours. A court neglected no element of showmanship that could possibly convey its message of might and magnificence).

When in 1471 Galeazzo Sforza, Duke of Milan, came to Florence with a train of fourteen chariots canopied in gold and silver, with an escort of 500 foot soldiers and 2,000 mounted men, with hounds and falcons and sparrowhawks innumerable, and his horses saddled with cloth of gold, Machiavelli criticized his ostentation in a republican city. Yet that very year ducal Urbino hailed with rapture the no less immoderate parade of Borso d'Este as a *grandissimo trionfo*.

As more and more the civic greeting of the important guest, which was already termed a "triumphal entry," approximated to the Roman triumph, with ever-increasing symbolism enshrined in the processional floats, this conception of the triumph as a sequence of allegorical "pictures" reflects its literary models – Petrarch's *Trionfi* in the fourteenth century, the illuminated manuscripts and early prints in the fifteenth. The personified abstractions of the pictures – Justice, Strength or Victory – would be relevant to the qualities and achievements of the hero of the day. For the *joyeuse entrée*, devoted to the theme of the high birth and praiseworthy virtues of a prince's bride, Love, Chastity, Prudence and Mildness rode the triumphal cars.

Sculpture, and analogous illustrations, record these triumphal arrivals and the equally ostentatious retinues which set out to welcome them. At Castel Nuovo in Naples, on the central section of the main gate is a bas-relief by Laurana of Alfonso of Aragon's entry in 1443; the manuscript *Grammar of Aelius Donatus*, from the Sforza library, contains a miniature of the Triumph of Massimiliano Sforza, son of Ludovico il Moro. Most famous of painted Triumphs are those of Federico da Montefeltro and Bianca Sforza by Piero della Francesca,

Courtly and ceremonious festivals in the fifteenth and sixteenth centuries – jousts, tourneys, palio races, state entries, masquerades and mock battles – were upper-class affairs in which the populace, though in attendance, took no active part. Foremost among the typical elements of these pageants was the triumphal car, modelled on the chariot of the triumphator *of ancient Rome and loaded with Renaissance symbolism.*
There would be literary allusions in its decoration, drawn, pehaps, from Petrarch's Trionfi; *abstractions might be personified – Justice, Virtue and Fame, or the attributes of the processional hero. Draught animals were usually disguised or concealed; or the cars were propelled by manually-operated winches hidden inside.*
We know what such chariots were like from illustrations to the text of Petrarch: the triumphal car of Fame, for instance, in a miniature (left) from a fifteenth-century MS in the Biblioteca Nazionale, Florence; or from prints and engravings such as that of Raffaello Gualtierotti (opposite, bottom), from a drawing by Accursio Baldi of the tourney at the Pitti Palace on 14 October 1579. It shows the car of the three "Persian knights;" a white chariot, varied with many subtle hues with enamelling and much gold – "a stately Persian throne, in our Tuscan fashion," as Raffaello Gualtierotti, also chronicler of the scene, describes it.

each on the reverse of a portrait panel, with duke and duchess enthroned on their respective chariots.

Mantegna's *Triumphs of Caesar*, intended for the ornate decorative schemes of the palace at Mantua, are evidence for the procession of welcome as, for the bridal procession, are the panels of *cassoni*, or dowry chests, and several manuscripts of Petrarch. The triumphal cars described at the wedding of Costanzo Sforza and Camilla of Aragon at Pesaro in 1475 seem, in fact, with their laudatory allegories for the bride, to have resembled those in a Petrarch manuscript in the library of Federico da Montefeltro.

The triumphal entry had a provisional decor of its own. Hangings and carpets were carefully draped over palace balconies on the processional way, against the more permanent background of the frescoed walls, while dominating the scene throughout the sixteenth century was that chief of tributes – revived in the humanist rediscovery of the classical world – the triumphal arch.

The arches, obviously ephemeral as they were in canvas, lath and marbled plaster, at once superimposed an imaginary city on the everyday reality. They were unexpected. They hid the boring bits, and framed foreshortened views, perspective panoramas, *trompe-l'oeil* streets. What people saw through them was a kind of theatrical townscape, half-dream, half-recognizable, which added to the festival atmosphere and the sense of the extraordinary.

Paintings on the arches referred to the lineage and merits of the visitor, or alluded to him

The desco da parto *(birth tray on which gifts were presented to a newly-delivered mother) of Lorenzo the Magnificent, painted with an allegory from Petrarch's* Trionfi.

with incidents from Plutarch's *Lives* or Petrarch's *De Viris Illustribus*. Encomiums were mimed or rhymed from the side niches or from above the arches. When Federico da Montefeltro visited Rimini in 1475, Hercules, Caesar and other Greek and Roman heroes sprang to life on the cornice of an arch and Caesar Augustus, as a demigod, "gestured towards a place prepared for the most virtuous and magnanimous of warriors," implying that the duke also was a demigod and entitled to sit among his peers.

The temporary structures were built, and often designed, by the court scene painters with the cooperation of technicians, for whom the men of letters, scholars and experts on iconology chose the subjects and the classical inscriptions. (These experts, in fact, held down important jobs at court.)

Shortest-lived perhaps but nonetheless a marvel of its kind, was Leonardo da Vinci's setting for the wedding procession in Milan in 1488 of Duke Gian Galeazzo Sforza and Isabella of Aragon. The garlanded streets of tradition he turned into a garden – what better place for a wedding? – and the couple made their way to and from the Castle and the Duomo beneath arches of juniper, laurel and ivy, with small girls dancing in their path.

Among the supreme state entries were those of Charles V on his progress through Italy in the sixteenth century. Each city, fully aware of the political and diplomatic import of his visit, and of the favour he conferred, tried to outdo the others in the magnificence of its decorative schemes.

But despite its ancient roots, the externals of pageant-architecture changed with the increasing taste for fireworks in the seventeenth century. Time and again the hero in the allegory, with the moral ardour of the Counter-Reformation, rejects the wiles of sin; promptly the Garden of Pleasure or the Enchanted Wood goes up in flames. And in that ultimate transience perished the dramatic "wonders" of the age of Baroque.

The palio at Ferrara. This included footraces as well as races for horses and donkeys. There was even a women's race until Duke Borso banned it because prostitutes entered in droves and unseemly incidents followed. (His decision was reversed five years after his death, and all was as before.) Rules for the event, which is mentioned in the records as early as 1279, were written down at the end of the fifteenth century. "We hereby establish and ordain that yearly on the feast day of the Blessed St George, patron of our beloved town, and to his honour and glory, horses shall race in the Palio d'oro, that is for a palio of cloth-of-gold, for a sucking pig and a cockerel, in the morning before lunchtime, on the via Grande. The race to begin at the usual point in the contrada della Pioppa, and to finish as usual near Castel Tedaldo, the horse reaching the palio first, if only by a head, is the winner; the second wins the

Castles of sugar

The banquet of honour was the great private, as the state entry was the great public, ceremonial entertainment. Its brilliance grows, in obedience to fashion, but essentially it differs little from court to Renaissance court in Italy or anywhere in Europe and no occasion, of politics or ceremony, had stricter rules. Food and wine and table furnishings, music (to be played on certain instruments only), flowers, dancing – all were regulated as by hallowed ritual.

A banquet was essentially theatrical, and the brief scenes recited, mimed or danced between the courses were not interruptions, but gave it continuity. The surroundings, customarily the great hall of the palace, but on occasions the ruler might feast his bride, or a very distinguished guest, in the palace garden. The idea of the garden of delights came to be deliberately echoed – with swags and festoons of greenery and flowered tapestries, in the indoor banqueting hall. From a painted ceiling, signs of the zodiac, starlike, showered their benign influence on the gathering below. Often we hear of seating provided for outsiders who were

pig, the third the cockerel; there are other things for the one that comes in last." The owner of the winning donkey received a length of white cloth, a pink cloth for the winner of the men's footrace, and green for the victress in the women's race. Above: Francesco del Cossa's famous fresco in the Salone dei Mesi at Schifanoia captures to perfection the excitement of the palio: the straining of the competitors, the concentration of judges and spectators as they watch.

allowed to be present at the banquet. And always there was the tiered wooden *credenza*, on which were displayed ewers and platters of gold and precious stone, intricately chased and ornamented – treasures on which the artists and goldsmiths in the prince's employ had expended their genius and craftsmanship.

The tables were arranged along three sides of the room, that of host and guest raised above the others, and the space in the middle free for an army of butlers, pages and subordinates. Faultlessly drilled, ever on the spot when wanted, these "officials" saw to it that the company was properly and politely looked after and that players, mimes and dancers, during whose interludes the courses could be served, did not miss an entrance.

Much of the "scenery" consisted of spun-sugar confections – buildings, statues, trophies and triumphal arches designed by court artists; and the seneschal at Ferrara, Cristoforo da Messisbugo, commends the "heavenly diverse patterns" into which napkins could be folded. Diverse they were indeed. Starched linen was shaped into birds or fish or fans, and the knack could be learned from printed instructions. Mattia Giegher wrote a manual on these "frivolities" in the seventeenth century.

The *Galateo* or book of etiquette, of Giovanni della Casa, and similar handbooks, had been teaching court table manners and how to set the table a hundred years before. At least three cloths were laid, in layers one above another, and removed in turn during the meal. There was a correct succession of courses – which could number 15 or 20 each with a minimum of 10 dishes to choose from – and they should be presented so as to elicit surprise and admiration. Rabbits and birds, released from pies and pasties, bolted and fluttered, to general commotion and amusement. Cooked, with skins or hides restored, animals and birds were borne in, propped as though alive on enormous salvers, and carried round before the carver demonstrated his ability.

The carver, or the general supervisor, the equivalent of a modern theatrical producer, was responsible for the banquet's orderly conduct, decorative theme and illusionist effects. These, too, were theatrical: sensation followed sensation when small birds flew from the table napkins at the banquet on the Capitoline Hill in 1513, leaving the diners speechless; sensation, too, when, at Mantua, ladies anticipating food saw their table metamorphosed into a fishpond with fishes swimming in it. At Florence in 1600, at the wedding banquet for Marie de' Medici, the table top revolved mechanically, revealing "a pretty garden in miniature, with trees, and singing birds which the Queen caught and distributed among the ladies."

For yet more drama the "producer" might invite allegory as a table guest. At Tortona in 1489 Jason spread the Golden Fleece on the table before the bridal pair, Isabella of Aragon and Gian Galeazzo Sforza, while Mercury donated a calf and Diana a stag – Actaeon himself, as she explained, whose enviable fate it was to be bestowed on such a princess.

Better still, when Costanzo Sforza married Camilla of Aragon at Pesaro in 1475, a couple related to the foremost ruling houses of fifteenth-century Europe, it was the Olympian gods themselves who personally supervised the banquet. Sun and Moon descended from a gap in the clouds – the Sun to serve the hot dishes,

Magnificence, fantasy, marvel and surprise were the keynotes of the settings and costumes at jousts and tournaments. The decorative halberds (above) and positively monumental crest (opposite) are from watercolour designs in the Biblioteca Ariostea, Ferrara.

the Moon to distribute the cold – and titbits were delivered by envoys from the other gods: from Venus by the muse Erato, from Jupiter by Perseus, from Juno by Iris. Neptune had Triton for a messenger, and Mars had Romulus. The celestial waiters are pictured, in their splendid robes, in the official record, the *Ordine delle nozze*.

But most popular of dramatic attractions at a nuptial banquet was the debate on Married versus Vestal Love, or Modesty versus Wantonness, between Juno and Diana, Juno and Minerva, or Penelope and Cleopatra. Cupid might be arraigned before Justice to be absolved or punished for the mischief he caused; and Chastity and Lust were arguing at marriage-feasts well into the dawn of the Baroque age.

The symbolic images recur at these courtly celebrations, all with the same tale to tell – how brave the noble guest, how virtuous the bride. The content of courtly spectacle – or, rather, ceremonious revel – is, inevitably, static and repetitive. Boredom and impatience were frequently the lot of host and spectator. Diarists and chroniclers in the fifteenth century report their sufferings from monotonous and prolix entertainments, stinking, over-heated rooms, and diminishing interest. Yet Mannerist artists, technicians and stage designers were soon to galvanize and fascinate them; while the banquet – ideal field for dramatic experiment, since "theater" of any kind could be incorporated – was to attain the height of magnificence in the seventeenth century.

Games of chance and chivalry

There is in the Corte Vecchia at Mantua a fresco-series by Pisanello which exactly illustrates Huizinga's phrase, "the dream of a more exquisite life." The scenes are freely interpreted from the Arthurian cycle of chivalric romance that was the chosen reading for leisure hours in courtly halls and gardens (to say nothing of bourgeois halls and gardens) in the fifteenth century.

Of ladies, cavaliers, of love and war,
Of courtesies and of brave deeds I sing, . . .

wrote Ariosto. And these would be the material

The tournament at the wedding of Vittorio Amedeo of Savoy and Marie Christine of France, in 1620. From a painting by Antonio Tempesti.

of court poetry for many years to come.

They are all in Pisanello's paintings: the handsome knights, and ladies leaning graciously from balconies; the lances splintered in combat and champions in search of adventure, riding over the countryside to distant woods and castles. There is even – predictably, in a Gonzaga palace – a dwarf knight, fully armed, with a towering crest on his helmet, and we remember the moral tales and *novelle* of Franco Sacchetti, deploring the "corruption" of chivalry in the late fourteenth century: who is there who does not style himself knight? Children are knighted, dwarves are knighted! (And we have accounts of the knighting of a dwarf, with the gravest ritual, at Venice.)

But Pisanello's subject at Mantua is not the dew-of-the-morning warfare that earns renown for princes; much less the twilight of chivalry, the decline into court jesting, with dwarfs in armour. Neither glory, nor mockery, it is simply a game, the favourite game of court and courtiers. In this game the prince and those who would once have been his fighting men – now his intimates and household – could dramatize and restate the knightly *Weltanschauung* whose expression was ordinarily restricted to emblems and externals. They were dressing up in knightly panoply, playing soldiers, *milites unius diei* "knights for a day."

By the end of the Middle Ages the Church was more tolerant of tournaments than it had been, largely because they were less savage and no longer the best of training grounds for war. The "mimic" – and too often appallingly realistic – onslaught that could mask the private duel or vendetta, was reduced to a courtly or a public entertainment.

Authorities, from King René of Anjou in the fifteenth century to the Jesuit Claude François Ménestrier, Vulson de la Colombière, Favyn and others in the seventeenth, wrote on the combat *en champs clos*, or lists; but we should perhaps revise as inadequate our division of these combats into two types – the tournament, between two groups and culminating in the *melée*, and the joust, between single knights. The tournament, for instance, must have generated the increasingly stylized military exercises of early modern Europe that led to the matchless spectacle of the Baroque carousel.

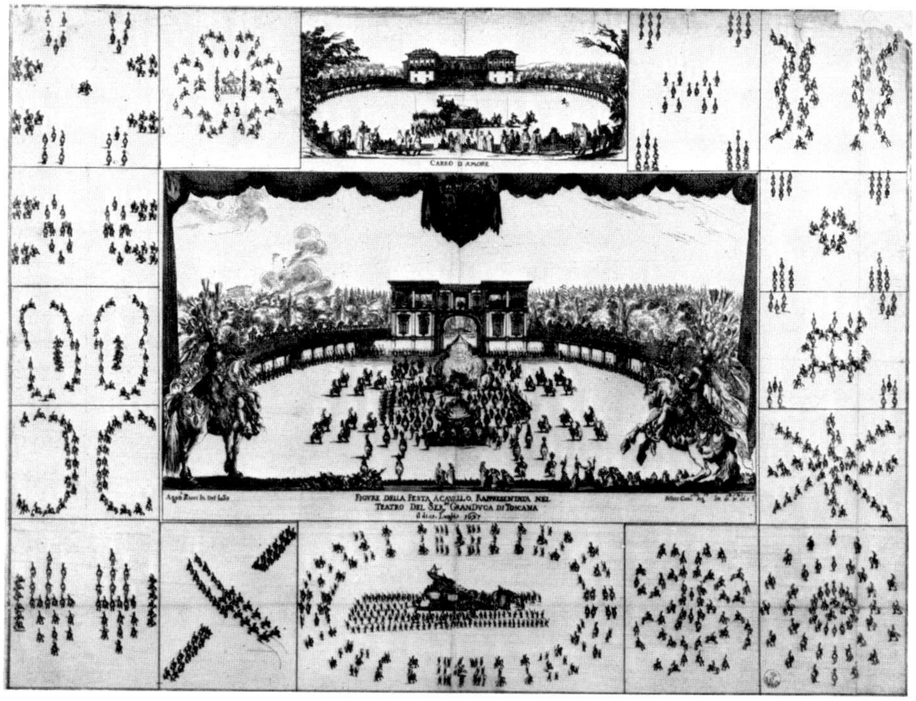

Right: detail of a tournament in the courtyard of the Belvedere, Rome. From an anonymous sixteenth-century painting in the Galleria di Palazzo Braschi, Rome.
Above: an engraving by Stefano Della Bella of the settings and figures of the carousel, held on 15 July 1637, in the amphitheater of the Boboli Gardens, culminating festivity for the wedding of the Grand Duke Ferdinando II. The theme was the Armida episode in Tasso's Gerusalemme liberata, *and the choreography was designed to dazzle. "Many things united to make it a truly memorable occasion," as Ferdinando de Bardi's* Descrizione *tells us; "the beauty of that theater, with room for so many people, the ingenious lighting, the fine* macchine, *the great number of riders and their different maneuvers, the sumptuous costumes, exquisite music and, in short, the perfect coordination of the whole."*

But in the fifteenth and sixteenth centuries both joust and tournament were preeminently parades, celebrations of and for the ruling class; exhibitions of athletic prowess, heraldry and symbolism, anchored to a plot, some tale to connect the different battles between individual knights or armed bands. The lists, or battlefield, would be equipped with props and scenery – pasteboard castles, fountains, bridges, forests as well as tents and stacks of weapons and armour – and each contestant played the hero in one of the adventures. This was what the French called a *pas d'armes*, the Spaniards a *paso honroso*, and whose allegorical content grew as steadily as that of late-medieval chivalric romance.

In France were fought the *Pas d'Armes de la Fontaine des Pleurs*, at which challengers came to an island in the river near Chalon, where a lady sat in a pavilion beside a spring and knights jousted round her; and in the *Pas d'Armes de l'Emprise de la Gueule du Dragon*, the challenge-bouts mimed the archetypal "passage perilous" (the *pas* here a pass, though it could be a bridge) beyond which one could not pass without accepting battle. The *Pas d'Armes de la Joyeuse Garde* ("sir Launcelot brought sir Trystram and Isode unto Joyus Garde, that was his owne castell") went on for 40 days; and in the *Pas d'Armes de la Bergière*, at Tarascon, knights and ladies, dressed as shepherds and shepherdesses anticipated many an Arcadian fête.

The knightly challenge was now nothing more than a theater cue, the excuse for a masquerade. Gangs of bold young men, whose forebears were the combative, almost hooligan *societates* of the early Middle Ages and the roisterers of twelfth- and thirteenth-century Italy, caught the eye in ever more resplendent attire. "We wore green damask, with pearl-embroidered sleeves and hose," wrote Francesco di Tommaso Strozzi, who had been a member of the Brigata del Pappagallo, or Parrot Gang, in 1421.

The Renaissance *tornei a tema*, or *tournois à thème*, had their popular equivalents in the raiding conflicts which, in their way, were "tournaments," when a city was split into rival imaginary "kingdoms" at the pre-Lenten Carnival. In Medici Florence this local strife was thorough-going invasion, defense and occupa-

Triumphal entry of Cosimo II; a cameo of white onyx carved by Domenico Compagni who was known as Il Romano. (Florence, Museo degli Argenti, Palazzo Pitti.) A wedding, the welcome of a distinguished guest, or a ruler's formal entry into a city, would be celebrated with spectacular public ceremonies, complete with tableaux, allegorical chariots, gorgeous, temporary decorations and artificial "triumphal arches."

tion of territory. This was Carnival, the world turned upside down, parody of the absolutist polity and a further facet of the mirror-dream which forced the ruler to contemplate his double, his reverse image, twin, conscience or Junghian shadow. What he saw was a counter-figure; and the counter-figure, properly understood, explains the Carnival.

There was much in princely festivals of the fifteenth century that was public, if not "popular." Lorenzo and Giuliano de' Medici joined in many public jousts, one of which, thanks to verses by Agnolo Poliziano, blended humanism and chivalry. Yet Giuliano's murder was to demonstrate how unsafe it was for a prince to step, unprotected, beyond the magic circle of the court. Court and public festivities in the sixteenth century are parallel to the point of inter-reflection, but they do not coincide. The hallowed rôle-switching and confusion of Carnival might from time to time bring commoners, and worse, to court and send the prince to seek amusement in disguise among his subjects. But these were Carnival excesses, *libertà di dicembre*, and asserted, rather than abolished, social distances.

The popular burlesque tournaments are thus substitutes for those at court, much as the herbs and humble ingredients of the *medicina pauperum* were substitutes for the powdered gems and costly spices prescribed by the medical establishment. There was a similar relation between the nocturnal feast in a palace garden, graced by classical nymphs and spirits of chivalry, and the witches' sabbath. Witches, too, had banquets and diversions by night; they, too, were acting out a dream of power.

On the other hand, neither tournament nor single combat, rules for which were collected in such books as the *Fior di battaglia*, written in 1410 by Fiore dei Liberi di Premariacco, was to be seen as merely a game or knightly pageant, but a competition, with glory, or honour at least, to be won. It was commended in Baldassare Castigliano's *Cortigiano*, and it scored as sheer hard physical exercise, which Vittorino da Feltre and Leon Battista Alberti had considered vital. Moreover, since physical prowess was, in the context of humanism, allied to intellectual accomplishment, the tournament naturally

Types of processional arches. Top: "arch of the sun," from the engraving of a sixteenth-century decorative scheme in Mantua.
Above: Polidoro da Caravaggio's sketch of an arch for Charles v's state entry into Messina in 1535.
Above, right: Philip II's entry into Mantua, 1549; painting by Domenico Tintoretto.

finished by dramatizing philosophical ideas as it had dramatized chivalrous romance and classical mythology. In poems ancient and medieval, from Prudentius onwards, battle had been the metaphor for the conflict of vice and virtue, the *pugna spiritualis*; and at Bologna in 1490 the much-debated humanist *quaestio*, Whether Wisdom or Fortune is to be Preferred? was the theme of a tournament. Supporters of Wisdom, uniformed in blue, were captained by Count Nicolò Rangone, those of Fortune, in green, by Annibale Bentivoglio, and there are detailed contemporary descriptions of triumphal cars, helmets and the exploits of the contestants.

Chess, the paramount board game since the Middle Ages, was not unlike a battle or a tournament. It was the Royal Game. Of ancient Indo-Persian origin, it had kings and knights and castles; its tactical problems were those of power and war, demanding intense concentration, shrewdness, brains, the ability to read an opponent's mind; necessary, too, was a retentive memory and an aptitude for mathematical thought. Jacopo di Cessole, in his *Liber scaccorum* of 1475, sees chess as a political allegory of the social order, while the mathematician Luca Pacioli writes of it in mathematical terms, as founded on the laws of probability.

For card games other skills were needed. Shrewdness here could smack of roguery, and brains without luck were of no avail. And the pack of cards was innocent of military flavour. Its lords and ladies, far from being power symbols, exemplified the old image of Fortune's Wheel and the vagaries of human life. Cards had an aura of witchcraft into the bargain. They were instruments of magic and divination, shuffled and dealt at hazard, as random as any sibylline scribbling. The tarot pack Mantegna painted (perhaps in 1459–60, when Pius II was in Mantua to discuss his hoped-for crusade) seems, in the balance and numerical relation of its figures, to propound some cosmic harmony which fate – the game – may demolish in an instant. And the players are as insecure: gods though they are of this number-and-image cosmos, the gods above them can, in an instant, tumble them to ruin.

Hunting scene by Lorenzo Leonbruno. Mantua, ducal palace; frescoed lunette in the Sala della Scalcheria. Hunting was one of the great courtly activities, the "third component" of court life, after le armi e gli amori, *arms and love.*

One devotee was Filippo Maria Visconti, Duke of Milan. Pier Candido Decembrio in his biography lists among the duke's youthful pastimes *palla*, *pallone* (football and volleyball), dice, the Homeric game of knucklebones and, as was to be expected, chess. But cards were his great love and a complete pack, finely decorated by his secretary Marziano da Tortona, cost him 1,500 ducats.

The addiction to cards, whether played with the tarot or the standard packs, such as the "Neapolitan," spread widely between the last quarter of the sixteenth century and the first of the seventeenth, and *palla* was as popular. This, too, required skill, and the spherical leather ball had its metaphysical connotations. In 1553 Antonio Scaino dedicated a treatise on *palla* to the Duke of Ferrara.

Games of risk and chance might have been condemned on moral grounds but possibly, to most people – at the courtly level at any rate – they were either paradigms of other activities, or civilizing agents, or metaphors for the fluctuations of life.

Yet, if this were the world seen as a game, the game was also seen as the world. In Pompeo Ulisse Ringhieri's *Cento giochi liberali e d'ingegno*, of 1553, the game has ceased to symbolize the world. The relation is reversed and the entire world symbolizes the game. Riches, power, war, love, art, folly, have their aspects of charade. Nothing is in earnest, or important. Everything is reducible to a game, played for its own sake and as its own reward. And when that happens the game, existing in its own right, is indispensable.

The court, then, had diversions – *palla*, dice, chess, cards, and colossal snowball parties in the winter. (St Francis of Assisi and his non contemporary, the poet Folgore da San Gimignano, are known to have been particularly fond of playing in the snow.) But the court's diversion was to become the court's one serious business and *raison d'être*, for, as absolutism prevailed, it had no function save as a setting and a game. With justification, Jean de la Bruyère wrote of court life in the seventeenth century as "a serious, melancholy and demanding game. One must marshal one's batteries and pieces, have a plan and follow it, blocking that of the adversary; be prepared for the occasional risk, or impulse and, after all the thought and all the precaution, expect a check – if not, at times, checkmate."

The third component

Of what, in fact, did the life of the court consist? What were the ingredients of the image, and when the prince gazed in his magic mirror, what did he see? The best short answer is that of the Catalan *trovador*, Peyre de Rius: *Armas, amors at cassa* – fighting, love, and the chase.

And so hunting is the third component, constantly reflecting and entwined with the other two in courtly metaphor. Love was literarily a metaphor for warfare as the plots, or *fabulae* of tournaments became in essence love stories. Hunting was no less a battle, and amorous pursuit a matter of hunter and quarry, lures and traps.

In court life the hunt was omnipresent. It is in music, from the Ars Nova of the fourteenth century to music for the Roi Soleil at Versailles. It is in poetry, pictures and tapestry. Lorenzo the Magnificent, Poliziano and Luigi Pulci wrote hunting poems. We see the hunting cheetahs, as in Gozzoli's procession of the Magi in the Medici palace, clinging to the saddles; the deer tracked on the rocky steep, the coursing greyhound and the big, white-breasted falcon plummeting on the hare. In 1472 Galeazzo Maria Sforza, in whose castle at Pavia a room was decorated with hunting scenes, planned a similar series for the Castello at Milan. The hunt was shown in both as a ritual of his life, together with the religious ceremony, the banquet and the public appearance.

But even as a courtly diversion and spectacle the hunt retained much of the ancient myth and magic. It was adventure in the forest, an encounter with sacred and ferocious beasts; for the prince hunted nothing less than stag, bear or boar, save when he flew his hawks, and they were noble birds. It had links with Teutonic legends of the *wilde Jäger*, associated in Italian folklore with the *caccia feroce* mentioned by Dante, Passavanti and Boccaccio. Its atmosphere lies between that of the outdoor court banquet and the uncanny pinewood at Classe in Botticelli's scenes (three of them in the Prado) from Boccaccio's tale of Nastagio degli Onesti: and in that tale, reminding us of the close sexual metaphor, the prey is a woman, naked and beautiful.

A darker magic pervades Paolo Uccello's *Hunt in a Forest*, in the Ashmolean Museum, Oxford: a hypnotic, frightening picture, with a sorcerer's spell on the wood, the night and the animals – dogs and horses, neither demon creatures nor quite real. Or Pisanello's *Vision of St Eustace* (in the National Gallery, London). Here, again, is the atmosphere of legend: the stag with the luminous cross in his antlers, halting the saint's fine horse, panicking the hounds, fixes attention on the mystic, transcendental colloquy. Christ talks to the rider in the depths of the forest, and the hunt is recognized as a source of private contemplation. Communing in the forest with a hawk, a horse, a hound, the prince might feel he was indeed "a new Adam," representative of Christ. In contact with nature and animals, he was lord of the natural world and of its symbol, the land that God had given him to rule.

Hunting scene with boar hounds, and an impresa *used by Gian Galeazzo Visconti; from a sketchbook of Giovannino de' Grassi, late fourteenth century. Bergamo, Biblioteca Civica.*

Hunting, the princely privilege, was also, in the *hortus conclusus* of the court, the knightly *aventure* or enterprise that simulated travel and warfare. (Both of which were ancient Christian metaphors for the journey through life.) *Venatio*, the chase, and *inventio*, the power of imagination, combined to make the hunt a quest, a foray into the unknown, the confrontation with fear and danger. For this reason the *senior*, or lord, disdained, until the end of the feudal period, to take small game or resort to

the traps and birdlime of the peasant. For the unferocious quarry – birds and hares – he employed the falcon as an aerial extension of his will and power; it was his double, hunting in the sky. Francesco Sforza wept for grief when his best and treasured falcon died, and his court poets had to write memorial verses. Emblems regularly included Diana, Actaeon, the greyhound and the hawk.

The ruler's privilege, synonymous with freedom and thus with non-utility, ranked as an amusement because it had no practical purpose. The court might be entitled to the meat, but it was not the prince's hunt that supplied the prince's kitchen, unless with purely token contributions. Hunting could be said, at most, to be a good school of horsemanship and to cultivate the soldierly instincts. In 1450 Aeneas Silvius Piccolomini, the future Pius II, dedicating his *Tractatus de liberorum educatione* to Ladislaus, king of Hungary and Poland, praised the hunt as the young noble's training ground for war, and quoted Vergil in support of the argument.

But though one did not hunt for the sake of the ensuing banquet, and hunted less for prey than for the excitement and the exercise, the banquet notwithstanding revealed the courtly meaning of the chase. For the carver, as for the herald, there were "noble quarterings," the noblest being dexter chief. Flesh from the off foreparts of the animal was thus cut first and this, though scarcely the tastiest, was the prince's helping. In the etiquette of the meal his quarry, yet again, endorsed the social hierarchy.

And so the hunt, especially of noble beasts such as boar and stag, was, as Castiglione said, an occupation for gentlemen, "a pleasure for great lords." It was their pleasure, and theirs alone. Feudal restrictions on the once universal right to hunt were gradually and generally increased between late medieval and early modern times. Uncultivated land was preserved. Certain animals might not be hunted – Gian Galeazzo Sforza forbade the hunting of stags near Vigevano in 1385 – nor might the peasants lime or net lesser game.

Game accordingly disappeared from the none too plentiful diet of the lower classes and multiplied under protection for the sport of princes, their guests and courtiers. The peasants were neither allowed to destroy, nor did they know

Dancing was a much-favoured pastime at court. Gaspare Visconti described a ball at the Sforza court as "a slow movement of nimble feet." The many treatises on dancing included De arte tripudii *by Guglielmo Ebreo of Pesaro, written in the latter half of the fifteenth century, and the* Libro dell'arte di danzare, *by Antonio Carnazzano; but most famous was Fabrizio Caroso's* Il Ballarino, *published in 1581 and reissued, enlarged with new music, as* Nobilità delle dame *in 1605. From this second edition, whose frontispiece (left) carries a dedication to the Duke and Duchess of Parma (below), are also taken the illustrations (opposite) showing steps and figures.*

how to exclude, marauding animals and as late as the eighteenth century the historian Ludovico Antonio Muratori heard of complaints that boar from the Farnese hunting park at Colorno near Parma were devastating crops. Almost everywhere in the princely domains of Italy it was the same. The houses of Este, Gonzaga, Savoy and Medici competed to have more and vaster parks, and almost everywhere the ancient hunting rights, and equally venerable rights to pasture, wood and water, were diminished. Popes and cardinals were mighty hunters, for the chase had ceased to be mimic warfare and was primarily an adjunct of power. Domenico Boccamazza, whose *Trattato della caccia* was one of the most noted essays on his craft at the beginning of the sixteenth century, was chief huntsman to Pope Leo X.

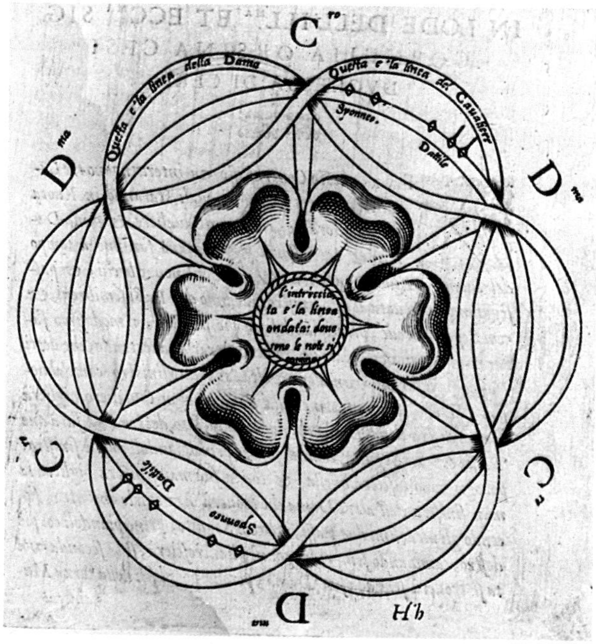

Hung be the heavens with black

Scholars have come to regard the state funeral as a state pageant, for its ornate decoration, the processions and the splendour, which place it among the artistic spectacles of the princely court.

A funeral was a political and dynastic opportunity which utilized superb temporary decoration (as did any exceptional event), and stressed the innate drama of the actual ceremony. The customary court artists and stage designers were responsible for its individual character; a court scholar composed a suitably eulogistic funeral oration and the propaganda messages in the official *descrizione*, and planned the symbolism and allegory.

Decoration, pomp and splendour had one object – to emphasize the superhuman qualities of a prince who achieved in death the historic legitimacy of his rôle as an elected one of God. The final political and dynastic observance was enacted in two phases in the joint theater of public street and church, each phase separate and distinct: the solemn civic procession through the town, the religious ritual in church.

For diplomatic reasons a court might hold the obsequies in effigy of some great personage with whom it had ties of friendship or alliance. Thus, in 1558, when Charles V died in Spain, the sovereigns of Europe honoured him with grand and formal obsequies at Brussels. To judge from the vivid engravings, they had a military triumph for the soldier-emperor, rather than a funeral; and there were many, less exalted, examples.

To allow time for guests to travel, and for their lodgings and the *mise-en-scène* to be prepared, a month or more might elapse

THE WHIMS OF FASHION

1

The general fashion picture seems fairly simple. "Almost to the beginning of the twelfth century," says Fernand Braudel, "European dress remained what it had been in barbarian times." Fashion might be said to start with the changes which followed economic revival, itself dependent on Western control of the Mediterranean trade routes.

"Towards 1400–50 princes dressed more or less identically in the four corners of Christendom:" Their style, that is, was elegant International Gothic. In the sixteenth century the "black" fashion, Spanish and severe, replaced the modes of Renaissance Italy – that period when the historian Corio could write of the glittering court of his native Milan, of its "new fashions in clothes and civilized amusements;" when François I could beg from Isabella d'Este a mannequin-doll whose attire he might have copied for presentation to ladies in France.

The triumph of the "Spanish" mode was really more the triumph of Burgundy, for Charles V, with his Burgundian breeding, had carried it to Spain, and it spread with the political and military dominion of the Spanish-Habsburg dynasty. Black – bigotted, Counter-Reformation black, as it might with some justice be described – was valued as being the most difficult of colours to dye.

Then, suddenly, there emerged one of the great laws of fashion: one had to look different, be set apart, dress according to one's rank. By the eighteenth century, as Braudel notes, "nothing made the nobles dislike cloth-of-gold so much as to see it on the lowest of the low." Black and the Spanish fashion went out, superseded by "French modes and bright colours." Isabella d'Este's mannequin model returned to Italy as the *piavola de Franza*, the latest thing from Paris.

We here illustrate this very brief summary, at least in a few of its Italian aspects. At the wedding in 1473 of Count Roberto Sanseverino and Lucrezia Malvolti, painted by Sano di Pietro on a Sienese *biccherna*, or account-book cover (1), the male guests are very smart and the ladies wear clothes which do very little for them – unlike the ex-queen of Cyprus and her gentlewomen, lined up, 30 years or so later, on the Venetian *fondamenta* in Gentile Bellini's "Miracle of the True Cross"(7).

Galeazzo Maria Sforza is portrayed (2) with a dandified air, his gloved right hand holding his other glove, *saglio* (a *saio*, or tunic) embroidered with the lily *impresa*. His hair is

2

3

4

5

6

7

8

long, his cheeks clean shaven. It was Julius II, imitated by François I and the Emperor Charles V, who launched the vogue for beards, moustaches and short hair. The Church nevertheless disapproved, though when the fashion swung back to clean shaven in Louis XIV's reign the priesthood alone was to persist with beards.

Piero de' Medici – Piero the Gouty – in Gozzoli's *Procession of the Magi*, wears a plain cap, *beretto all'antica* (9); in a portrait by Bernardino de' Conti il Giovane (10), the *beretto* is adorned with a medallion or badge. The custom of removing, and thus drawing attention to, one's hat in greeting was perhaps introduced at this period; certainly it was new to the French when the gentlemen of Naples employed it in the presence of Charles VIII.

Details of feminine fashion are seen in Luini's portrait of Bianca Maria Visconti (6), her hair shaved high on her forehead and worn in a bun at the back, with a short veil; and in another portrait by Bernardino de' Conti (3) and in that, said to be of Beatrice d'Este, by Leonardo da Vinci (4), in which both subjects wear the *lenza*, a ribbon or chain tied round the head. (This was known in France as a *ferronière*). Beatrice has the pearl-edged coif, or *cuffia*, which, in Ambrogio Noceto's portrait of Francesca Magna (5) has become a braided net.

In the Pala Sforzesca, Beatrice d'Este is shown with the *coazzone*, a long plait braided in ribbon and worn down the back (8). Silken braid, as we can see (3 and 5) was immensely popular and it is easy to see why silkworms and mulberry trees were widely cultivated in Renaissance Italy.

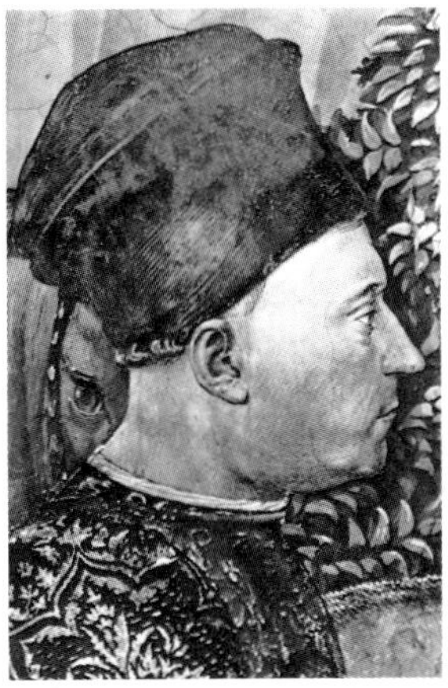

9

10

Drawings by Pisanello (above), from the Biblioteca Ambrosiana, Milan

between a prince's death and burial. For several days his embalmed body, robed as in life and with his royal emblems, lay in state to be venerated by the people before it was conveyed, in a melancholy cortège by night, to the court chapel, there to await the funeral.

This began with a procession which passed by every building of symbolic importance and through every quarter of the town as citizens crowded the streets, testifying unanimous assent to the rule of the prince and his successors. Palaces and mansions were draped in black and gold, with black-bordered heraldic hangings; the division of the procession into groups was dictated by rank and strict court etiquette.

From the mid sixteenth century there is a flood of material on state funerals, their ceremonial, the decorations and the detail. Descriptions, drawings and engravings show us, as it were, what the courts of Italy were aiming at on these occasions.

We may choose an example from Florence in the late Mannerist period. When Grand Duke Cosimo I died in 1574 his son Francesco found it politically inexpedient to have the official ceremonies in the Salone dei Cinquecento in Palazzo Vecchio, but he took the procession on a very circuitous route from that palace, the seat of government, to the Medici family church of San Lorenzo – as far as Palazzo Pitti across the Arno. At its head, in brilliant uniform, marched trumpeters with muted instruments, men carrying black-swathed standards, servants with torches and emblems, ecclesiastical dignitaries and the town magistrates with their flags.

This pageantry was followed by a less colourful mourning contingent of the poor in rough, drab clothes, by standard bearers trailing their banners, by the dead duke's horse with black trappings and funeral plumes. At the center of the cortège came the gilded coffin and on it, raised a little the better to see his subjects, a life-size plaster efigy of Cosimo beneath a canopy. After him, wrapped majestically in a sweeping black cloak, rode his legitimate heir Francesco whose presence at that point, as if in partnership with the effigy, verifies the transfer of power – a propinquity of death and triumph making tangible the strange, and later

Drawings by Pisanello (left) from the Biblioteca Ambrosiana, Milan, and opposite, from the Musée Condé, Chantilly) give some idea of upper-class fashion in the first half of the fifteenth century. (One should allow for the exaggerations of personal, artistic style). The favoured colours were cremisi, *a brilliant red, purple and saffron. Blue was obtained from indigo, and different shades of red from brazilwood, madder and cochineal. Garments were usually multicoloured, made up in vertical strips, or colours might be combined in intricate patterns, in wavy lines, in checks or quarterings; or the basic garment might be of one colour, with sleeves, close-fitting hose and trimmings in another colour.*
In the sixteenth century black was adopted from Venice as the fashion for ceremonial dress.

proverbial, popular shout, "The king is dead, long live the king!"

The procession ended with men of the duke's household (no women), the nobles and foreign delegations. The scholarly Vincenzo Borghini, who had a genius for these things, had organized it all, as he organized so many of the most dazzling Florentine state entries.

Next, the second phase, for which the secluded – the essentially private – scene was San Lorenzo. The huge church, transformed with hangings, had the gloomy magnificence proper to a moralizing discourse on the Art of Dying; and as the ceremonial dialogue unfolded between Power and Death the macabre motifs – coffins and scythes, skulls and grinning skeletons – drove the lesson home: *memento mori*.

Visual focus of such a funeral was the monumental catafalque. This *macchina*, on which the coffin was laid, symbolically housed the dead man's remains and bore allegories of his imperishable glory here below and that of his soul in heaven above. The catafalque was a version of the medieval *castrum doloris*, "in the antique style," as the *descrizioni* say, with its personifications of the Moral and Theological Virtues, and other imagery. It was more frequent in Italy from the later sixteenth century, a soaring, moveable structure of wood and painted plaster – *tempietto*, pyramid or triumphal arch, with a forest of candles on top, on a stepped plinth in

A finely-decorated music MS with a madrigal, Arboro son che li miei rami persi *("Withered at the roots, my branches fall") is said to be by Isabella d'Este, Marchioness of Mantua, a woman of many cultural interests.*
Left: frontispiece of a late fifteenth-century edition of the Canzoni per andare in maschera per carnasciale facte da piú persone *"Carnival songs by Several Hands". One of the figures resembles Lorenzo the Magnificent who was himself a poet and wrote such songs.*

the middle of the nave. (No bier but a pope's might lie in the chancel.)

A church was adapted for a funeral with the same decorative elements as those of palace festivals but here, in tone, colour and significance, they breathed the gruesome pietism of the Counter-Reformation.

The richest and most elaborate hangings, gleaming with gold thread, swathed the columns and curtained the walls inside and out. On them chiaroscuro paintings extolled the family, the illustrious dead and even, at papal interments, the officials and the man in charge. Allegorical statues were clear and distinct against the sable background, silvered plaster skeletons flickered disquietingly in the candlelight. And the whole thing, entrusted, as always, to the experienced scenographers and artists of the court, was concentrated on the coffin beneath the candle flames where the catafalque blazed like a hero's pyre, the epiphany of the prince.

At St Peter's, by contrast, the austere ceremony and decoration for the funeral of a pope were governed by Agostino Patrizi Piccolomini's *Caeremoniale Romanum* of 1516. Soon, however, it was thought desirable that the obsequies should not lag behind those of a secular prince and the new high altar, over which Bernini's baldacchino rose in 1633, both provided the setting and served as a catafalque. The papal bier rested, as it rests today, on the

Michelangelo's first sketch for the tomb of Julius II in St Peter's. The design was never carried out in its original form and the actual tomb, in San Pietro in Vincoli, is of more modest proportions. Grandiose tombs and funeral rites were yet further pretexts for magnifying the prestige and "image" of Renaissance rulers, and great artists and court scenographers would have the task of creating appropriate settings and ceremoniously glorifying a departed prince.

first step of the base.

In the metaphorical language of seventeenth-century decor the colossal catafalque was a fiery apotheosis, alight with candles, festooned with ornament, symbol and allusion. But still it was the *castrum doloris*, a sepulcher. It suggested the *coemeterium* – literally, sleeping place – where the prince would be portrayed, as if in earthly slumber until the Judgement Day, beside his kin in the family vault. And the vault itself, demonstrating his power and glory in the shadow of death, was a rhetorical image of the court.

Where fashion rules

The Renaissance court developed chronologically, in diverse forms, from the small clique or household group around its lord to the full-blown signorial establishment. Consolidating its wealth and power, each type of court becomes an administrative body within the hierarchy of a sovereign state, and spectacle had its part in the process. Luxury, as a cultural manifestation, went with spectacle, and would reach its climax at courts of the Baroque era.

Bureaucratic ritual maintained a court's authority, not only in its own circumscribed sphere but in its continual, competitive foreign relations, and the most obvious external expression of that ritual was dress. It was dress that showed the repetitive, infinite graduations of rank under stricter and stricter rules of etiquette, and dress that constantly announced degree. The princes, leading actors and spectators of the play, were sacred figureheads who dictated and disseminated fashion, including the fashion in clothes. They did so through their often interconnected political and kin relationships

Above: the catafalque of Grand Duke Francesco I of Tuscany in the church of San Lorenzo in Florence; etching attributed to Teodoro Crüger, 1587. Below: pencil drawing by Maso da San Friano, second half of the sixteenth century; typical of the often macabre taste of artists in the Counter-Reformation period.

which were conducted with an eye to aggrandizement and in a spirit of self-approbation.

When the court was a feudal household its apparel was no more than a necessary household expense. But as external show acquired significance, and the signs of allegiance – the badges, emblems and *divise* worn by courtiers – acquired symbolic value, it was a matter of privilege. Ceremonial differences in dress, originated by the Romans, were inherited by the Church and survive as liturgical vestments. The privilege of wearing certain dress or insignia was granted by an emperor to officers or officials; and later a medieval retinue might be clad – economically, we presume – in the lord's *livrée d'honneur*, of one pattern and material. From this, later still, descends the "lord's badge," or *divisa*, with its precise colour-symbolism, subject of perennial argument among the more erudite sixteenth-century commentators.

Dress, then, is both something to wear and something valuable, with a double rôle as clothing and mark of favour. (The *palio*, or bolt of precious cloth, had been among the most coveted of gifts since antiquity, and gave its name to the race or contest in which it was awarded). The evolution of dress in this double rôle, with all the other sumptuary accessories of power, can be traced in the alternations of fashion at the courts of the Renaissance.

Early fifteenth-century taste was for antique simplicity, in clothes as in everything else. The keynote was masculine, sober, severe. By the late sixteenth century luxury was in demand, pomp and splendour that were to confound illusion and reality.

The court of Ferrara in Leonello's time, lived a frugal life. Its rooms were scarcely palatial, its furniture of the plainest. In the realm of cultural progress it was an age of "private" learning, of rare books in private libraries. Yet in the reign of Borso his successor – that is, before Borso's successor Ercole made his prestigious marriage with Eleonora of Aragon – luxury had reared its head at the Ferrarese court.

There is the evidence of Borso's gorgeous illuminated Bible, the Bibbia di Borso, and of his gorgeous wardrobe, so lovingly depicted in the celebratory Ciclo dei Mesi at Schifanoia.

French costumes in these frescoes indicate that Ferrara borrowed modes and refinements from Burgundy, and there were literary borrowings besides. Ariosto wrote *fables courtois* in the "chivalric" style, and the court poet Ludovico Carbone, using the *volgare illustre*, echoes the French vernacular revival. These influences included a devotion, shared with Florence, to the renewed concept of *varietas*.

In Florence Piero de' Medici, too, commissioned a self-celebratory fresco – Benozzo Gozzoli's stupendous, elegant procession of the Magi on the walls of his chapel in the Via Larga palace. Here he and his court ride by in ultra-fashionable French clothes, or dazzling Oriental garb. By now the scholar-prince does not rely on "classical" costume for his air of authority, but dons the smart, close-fitting doublet which, as we may see in Carpaccio's *Legend of St Ursula*, came from France through Venice.

Black was also a Burgundian taste, though Castiglione says the somber Spaniards brought it into Italy. But Charles V and his suite had taken it to Spain from the Habsburg court, which copied Burgundy, where there were special regulations for the difficult dyeing of black cloth.

Prized the more because of this difficulty, black was the colour of magnificence, not only for mourning, but at fêtes and weddings. Lucrezia Borgia's black and gold dress for her marriage to Alfonso d'Este in 1502 was much talked of, though for her state entry into Ferrara the previous February, she had chosen "her morello," a purple, gold-striped satin. The guests from Mantua, Milan, Urbino and Rome were most of them in black. Black velvet, black brocade, black *tabí* (a kind of moiré taffeta), black dripping with gold and pearls, are repeatedly mentioned in the many accounts of that well-reported wedding feast.

A vogue for colour in the years that followed lasted through the Reformation period, and black was relegated to ceremonial wear. Even the Spaniards succumbed, and Charles V had a coronation procession that rivalled the rainbow, at Bologna in 1530.

There were, of course, economic factors in the wholesale adoption of black, for they are never absent from questions of fashion and its sources of supply. The heavy Genoese velvets had been ideal for the so-called "Spanish" and sumptuous Italian styles of the sixteenth century. The perfect cut was perfectly displayed by the rich fabric and these styles were unchallenged until Colbert established the silk industry in France and fashion changed completely. Henceforth the gossamer materials, and the French taste, reigned supreme.

The court itself was constrained to obey fashion and the economic interests by which fashion was, to a large extent, determined. Often it contributed to those interests with *nove foze*, or new styles introduced, as the chroniclers tell us, by the aristocracy. Thus Mantua manufactured headdresses – the *schofioto*, an embroidered cap of felted Lombard cloth, *conzature de testa* and the *capigliara*, a renowned invention of the Marchesa Isabella. Her proverbial elegance may have had much to do with the launching of the Mantuan textile industry which from 1523 onwards produced some of the most sought-after velvets, satin and damask.

Isabella's reputation as the accepted arbiter of fashion matched her reputation for culture,

Reconstruction by Sandro Gallieri and Giorgio Beretti of the black-draped façade of San Lorenzo, Florence, for the vicarious "funeral," on 10 November 1598, of Philip II of Spain. Opposite: sectional reconstruction of the interior of the church, showing the ornate catafalque, erected on the order of the Grand Duke Ferdinando I, in honour of the deceased Spanish monarch.

charm and political intrigue. In 1519 François I was urgently begging, through his son Federico, for a *puva*, or wax doll, "clad in your patterns of sleeve and bodice, and the under- and over-dress you wear, with the headdress and hair the same . . . for his Majesty wishes to have several of these fashions made up as gifts to ladies in France."

So overwhelming was Italian chic that Anne of Brittany, expecting to accompany her husband Louis XII to Italy in 1510, was fearful of comparisons. Jacopo d'Atri, the Mantuan ambassador in France, wrote on 14 January to Isabella that the queen had decided she would have "nothing but black or tawny cloth" and keep it plain, to minimise the competition.

In the sixteenth century mannequin-dolls were sent to demonstrate the latest Italian court fashion in the capitals of Europe, and it was 200 years and more before they were displaced as top models by the French *poupées*, "Big Pandora" and "Little Pandora." By then all eyes were on Marie Antoinette's *modiste* in the Rue Saint-Honoré. The fashion-conscious desired to know only what Rose Bertin was doing.

Italian courts in the sixteenth century witnessed a ferment of female interest in everything relating to fashion, of which ample evidence exists as in the correspondence of Isabella d'Este with sources in Venice, Rome and Florence, which in large part consists of questionnaires on the *nove foze*. A veritable espionage system, which amounted to a diplomatic market in fashion secrets, existed between the various courts. The Marchesa and her brother's wife at Ferrara were notorious rivals. Each desired to know only what the other was wearing, and each had her pet accessories: wimples, Isabella's *capigliara*, Lucrezia's "Spanish" bodice.

The clothes that distinguished the lady of rank were so extravagant and so extreme as to be fantastic. The fantasy increases with the ritualization of court etiquette which, restricted at first to grand ceremonial occasions, is elaborated until the self-imposed rules are an immutable code that culminates in the exaggeratedly detailed precepts of Versailles.

This passion among noble ladies of the sixteenth century to outsmart their rivals in mat-

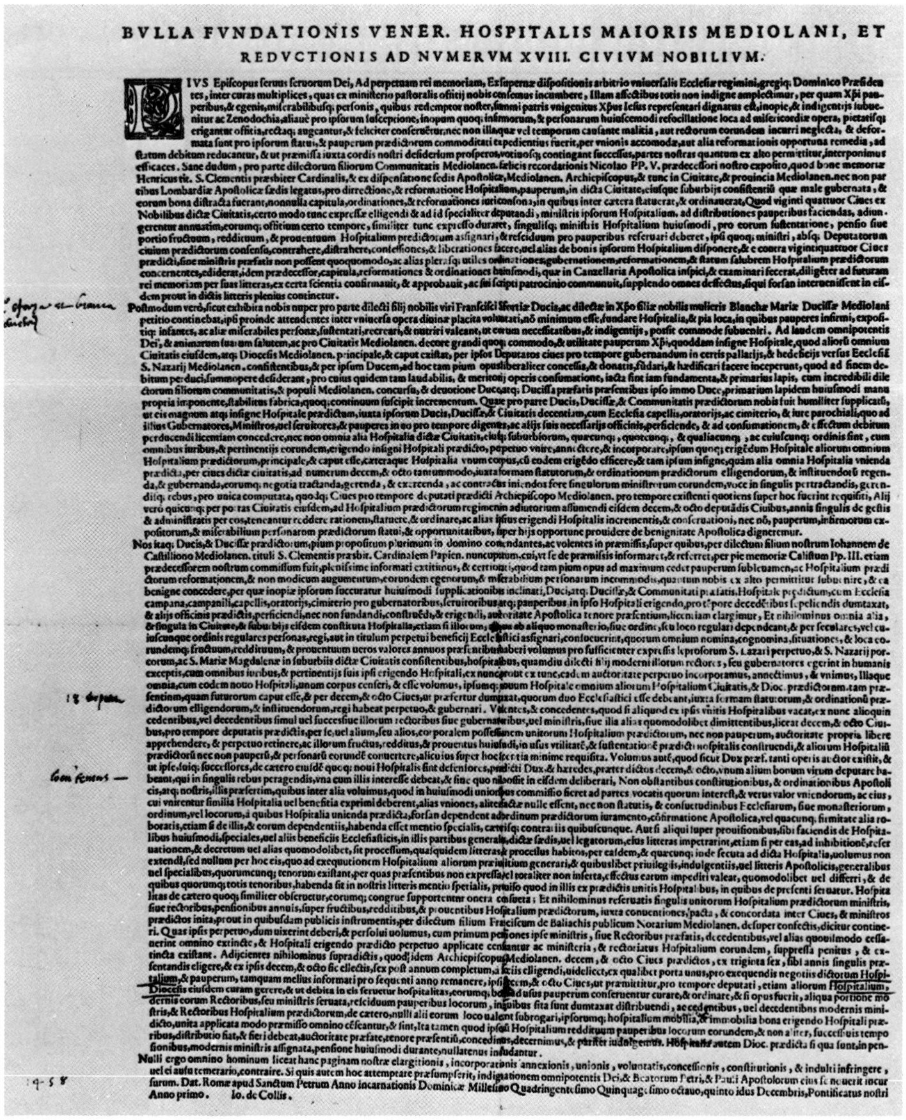

BVLLA FVNDATIONIS VENER. HOSPITALIS MAIORIS MEDIOLANI, ET REDVCTIONIS AD NVMERVM XVIII. CIVIVM NOBILIVM.

PIVS Episcopus seruus seruorum Dei, Ad perpetuam rei memoriam, Ex superæ dispositionis arbitrio vniuersalis Ecclesiæ regimini, gregiq; Dominico Præsidentes, inter curas multiplices, quas ex ministerio pastoralis offitij nobis censemus incumbere, Illam affectibus totis non indigne amplectimur, per quam Xpi pauperibus, & egenis, miserabilibusq; personis, quibus redemptor noster, summi patris vnigenitus Xpus Iesus representari dignatus est, inopie, & indigentijs subuenitur ac Zenodochia, aliaue pro ipsorum susceptione, inopum quoq; infirmorum, & personarum huiusmodi refocillatione loca ad misericordiæ opera, pietatisq; erigantur offitia, rectaq; augeantur, & feliciter conseruentur, nec non illaquæ vel temporum causante malicia, aut rectorum eorundem incurri neglecta, & deformata sunt pro ipsorum statu, & pauperum prædictorum commoditati expedientius fuerit, per vnionis accomodæ, aut alia reformationis opportuna remedia, ad statum debitum reducantur, & ut præmissa iuxta cordis nostri desiderium prosperos, votiuosq; contingant successus, partes nostras quantum ex alto permittitur, interponimus efficaces. Sane dudum, pro parte dilectorum filiorum Communitatis Mediolanen. fælicis recordationis Nicolao PP. V. prædecessori nostro exposito, quod bone memoriæ Henricus tit. S. Clementis præsbiter Cardinalis, & ex dispensatione sedis Apostolicæ, Mediolanen. Archiepiscopus, & tunc in Ciuitate, & prouincia Mediolanen. nec non partibus Lombardiæ Apostolicæ sedis legatus, pro dirrectione, & reformatione Hospitalium, pauperum, in dicta Ciuitate, eiusque suburbijs consistentiũ quæ male gubernata, & eorum bona distracta fuerant, nonnulla capitula, ordinationes, & reformationes iuriconsona, in quibus inter cætera statuerat, & ordinauerat, Quod viginti quattuor Ciues ex Nobilibus dictæ Ciuitatis, certo modo tunc expressæ elligendi & ad id specialiter deputandi, ministris ipsorum Hospitalium, ad distributiones pauperibus faciendas, adiungerentur annuatim, eorumq; offitium certo tempore, similiter tunc expresso duraret, singulisq; ministris Hospitalium huiusmodi, pro eorum sustentatione, pensio siue portio fructuum, redditum, & prouentuum Hospitalium prædictorum assignari, & residuum pro pauperibus reseruari deberet, ipsi quoq; ministri, absq; Deputatorum …

Above: printed sixteenth-century copy of the Charter, or Bull, of the Ospedale Maggiore, founded by Francesco Sforza in Milan. The fifteenth-century parts of the buildings are by Filarete.
Right: a page from Fundatio magni hospitalis Mediolani *(1508), by G.G. Gilino. God the Father blesses the enterprise and above the great hospital hover the Virgin and the Archangel Gabriel.*

ters of dress found expression in the current *literatae* fashion-garments embroidered in unknown cufic script and undecipherable ciphers, each garment an esoteric message in a mystery language. Colours and flowers, variously interpreted, were related to family *divise* and emblems: the Medici green, the Sforza black and white.

The alternations of fashion are thus reflected in the history of the courts, which are perpetually alert to stabilize their power and whose rigid internal etiquette is the instrument by which power is affirmed to an attentive world. Etiquette in its turn is responsive to the currents, the "fashions," of history. The sober routine of the early fifteenth century is succeeded by the opulence of Mannerism, as the grave, much-vaunted *virtus* of the Roman *dominus* had been succeeded by the luxury of the Byzantine court, where unbelievably subtle and mind-boggling "effects," comparable only to the "marvels" of Baroque theater, were designed to exalt and glorify the sovereign. Ambassadors admitted to the sacred presence were stunned to see the Basileus high in the air above them. (The mechanisms are described by Hieron of Alexandria.) Chroniclers dwell at length on the countless ceremonial vestments at the court of Constantine Porphyrogenitus; in 1627 Gasparo Bragaccia, in his book *The Ambassador*, advises what to wear for a princely audience "at the court to which one is accredited."

His advice bears out what we have said of the importance of fashion. The ambassador should, as far as possible, dress in the mode of the court he visits – *alla Spagnola* in Spain, *a la francese* in France. In Italy he should lean to the Spanish style rather than the French and in northern lands will find the Italian fashion "agreeable to both English and Flemings, the latter having no wish to resemble their German neighbours, nor

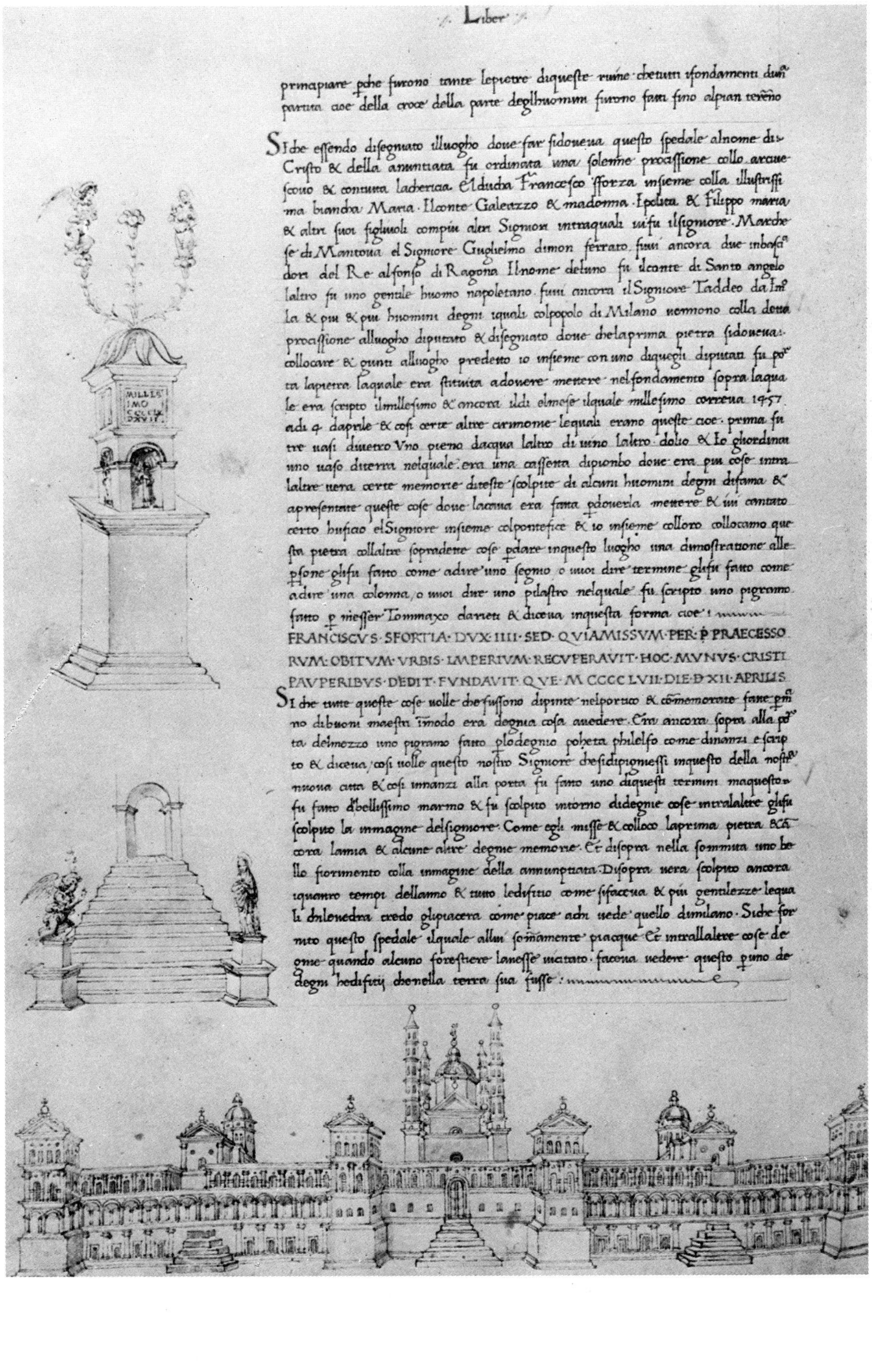

A page from the Magliabechiano ms of Filarete's Trattato d'architettura. *The façade of the Ospedale Maggiore is reproduced, and a sketch of the commemorative pillar designed for the foundation ceremony.*

the former to look like Frenchmen." There is a last plea for the "ancient traditional" ceremonial attire, which takes precedence over the foibles of fashion.

"If the Ambassador is an ecclesiastic, let him dress as one . . . decently, *alla romana*; if a Venetian Senator, then in the long Venetian gown, and he may fittingly appear before any King on earth. His Suite should be clad, as nearly as may be, in the mode of the Court he visits, and to Princes he should pay the customary honours of their Courts."

The Courtly Life

The tiny, elegant studiolo *of Grand Duke Francesco I in the Palazzo Vecchio, Florence, was created by Vasari, and part of the decoration is a series of pictures by his pupils on the theme of "human activities in relation to the natural elements."* Pearl Fishery *(opposite) is by one of these collaborators, Alessandro Allori.*
Vasari took some of his ideas for the decoration of the studiolo *from the historian and philologist Vincenzo Borghini, a learned Benedictine, secretary to the Medici, and at the same time member of a commission appointed to "correct" the* Decameron.

"To shape in wordes a good Courtier"

Poets and magicians make things, and the images of things, with words; the sorcerer Atlante in *Orlando Furioso*, with his kingdom of magical words and the vapour of his cauldrons, is Ariosto himself. Poet and sorcerer are one, as the Siberian shaman proves. Words are their tools of creation, and the illusions are stronger, in the end, than reality.

And so we glimpse the courts of chivalrous romance, wavering and evanescent, in the fumes of a writer's magic cauldron – that of Baldassare Castiglione, man of letters, knight, diplomat and Papal Nuncio to Spain, and the magician who, in the early sixteenth century, best evokes the courtly world. In his day that world was a new phenomenon, and he sought to imbue it with the antique, humanist, Christian and chivalric spirit which is, perhaps, the most attractive emanation of court culture, its finest and most lasting dream.

Pastime is magic – free as art and magic are, insubstantial, lovely for its own sake; and for its sake the group of lords and ladies in Castiglione's book, *Il Cortegiano*, gathers, one calm evening in Duke Federico's palace at Urbino, in the reign of his son Guidobaldo. Their pastime is with words: "that one of them should 'shape in wordes a good Courtier.'" The very phrase (quoted here from Sir Thomas Hoby's translation of 1561), is magical. Yet the word creates, and it evaporates. Through words we think we have grasped things, but that is illusion; words have merely brought them nearer. And at court – a theater of hard political

The courtier, wrote Castiglione, "beside noblenesse of birth" – which was his first requirement – should have "not onely a wit, and a comely shape of person and countenance, but also a certaine grace, and (as they say) a hewe, that shall make him at the first sight acceptable and loving unto who so beholdeth him." (For "hewe" we would perhaps, say "air," or "bearing").
Above: sixteenth-century gentlemen, in a fresco by Girolamo Romanino in Cremona cathedral.
Right: ladies and gentlemen of the Ferrarese court in a fresco at Schifanoia. Castiglione looked back to Duke Borso, for whom the palace of Schifanoia was decorated, as a model prince.

Mount Olympus, immune, so it was thought, from wind or storm, was among the 36 imprese *used by the Gonzaga and listed by Jacobus Typotius in his* Simbola varia diversorum Principum. *Often the motto* ad montes duc nos – *Lead us to the Mountain – added a religious note. From the palace in Mantua, this picture shows Olympus rising from a lake in a landscape where there are waterfalls, and people engaged in various pursuits. Allegory is piled on allegory – the spiralling road to the summit, the water maze at the mountain's foot – to remind us of the allegorical thread running through court life.*

fact, of power games played to Machiavelli's iron rules – the courtier supplied illusion. He was there to mask and soften the sharp edges, as did the gardens and the tapestries. He was both necessary and complementary to the court, though Castiglione manages to persuade us, as Burckhardt says, that the court existed for this "ideal man of society," rather than he for it.

The author's avowed aim is to describe "the trade and maner of courtiers, which is most convenient for a gentleman that liveth in the Court of Princes" and, in a discussion both philosophical and phenomenalist, "to picke out the perfectest trade and way, and (as it were) the floure of this Courtiership." The first of the four books treats of gentlemanly birth and education, the second of a gentleman's behaviour in social and courtly life, the third of his counterpart, the *dama di palazzo*. In the fourth, Pietro Bembo – who else? – examines the relations between prince and courtier and dissects Platonic love.

Il Cortegiano may be said to wind up the debates initiated by Lorenzo de' Medici and Marsilio Ficino in the gardens at Careggi (where Plato was reintroduced to western Europe), and pursued in those of a dethroned queen at Asolo. (As guest and prisoner of Venice, Caterina Cornaro recalls the fair heroines, guests and prisoners in the enchanted gardens and palaces of chivalrous romance).

The ceremonial of court was thus a Platonic mimesis. It was an image of the Christian paradise, and of the court of Olympus, and the individual courtier was the image, imitator or "double" of his prince. The city, with its environing lands, was an image of the ruler environed by his court. The accomplishments of the courtier – proficiency in arms above all, that links him to the chivalrous world surviving in courtly insignia, and in the tournaments – have a tinge of studied artifice. This goes with the wish to conform, to assume a natural air which is the height of artificiality, to display imitative "grace" towards others, and towards the prince especially.

Castiglione is aware that the court he talks of is a myth. He is honest, and intelligent enough, to warn us not to credit those who "extoll with infinite prayses" the courtiers of Filippo Maria Visconti and Borso d'Este, and believe that "in Courtes at that time there raigned such good conditions, and such honestie, that the Courtiers were (in a manner) religious folke," whereas "in these dayes every thing is cleane contrary." The lamenting of ancient chivalrous virtue was a hoary reactionary trick. The Golden Age had never been; *tempus illud* was a vision, an archetype, and, as history, utter fraud. But "nature nowe bringeth forth much better wittes," men are better judges of good and evil, with a better conception of their rôle. The court is the court; those who play the court game know what to contribute and what they can expect, and though one plays with magic mirrors and extravagant dissembling, it has its rules, its decorum and inexorable inner purpose.

One of the group at Urbino objects that "now adaies very few are in favour with princes, but such as be malapert" – the boastful and presumptuous, rather than the able and good. Not inevitably so, replies Federico Fregoso, who speaks for Castiglione; and "if it fell to our Courtiers' lot to serve one that were vicious and wicked... let him forsake him." This, we may be sure, is pure *pietas* and pure hypocrisy. No courtier would voluntarily abandon the court and could but testify, in staying, to the prince's virtue.

Questa fu facta per noi ragazi
E anchor perquei che son bestial e pazi

Rules, precepts, regulation. Niccolò Machiavelli codified the rules of politics in *The Prince*; Pietro Bembo those of love in the *Asolani*, and of courtly speech and writing in his *Prose della volgar lingua*. Giovanni della Casa did the same, in the *Galateo*, for mannerly behaviour. These texts appeared within a short space of time, when art and learning, too, were tending, in theory and practice, to abandon "progress" in favour of an idealized and seemingly attainable perfection. In this climate, in the shadow of princely power, the courtly virtues are codified as those of the modern courtier. An ethos became an etiquette.

Not by chance is the sixteenth century that of the guide and teacher. (As it was, more brutally, the century of the Inquisition, censorship and police spying in the wake of the Reformation.) The medieval *conversatio*, the practice of religious life after a deliberate renunciation of the world for God, is, in Castiglione, conversation – the normal language – the very yardstick – of court life.

But in the court, though the prince is above the law and may "kill not one man alone, but ten thousand" and "doe many other thinges, which if a man waigh them not as he ought, wil

Princely education. The most comprehensive "Latin course" that has come down to us is by the mid fourth-century grammarian Aelius Donatus, and an illuminated MS of his Ars minor *and* Ars major *was prepared for the lessons of Massimiliano Sforza, son of Ludovico il Moro. One aspect of schoolroom life is forcibly illustrated (left) by a scourge and the words, "This was made for little boys."*
Ludovico il Moro had usurped his nephew's duchy of Milan and given his niece Bianca Maria in marriage to the Emperor Maximilian for the sake of imperial support; but he was overthrown by Louis XII and died, a prisoner, in France. The duchy was recovered, largely by Swiss mercenary troops of the Holy League, and Massimiliano reinstated, only to lose it again three years later, after the victory of François I at Marignano. He was still a young man when he, too, like his father, died in France.
Left, below: the young prince meeting the emperor, his namesake.

appeare ill, and yet are not so in deede," the courtier, by contrast, has little or no independence. The chorus of "I want," "you must," "you have to," is deafening. He can do nothing but perpetuate princely rule and the princely consciousness of power, and with it his subordinate position. But for Ottaviano Fregoso (brother of Federico), the mature courtier will "come by his end at length, to instruct well his prince;" and for Castiglione – "the best knight living," said Charles v, who knew what he was talking about – the subordination was obviously pervaded with Christian and Platonic significance and the chivalrous belief that the greatest honour is in loyalty to one's lord.

The courtier was both to emulate the knight of yore and be an esteemed counsellor. Incipient absolutism would be conditioned by aristocratic experience – that of the prince's friends, noble, sage and courteous. In the long run, a courtier was a minister. He could be a minister in the medieval sense, in a ceremonial household post, but already there was no genuine nearness to the ruler, his was the humdrum intimacy of the dogsbody, with small thanks attached.

The romantic nineteenth century saw the Renaissance in unholy alliance with slavery, and Rigoletto can sing of "the vile, damned race of courtiers." It was not damned, perhaps, but certainly contemned. Under the thin veneer of gold, court life was a succession of humiliations: bad lodgings, poor food, cast-off clothes to wear, crumbs and paltry donations and modest pensions to solicit. The princely sun was often niggardly of his beams, and away from the rooms of state there were dark holes and corners.

The man of courtly accomplishments may, then, exemplify one type of culture. Its opposite, not surprisingly, is seen to be in nature, in the freedom of woods and meadows – the Golden Age regained. This freedom Erminia finds among the shepherds in Tasso's *Gerusalemme liberata*, with the wise old man who has renounced the splendours, miseries and falsity that must attend a prince. But these things have their rules and regulations, and their conventions dominate the banquet, and the life of the country villas, and the travels of the court.

Education was also represented symbolically. It is seen (above) as a choice between vice and virtue. Unfortunately Massimiliano Sforza, here choosing correctly, was to lead a dissipated life.

166 Iconologia del Ripa

DOMINIO DI SE STESSO.

per moſtrare, che la ragione deue tenere il freno all'animo, oue troppo ardiſca, e pungerlo, oue ſi moſtri tardo, e ſonnolento.

DOTTRINA.

DOnna d'età matura, veſtita di pauonazzo, che ſtia à ſedere con le braccia aperte, come voleſſe abbracciare altrui, con la deſtra mano terrà vno ſcettro, in cima del quale vi ſia vn Sole, hauerà in grembo vn libro aperto, & ſi veda dal Cielo ſereno cadere grá quantità di rugiada.

L'età matura moſtra, che non ſenza molto tempo s'aprendono le Dottrine.

Il color pauonazzo ſignifica grauità, che è ornamento della Dottrina.

Il libro aperto, & le braccia aperte parimente denotano eſſere la Dottrina liberaliſſima da ſe ſteſſa.

Lo Scettro con il Sole è inditio del Dominio, che hà la Dottrina ſopra li horrori della notte dell'ignoranza.

Il cadere dal Cielo gran quantità di rugiada, nota ſecondo l'auttorità de gl'Egitij, come racconta Oro Apolline, la Dottrina, perche, come eſſa intenериſce le piante giouani, & le vecchie indura, coſi la Dottrina gl'ingegni pieghеuoli, con il proprio conſenſo arricchiſce di ſe ſteſſa, & altri ignoranti di natura laſcia in diſparte.

DOTTRINA.

DOnna veſtita d'oro, che nella ſiniſtra mano tenga vna fiãma ardente alquanto baſſa, ſi che vn fanciullo ignudo accenda vna cãdela, e detta donna moſtri al fanciullo vna ſtrada dritta in mezzo d' vna grande oſcurità. Il veſtimento d'oro ſembra la purità della Dottrina, in cui ſi cerca la nuda verità, moſtrandoſi inſieme il prezzo ſuo.

La fiamma nella mano, alquanto baſſa, onde vn fanciullo n'accenda vna candela, e il lume del ſapere cõmunicato all'intelletto più debole, men capace, inuolto ancora nelle coſe ſenſibili, & materiali, & accomodandoſi alla baſſezza, moſtra al fanciullo la buona via della verità, mouendolo dal precipitio dell'errore, che ſtà nelle tenebre oſcure della commune ignoranza del vuolgo, frà la quale è ſol beato colui, che tanto può vedere che baſti per non inciampare caminando. Et ragioneuolmente la Dottrina ſi aſsomiglia alla fiamma, perche inſegna la ſtrada all'anima, la viui fica, & non perde la ſua luce, in accendere altro fuoco.

DVBBIO.

GIouanetto ſenza barba, in mezzo alle tenebre veſtito di cangiante, in vna mano tenga vn baſtone, nell'altra vna lanterna, e ſtia col piè ſiniſtro in fuora, per ſegno di caminare.

Dubbio è vn'ambiguità dell'animo intorno al ſapere, & per conſeguenza ancora del corpo intorno all'operare.

Si dipinge giouine, perche l' huomo in queſta età, per non eſser habituato ancora bene nella pura, e ſemplice verità, ogni coſa facilmente riuoca in Dubbio, & facilmente dà fede egualmente à diuerſe coſe.

Per lo baſtone, e la lanterna ſi notano l'eſperienza, & la ragione, cõ lo aiuto delle quali

due

A page from the Iconologia *of Cesare Ripa. A native of Perugia, Ripa published his "Descriptions of sundry images derived from antiquity and from imagination" in 1593. The emblem above illustrates the virtue of self-control,* dominio di se stesso.

The protocol of the banquet

The complete social structure of the Renaissance court is visible in the etiquette and ceremony of its banquets. The table is a place of public meeting; guests are there by agreement and all, by implication, courtiers, but there are delicate discriminations. Some courtiers are demonstrably more equal than others.

First the prince, the pivotal figure, is isolated. There was symbolism in the table vessels reserved for him, and in the barriers and distances behind which he sat, as ruler and sacred being, in an imaginary enclosure. And, as his magnificence was measured by that of his guests, he had circumstantial *descrizioni* written of his feasts, for circulation, by his *maestro di casa* or resident men of letters.

And his banquets, proclaiming his status, clarified that of his courtiers. He sat in isolation; they sat as near to him as their rank permitted. The courtly structure was reflected at the dinner table, and good manners asserted social identity. Manners are heavy with meaning.

Seating was anything but casual. The rules were rules of precedence, with everyone where he should be, though as the manuals of good behaviour tell us, where the "head" of the table sat, was somewhat different before the Renaissance.

In the antique world the seat of honour was the *lectus medius*, or central couch in the triclinium (the lateral couches were the "upper", and "lower", *lectus summus* and *lectus imus*). In hellenistic Greece, host and chief guests were probably at either end of a sigmoid table (from the Greek letter sigma, originally C-shaped). When the rectangular table, of differing lengths, was introduced in the early Middle Ages as an alternative to the half-moon, oval or circular Eastern patterns, the head seat could be for many years, as we see in Duccio, Buoninsegna and Giotto, either in the middle of the long side – a possible reminiscence of the central Roman couch – or at one of the shorter ends, which approximated to those of the sigmoid table.

Later rule books were very precise on the seating plan, and on where the head of the table should be. Vincenzo Nolfi, in his *Ginipedia* of

Two more pages from Cesare Ripa's Iconologia, *picturing Fraud and Hypocrisy. Ripa's erudite work, with its illustrations of myths and allegories and its personified abstractions, was enormously influential. Knowledge of this kind was endlessly useful at court, supplying themes for state entries and palace decoration as well as ideas for ordinary objects – even the shapes into which table napkins were folded. Acuity in such matters,* Acutezza recondita, *gave food for thought, as Castiglione said. Ripa illustrates* Dottrina *– Learning, or Education – as a mature woman in a purple gown, for learning is acquired with time and purple is a colour signifying seriousness, "the ornament of learning." Dew falls in quantities from a clear sky above her because "the Egyptians" say that dew nourishes young plants and strengthens old; and thus we see that "flexible minds are enriched by learning while those unwilling to learn are unregarded." The depiction and the commentary are fair examples of Ripa's method.*

1631, says, "When taking your place – if this has not been allocated by the *padrone di casa*, who is to be obeyed implicitly – do not forget my instructions, and sit neither near the top nor at the bottom of the table. The most important person sits at the top (farthest, that is, from the main door to the kitchens), with the next in importance on his right, the third at his left and so on, from rank to rank." Or rank might be underlined by distance. When King Christian I of Denmark was feasted by the *condottiero* Bartolomeo Colleoni, no one sat near him at the head of the table.

Though the less hierarchical round table was practically ousted by the rectangular during the Renaissance, it might, having no "head" place, be used for a brotherly union of peers. Derived from the Round Table of the King Arthur stories, it endured in pictures of Arthur's court, and of the Last Supper. Clearly, the shape of a table was significant. At a banquet in Florence, the (non-courtly) Accademia della Crusca (an academy of purists given over to the separation of literary wheat from *crusca*, bran), the long oval table was "cut out on the side facing the *credenza*, into a capital C . . . for Crusca."

As we have said, no one sat near the royal guest at Colleoni's banquet, and a prince might further distance himself at an entirely separate table. This "high table" – literally high, on a dais – was placed at right angles to the other tables, like an extended seat for the ruler and his most prominent courtiers. The wedding feast for Cosimo de' Medici and Maria Magdalena of Austria in 1608 was "in the *salone*, where there is a dais, five steps up, for public audiences and state ceremonies, and on this was the princes' table, slightly curved, so they could see and converse easily." Its height, and the grading by ranks of the tables at floor-level, are to be seen in Greuter's engraving.

A canopy over his seat or his table might also distinguish the ruler. Or the table might be so far separated and elevated that it was a rostrum:

232 **Iconologia del Ripa.**

FRAVDE.

Sic transit gloria mundi Pater Sancte

onde sopra di ciò mi par che sia molto a proposito il detto del Petrarca.

La vita fugge, & non si arresta vn' hora.

Le rose nella guisa che habbiamo detto. Pierio Valeriano nel lib. 55. narra che questo fiore sia Geroglifico dell'humana fragilità, & segno del ben fugace, & della breuità della vita nostra non essendo che in quello istesso giorno che egli fiorẽdo, & mostrando il suo vigore, tosto nel medesimo tempo sfiorisca, languisca, & more, e però Iob. cap. 14. *quasi flos egreditur & conteritur*, molto si potrebbe dire sopra della rosa a questo proposito, ma per non essere lõgo, ne tedioso nel dire, rimetto al Lettore a quanto in diuersi luoghi della nostra Iconologia habbiamo detto spetialmente nella vita breue. Ma non lassarò in disparte vn madrigaletto, che mi pare molto a proposito a questo suggetto.

Vane son le speranze, & il desio,
D'accumular ricchezze, e gran tesori.
Per ciò che'l tempo vola fugge, & passa,
Onde tutto si lassa
A viua forza, & l'huom resta in oblio.
Mà se brami acquistar grandezze, e honori,
Et dopo morte ancor viuer vorrai
Senza tormenti, e guai.
Segui pur la virtù, che tanto vale,
Che fà l'huomo immortale.

quando l'huomo più pensa di arriuare al segno, & però si può dire.

O speranza, ò desir sempre fallaci.

Il Petrarca nel primo trionfo della morte.

Miser chi speme in cosa mortal pone.

& Silio Italico lib. 7. vel Pun.

Spes heu fallaces, oblitaque corda caducum.
Mortali quodcunque datur.

La diuersità delle gioie sopra il vestimento, & la corona d'oro, ne dimostrano l'alterezza, & le grandezze con lequali la gloria mondana si adorna, l'acceso, & sfauillante razo che tiene con la destra mano co'l motto sopradetto, ne significa che le nostre grãdezze, & l'humana gloria sia simile ad vn razo, che non si tosto acceso sparisce, scoppia, & more, onde à questa similitudine per mostrare che l'huomo nõ si debba insuperbire giunto che sia a qualche grado non solo di ricchezze, ma d'essere superiore a gl'altri, nella Creatione del Sõmo Pontefice, li deputati auanti di esso in S. Pietro mettano sopra d'vn'hasta della stoppa la quale accendendola dicano ad alta voce.

FVRIE.

Dante nell' Inferno dipinge le Furie donne di bruttissimo aspetto, con vesti di color negro, macchiate di sangue, cinte con serpi, con capelli serpentini, con vn ramo di cipresso in vna mano, nell' altra con vna tromba, dalla quale esce fiamma, & fumo netro, son finte da gli Antichi Poeti donne destinate a tormentare nell' Inferno l'anime de' malfattori.

FVRIE.

Statio così dipinge.

Cadendo giù fan ombra all' empio viso
I minor serpi del vipereo crine
E gli occhi son sotto la trista fronte
Cacciati in due gran caue onde vna luce

Spa-

Libro Secondo. 257

HIPPOCRESIA.

dicendo. *Cum ergo facis eleemosynam noli tuba canere ante te, sicut Hypocritæ faciunt, in synagogis, & in vicis, vt honorificentur ab hominibus, &c.*

Le gambe, & i piedi simili al lupo significano, come dice S. Matteo 7. che gli Hippocriti nell' esteriore sono agnelli, & dentro lupi rapaci.

gli Hippocriti non si curano di estenuare il corpo per essere tenuti, & stimati buoni, & S. Matteo al cap. 6. *Cum ieiunatis nolite fieri si.. t Hipocritæ tristes; exterminant enim facies suas, vt videantur ab hominibus ieiunantes.*

Il vestimento come dicemo, essendo composto di lino, & di lana dimostra (como dice il sopradetto S. Ambrosio, nel cap. 8. de morali) l'opera di coloro, i quali con parole, & attione di Hippocrisia cuoprono la sottigliezza della malitia interna, & mostrano di fuori la semplicità dell' innocenza; questo si mostra per significato della lana, & la malia per il lino.

La testa china, con il velo, che la cuopre la fronte, & la corona, & l'offitiolo dinotano, che l'Hippocrito mostra d'esser lontano dalle cose mondane, e riuolto alla contemplatione dell' opere diuine.

Il porgere la moneta ad vn pouero, nella guisa che si è detto dimostra la vana gloria de gli hippocriti, i quali per acquistar fama, & gloria del Mondo fanno elemosina publicamente, come ne fa fede S. Matteo al 16. così

HOMICIDIO.

Huomo bruttissimo armato, col manto di color rosso per cimiero portarà vna testa di tigre, sarà pallido, terrà con la sinistra mano per i capelli vna testa humana tronca dal busto, & con la destra vna spada ignuda insanguinata. Bruttissimo si rappresenta l'Homicidio: percioche non solo e abomineuole alle persone; ma quello, che molto più importa, al sommo Dio, il quale tra gli altri comandamenti, che ci ha dati, ci proibisce l'Homicidio, come cosa molto dannosa, & a lui tanto odiosa, che come si vede nell' Exodo 21. comanda che non si lascia accostare al suo altare l'homicida.

Si quis per industriam occiderit proximum suum, & per insidias, ab altari meo auelles eum, &c.

Si dipinge armato, perche l'homicidio genera il pericolo della vendetta, alla quale si prouede con la custodia di se stesso.

La Tigre significa fierezza, e crudeltà, le quali danno incitamento, & spronano l'homicida: la pallidezza è effetto dell' ira, che conduce all' Homicidio, & del timore, che chiama a penitenza; però si dice nel Genesi, che Caim hauendo vcciso il fratello, andò fuggendo temendo il castigo della giustitia di Dio.

HONESTA.

Donna con gli occhi bassi, vestita nobilmente con vn velo in testa, che le cuopra gli occhi.

La grauità dell' habito è inditio ne gli huomini d'animo honesto, & però si honorano. & si tengono in conto alcuni, che nõ si conoscono per lo modo del vestire, essẽdo le cose esteriori dell' huomo tutte inditio delle interiori,

R che

at a birthday banquet for the Duchess Christine of Savoy, she and a selected handful sat aloft, toasted by courtiers below.

Hierarchy ordained the precedence of those at the prince's table, as well as their presence there. He was at the center, the chief guest on his right, and so in order. At the wedding of Margherita de' Medici and Odoardo Farnese the seats of honour were, by the laws of etiquette, those of the bride and the two co-regents of Tuscany, Maria Cristina of Lorraine, widow of Ferdinando I, and Maria Magdalena of Austria, widow of Cosimo II, since the latter's son, Margherita's brother the Grand Duke Ferdinando II, was a minor. On the dais, "under a canopy of dyed material," the bride had the head of the table, with her mother and grandmother, "the most serene archduchess and the most serene madama," next to her, and Ferdinando in fourth place.

Rank, as we know, determined a courtier's nearness to the prince. The elite were at his table; then came the privileged occupants of lower tables in the same room; then those who ate in the *tinello*, a separate room; and underlings who ate in the kitchen.

The *tinello*, an extra barrier between prince and courtiers, is rosily sketched by Francesco Liberati in *Il perfetto Maestro di casa*, of 1658, as "a good, spacious room, with tables and benches, sideboards and all necessities," where courtiers and staff were fed. But though the prince's table, as at the banquet for Henri III of France at Ferrara in 1574, could be described as "a profusion of the whitest linen, plates and dishes of gold, silver and majolica, and carvers and *camerieri*," the arrangements in the *tinello* left much to be desired. There "ladies were eating from coarse earthenware, with no knives or forks, with thieving knaves, who jostled and pushed, instead of servants," Aretino compares a court dining room, disparagingly, with a prison, whose temperature, at least is less extreme. The *tinello* is "an oven in summer, and in winter you are too cold to talk." Comfort was scant, and the food as awful as the service.

The seat you sat on was another signal. The most important person might not only be at the head of the table but in a separate chair, which could have the semblance of a throne in its own right. The individual chair, with arms and back, would be for years sacred to princes and *signori*.

"A chair for the noblest, and for the lesser, a bench," says Giovanni della Casa in the *Galateo*. And so it was: the chair, the stool – a stool with a back outranked a backless one – or the long, undifferentiated bench, as in the *tinello*. While the stool might be for the humble and reviled (a servant, when permitted to sit, sat on a stool, like Judas in religious pictures), the individual chair, of the grandest sort, could be a courtesy towards ladies. "The guests proceeding to table, the ladies had chairs with arms, and while they were there the Gentlemen sat on stools between them . . . " Or it was for the guest of honour alone, a reminder of his rank and sacred status under the ancient laws of hospitality.

Grand Duke Cosimo I, who received guests, we are told, as a "welcoming, courteous, great and prodigal host," omitted no gesture of "amity and respect" when entertaining the Archduke Charles of Austria. At table "he made as if to refuse a chair and take a stool;"

Below left: a game of chess, by the fifteenth-century painter and illuminator Girolamo da Cremona, a follower of Mantegna. Pietro Cataneo, author of I quattro primi libri di architettura *(1554) mentions "fishing, hunting, singing, dancing, evening entertainments and card-games," all or most of which, he says, were more easily indulged in at the country villa than in the town. Perhaps in anticipation or remembrance, these pastimes were the theme of paintings and decoration in the villas. The lady (opposite), playing* palla *with a* mazza*, or bat, is frescoed in the Palazzo Borromeo, near Milan.*

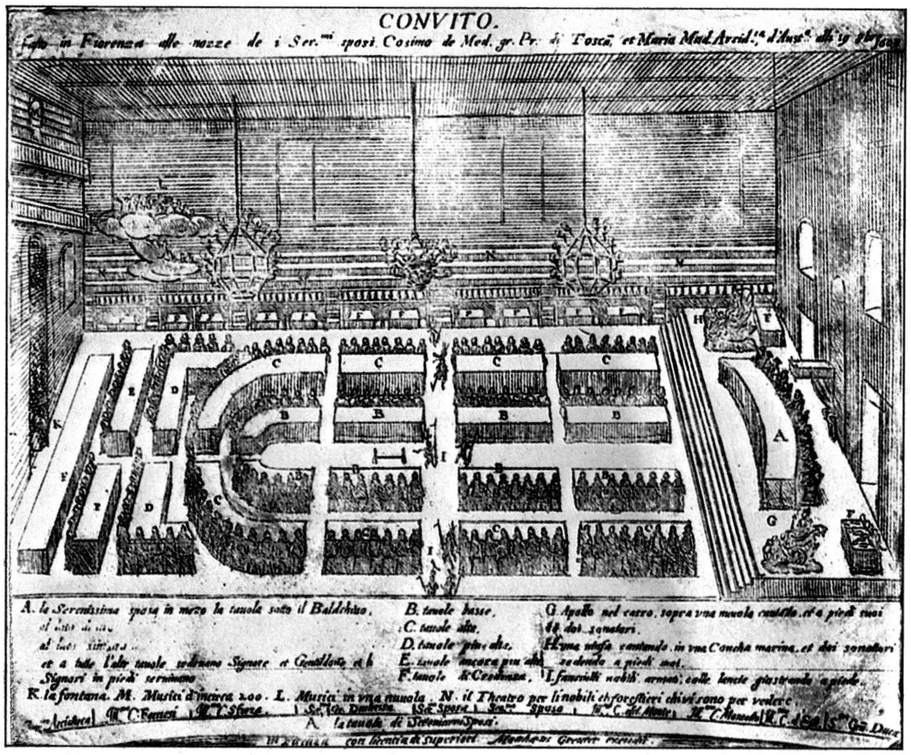

Above: table plan at the wedding banquet in Florence in 1608 for Cosimo, hereditary prince of Tuscany, and Maria Magdalena of Austria. On a dais, the princes sit at a table "slightly curved, so they could see and converse easily."
Right, below: table layout in the shape of a fishpond, entirely composed of comestibles. The illustration is from a treatise by Bartolomeo Scappi, one of many such books, consulted at princely courts, on how to stage a banquet.
Opposite: sketch of a Venetian banquet. Again we note the raised, semicircular high table. The host is, presumably, the Doge and it has been surmised that the woman beside him is Christina of Sweden, though she never visited Venice save, perhaps, in 1657 when she may have been there incognito.

but though this was the act of a gracious host it was beneath the dignity of a grand duke, and the archduke would not hear of it.

Precedence, the paramount obsession, could lead to diplomatic incidents. When Pope Julius III had a stool fetched for Cosimo I and bade him sit on the right of the papal throne, the ambassadors of France, Portugal and Urbino, who, strict observers of papal protocol, stood bare-headed before the pope, stalked from the chamber in dudgeon. Cosimo had not even a papal charge; he was not entitled to sit. Nobody was so entitled, save emperors and kings, and they on chairs, not stools. Protocol had been breached.

Besides the chair, the canopy and the seat at the head of the table, a multitude of niceties – of services, of implements and dishes – indicated rank. Thus, after the official announcement of Marie de' Medicis's betrothal to Henri IV, when the grand duke "and many noble persons" dined in the *sala delle statue* at the Pitti, the French ambassador presented the napkin to his new queen, escorted her to the head of the table under the *baldacchino*, and stood bareheaded until she was for the first time served with wine by the *Signor luogotenente* of Signor Antonio Francesco Bondi . . . a veteran of the Grand Duke's household. The ambassador then withdrew to dine in his own apartments.

"The Grand Duke sat two arm's lengths from the Queen on her right, with the Grand Duchess opposite; below him was the Duchess of Bracciano, who had a chair, then Signor Don

Virginio her husband. Opposite them were the most excellent Signor Don Giovanni and Signor Don Antonio de' Medici, uncle and brother respectively of the Queen. But they were seated on stools and served from open dishes, and their goblets lacked *sottocoppe* (coasters). As in France, no one drank unless the Queen did so; and after the meal the Princes rose, the most excellent Signor Don Virginio passed her the napkin, and they returned to the Grand Duke's quarters."

This account tells us who sat on what, who had a napkin, a *sottocoppa*, or dishes with covers (a safeguard against contamination, if not poison); who rose first from table and, above all, the system of serving and being served. In practice, the higher the rank, the higher that of the ministrants. "Thieving knaves" had no place in such an atmosphere, and Marie de' Medicis was emphasizing her new dignity and that of the French ambassador in allowing him to pass her a linen napkin. It was an honour thus to serve the great. Duke Ercole II d'Este rode on the emperor's right when Charles V came to Lucca, yet tendered him a napkin at the banquet. (A diplomatic incident ensued, as Cosimo I protested, through his ambassador – the Medici had precedence of the Este at public ceremonies – speaking of an attack on rank and honour.)

But the symbolic services at table were in excess of requirement, as anyone could see. A feature of banquets was the almost balletic performance and faultless drill of the superabundant personnel, appearing and disappearing with the dishes. And this corps, too, had its hierarchy of privilege and reward, from those at the prince's table to those who toiled in the *tinello*, or for yet lowlier diners. In the branch of his household responsible for meals, the prince had what Vincenzo Cervio calls "three offices of most honour, those of Steward, Carver and Cupbearer," and chose for them "noble, known and trusted persons;" vouching for his food and drink, they had his life in their hands.

Directly under the steward were bursar, butler, cook, and the private cook to the prince. Under the cupbearer were the cellarmen. It was for the steward to see that an animal was

Above: menu, for a banquet, with sketches by Michelangelo.

correctly carved, that helpings matched rank and reached the proper people: the head, for instance, as emblematic of leadership, to the lord. One might say that every morsel had its own symbolic message and was scrupulously allotted among the scrupulously graded guests.

When the dish itself was on the table, the business was still hedged with protocol. The prince, the ranking guest or the master of the house took, or was given, first helping. Renaissance manuals insist that to serve a guest first, *per cortesia*, in recognition of his "sacredness," is the crown of hospitality, but the quantity, quality and order of servings were otherwise decreed by social identity. Best fare to the top table, and inferiors must be content with the leftovers from the top table, or with scraps of offal. At Mantua, as in other Italian courts, it was a rule that "surplus from the table of the Serenissimi Padroni is for the third and lesser tables," though if there were "some noble dish that could be eaten cold in the evening, the Steward of the guests' dining room will remove it on a silver platter to the *credenza*, and trim

Above: illustration on a fifteenth-century cassone, *depicting a scene from a Boccaccio novella; it shows screens in front of the high table, and the four-stepped dais on which it is mounted.*
Below: a banquet of the early 1500s. The table still looks medieval; the cloth hangs to the ground and is full enough for the folds to be used in lieu of napkins; food is eaten with the fingers, and the copper receptacle in the foreground is for bones and other débris. The picture may be from the school of the Brescian painter Romanino.

Above: painting by Marcello Fogolino of the banquet offered by Bartolomeo Colleoni in honour of King Christian of Denmark who, as guest of honour, sits alone at the head of the table.

and garnish it as he thinks fit, to look fresh." As for the elaborate sugar confections on the prince's table, these percolated as débris to the courtiers. To quote again from Mantua: "anything unbroken the Butler is to save for reuse . . . and the Master of the *Tinello* may have the broken bits to distribute." The joys of court-life indeed! . . .

The prince, then, was distinguished by the quality of his food and his table appointments – bread-baskets, silver and precious objects, many in crystal or gold, and the blindingly white linen (this in the days before chemical bleaches). The banquet was no private pleasure, but a public projection, a statement of rank. Its lavishness, the gold and silver on show, the attire and number of the servants, were all marks of status. The banquet and all the magnificence that went with it were a continual dramatization of power and of the social and political establishment that was the background and setting for power.

The court in the country

The most widely-read authority on architecture during the Renaissance was undoubtedly Leon Battista Alberti, but neither his *De re aedificatoria* nor the majority of later – and largely derivative – works on the subject laid down hard-and-fast rules as to what the courtly villa should be. He merely differentiated, as for the town palace, between buildings for prince and private citizen, the difference being fundamental and intrinsic. "Princely palaces (and villas) are to harbour many people; the rooms should be many and spacious and, even when they are for individuals, should be stately, since they are always crowded. But in a private house it is enough that the busiest rooms are seen to suffice for the master's wants."

Pietro Cataneo, in *I quattro primi libri di architettura* (1554), had classified buildings by the owner's rank – for "King, Prince, Prelate, Signore or honourable gentleman," with cost and magnificence suited to "income and dignity." In the second half of the sixteenth century Anton Francesco Doni names five types of

THE VILLA; FOR PROFIT AND PLEASURE

1

Towards the end of the fifteenth century, the villa emerges as an architectural type distinct from the medieval signorial stronghold; a new relation with the surroundings is chiefly indicated by the number of doors and windows giving onto the outside world. The villa is no longer shut-in and defensive, for the outer world is no longer savage, dark and, therefore, menacing. Nature has felt the hand of man and is rationally arranged; the villa overlooks a garden.

Fortress features, such as battlements, become mere decoration (1, the villa of Cafaggiolo, built by Michelozzo for Cosimo the Elder in 1451); the twin-window was introduced at the ground level of the façade. Once thought to have been invented by Michelangelo, this type of window is now considered a Michelozzian innovation, used in rural villas before it was seen in the town. It belongs to the new concept of villa life in the country.

The basic plan of a villa

2

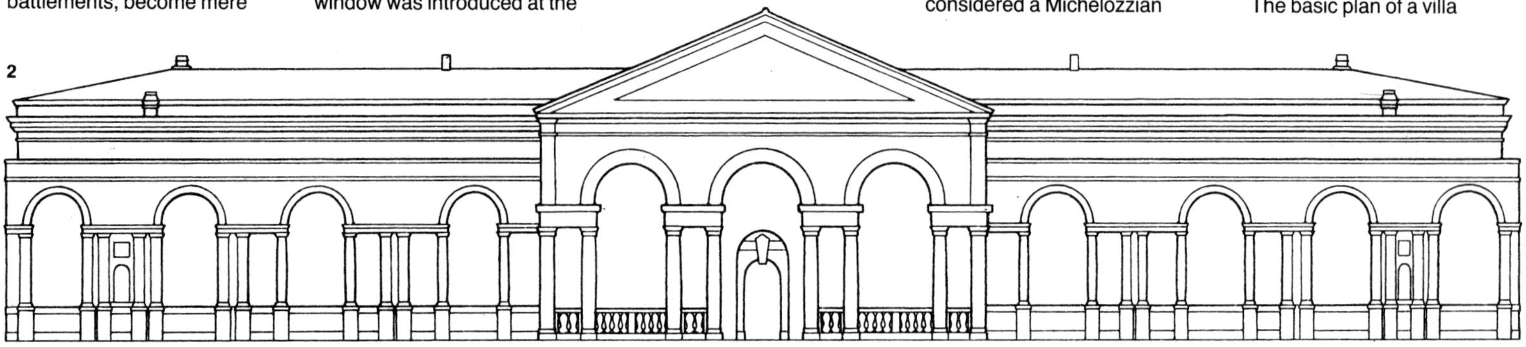

3

4

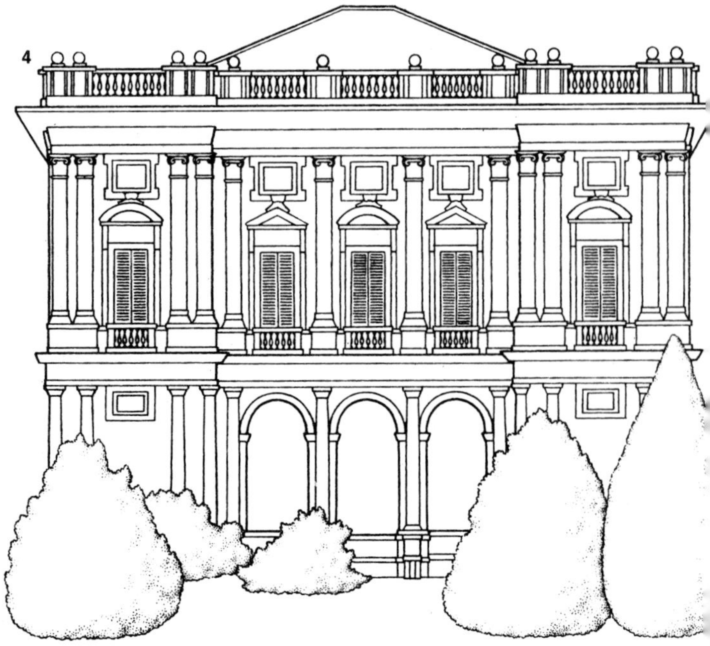

would reflect the new relation with the setting. It might be one square block, with or without a courtyard (4, Villa Cambiaso at Albaro, built in 1548 by Galeazzo Alessi for the Giustiniani family); it might have lateral wings, a type of which there are many rural examples, as well as the Palazzo Pitti in Florence, and which had great influence on Roman villas (5, Villa Farnesina, below the Gianicolo; built in 1508–11 by Baldassare Peruzzi for the Sienese banker Agostino Chigi, it passed to the Farnese in 1580).

Or design could be married to surroundings in other ways: by the courtyard, which Alberti says, in *De re aedificatoria*, is fundamental to villa architecture; or by a loggia at ground level, or a terrace above (3, the garden frontage of Villa Gamberaia at Settignano, a fifteenth-century building, later altered; 2, the loggiaed garden-front of the Palazzo del Te at Mantua, built in 1525–35 for Federico II Gonzaga by Giulio Romano; 6, loggia and double, great stairway entrance at Artimino, hunting lodge of Grand Duke Ferdinando I, built by Buontalenti in 1594, and betraying elements of the ancient tower motif).

Such elements might be more than residential amenities and have their practical purpose in the productive running of the estate. (7, plan of the Palladian villa at Fratta Polesine, built in 1568–70 on a "conspicuous site," for "the magnificent signor Francesco Badoero" and known as La Badoera; the central block is connected by curving colonnades to left and right to the level where farm manager and bailiff had their quarters, and to the stables and other necessary outbuildings).

The Rotonda, near Vicenza (8), is also by Andrea Palladio, who built it in 1570 or so, for Paolo Almerico. Here the utilitarian additions are quite separate from the main house and the two basic themes of villa architecture, the solid block and the open prospect, are resolved by means of the four identical loggiaed porches, each jutting from the middle of one façade and approached by stone steps. They are on the vertical axes of the villa, which run through the cupolaed central rotonda – a pattern characteristic of Renaissance humanist architecture and derived from the Pantheon in Rome.

Palladio himself wrote that the Pantheon was so-called "because it was dedicated, after Jupiter, to all the gods or, as others would have it, because it is a model of the world." Certainly every element of his rotonda breathes the two-fold *utilitas-delectatio* ideal which underlay the humanist conception of villa life in the country.

6

5

7

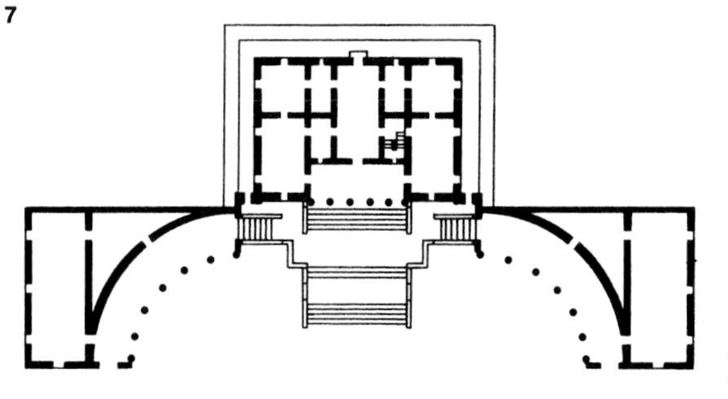

8

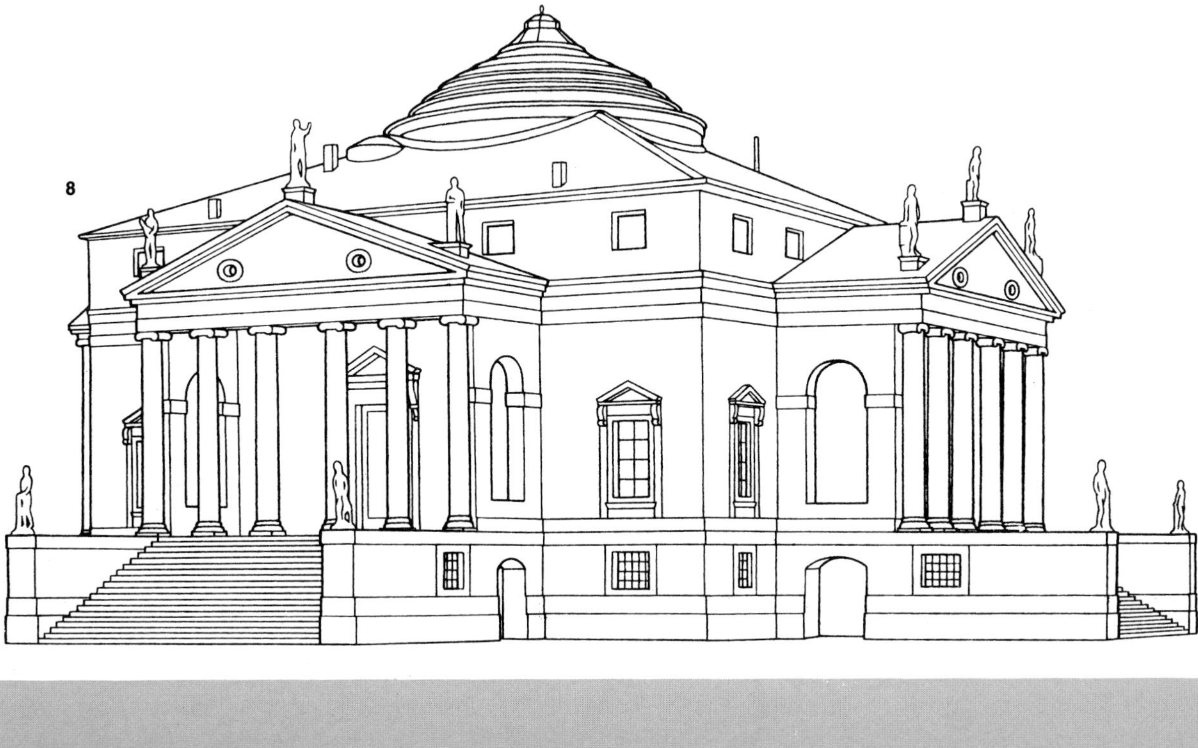

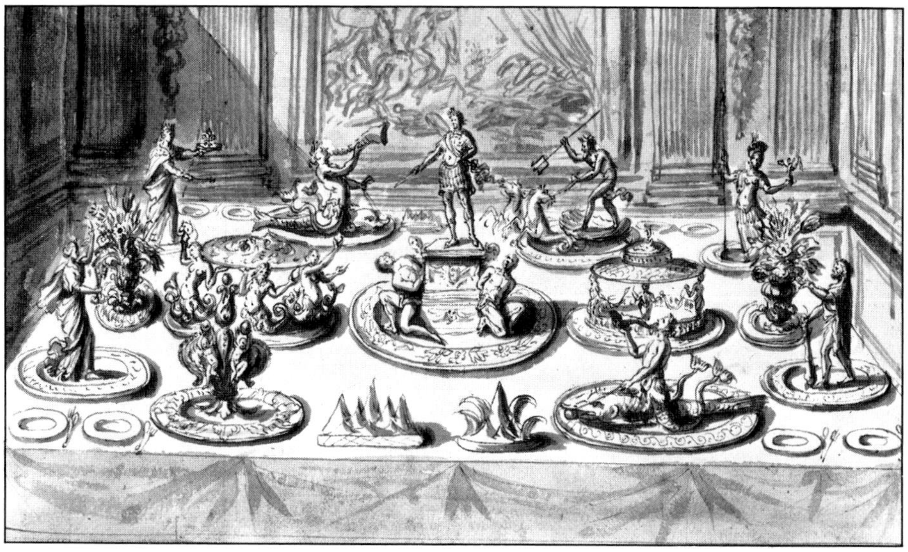

The trionfi *of a table decoration, probably in honour of Cardinal Leopoldo de' Medici, son of Cosimo* II. *The centerpiece is a miniature of Giovanni Bandini's statue of Ferdinando* I, *set up in Leghorn in 1595. Pietro Tacca added the "four Moors" later.*

country dwelling in his book *Le Ville*. The princely villa, "for King, Duke or valiant and powerful lord," is the twin of the town palace, consisting, as it may, of the same architectural elements. Next is the "rural retreat" of the scholarly gentleman; then the villa as profitable enterprise – a farm, that is; and lastly the *casa di risparmio*, or investment property, and the peasant's hut or *capanna dell'utile*.

Though there was no definite technical literature on villa building, prince and architect were certainly influenced by these and similar books, which urged a very careful choice of site. Not too far from a city, Alberti advised, and on fertile soil "for an abundance of produce;" somewhere with good air and water and a mild climate. But though emphasizing the productive side in the case of the ordinary villa, for a prince's, he counsels that the amenities and opportunities for recreation must be thought of, and consequently the site chosen should not be a particularly fertile one, but notable for other advantages such as the air, its siting as regards the sun, and the view. Access was all important, with decent roads for the reception of guests. The noble villa will stand well. It will have vistas, "of a town, or of fortresses, the sea, a rolling plain, perhaps a bold line of hills or mountain crests, or beautiful gardens; and plenty of fishing and hunting."

For the prince, the prime consideration, therefore, is the site – a peaceful spot in which to escape from the summer heat, but, as Alberti

Below and opposite, left: examples of the fantastic art of folding dinner napkins, from Mattia Giegher's treatise on the subject. Some of the possible results are shown, with the correct way of working. Different patterns were made for guests of different rank.

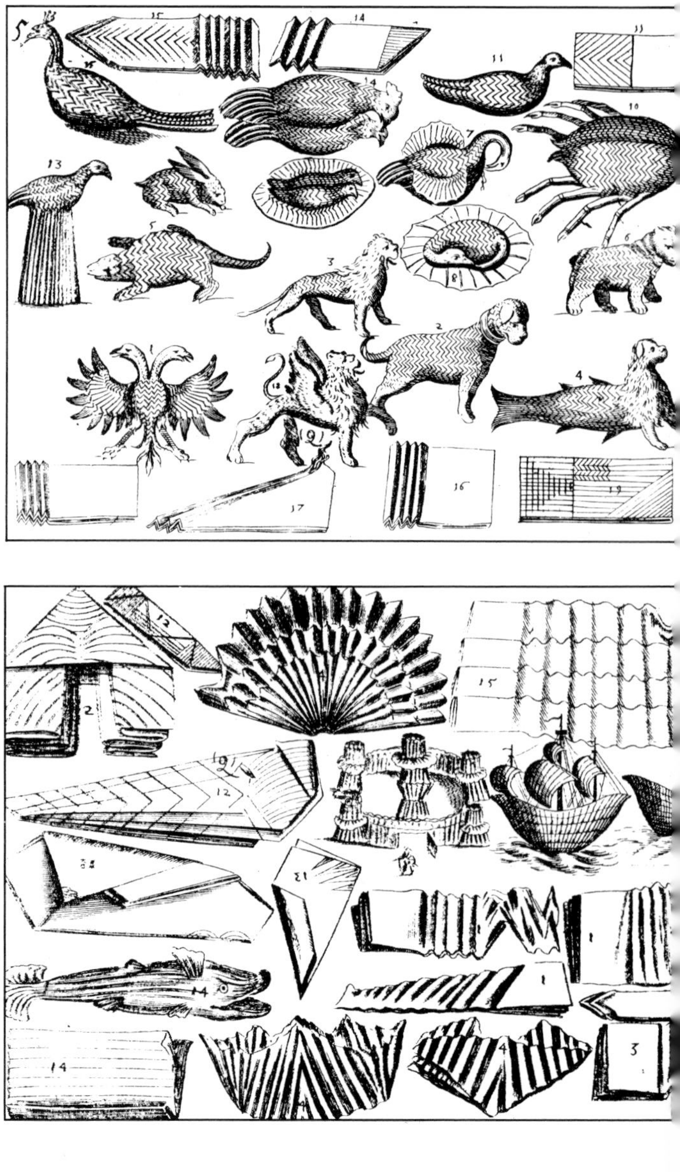

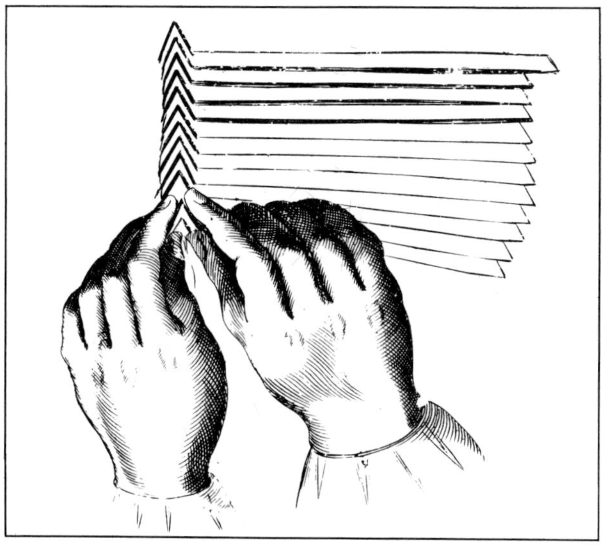

points out, not too far away from the city, the best examples being the Medici villas of Petraia, Castello and Careggi in the vicinity of Florence, between Sesto and Castello. Or they might consist of a series or circuit within the city boundaries, such as the Este "delights" at Ferrara.

The courts of Rome and Naples – territories exposed, as Cataneo says, "to heat rather than to cold" – had summer refuges "in the hills and mountains, with cool air, and trees, and flowing streams." The Roman court might retire to Frascati, Tivoli or Viterbo – to the villa Aldobrandini, or the villa d'Este, or the villa Lante at Bagnaia near Viterbo; and the court at Naples could spend the hot months "in the cool towns and hills of the Abruzzi, and similar resorts in that kingdom."

But villa life had other attractions to supplement the freedom from stifling urban heat: "sundry diversions," Cataneo tells us, most of which were easier to come by in the country. "Honest and laudable pastimes" were fishing, hunting, singing and dancing, evening entertainment and card games. But hunting was unquestionably the lure that drew the lord and his courtiers to the country. Many villas were really hunting lodges; the villa of Ferdinando I de' Medici at Artimino is an example. Beneath the arcades of their clipped "Italian gardens" the feasting would go on, and their decorations are appropriately of hunting scenes, pastoral scenes and idyllic *concerts champêtres*.

Above: detail from a painting by Pier Francesco Cittadini, showing the kitchen shelves of a seventeenth-century palace, laden with plates, utensils, cooking pots and candlesticks. Maids are busily preparing chickens and vegetables, and the scene as a whole is very lavish. Yet the courtiers – or those of them relegated to the tinello *– ate broken meats and leftovers.*

Villas were used seasonally for their appropriate diversions. Ferdinand I would pass the spring mainly at Poggio a Caiano, "where a resident troupe of players performed for him." In summer he preferred the villa of Poggio Imperiale, and would be at Pratolino in the autumn to hunt and listen to music.

On a deeper level the phenomenon of villa life partook of a philosophical and literary predisposition which had much to do with the study of antiquity, and is in tune with the princely culture of the Renaissance. Leon Battista Alberti's writings begot whole volumes on the villa as sanctuary, a country retreat, that is, of unconditional happiness, intellectual bliss, of relief from mundane care. The lord in his villa is a practicing humanist, his life is one of leisure and contemplation. Two of the Medici villas exemplify this attitude: Careggi, where Cosimo The Elder presided over the Platonic Academy, and Poggio a Caiano, that "temple of Florentine intellect and humanist learning," a model institution.

But the villa-for-delectation was surely realized to perfection at Ferrara. Schifanoia and the Paradiso, as their names tell us, were built (by Alberto d'Este, who reigned from 1388 to 1393), solely for pleasure, though later they were ducal residences; and the scattered pleasure-villas, the fishing and hunting lodges of the Este, were in reach by road or, more often, by water. The *delizie* of Ferrara were legendary for the villas, gardens, fishponds and parks, of which it had more than any other town, that existed, albeit in curtailed form, within its walls. Other villas, built by successive princes beyond the city confines and absorbed into the Herculean Addition, reached their maximum splendour under Alfonso II. It was he who had a connecting road built, reminiscent of Vasari's *corridoio*, so that the court could interchange visits to the various villas, free from the gaze of the townspeople.

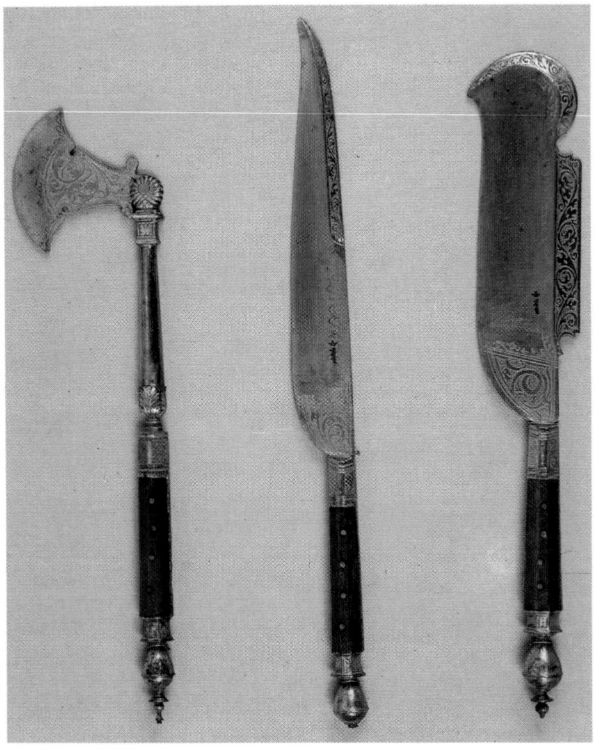

Objects of great beauty and value were used at the princely table. Above: a plate of Urbino ware, decorated with the wedding impresa *of Alfonso II, Duke of Ferrara, Modena and Reggio, and his third wife, Margherita Gonzaga, whom he married in 1579. Left: sixteenth-century utensils for cutting up game, made in Lombardy. Opposite: fifteenth-century goblet from Murano.*

This road of Alfonso's is on a map of 1597 of Ferrara. It had a central canal (fed from the castle moat, and so from the Po river), with a fleet of white swans and water birds, and beside it were carriage tracks and gardens, protected from prying eyes by an avenue of tall olives and vines. The ordinary streets were borne on bridges overhead, and prince and courtiers could sail or drive or walk, unobserved. The scheme might have been designed specifically to illustrate Alberti's ideas: the villa at no great distance from the town palace, "on an easy route where one could walk, drive or sail unimpeded, summer or winter; and this route to be if possible near the city gates, so that one can go to the villa when one pleases, with one's wife and children, with no dressing up and nobody staring."

Leaving his castle, the Duke of Ferrara would turn west to reach the Castellina, a pleasure-pavillion with garden, orchard and fishpond; then on to the Cedrara, a grove of what were then rare and remarkable trees – cedar, orange and lemon – and an ilex-wood, with birds for shooting. North, then, to the villa of Belfiore, begun by Alberto d'Este towards the end of the fourteenth century and a favourite of the later princes, Ercole and Borso among them. Borso would receive ambassadors there, and indulge in learned conversation with poets and artists. It had gardens, groves, orchards and fishpools, and nearby, girdled in trim greenery, was the *barchetto* with stags and deer and goats "for household sport." After the man-made pleasure-grounds of the Montagnola and the Montagna was the villa Belvedere, one of the loveliest of the *delizie*. Alfonso I had built it in 1520 or so, and engaged Ariosto himself to write of it.

The walled estate, on an island in the Po, comprised every delight: "gardens, fountains, woods, meadows and vineyards; there were many animals, native and foreign, and the views and paintings were enchanting." Within a mile or two lay the Barco, a vast wood of wild game for the duke's hunting, and south of the city rose the villa of Belriguardo. Dating from 1435, in Niccolò III's reign, this was the jewel of the Este villas, beloved by all the succeeding dukes. "Truly a royal palace, with as many rooms as there are days in the year;" and in its ponds

ladies, using hooks and harpoons, achieved "incredible catches" of fish.

The notion of the villa as *luogo di delizia* was not limited to Ferrara. On the outskirts of Mantua, Federico II Gonzaga had Giulio Romano construct the Palazzo del Te, designed specifically for pleasure and diversion including theatrical entertainments. Naples, Serlio tells us, was "as rich in gardens and pleasure retreats as anywhere in Italy," and of these agreeable places near the city he names "the palace of Poggio Reale, built by King Alfonso for his recreation." Serlio's engravings, modified though they are by his personal style, are one record of this vanished villa of the Aragonese court, the most famous Renaissance building in the Kingdom of Naples. The plan is influenced by the Medici villas near Florence (the workmen employed were Tuscan), and there was a courtyard with a staircase. But the striking elements are four corner pavilions – separate "noble suites," where high-ranking guests were housed.

For the court at Ferrara, the tour of the *delizie* by Alfonso's internal road was merely a token trip round its own back garden, but for more distant destinations the court embarked on a journey in earnest. The prince, living for several months of the year between his villas quitted the urban palace with his numerous court and the essentials for comfort and luxury. Furnishings, of course, for these were scanty when a villa was empty; but chiefly he brought with him the insignia of power. For months he would rule from a base in the country. It was logical publicly to transfer the symbols and instruments of authority, thus making the villa the equivalent of the palace in his capital. This was something all rulers did, the pope included.

The proliferation of pontifical court villas near Rome owed as much to cardinals as to popes, for the cardinalate courts, though satellites, were powerful and relatively independent. The scions of princely families – Scipione Borghese and Ippolito d'Este are examples – would build near Rome on becoming cardinals; and when cardinals became popes, the villas were beloved country residences. Cardinal Giulio de' Medici, as Clement VII, still prized his Villa Madama.

The Medici family dogs (with cat and rabbit) in an anonymous painting in the Palazzo Pitti. Opposite: portrait of a young woman, also in the Pitti, by an anonymous Florentine artist of the first decade of the seventeenth century. The inset view probably shows the palace as originally designed by Brunelleschi.

The rural installations of a Renaissance court revealed its social structures, most clearly when an existing building was adapted. Many villas – including princely villas – had been medieval strongholds, where modernization could mean changes of function: a watchtower preserved as a dovecote, with *altane*, or roof terraces; big windows inserted even on a ground floor, altering the relation of architecture to environment; a new plan hinging on an inner courtyard. And much more was involved than a multiplication of lodgings, unenvisaged by the small medieval community; thus are structural changes imposed by social ones. At La Petraia, restored in 1576–89 by Buontalenti for Cardinal Ferdinando de' Medici, a square tower dominates the façade: the fortified tower of the original fourteenth-century *casa da signore*, disguised as a sixteenth-century belvedere, its corbels retained for decoration.

La Simonetta, near the Porta Comasina of Milan, was a bourgeois mansion, rather than a stronghold, enlarged for a princely court – first in early Renaissance style for Gualtiero Bescapè, chancellor of Ludovico il Moro, then for Ferrante Gonzaga, governor of Milan, who acquired it in 1547. His architect was Domenico Giunti (or Giuntalodi), a disciple of Giulio Romano and Vignola. Giunti's plans, derived mostly from those of Roman villas, embraced the decorations and the gardens, where he positioned the fruit trees, in the process planting a *giardino all'italiana*, a reorganizing of nature into an overall design; what he created was a *luogo di delizie*.

Guests at court

Rightly to comprehend the princely hospitality of the Renaissance we must remember that a state was, to its absolute ruler, an extension of his own house. The guest was under his roof, from the moment of entering to the time of leaving his domains, and every foreigner of requisite rank – the gentleman travelling privately or the diplomat on a mission – should be welcomed.

"Emblems, hieroglyphs, fables and mottoes," said Balthasar Gracián, the seventeenth-century Spanish Jesuit in his Agudeza y arte de ingenio, *"are as precious stones in the gold of elegant discourse." It took as much* ingenio, *one would think, to coax precious stones – or rather, hard marbles,* pietre dure *– into the appearance of flower stems and petals, of juicy fruit, or the delicate tones of sea and sky. Late in the sixteenth century, the Medici established a workshop for this art, the* Opificio delle pietre dure, *in San Marco in Florence; its products were much sought after by Italian and foreign courts.*
Opposite and above: tabletops in pietre dure *inlay.*
Right: an upright table clock of the later sixteenth century.

Court jewellery. Below and opposite bottom: thirteenth-century pieces that belonged to Cangrande I Della Scala, lord of Verona.
Right: front and back of a sixteenth-century pendant in gold, enamel, pearls and precious stones.
Opposite, top: seventeenth-century brooch with a large irregular pearl. This, like the pendant, was in the collection of the grand dukes of Tuscany.

Not that treatment was identical, nor the prince's bearing the same for each. Precise rules of ceremony were fitted to the relevant social grading of each guest. Diplomats fell into the broad categories of ambassador, special or resident ambassador, and the degree of friendship desired with the country in question counted for much. Needless to say, the more powerful the country, the more fulsome the reception for its emissary.

From the official reception to the official adieu, the visit was dominated by ceremonial. To begin at the beginning, the greater the guest, the further a ruler went to meet him; the lower he was on the scale, the fewer miles the ruler would condescend to go to meet him. The greatest were met at the border and conducted in pomp to the capital. Lodgings, if necessary, were provided on the road – in castles, religious houses, or with noblemen; in inns if all else failed. At the city walls there might be troops paraded, a reception committee, or somebody's servant waiting. For the star guests, the forts might fire a salute, and a carriage procession drive through decorated streets.

The reception committee, too, was made to measure with different vehicles for strangers of differing rank. A ruling sovereign was met by the prince in person, his officers of state and a concourse of coaches and carriages.

These rules applied as rigidly if the guest were simply passing through. The prince paid food and lodging, despatched servants, provisions and transport to smooth the journey; and the higher the guest's rank the farther away was he joined by the obligatory attendant. It was as though the city were the heart of a system of concentric circles which, from zone to zone, qualified the host's duty towards him.

Social position dictated the programme. Contrast, for instance, the reception of two visitors to Florence: the king of Spain's treasurer, and the ambassador of the Duke of Parma.

The first was in 1607. "On 20 January, there arrived in Florence, posting from Rome, the most illustrious and most excellent signor Don Francesco del Castro, valet to the king of Spain. Signor Matteo Berti left Florence ("the 24th hour"), with a coach and six horses, to meet him. His Most Serene Highness (Cosimo II) sent

signor Paolo Orsino, of the Ambrosian Academy, to receive him at the gates with the maestro di casa and majordomo. They escorted him to the Cardinals' apartments in the Pitti, where he dined, with signor Paolo in attendance . . . and after dinner he saw the Galleria, then the defenses and the Santissima Nunziata, which was opened for him; from there he was escorted to the gates, for he supped at Scarperia . . . and his travelling expenses were paid throughout by the state, and he was supplied with grooms, and an enclosed litter for the journey over the Alps . . ."

Then, on 26 April 1609, Count Giovanni Torelli, ambassador of the Most Serene Duke of Parma, is at the Campana inn, "where he was collected that evening by signor Sinolfo Otterio, who took him to the Pitti, to the rooms above the *sala delle statue*. Signor Benedetto Rucellai was his steward, with pages and a carver; he had a covered dish; for his brother and a gentleman with him the dishes were uncovered . . . he left on 1 March . . . on his way to Pisa."

Of these two very important individuals, it is obvious which one carried the more weight. The Spanish treasurer is met at the city-gates and escorted to the palace immediately. The Duke of Parma's ambassador is stuck at an inn for the day before being fetched, less ceremoniously, to the Pitti. When he leaves, he leaves alone, while the King of Spain's man has a litter in which to navigate the Alps.

The critical dividing line was between those who had the right, and those who had not, to lay their heads in the palace. If they had not, they were sheltered by nobles of the court (in whose town houses their master seems to have allocated guest rooms at will), in villas belonging to the prince, or in convents. A lordly suite, or a minor guest, might go to an inn. We read in the *Ordini et officii della Corte del Serenissimo Signor Duca d'Urbino* (in the early decades of 1600) that the duke should have, initially, "a private inn, or one where he may board people for whom he merely pays expenses; then a house, or several houses, for those who merit both lodging and a certain respect. Such a house should be near the palace, and for none but honoured guests."

Audience with the prince was a coveted

distinction, reserved for diplomats on very confidential errands, for great prelates and nobles and the envoys of very powerful states. It was not for all comers, and the minutiae of its etiquette were crucial. Titles and forms of address, the granting or not of a hand, the doffing or not of headgear; how one was received and how escorted; how many rooms the prince walked through to meet a guest, and whether or not he walked back with him; whether the guest sat by the host at a banquet, and what food was on his plate – all these told of the regard in which he was held, or the regard the ruler wished him to infer. And courts, like courtiers, had their hierarchy.

The sojourn of an illustrious visitor was beguiled with the gamut of courtly festivals: hunts and tournaments, drives in the town, plays, balls and banquets. He viewed the churches and buildings and sights of the capital; made the rounds of the prince's treasures, the art collection, the glories of the palace. He did so accompanied by his host, or the bevy of attendants allotted to serve and entertain him throughout his stay. And the programme prepared for him was neither free-and-easy nor spontaneous. Every detail of protocol was worked out beforehand, nothing was left to chance; everyone was briefed, and the ground plan drawn up in the finest detail: the officials he would meet, the places to be visited, the hospitality he was entitled to expect from his hosts.

As the etiquette of hospitality in Italian courts grew ever more rigid, guest quarters tended to be confined to princely palaces, with the result that lodgings were better and more permanently arranged, and the duties of courtier and domestic were more specifically categorized. The reorganization of guest quarters in the early 1700s, proved a boon at Mantua, for instance, where, on at least one occasion, the court was left red-faced in its handling of an important foreign visitor. This happened after lodging arrangements misfired during an archducal visit from Austria.

To the same end, each court had a senior official – master of ceremonies or maestro di casa, though not necessarily styled as such – to supervise guest entertainment. Banquets, decor

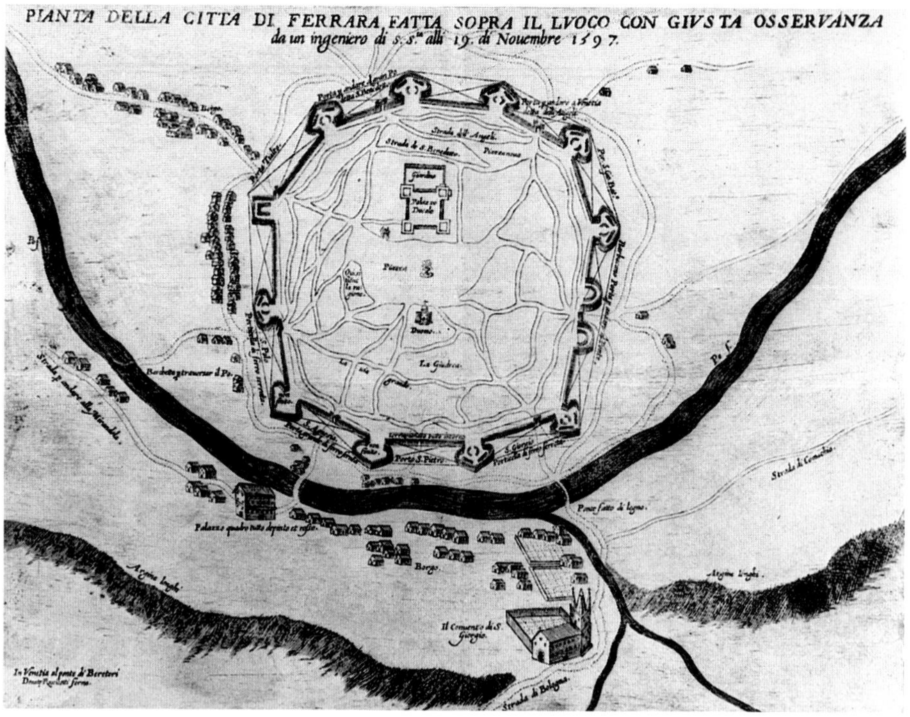

Plan of Ferrara in 1597. A canal, fed from the River Po, surrounded the castle. Along it the duke and his court could sail – or walk or drive on pathways beside it, screened by tall olive trees and spaliered vines – to any of their villas nearby, "without dressing up" or having to appear in public; and this, said the humanist Leon Battista Alberti, was a great convenience.
Opposite: view through the entrance gate of the Palazzo del Te, the Gonzaga villa at Mantua, built for Federico II. The name may be derived from an old word, tejeto, *for a group of peasant huts.*

On these pages are shown frescoes from two of the rooms in the Palazzo del Te, the huge "suburban" villa which Giulio Romano both built and decorated for Federico II, fifth marquess and first duke of Mantua, in 1525–35.
Above: a corner of the Sala dei Giganti. *The frescoes,* The Fall of the Giants Struck by the Thunderbolts of Jupiter, *were designed by Giulio Romano and executed, from his cartoons, by Rinaldo Mantovano and others. Walls and ceiling are treated as one pictorial surface.*
Opposite: the Sala di Psiche, *frescoed with the nuptial banquet of Cupid and Psyche.*

and staging came under his supervision. He was the billeting officer; he saw that people had the right complement of servants; he checked precedence and procedure. And to avoid chagrin and complaint he had, as director of etiquette, to be thoroughly versed in the history of previous visits.

For this reason he kept, or caused his staff to keep, records, so as to have concrete examples at his fingertips in case of doubt or difficulty. When expecting an ambassador or foreign notability he thus knew exactly how he, or an equal in rank, was treated before, and what the nuances of etiquette had been. The records were evidently compiled for this purpose, for descriptions are lengthy and much space is devoted to the names and offices of the suite, to table settings, precedence, greetings and salutations and the distribution of rooms – down to the colour of wall hangings, and how the carriages were ornamented.

Nor was this mere irrelevant preoccupation with externals, for the nuances proclaimed rank and rating and slotted the guest into his niche in the social ladder. On that ladder each rung had its social significance. Personal dignity was insulted, personal concord wrecked, for the slightest prevarication or chance slip of memory, in a world whose words and gestures were conceived, and interpreted, as very serious things. And so they were. In words and gestures reality was encoded.

Saying it with gifts

Closely connected with court hospitality was the reciprocal obligation of present-giving. Princes, lords and prelates were habitual gift-givers; it mattered not whether the dignitary in question was merely travelling through a foreign domain or on a state visit to the court. It would be equally unthinkable in either case not to mark the occasion without an exchange of gifts.

If a guest were to stay for some time, he was the recipient of a gift at the first opportunity which presented itself – the banquet, audience or meeting with the host; and on departure he reciprocated in like manner, not forgetting to suitably reward the suite of servants appointed to look after him during his stay. If he were not breaking his journey, but only passing through, the gift would generally be in the form of assistance on the road – servants, military escort, transport or victuals. Cardinal Aldobrandino, on a journey through Tuscany in 1559, is logged in the *Diari di Etichetta del Guardaroba* of the Medici court as having been presented with "12 spring chickens, 22 salami, 40 pounds of sausage, 20 flasks of Trebbiano wine, plums, medlars, peaches and snow. [The snow was for refrigeration purposes, presumably.] Total delivered to Casteldellapieve." On a similar occasion, in 1608, the beneficiary is Cardinal Mellini, "to whom His Most Serene Highness [Cosimo II de' Medici] gave "three bay mules, and a litter . . . of red damask with gold fringes, together with harness and fittings."

More often, however, the gift was in the nature of a private congratulatory token between members of the various reigning families. The prince would send his gift through an envoy, be it for a birth or baptism, coronation or wedding, or as condolence in a protracted illness, or other such eventful family vicissitudes. Martial or diplomatic success was hailed with gifts or, if warranted, with civic and popular jubilation. These were expressions of solidarity, elicited by the personal or political fortunes of princes, and contained within a wider network in which gifts spelled peaceable intention, either the launching of new friendships or the cementing of old ones.

As the seal of any satisfactory negotiation, the gift was a major item in official court diplomacy. An alliance, treaty of commerce or marriage, or ordinary neighbourly agreement, warranted an exchange, as did quite trivial mandates. It was unthinkable that an ambassador should turn up with no gifts from his lord, or even from himself; and equally unthinkable that he should receive none. He, by custom, gave first, with his lord's greetings, at his official reception, or at the princely audience when that was accorded; and not until the rite was over would he mention politics.

The gifts would be costly objects or rareties and "marvels" – uncommon gemstones, mechanical and scientific curiosities, veritable *mirabilia*. A happy choice was a finely-bred animal – horse or hound – but nothing was neglected that might tempt admiration and goodwill. We hear of a parrot offered to Cosimo II, "the most beautiful parrot ever in these regions, of six colours: fiery red on beak, head and breast, yellow below, with shades of green and blue in its wings, and a black tail."

The bearing of a gift might be the sole reason for a diplomatic mission, and this gesture, repeated, perhaps, at regular intervals, helped to maintain the bonds of friendship or alliance; it implied harmony, now and for the future. The quality and frequency of such ceremonial exchanging of gifts were predictable indicators on the diplomatic barometer of how matters stood between the participating courts.

The gift was, besides, the internal currency at court. A prince's court must be ample, and eminent. Ideas might alter as to what a gentleman should be, or do, but the relation of prince and courtier continued as one of mutual profit. Honours, titles, revenues, offices (as well as tangible gifts) from a ruler were the guerdon of service, acknowledgement of the luster his court lent his crown.

Above all, the court had to be seen. In 1468 Galeazzo Maria Sforza (Duke of Milan from

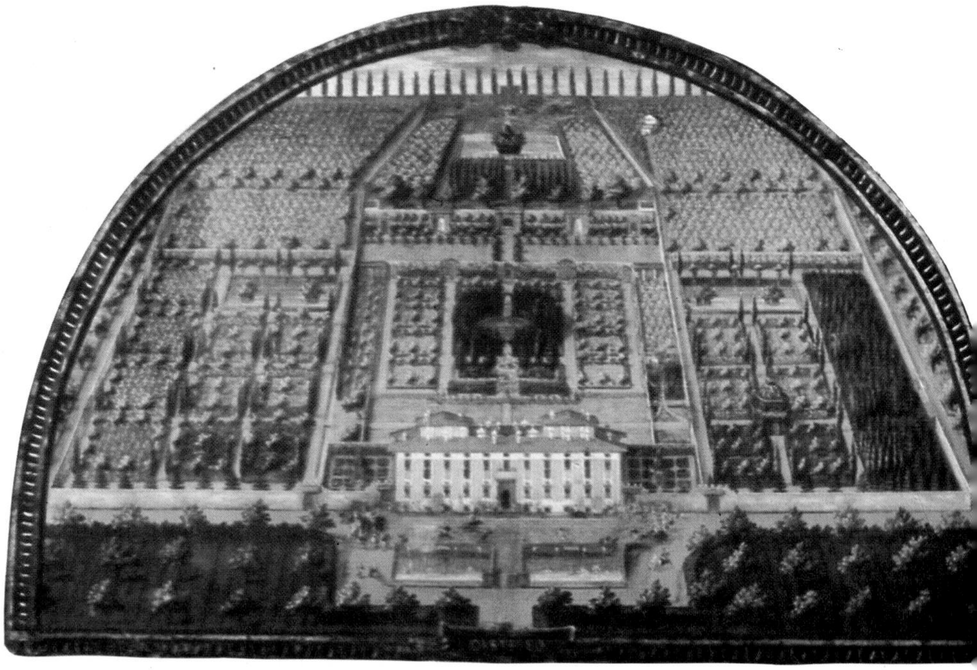

The Medici villa at Castello, depicted (above) by the Flemish painter Justus Utens. This villa, known as "il Vivaio" (the Fishpond), came into the possession of the Medici in 1480, was sacked and burned on their expulsion from Florence, and restored by Cosimo I. It had belonged to Lorenzo il Popolano and his brother Giovanni, descendants of Lorenzo the Elder (Cosimo's brother; these two, cousins of Lorenzo the Magnificent, were called the Medici di Castello and from this branch descended the grand dukes of Tuscany. It may have been for Lorenzo il Popolano, and for this villa, that Botticelli painted the haunting Primavera.

Machiavelli, writing of the houses owned by Cosimo the Elder, says he had one in the city – "and very appropriate for a citizen of his status" – and four in the country outside, at Careggi, Fiesole, Cafaggiuolo, as he spells it, and Trebbio: "all of them palaces, not for private citizens, but kings." (Right, the villa at Trebbio, and (opposite, bottom) Cafaggiolo, originally a Florentine fortress, altered by Michelozzo in 1451. Both pictures by Justus Utens). "Yet," Machiavelli goes on, "although these houses were regal, as was everything he did . . . his actions were so tempered with native prudence, that he never passed the limits of good-natured modesty. Whether he were talking, or riding, or dealing with servants or arranging family alliances, all he did he did like a simple citizen; knowing that constant ostentation will attract more enmity than will things done in a plain and ordinary way."

1466 to 1476) made it obligatory on his feudal vassals to be present at court for Christmas, Easter and the feast of St John, thus ensuring the most consummate splendour for these celebrations. His "family" was thus periodically summoned to do him honour and to ratify his political and social supremacy, and his bounty in response was infinite. He recompensed noble and lackey as each deserved, with magnificent gifts all round.

The gift, at one time or another, was bestowed on scholar, artist and astrologer as often as on official, diplomat or menial; but it was, too, the sign of gratitude from lord to vassal. "The brave and loyal subject," wrote Carlo Emanuele I of Savoy in a patent of nobility of 1587, "can and should expect, as the best

reward of noble and honourable deeds, their public recognition by his natural Prince." The "good Prince," therefore, "is at pains to recognize and requite him, not only with royal gifts but with titles, rank and dignities to bring universal honour to him and his posterity."

Whatever the ruler's gift, it conveyed benevolent esteem. The prince's patronage, direct or indirect, adorned his court and enhanced his entourage; his gift was an envied promotion which sustained the courtier's hierarchical values and prestige. The prestige depended on the present. It was the stick-and-carrot method.

The very act of giving was symbolic. Shades of meaning in the type of present, the circumstances and ceremonial were translated as vital messages by the recipient and those about him. Most honourable and most flattering was presentation "by the ruler's own hand," rather than by that of some delegated inferior. Nothing could rival that.

More often than not the gift was jewellery, its *nobilità*, in terms of money and beauty, proportioned to the status of the man, or the deed, to be rewarded. Gold necklaces, earrings or medallions were given, and luxury articles whose craftsmanship and decoration were, from the accounts, superb. But an object was not just to be appraised for its cost or usefulness: the reality was the meanings to be drawn within the confines of the court; the gift could be of honours, privileges, court offices or diplomatic or administrative posts. Even a career in a prince's chancery was built, not on personal ability, but on his generosity and willingness to compensate devotion.

Payments to lesser functionaries or to domestics might be disguised as gifts when "wages" were not to be spoken of in so many words. In the *Trattato degli uffici communi tra gli amici superiori e inferiori*, of 1546, monsignor Giovanni della Casa (who was an archbishop) speaks of "sums to remunerate those who pass their lives in our service" and warns the great that their money is not largesse but straight payment for services and honour received, and it should be appropriate to the effort and industry expended or demanded, as the earth yields her heaviest crops to the most diligent husbandman. People will then do anything for

Michelangelo is said to have suggested the Mannerist rhythms of the inner façade of the Roman Villa Medici (above). The villa was built in 1544 by Annibale Lippi for Cardinal Ricci of Montepulciano, bought by the Medici, whose name it still bears, in 1580, and subsequently by Napoleon. It is now the Académie de France in Rome. Opposite, top: the Villa Ferdinanda at Artimino, built by Buontalenti as a hunting lodge for Grand Duke Ferdinando I in 1594. Bottom: the villa at Careggi, with the battlemented gallery recalling its origins as a feudal fortress. This villa belonged to the Lippi, then to the Medici, and when there was a division of family property, in 1457, it fell to Cosimo the Elder, for whom Michelozzi altered it. Cosimo gave a small property "near his Careggi," as Machiavelli tells us, to Marsilio Ficino, "the second father of Platonic philosophy."

you, he says, and you gain the reputation of a benign and generous master. This is much to the good, since it disposes your friends to assist and obey you, with the best of care and attention.

A prince on tour

The Renaissance court seldom went far afield, for by now the princes of Italy had fixed dwellings and resided in them, or in nearby villas, palaces and castles. In this they differed from their medieval predecessors, most of whom were constantly patrolling their lands, from one castle to the next. But Renaissance princes visited each other only when necessary to do so, and even then it would have to be for a very special reason such as a diplomatic mission. They moved between town palaces and country villas as the seasons dictated; or they might from time to time carry out inspections of the princely domains. There was also the odd pilgrimage or two to be considered.

Foreign travel, however, when it did occur, was regarded as one of the most fundamental

KITCHEN AND TABLE

When the prince sat down to dinner there were some light and ephemeral touches in the table decoration – sugar figures fancifully and delicately modelled, less realistic shapes in folded linen, tiny fireworks imported from Japan. But the more solid objects, useful and constantly used at these spectacular scenes, were handled with equal care and skill.

Officials responsible for the success of the banquet, the *Festa magnifica*, could refer to manuals of the kind from which our illustrations are taken. They had manuals on cooking and etiquette, on the rules for festive occasions, on how to equip a kitchen, a *credenza* or a table.

Guides to the art of carving, recipe books, detailed memoranda on dinners and luncheons and parties, were written by stewards in princely service or private cooks to the papacy. The best-known publications by such *segreti*, or confidential experts, were those of Messisbugo (2, 5, 6, 7, 9), Scappi (1, 4), Cervio and Fusoritto. Often they resemble directories, with their lists for kitchen and banquet and their accurate pictures (8, from the *Trattato dell scalco*, by Mattia Giegher).

A *siniscalco generale*, or majordomo, was in charge of the *offiziali* who saw to the

1

2

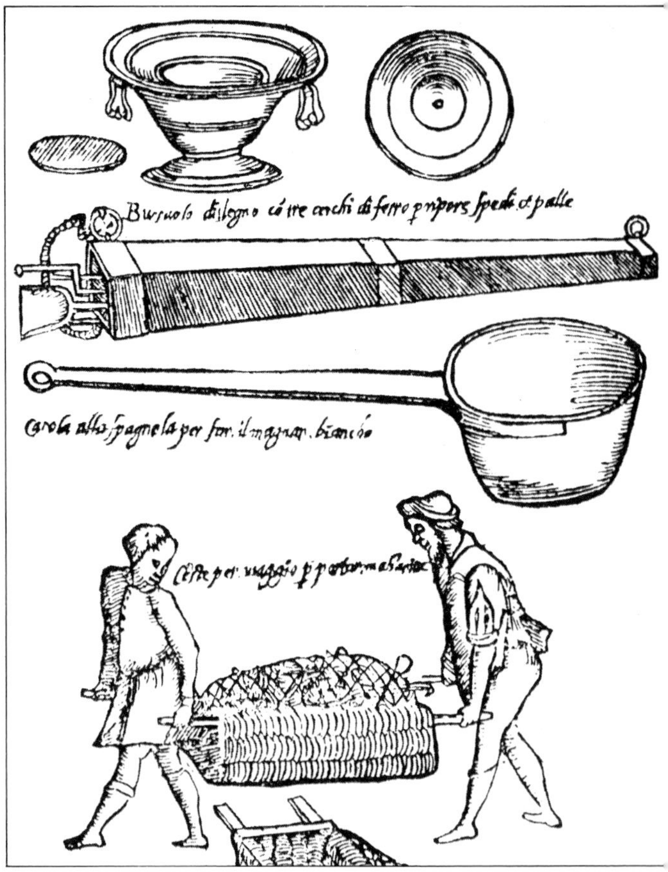

3

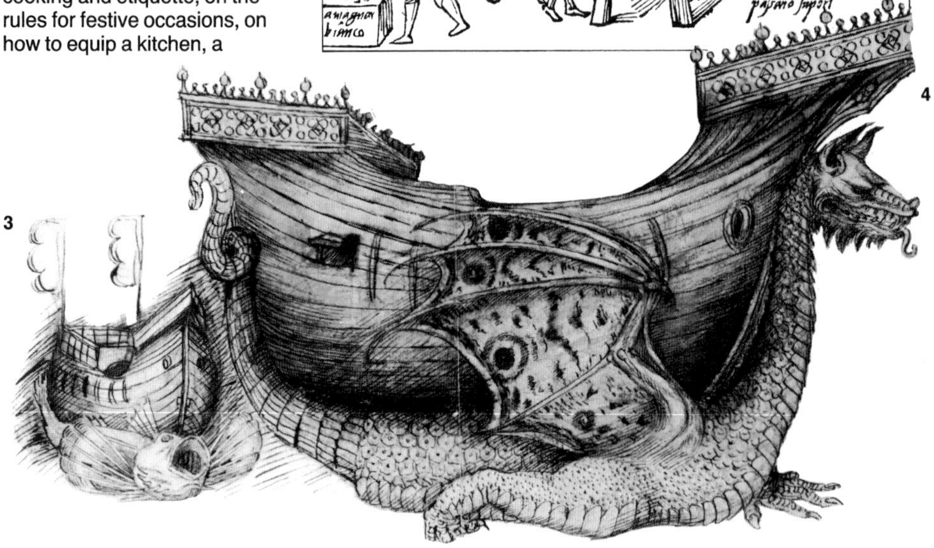

4

5

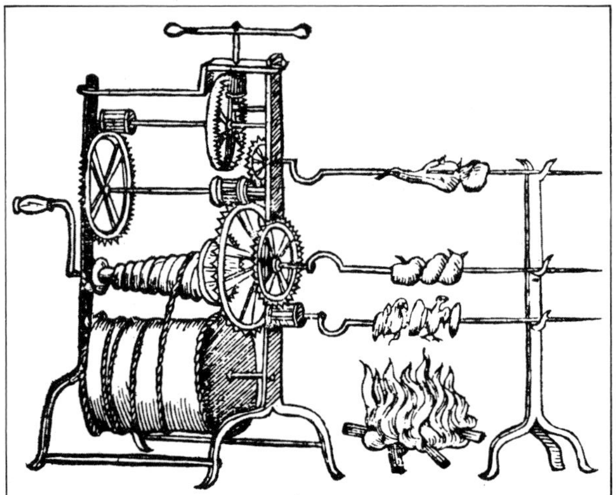

tables and benches, linen and fingerbowls, scented water and candlesticks. Skilfully he supervised the timing of the courses so as to interrupt none of the dramatic interludes; and when the table setting was changed – probably more than once during a meal – he ensured that fresh cloths, spotless napkins, plates, salt cellars, knives, bunches of flowers (either of silk or fresh according to the season) and scented toothpicks were ready on hand.

Food came to table in huge platters, each of which held enough for several people. Meat was already carved, forks were provided and guests helped themselves onto their own plates. These, and the dishes, would be decorated with armorial or other appropriate designs by artists who had patrons and customers at every court in Europe. A large receptacle on the table – a ship, perhaps, like that in Pisanello's drawing (3) for Alfonso of Aragon – contained clean plates and glasses, while smaller bowls and baskets received the debris. The first rule in the etiquette book was that no mess or unpleasantness should spoil the repast.

Illustrations to Bartolomeo Scappi's *Arte del cucinare*, of 1610, introduce us to an array of kitchen utensils and implements and a rich vocabulary of names. The cooking pots, or *vasi*, include the *navicella* (rather like a fish kettle, with or without feet, having a perforated rack on which to lay the food), and various stewpots with tight-fitting lids. There were frying pans "for eggs," and cake tins. There were baskets for carrying these things, and special baskets, called *cornute*, for spits and crockery. There were meat hooks and other moveable gadgets, carving knives and strainers, sugar and nutmeg graters, and little rollers for trimming pastry. There was apparatus for regulating the heat of kitchen fires and for turning spits; even, surprisingly, a sort of mechanical pulley, with ropes and levers, "for lifting big pots from the fire."

Very grand Renaissance kitchens might have auxiliary cookhouses for whole, large animals. Wreathed in garlands and propped upright, the beasts would be paraded before applauding guests and earn a mention in official records as having appeared, "cooked, in their hides and on their feet, in splendid fashion."

6

7

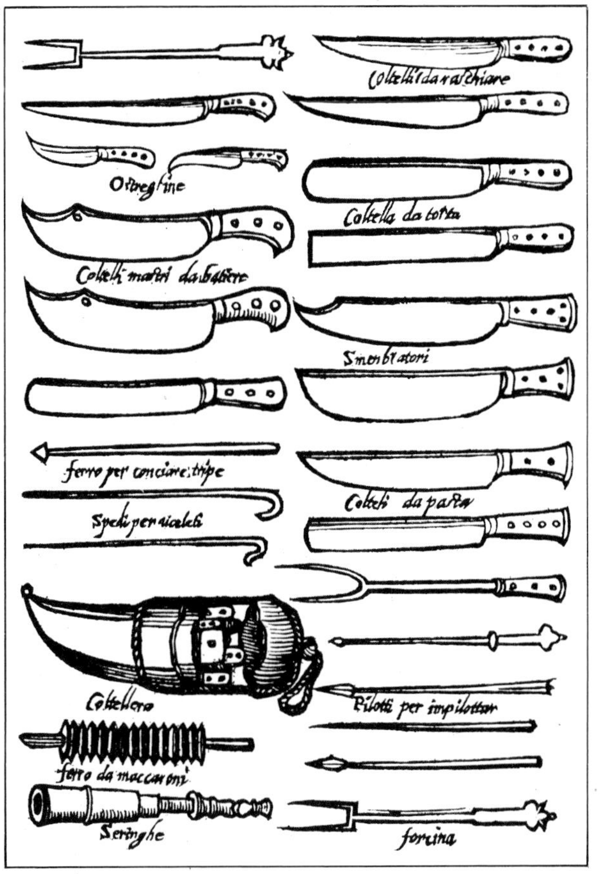

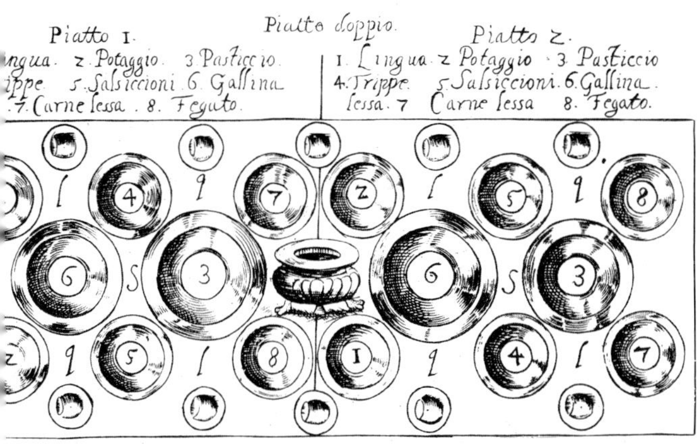

9

moments in the public life of the court, involving, as it did, the wholesale uprooting of the princely household.

Everywhere the prince took with him his court and his comforts and all things seemly for his rank in the hierarchy of princes. There is, for illustration, Cosimo Priè's journal of the progress in Lombardy of the future Cosimo III – a diary so informative that we may consider it typical, as the educative tour was customary for an heir before succession.

"The Most Serene Prince, Cosimo III of Tuscany, being 22 years of age, wished to travel abroad in Italy, to see the fine cities and country of Lombardy. He was resolved on this, and the Most Serene Grand Duke, his Father [Ferdinando II], in his wisdom agreed, advising the Most Serene Prince to go incognito, since he might then have fewer princely receptions and official visits, and fewer servants and companions. The latter were therefore reduced to a minimum . . ."

Reduced or no, they made a healthy tally. Some twenty gentlemen-in-waiting, as many

The hemicycle façade and fountains of the villa at Frascati built in 1598–1603 by Giacomo della Porta for Cardinal Pietro Aldobrandini, nephew of Clement VIII.
Right: eighteenth-century print of the Villa Simonetta near Milan, built late in the fifteenth century for Gualtiero Bescapè, chancellor of Ludovico il Moro, and rebuilt almost completely in the sixteenth for Ferrante Gonzaga, duke of Guastalla and governor of Milan. There were rumours of sumptuous and obscene festivities held here, but better known was the 56-times-repeated echo directed from the garden towards the frontage of the villa.

head servants, and a hundred or so domestics, grooms, muleteers and odd-job men. Priè lists the train, in order, from "the Signor Conte Ferdinando Bardi, Councillor of State to His Most Serene Highness" and "the Signor Conte Silvio Albergati, his cupbearer," to the scullions and stableboys.

First are the nobles with their ceremonial duties, then the gentlemen, of the royal

Right: the pentagonal palace, or villa, at Caprarola, approached by two theatrically-conceived piazze and a magnificent courtyard, was begun, on its spur of rock, by Antonio de Sangallo the Younger, Cardinal Alessandro Farnese, for whom Vignola completed it in 1559–75, was the son of Pier Luigi Farnese, bishop of Parma, Avignon and Tours, a great patron of the arts and protector of Bembo, Della Casa and Vasari.
Below, right: the gardens of Villa Lante at Bagnaia, near Viterbo. Cardinal Raffaele Riario, nephew of Sixtus IV, first laid out a hunting park here, much favoured by that keen sportsman Leo X for its wealth of game. Later, Cardinal Giovan Francesco Gambara engaged Vignola, who had built Caprarola for the cardinal's Farnese relations, to create the Italian garden and one of the twin palazzine *(1566–78). Work on the second projected pavilion was cancelled in the reign of Pius V, on a wave of austerity following a visit from St Carlo Borromeo, who disapproved of the extravagance. But it was resumed by later tenants, and the villa's name goes back to 1656, when it was acquired by Cardinal Ippolito Lante in the reign of Alexander VII.*

chamber, under-cupbearers, and valets. There were a majordomo, a personal page, and an extra wardrobe-valet who doubled as cashier. The prince had a chaplain for spiritual solace. He had his barber, his druggist, nine grooms, two footmen, a paymaster, a wine-steward, butler, almoner, cellarman, a full staff of cooks. For each carriage he had a coachman. He had litter bearers, muleteers, drivers, with an indispensable army of auxiliaries, for each of these had his juniors and assistants. The suite was practically self-sufficient, a travelling court in miniature, equipped for any ceremonial occasion, should it arise, and for whatever day-to-day eventuality.

Interesting, too, is the account of the diversity of vehicles and hordes of animals needed to transport the royal equipage. The two state carriages were drawn by six horses apiece, with two extra in case of accident. In the first carriage rode the prince and his intimates, while the less privileged crowded into the second. Four litters were available for His Highness if he wanted them, and two riding horses, *cavalli di rispetto*, for parades and state entries. There were 16 horses for the gentlemen's servants, eight mules for the unarmed waggons with His Highness' private luggage, and another eight for his household luggage, provisions, plate and wine; and eight more for the luggage of "gentlemen and assistants."

If these were the impedimenta for a journey

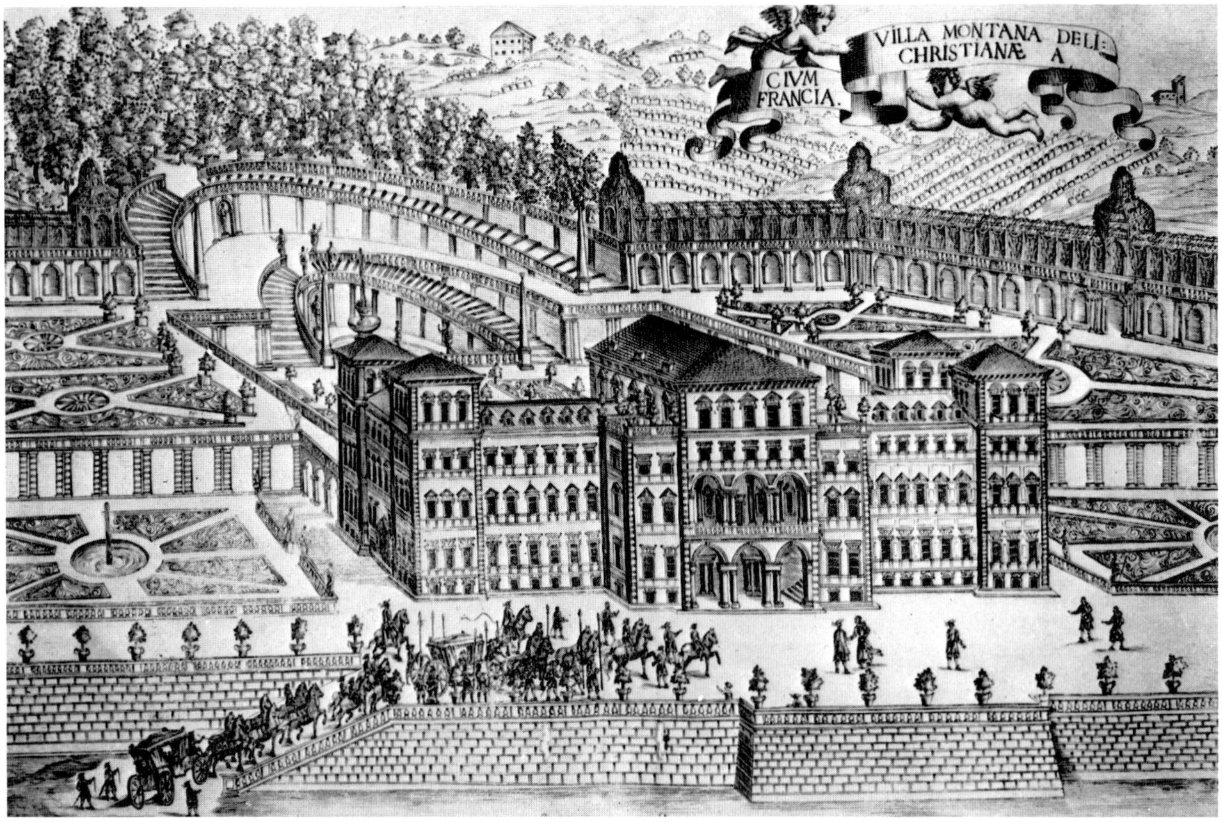

ostensibly incognito, what, we may ask, would it be for a diplomatic expedition or an official visit to a fellow ruler? And let us not forget that this retinue, which might do very well for a cardinal, the ambassador of a large court, or a minor prince, was scarcely up to the standard of a future grand duke of Tuscany, unless, that is, as in this case, he wanted to keep a low profile, at least outside his own domains.

Yet what a train it was, crawling over the landscape and through the villages, nose to tail in single file from the prince's coach in front to the last pack mule weighed down with rations. It was watched open-mouthed, we may presume, from the roadside, and the wonder grew as an equerry dispensed alms, on behalf of His Highness, to the poor.

For the prince, it was an opportunity to show himself to his subjects, magnificent, munificent, majestic. Popular acknowledgement was a ritualistic confirmation of his power and this aspect of the journey, too, had been planned.

Not that planning was easy. Each day's march must finish where lodging was to be had. Bad weather must be reckoned with, as well as difficult or dangerous roads. There might be difficulty over animal fodder, or organizational problems; there was also the need to maintain strict dicipline within the travelling party.

Any official journey abroad could involve diplomatic wrangles and arguments over etiquette: the quality of entertainments, state entries, receptions and gifts were fertile ground for rancour and bad feeling. And, to be fair, the burden fell heavily on those at the receiving end, the subjects so fortunate – if fortunate is the word – to have the necessary resources: feudal lords in their castles, monks in their convents, city governors, innkeepers – they had to find room for multitudes of men, with beasts and baggage. They had to clean and polish and cook a dinner fit for a prince. The joys of hospitality . . .

The religious pilgrimage is in a category of its own, and was usually to Rome, though some princes visited the Holy Land. The Marchese Niccolò III, leaving Ferrara on 15 April 1413, reached the Holy Sepulcher at Jerusalem after exhausting marches overland and a long sea passage. The days in Jerusalem were spent in meditation and penitential exercises, and he arrived back in Ferrara on 5 July, an absence of nearly three months.

In a diary kept by Niccolò's chancellor, Luchino del Campo, he tells us how his master chose a court-in-little for the expedition, and how its functions and hierarchy were tailored for pilgrimage. But he chronicles the pilgrimage as if it were an epic, the enterprise of a prince errant in the realms of exoticism, magic and adventure. The chivalrous virtues, power and valour of the hero come into play at every halt of the caravan. What we read is not a pilgrim record by any conceivable yardstick, but a paean of praise for Niccolò, the beams from whose countenance blind out everything and everyone else around him.

We also have Cosimo Priè's diary of a similar journey made by Cosimo III. In his dedication he flatly reports that his diary is "truly to exhibit the mind and behaviour of so worthy a Prince, as revealed on this journey: the wise prudence and peerless liberality, the majesty and decorum, his absolute kindness and courtesy, with an affability and ease of manner that won all hearts; for he combines the virtues and gallantry of his great Ancestors..."

Prince and court were virtually inseparable, living and journeying together, always within their own sphere.

Villa expeditions. Opposite: a print from the latter half of the seventeenth century shows carriages ascending the ramp to the Villa montana delicium Christianae a Francia *– the* vigna di Madama reale, *or Palazzo Madama, at Turin. This villa was named after Marie Christine, daughter of Henri IV of France and Maria de' Medici; she was married at the age of 13 to the heir of Carlo Emanuele I of Savoy. Her husband succeeded as Vittorio Amedeo I, and after his death she was regent for their sons. Her life was complicated by the quarrels of her party, the* madamisti *(in Italy she was Maria Cristina,* Madama reale*) and the supporters of her brothers-in-law, Tommaso of Savoy—Carignano and Cardinal Maurizio.*
Above: another expedition scene. Eleonora of Toledo is shown arriving at Poggio a Caiano in a decorative painting by Vasari for the apartments of Cosimo I, in the Palazzo Vecchio, Florence. Eleonora, daughter of the Spanish viceroy of Naples, Don Pedro de Toledo, married Cosimo in 1539 when he was Duke of Florence. She bore him 11 children and died of consumption at the age of 40.

Faith in God – and the Stars

Ceiling-decoration by Perin del Vaga and Giovanni da Udine in the Sala dei Pontefici in the Borgia apartments of the Vatican; mythological figures surround a central tondo of dancing angels. The frescoes of this room were commissioned by Leo x, Giovanni de' Medici, second son of Lorenzo the Magnificent. His father had him made a cardinal in pectore, *that is, the appointment was, for the time being, undeclared. "All the more remarkable," comments Machiavelli, "since, contrary to any known precedent, he was less than 14 at his elevation; a step on the ladder, enabling his house to scale the heights – as, in later years, it did."*
The princes of Italy would endeavour, often with success, to have their "representatives" in the Sacred College: cardinals of their own blood who could speak on their behalf with the pope, who could vote in the conclave, or – as in Giovanni's case – ascend the papal throne.

Almoners, chaplains and confessors

All over Europe, before and long after the French Revolution, Catholic rulers and nobles found it necessary to surround themselves with priests; nor did the holy men underestimate the value of a presence in the palace. Until the end of the twelfth century, and for much of the thirteenth, the imperial, royal and feudal chancelleries of Europe were staffed by priests and monks, who alone had the necessary learning.

However, the rise of the universities brought about great changes in the rôle of the clergy. Clerics were still involved in certain areas, even in the government of city communes, but priests, monks and friars were no longer as numerous in their administrative or secretarial personas – the friars in particular lost ground after the mid thirteenth century, and from the late sixteenth century onwards were supplanted by the new Counter-Reformation orders, above all, the Jesuits. The posts they retained, however, were perhaps more delicately balanced and, therefore, more important. They were still chaplains and spiritual advisers. Serving the prince and his family, celebrating Mass for him and hearing his confession, they had access to the *arcana imperii*, the secrets of state. Their power and influence were incalculable, despite the fact that "court priests" were often treated no different than any other courtier, and perforce might seem less powerful than they actually were.

It was, in essence, a two-way arrangement, for while some clerics were merely "attached" to ruling dynasties, many were actually connected by blood with the royal household, having for a variety of reasons, embraced the religious life. Since the eleventh century, when reforms spearheaded by the abbey of Cluny had

The sitter as saint. Left: Maria Magdalena of Austria, wife of Cosimo II, Grand Duke of Tuscany, and sister of Emperor Ferdinand II, here painted in the guise of Mary Magdalene, by Justus Susterman of Antwerp. Until recently, the portrait was thought to be of Vittoria della Rovere. Below, left: a small oval portrait on copper by the same artist, of Margherita de' Medici (daughter of Cosimo II and wife of Odoardo Farnese, Duke of Parma, as St Helena, who is traditionally associated with the finding of the true Cross.

Amedeo, eighth count and first Duke of Savoy (1383–1451), antipope of the House of Savoy, saying Mass. In 1422 he retired to the monastery of Ripaglia, founding the chivalric Order of San Maurizio. Elected antipope by the Council of Basle on the deposition of Eugenius IV, he took the title of Felix V, abdicating nine years later. Miniature from the Missal of Felix V, *in the Biblioteca Reale, Turin.*

removed monasteries, bishoprics, and the religious hierarchy in general from lay control, the great families had changed their tactics and succeeded to a certain extent in sidestepping the obstacles placed in their path by the *libertas Ecclesiae*, by filling the ranks of the clergy with their own scions. Bishops' thrones were occupied by noble members of the great feudal houses and canonical stalls by the sons of leading citizens. Ecclesiastical appointments, therefore, became the domain of the ruling classes who thus ensured that the local religious hierarchy remained firmly under their control.

This process was strengthened and legitimized as communal gave way to signorial, and then to princely, rule. And since the princes of Italy were in practice sovereigns *superiorem non recognoscentes* (who owed their crowns by a "feudal fiction" which really meant very little, to the Holy Roman emperor or the pope alone), it was natural that they should propose men they could trust implicitly to act as their representatives to the Holy See. By that they meant true princes of the Church chosen from their own ranks, who could negotiate for them with the pontiff face-to-face, whose votes would count in the conclave and who might themselves in time even aspire to the papal throne.

Between the fifteenth to the seventeenth century the upper echelons of the Church were a sort of "imperfect federal council" of Europe, in which every sovereign had his own cardinal or cardinals who built splendid, palatial residences, both in Rome, in the surrounding countryside and also in their native cities.

Sons of ruling families who had achieved high rank in the Church thus became involved in both dynastic and ecclesiastical politics, acting as a bridge between the two and becoming key figures on the contemporary scene – Alessandro, bishop of Pistoia, for example, who came from a cadet branch of the Medici. He was sent to Rome in 1569 by his kinsman the Grand Duke Cosimo as ambassador to Pius V, and in 1574 was appointed Archbishop of Florence. The pope, however, did not wish to be deprived of his counsel, and so for roughly a decade Florence had to resign itself to having an absentee archbishop, a practice which had been common prior to the Council of Trent, but had subsequently been frowned upon. On the other hand, Alessandro did not wish to abandon the running of his diocese, and so he entrusted its administration to a surrogate, Canon Sebastiano de'Medici.

As a result of this arrangement (not without its opponents in strict Florentine religious circles), Monsignor Alessandro was able to continue playing his part as grand-ducal ambassador to the Holy See for a good many years. This does not mean that his rôle as archbishop and the surname he bore did not cause him problems; when the affair of the adulterous relationship between Grand Duke Francesco I and Bianca Cappello broke out, for example, poor Alessandro did not know what line to

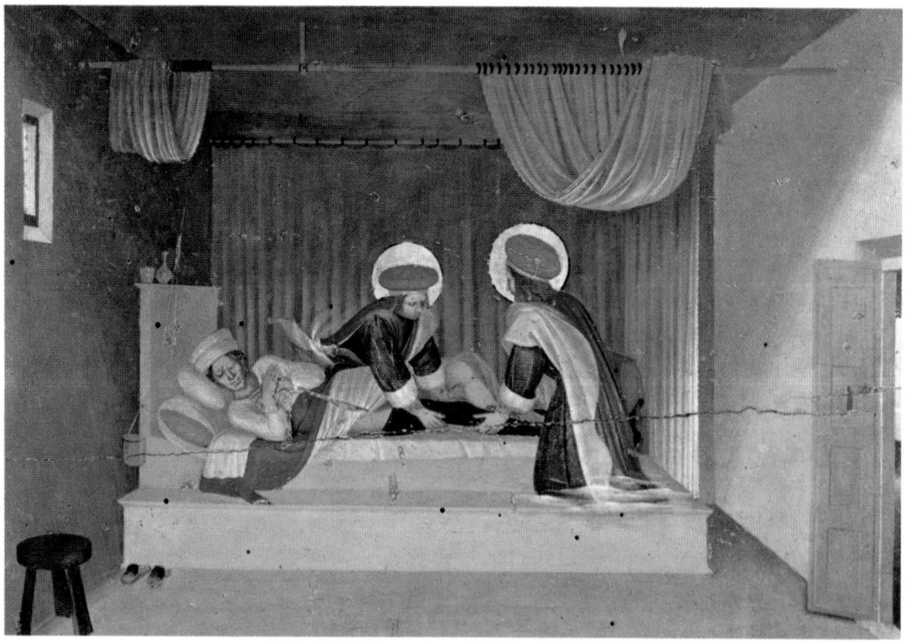

Painting by Fra Angelico of the performing of a miracle by the twin saints Cosma and Damian. From Syria, probably suffering martyrdom under Diocletian, the brothers were revered as miracle-workers after their deaths. Here they are replacing the leg of a white man with that of a black man. Cosimo de' Medici chose them as patrons of his family, less, perhaps, because his own name was a form of Cosma, than because they were said to have been medici – *doctors.*

take. His dilemma was heightened by the fact that, in Rome, the Venetian adventuress had a sworn enemy in the person of another Medici cardinal, a man who also wielded much more authority than the archbishop of Florence: Cardinal Ferdinando, brother of Grand Duke Francesco, and his designated heir.

The princely dynasties were well aware that their outward behaviour, particularly on solemn occasions, had to be surrounded by an aura of great religiosity: the occasions on which the ruling family appeared to the populace were for the most part religious by nature. Every dynasty had its own special relationship with a particular religious institution. Life at court was also the subject of careful spiritual regulation, and even in the fourteenth-century "Palatine laws" of Pietro IV of Aragon, the model for many later court rules, a special place was reserved for the chaplain, the almoner and the confessor. Later, when the Company of Jesus became firmly established in the courts of Catholic Europe, the rôle (albeit unwritten) of confessor became even more important.

"Living saints," family saints, and relics

As with the clergy and religious institutions, so the princes enjoyed a special relationship with the saints. Every dynasty had its own saint: the traditional calendar was not enough for them and new canonizations were made.

What is more, if the ambition of the male members of princely families was that of achieving glory in war, their womenfolk were correspondingly attracted to the ideal of saintliness. The Grand Duchess Vittoria della Rovere, wife of Ferdinando II de' Medici, had herself portrayed with the crown and cross – the saintly attributes of St Helena, mother of Constantine, to whom the discovery of the relics of the Passion in Jerusalem is traditionally ascribed.

This desire to possess a special relationship with the saints or even count one within the ranks of one's own family was not a recent phenomenon. The Middle Ages had produced famous examples of canonized rulers. Apart from Charlemagne, there had been St Edward the Confessor of England, St Henry II of the Holy Roman Empire, St Louis IX of France, St Ferdinand III of Castile, and St Wenceslas of the duchy, later kingdom, of Bohemia.

The various princely and signorial dynasties of Italy emulated these models; even families known for certain none too reputable members, such as the Casali of Cortona, for example, who "corrected" their self-inflicted reputation as fierce tyrants by parading their devotion to the great saint of their city, Margherita, and to one of their own number, Allegrezza, who, as Sister Marta of the Order of St Clare, was for some time abbess of the great Monastero del Paradiso in Florence at the end of the fourteenth century.

The relationship between the *signori* and the various patron saints of cities could prove a little more difficult. This was partly because the Italian principalities of the Renaissance were to a greater or lesser extent all territorial rather than city-based, and a prudent policy of regional balance advised against imposing the cult of the dominant city's patron saint on the subjugated territories as well, since the former had for too long been used as a symbol of hegemony. But it was mainly because the patron saint of the principality's capital was almost always linked in some way to family or political groups to which the ruler was either opposed or from which he at least preferred to distance himself.

Carlo Borromeo carrying the cross in procession during the Milanese plague of 1576–77. A "family" saint of the Lombard feudal house of Borromeo, he was a selfless and exemplary man, who believed in prayer and practical charity. He was canonized in 1610, 26 years after his death. Fresco in the Collegio Borromeo, Pavia, which he founded when archbishop of Milan.

Let us take the case of the Medici, for example. They could certainly not carry on the cult of St John the Baptist or St Zenobius in the same way as before: both of these were too republican, too closely linked to the republic to which the grand duke was the not universally popular successor; they were also both seen in Tuscany as symbols of Florentine rule. The house of Medici, therefore, promptly began promoting the cult of their dynastic protectors, Cosma and Damian, and Lorenzo, the patron saint of "their" basilica, and the Madonna of the Annunciation, for whom they built the huge sanctuary of the Santissima Annunziata in Florence. In addition, the ruling dynasty infiltrated the local religious life of other cities throughout the grand duchy, making great show of its own devoutness and promoting the cult of politically neutral saints and the foundation of new shrines.

And yet the ideal still continued to be that of numbering saints among one's family. In the thirteenth century, for example, of three Este ladies sharing the same name of Beatrice, one was canonized and two beatified.

Many of the holy ladies of noble birth chose to enter the Order of St Clare; the Blessed Camilla Pio di Savoia was a Poor Clare, as was the Blessed Sveva Montefeltro, who was unjustly accused of infidelity by her husband, Alessandro Sforza, lord of Pesaro, and forced to enter a convent, where she achieved sanctity. The

Este family founded a convent of Poor Clares at Ferrara in 1510 for Camilla, illegitimate daughter of Cesare Borgia, whom they had brought up. Later, against the background of the Counter-Reformation, it was another noblewoman, Maria Maddalena, sister of the Carafa pope Paolo IV, who founded the Sapienza convent of Dominican nuns in Naples.

However, among all the Italian families rich in saints and mystics, the House of Savoy stands out. In 1422 Amedeo, eighth count and first duke of Savoy, retired to the monastery of Ripaglia, where with six companions he founded the knightly order of San Maurizio (he emerged briefly only during the Council of Basle, as antipope with the title of Felix V); the Blessed Amedeo IX had for long sought to bring morality to court life which he later abandoned in order to devote himself to works of piety; and the Blessed Margherita, also a member of the House of Savoy, entered the Dominican order and founded a convent.

These religious foundations, organized and often led by representatives of the princely families, represented, among other things, a component of the elite's policy of control within absolute states: in fact, they provided shelter for the young girls of important aristocratic families who had never found husbands. But the most notable example of a "family saint" in the history of the Italian principalities is undoubtedly that of St Luigi Gonzaga, who died in 1591: a true saint of the Counter-Reformation who spent his brief life in deep and burning devotion. Mention should also be made of St Carlo Borromeo, offspring of the great Lombard feudal family, who governed the Church in Milan during a period of considerable difficulty and, inspired by prayer and charity, revealed qualities of great statesmanship.

One phenomenon exerted a fatal fascination over the princely courts of Italy: that of female "living saints," which was a widespread feature of life between the end of the fifteenth century and the first quarter of the sixteenth. In fact, there was a constant vein of superstition, a sort of pious fetishism, running through the relationship between some of these female saints (who often bore the stigmata) and certain princes. Such was the case of Ercole I d'Este, who in 1497 heard that a young Dominican tertiary living at Viterbo, Lucia Brocadelli da Narni, had received the stigmata: he immediately tried to persuade her to move to Ferrara, promising to found a convent for her. Lucia accepted, but the people of Viterbo objected: there followed a lengthy diplomatic exchange which ended up costing the duke 3000 ducats.

Ercole was very sensitive to mystical portents; a man who consulted astrologers and lived in an atmosphere filled with magic, he considered that a woman specially touched by God could act as a link with the mysteries of the unknown. But in 1503 Lucia's stigmata vanished as mysteriously as they had appeared, whereupon Ercole lost interest.

Often a sort of small court of friends, relations and mentors would gather around the object of mystical interest. Lucia Brocadelli, for example, arrived in Ferrara with her mother,

Faith in God and in the stars went hand in hand at the Renaissance court, with astrologer and chaplain in peaceful cohabitation under the same roof. In the Tempio Malatestiano at Rimini – the church of San Francesco renovated by Sigismondo Malatesta as a family chapel – many of Agostino di Duccio's delicate sculptured reliefs are astrological in inspiration.
Opposite, far left: the gemini sign of the zodiac, and (top left, and below) the chariots of the Moon and Venus respectively. Sigismondo intended the church as his burial place, and that of his mistress – later his wife – Isotta degli Atti, to whom he wrote poems.
O vaga e dolce luce anima altera!/Creatura gentile o viso degno/O lume chiaro angelico e benigno/In cui sola virtú mia mente spera.
She is all nobility and sweetness, her goodness alone sustains him:
Oh gentlest, fairest face,
And light of heavenly grace.
He besought the stars, the planets and the signs of the zodiac to help him to melt her heart with their music. Pius II, who had him burned in effigy for his impiety, yet acknowledges admiringly in his Commentaries *how much Sigismondo knew of the classical world and of philosophy, and "whatever he did, he seemed as if born to do it."*
Above: zodiacal frescoes in the Salone dei Mesi of the palace of Schifanoia, Ferrara, commissioned by Borso d'Este, are further evidence of astrology in court culture.

her brothers and her confessor, and other friends or acquaintances were later summoned from Viterbo. On the other hand, the Este family clearly had a thirst for sanctity, and the spiritual atmosphere permeating the Ferrarese court also affected those who came into contact with it; people such as the famous wife of Duke Alfonso, Lucrezia Borgia (aunt of the Sister Camilla mentioned earlier), who conducted a lengthy correspondence with a nun called Laura Mignani, whose prophetic abilities she admired intensely. Lucrezia's gradual development towards a spirit of deep religious piety is a hitherto neglected aspect of her character. She was a perfervid reader of devotional works, and in her time, Observant friars of the Dominican order often visited the Ferrarese court, keeping alive the cult of Gerolamo Savonarola, that great adversary of Pope Alexander VI, the father of Lucrezia.

When, in 1536, John Calvin arrived incognito at the Este court and was honourably received by Renata of France, wife of Alfonso's son Ercole II, and daughter of Louis XII, the ducal environment was still steeped in a mood of contradictory spirituality, tinged with devotionalism and superstition, but still definitely profound. In a certain sense, the seeds of the Calvinist adventure were sown in ground that had already been well prepared.

It was not only the Este court that became immersed in this devotional tide. In 1517 Elisabetta Gonzaga, the Duchess of Urbino, also turned to Laura Mignani, a fortune-teller, asking her to throw light on certain reports of unrest which had reached her ears.

For their part, the Gonzaga of Mantua set the greatest possible store by two Dominican nuns, Osanna Andeasi and Stefana Quinzani, who were regarded as "mothers" of the ducal house and of the state itself, living prophetic protectresses; after their deaths the princes did everything in their power to promote their cult. Isabella d'Este of Mantua was a devoted collector of relics of the Blessed Osanna and of her thaumaturgical virtues. In 1515, when the Holy See permitted her public cult in the diocese of Mantua and initiated the beatification process, it fell to Mario Equicola, who had already followed the episode of Sister Lucia Brocadelli da Narni at Ferrara and had now moved to the court of the Gonzaga, to compose a eulogy in which Osanna and the city of Mantua were joined in a single paean of praise.

The cult of saints, both old and new, found a natural adjunct in the veneration of relics. Ercole I d'Este, for example, was a skilful propagandist for the sainthood of Lucia da Narni: among other things, he circulated handkerchiefs stained with the blood of her wounds, her stigmata, throughout Europe. The da Correggio family, faithful to their patron saint, San Quirino, exalted both his powers as a miracle worker and also his relics, blending the account of the discovery of his remains with the miraculous healing of Beatrice da Correggio's son Tomasso.

On the the other hand, relics and precious reliquaries ended up by not only forming part of the endowments of princely chapels and of their

imerito uellem sere
nissime comes ad operis
tanti quod ego q q indi
gnus confitiendum acce
pi laudem explicandam

The astrologer Raffaello da Vimercate presents a horoscope to the young Galeazzo Maria Sforza, son of Duke Francesco and Bianca Maria Visconti. Technically, a horoscope is a diagram of the houses and aspects of the planets at the moment of one's birth, and may be interpreted to reveal one's destiny (the heavens being divided into twelve "houses," and an "aspect" is the relation, measured in degrees, of one planet to another).
Galeazzo Maria's destiny was to be murdered at the age of 32 by the conspirators Gerolamo Olgiati, Andrea Lampugnani and Carlo Visconti.

Right: the sign of Leo in the famous fifteenth-century MS of astrological tables, the De Sphaera, *in the Biblioteca Estense, Modena. Leo is a kingly sign, governed by the sun. The figure is crowned and bears a scepter and a book of laws. Below are scenes of military training, since a king should be a warrior. This codex contains the* Sphaera mundi, *or* Sfera di Sacrobosco, *an astronomical treatise by John of Holywood, an Englishman of the mid thirteenth century whose name is rendered as Johannis de Sacro Bosco. It was one of the first books on astronomy to be printed – the first edition was issued at Ferrara in 1472 – and was used and consulted up to the end of the sixteenth century.*

patrimony in general, and as such also suitable objects for giving, exchanging and even pledging or selling, but actually becoming miraculous "collector's items," objects destined for holy *Wunderkämmer*. This is the spirit, combined with the urge to collect sacred amulets, that pervades many princely collections of relics in Italy and elsewhere in Catholic Europe.

The repository of relics planned by Galeazzo Maria Sforza for the palace at Pavia, and never completed, took the form of an enormous coffer some 25 meters (c.81 ft) wide and four meters (13 ft) high, adorned with paintings, sculptures, precious stones and crystals. In the church of San Lorenzo in Florence is a precious and extraordinary reliquary assembled by the grand dukes of Tuscany. In the climate of the Counter-Reformation, the cult of the Holy Shroud became triumphantly established by the house of Savoy, whose members in 1578 arranged for the relic's transfer from Chambéry, its home for some 150 years, to Turin, while some hundred years later, in 1670, on the petition of Margherita di Savoia a plenary indulgence was granted to those visiting the relic.

Ruling the stars

Girolamo Scolari, an Olivetan monk, reminded Isabella d'Este in a severe letter that God is not subject to the stars and that if He wishes to reveal some secret of the future, he will do so only through the gift of prophecy granted to some privileged soul like the Blessed Osanna Andreasi.

This warning by Scolari, dated September 1505, clearly pinpoints the sort of competition encountered by "living saints" in obtaining the ear and favour of courts; he also hinted at the reasons for such favour and attention. The gift of prophecy was the great rival of judicial astrology, and it was also its great competitor, in view of the fact that princes used both methods to unlock the secrets of the future. Even though the latter treated the mystical "friends of God" as people it was prudent to have at one's side in order to curry favour with the Creator, that did not stop them from also summoning astrologers to gain control over the

stars as well, to harness their positive influences and obviate or minimize their negative ones. The theological incompatibility of prophecy and religious orthodoxy and belief in judicial astrology (meaning the sort of astrology on the basis of which responses are derived that control actions and choices), could be clearly demonstrated, but that did not stop rulers exploiting both these *instrumenta regni* at the same time.

From the thirteenth century onwards, astrologers infested the princely courts. In that century it had been mainly the Ghibelline rulers, like Frederick II of Swabia or Ezzelino da Romano of Verona, who became famous as patrons of those who read the stars, some of whom, such as Guido Bonatti of Forlí, enjoyed an extraordinary reputation. But the connection between the Ghibellines and the practice of arts suspected of having links with Satanism had been made much of for propaganda purposes by Guelph supporters: in reality, the belief in astrology was extremely widespread and even the pontiffs had their astrologers.

Already common in the Middle Ages, the phenomenon of belief in astrology became stronger between the fifteenth and sixteenth centuries, and it was no coincidence that the papal court was the authoritative model for this practice as well. Julian II had astrologers identify the appropriate day for his coronation; Paul III followed the same path in fixing the time for consistories; Leo X founded a chair of astrology in the papal *Università della Sapienza*, thereby adding to the list of other famous chairs at Bologna, Padua and Paris.

The use of judicial astrology undoubtedly led to instances which, seen from outside and without any understanding of its underlying rationale, may appear ridiculous today. Astrological calculations were consulted before founding a new building, before leaving a city, before launching an attack in battle or before conferring the insignia of command – the baton and the standard – to the commander of an army. Ceremonies were sometimes postponed for considerable periods or even put off altogether. Alessandro Sforza, lord of Pesaro, waited for the right astrological moment before consummating his marriage to Lucrezia Borgia.

But the basic astrological "point," from which it was possible to foretell the whole course of a life, continued to be that of birth. This was the "natal theme," the aspect of the heavens at the precise moment when the prince emerged from the womb of his mother, the instant that decided everything. This was an instant to be recorded and also be a subject of constant reflection because, although it is true that at that moment the stars had chosen the prince, it was also true that it was the prince who could manipulate the stars through using the counsel of those who knew their orbits and powers and were, therefore, in a position to assist him in exploiting their benevolent rays and avoiding the malevolent ones.

Near Parma, in the castle of Roccabianca, which Pier Maria Rossi began building in 1450, the so-called "Griselda chamber" (from the frescoes on the walls that tell Boccacio's famous tale) has a ceiling covered in astrological figures. A theory has been advanced that these represent the horoscope of the castle's owner; this is by no means implausible,even though it is not supported by any convincing proof. In Florence, however, both in the Old Sacristy at San Lorenzo and in the Pazzi Chapel at Santa Croce, the decoration of the interior of the domes represents stars and planets whose aspects repeat a precise zodiacal moment with great exactness; similarly, in Rome, the ceiling of the Sala di Galatea in the Farnesina reproduces the constellations as they were on 1 December 1466, the birthdate of the Sienese banker and patron Agostino Chigi, who had built the palace as his residence.

If the spiritual counsellors of the day did not hesitate to stigmatize belief in the stars, the learned men at court were quick to denounce the "lies, humbug" and so on (terms used by Ariosto) employed by astrologers to deceive people. There was a reason for all this acrimony, but it is certainly not to be found in any calmly, lucidly stated "scientific" or "rational" beliefs. That this was not the case can be seen in the writings of those same men of letters, which regurgitate astrological elements and clearly spring from the same cultural background. The fact of the matter was that astrologers were the most privileged and the best treated courtiers.

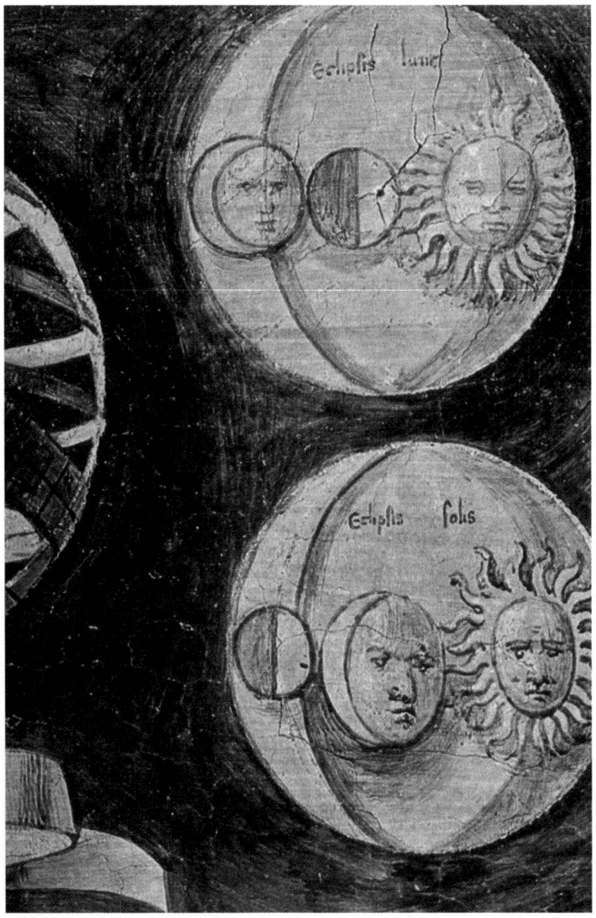

Astrology and astronomy as represented in art.
Opposite: the ceiling-fresco of the Sala dello Zodiaco in the ducal palace at Mantua (1579, possibly by Lorenzo Costa il Giovane). The chariot-borne Diana, whose name of Lucina the Romans interpreted as "bringer of light," is shown in a starry sky, surrounded by figures of the zodiacal constellations; myth, allegory and astrology meet and mingle.
Left: detail of a frieze by Giorgione in the Casa Pellizzari at Castelfranco, near Venice. Giorgione may have been born in this house, for he was an illegitimate member of the Barbarella family, to whom it belonged. The frieze is of various instruments, medallions, subjects relating to the liberal arts, and allegorical figures which critics have connected with those in the Venetian edition of Holywood's Sphaera mundi *of 1484–85. It is interesting to note, next to the armillary sphere, the accurate representations of the eclipses of the sun and moon. Astronomy was beginning to diverge from astrology. Copernicus had been in Italy, at Padua University, in 1496, when Giorgione was 19, and knowledge of his heliocentric system was first circulated in a manuscript of 1507.*

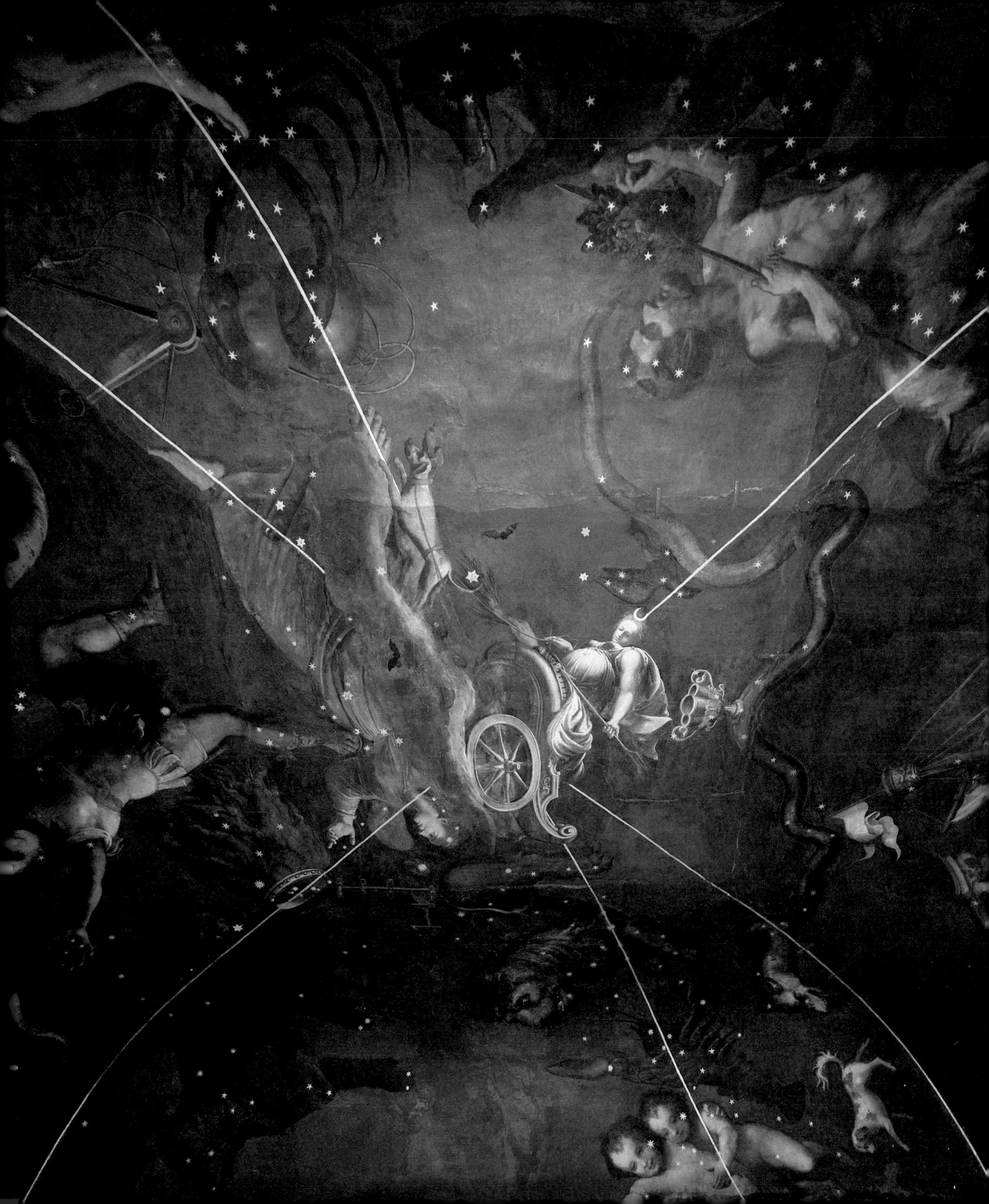

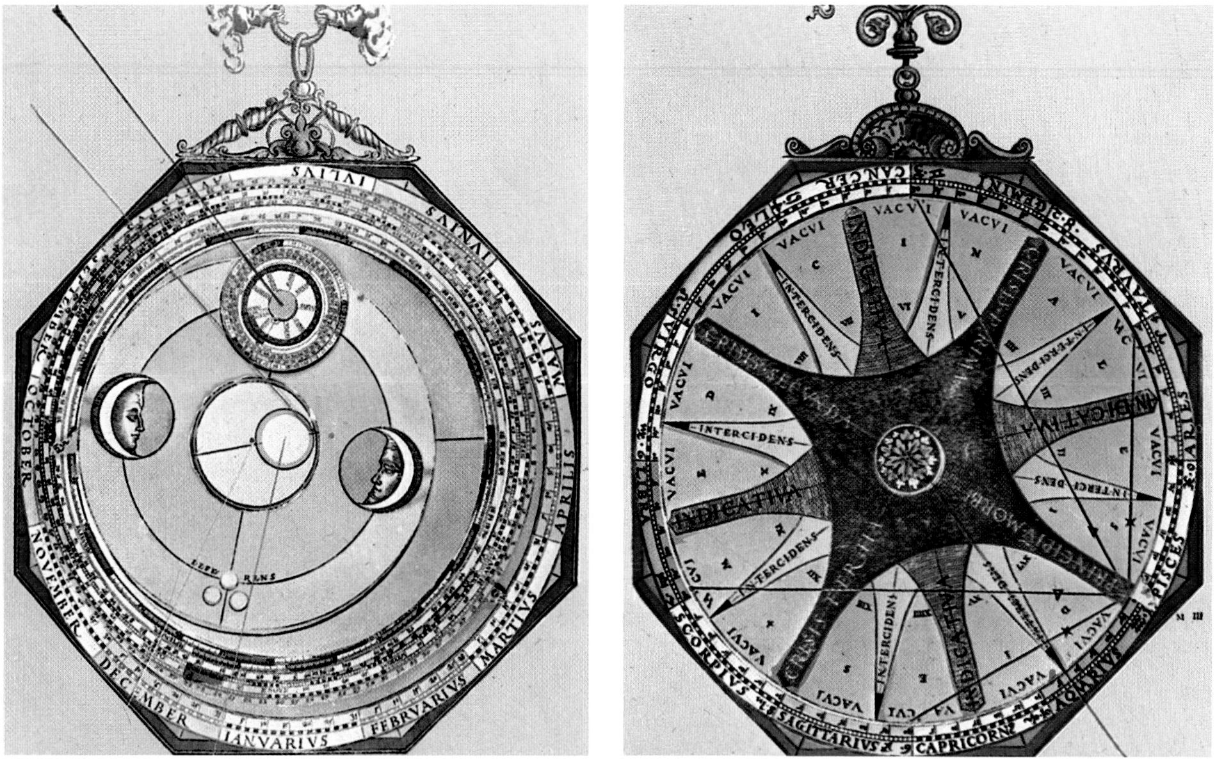

Illustrations of "analogical calculators," sixteenth-century astrological instruments resembling astrolabes. That on the far left was for measuring phases of the moon and other planets (for astrologers both sun and moon were planets), that on the left for measuring planetary "aspects," or angles of distance between two planets. When this distance is little or nothing, the planets are "in conjunction." If 60° apart – one-sixth of a perfect circle – they are "in sextile." When the difference is 90° or so, they are "in quartile," and "in trine" when it is 120°. (Inscribe three points at this angle on the circumference of a circle, and you can construct an equilateral triangle). They are "in opposition" when directly opposite, at an angle of 180°.

Nevertheless, there was often a reason behind this preferential treatment. The master astrologers sometimes consulted by princes were frequently the complete antithesis of the sort of charlatans maliciously portrayed in some literary descriptions. The Austrian Georg Purbach, who taught astrology at Ferrara in the mid fifteenth century, was an authority on Ptolemaic studies and the friend of Cardinal Nicholas of Cusa, the philosopher and scientist. In 1458 Giovanni Bianchini, who was born in Ferrara, published the *Tabulae caelestium motuum novae*, not many years before Johann Müller arrived in the city. Astrology at this level is indistinguishable from astronomy, and Müller, "*Regiomontano*," as he was called by the Italians, was the prince of German astronomers.

Between 1476 and 1506 another teacher of astrology at Ferrara was the scholar Pietro Bono Avogaro, who was also a renowned doctor and famous for having published the works of Ptolemy. Avogaro was a remarkable and highly learned figure, and yet he appears to have felt completely at ease in the superstitious atmosphere of Ferrara, where Duke Leonello d'Este had for a long time been wearing a different colour every day, based on the seven planetary colours, and where Pellegrino Prisciani, inspired by Abu Ma'shar, was formulating the iconographical layout of the astrological frescoes in the Schifanoia palace and, at the request of Duke Ercole's wife, Eleonora of Aragon, was calculating the most favourable astrological conjunctions.

We also know that Pietro Bono Avogaro published his prognostications daily, and not only for the Este family.

In the person of the erudite and intelligent Prisciani – administrator, librarian and diplomat – we find a well-balanced and keen connoisseur of astrology and particularly of the works of Ptolemy, of Marcus Manilius the Augustan author of the poem *Astronomicon*, and of Abu Ma'shar. A devout and sincere Christian, Prisciani carefully distanced himself from any black magic practices that might taint his astrological knowledge; at the same time he firmly and intelligently defended the dignity of astrology, his total abhorrence of any sort of sorcery and his firm belief that the stars were not only symbols of God's power, but actual links with it. On the other hand, as a courtier and politician, Prisciani was well aware that as-

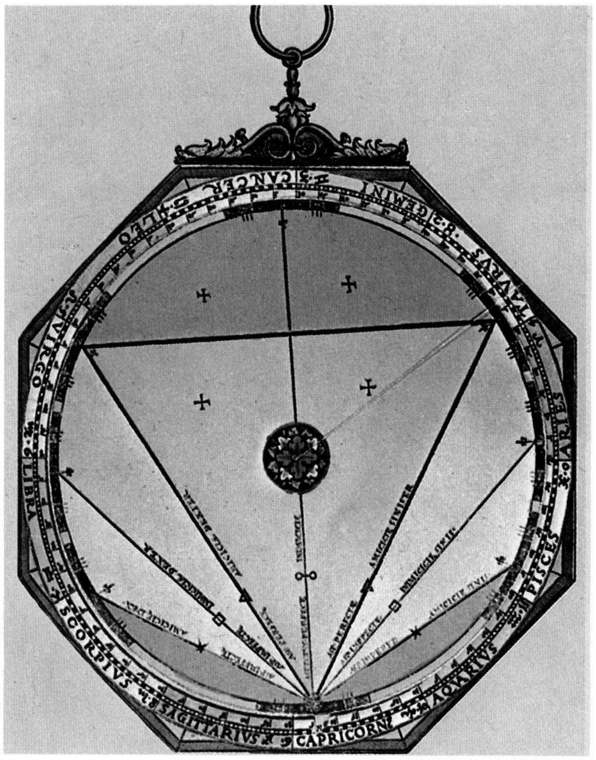

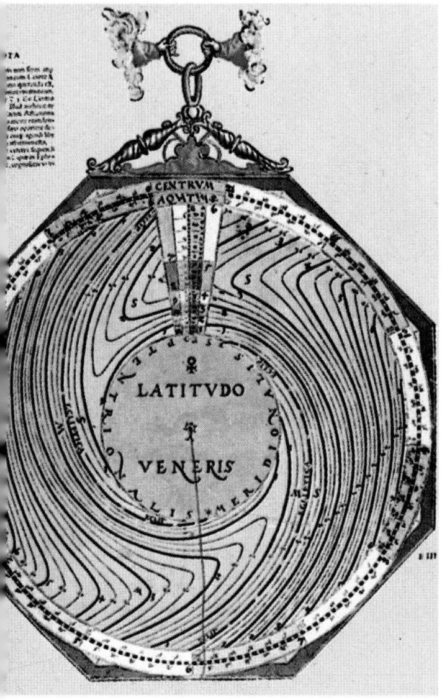

Sixteenth-century astrological instruments for calculating the latitudo veneris *(below), and (right), the aspects of the planets. In calculating a horoscope it was essential to know the date and hour of birth, since the heavens change with the rotation of the earth and the movement of the planets. Also, since the appearance of the skies depends on latitude, or angle of distance from the equator, the place of birth is important. Astrologers, like sailors, relied on the astronomical almanac.*

trological forecasts could also be used for political ends, and he himself did not shrink from providing the raw material for Este propaganda based on readings of the stars.

The fact that an astrologer could also act as political adviser and doctor shows very well how the relationship of astrologers with their princes was much more complex and intricate than we would tend to imagine, were we to assess it solely in terms of credulity and superstition. The latter are emotive abstracts which reflect a basically anachronistic and unhistorical view of the past; they are the result of concentrating too much on contemporary thinking and not being sufficiently prepared to understand the mentality of those who have gone before.

And yet magic, both "white" and "black," also cast a long, dark shadow over the courts of Italy: in fact, it would be tempting to say *particularly* over the courts. It infiltrated the iconographical themes inspired by astrology, as in the frescoes based on that most "magical" of ancient fictions, Apuleius' *Golden Ass,* in the castle of San Secondo near Parma. It even came close to the throne of St Peter, on which sat the same Leo x who listened to the words of the "necromantic" philosopher Agostino Nifo. It played dangerously with power, as was shown clearly in France in 1574 – albeit at the court of the de'Medici regent Catherine – when a plot against the king turned from politics to witchcraft following the implication of the Florentine astrologer and magician Cosma Ruggieri.

At the court of the devout and superstitious Ercole I d'Este there was a whiff of magic in the air, mingling with the astrological calm of Prisciani and the divine aura of Lucia da Narni, in the form of the astrologer Carlo Sosena, who worked in the duke's service and kept a devil trapped in a bottle. At Modena, in the early years of the sixteenth century, Don Guglielmo Campana had two parallel working areas in the church of San Michele: the holy area containing the altar on which he celebrated Mass, and the sacristy, which acted as a "back room" where he performed magical rites with a clientele that even included members of the city's ruling elite. Isabella d'Este and Elisabetta Gonzaga both avidly followed any news of witchcraft trials.

Religious devotion, prophecy, the cult of relics, belief in the stars and dabbling in the occult were all parts of the shifting kaleidoscope of power, elements in the perennial, age-old drama of how to gain power, how to hold on to it and how to live both with the constant fear of losing it and also the constant desire to increase it. Astrology and magic – even, in certain cases, outright witchcraft – further contributed to the tension. The power game developed in the enchanted, intrigue-ridden setting of the court; it followed the twisting, labyrinthine paths of gardens, spreading into the grottoes and hermit's caves, touching the threshholds of the *studioli*, endlessly reflected and reinterpreted through astrological metaphor. The court looked at its own reflection and, like the emblematic Hermetic Serpent, constantly threatened to devour and continually regenerate itself. A lavish setting for this princely drama, the court was a mirror in which the protagonists could watch themselves playing the part of both actor and spectator. It was a deadly serious game, for high stakes.

The Food of Conspiracy

Miniature from the De Sphaera *codex in the Biblioteca Estense, Modena, showing a man about to be beheaded, against a background dotted with gallows. As Machiavelli wrote in* The Prince*: "Men think less of offending a man who sets out to be loved than one who sets out to be hated; this is because love is retained by a bond of obligation which, because men are sorry creatures, is broken whenever the need arises; but respect is retained by a fear of punishment that will ever hold you in good stead."*

"... threat to property, to life, to honour"

"In dealing with this topic, first consider against whom conspiracies are made; and they are hatched, we find, against the fatherland, or against a prince ... and first we shall treat of those against a prince, inquiring into their many causes: but there is one which is far more important than any other, and that is being hated by everyone. If a prince has excited this universal hatred, it is logical that there will be individuals who have been offended more than others and these will desire to revenge themselves. This desire is intensified by that universal ill will he has excited ... The threat may be to a man's property, his life or his honour. Of injury to life, threats are more dangerous than executions; indeed threats are extremely dangerous, while in executions there lies no danger, for a dead man cannot think of revenge, while those who remain alive, more often than not, leave you in a state of uncertainty as to their intentions. But the man who is himself forced to either act or perish, becomes a very dangerous adversary to the prince ... Beyond this compulsive need for revenge, injury to goods and honour are the two things which offend men more than any other; and of these the prince must beware, because he can never strip a man so completely that he does not still have a knife with which to obtain his revenge; he can never so dishonour a man that he does not still retain a mind bent on vendetta. And of all the types of honour of which a man may be deprived, that relating to women is the most important; after this comes contempt for his person ... It is my experience that in history all conspiracies are made by important men or those very close to the prince: this is because the others, unless they are completely mad, are unable to conspire, and because weak men not

Left: Girolamo Riario in a detail of the fresco depicting the inauguration of the Vatican Library by Melozzo da Forlí. Great nephew of Pope Sixtus IV, lord of Imola and subsequently of Forlí, he organized the Pazzi conspiracy against Lorenzo and Giuliano de' Medici. He himself died as the result of a conspiracy in 1488. Francesco ("Checco") D'Orso sought an audience with him and, as Machiavelli relates, "after a few words of simulated discussion, killed him." Such was Lorenzo's revenge for the killing of Giuliano.

The obverse (opposite) and reverse (above) of the medal struck by Pollaiolo commemorating the Pazzi conspiracy. Beneath a likeness of Giuliano de' Medici (above) is the legend luctus publicus, *beneath that of Lorenzo (opposite) are the words* salus publica *– public lamentation, and the public weal. Giuliano was assassinated by Franceschino dei Pazzi in the cathedral church of Santa Maria del Fiore in Florence. "Lorenzo," says Guicciardini, "with the help of those around him and some priests, reached the safety of the sacristy, where the door was barred, lest he be killed."*

close to the prince lack all those ambitions and opportunities needed to carry out a conspiracy ... You will see that those who have conspired have all been great men or intimates of the prince ...."

These are the words of Machiavelli in the famous sixth chapter – on Conspiracies – of the third book of his *Discorsi*, which is devoted entirely to a problem that was central to a society in which all power was concentrated in the person of the ruler.

The private life of a prince that becomes confused with his public image; the doubtful legality, from the point of view of feudal law, of so many lords, further complicated by the not infrequent successions by legitimized bastards; the presence, within a single city-state, of several patrician families and old consular clans, all of them, until the advent of the *signoria*, as strong, powerful and wealthy as the ruling house; the jealousies and enmities of neighbouring *comuni* or other *signorie* and principalities ranged on different sides: all this made up a cocktail that was too powerful not to provoke internal upheavals capable of destabilizing a power which was, after all, basically precarious.

In this world of clans and patrician families, opposition could not help but express itself in sectional organizations and conspiracies, while the ruler had no alternative other than that of physically suppressing his most dangerous adversaries in order to stay in power. In a world based on honour, in which women and property were almost synonymous, abuses of power by a lord would trigger off a chain of feuds.

The blood feud

On 26 April 1478 a letter left Florence for Milan, as brief as it was dramatic in the news that it brought to the Duchess Bona Sforza and her son Gian Galeazzo Maria: "My most illustrious lords. Giuliano my brother is dead and I am in the direst danger, as is the state. My lords, now is the time to aid your servant Lorenzo. Send every man you can with all speed, that they may, as always, be my shield and the safeguard of the state. Your servant, Lorenzo de' Medici."

The Florentine apothecary Luca Landucci records in his diary: "On the 26th day of April 1478, at about the fifteenth hour, at High Mass in Santa Maria del Fiore, at the elevation of the Host, Giuliano di Piero di Cosimo and Francesco Nori were slain in the choir of the said church, by the door which leads to the Via dei Servi; and Lorenzo de' Medici was wounded in the neck and fled to the sacristy and survived. They were slain by a conspiracy planned by Messer Jacopo de' Pazzi and Francieschino de' Pazzi and Guglielmo de' Pazzi, the said Guglielmo being brother-in-law of Lorenzo de' Medici ... And privy to the plot ... was the house of Salviati, that is Messer Francesco, Bishop of Pisa, and Jacopo Salviati ... and Jacopo di Messer Poggio Bracciolini and Bernardo Bandini of the house of Baroncegli, and Amerigo Corsi, and many others. This conspiracy was led here by the Cardinal di San Giorgio [this was Raffaele Riario, great-nephew of Sixtus IV]."

Lorenzo immediately realized by whom the blow had been struck. He waited ten years before he could repay it, actually making use of one of the men who had conspired against him in 1478: Lodovico Pansechi an infantry commander in the service of the count of Forlí, Girolamo Riario.

On 14 April 1488, exactly ten years after the slaying of Giuliano, Checco and Deddo Orsi, Lodovico Pansechi and another soldier stabbed the foreign lord (the Riario family was originally from Savona) imposed on Imola and Forlí by the pope. "Having killed him, they stripped him and had his body thrown out of the window," as the Florentine agent in nearby Castrocaro hastened to report to Lorenzo. But let us leave it to an eyewitness to give an account of the events: the Forlí-born painter and diarist Leone Cobelli (1440–c.1500).

Above: the hanging of Bernardo di Bandino Baroncelli, one of the participants in the Pazzi conspiracy. The drawing, by Leonardo da Vinci, is dispassionately annotated "tan cap, doublet of black satin, black-lined tunic, deep blue coat lined with wolf fur, the collar trimmed with velvet appliquéd in black and red . . . black hose."

"How the count Gerolimo was slain"

The Pazzi arms – addorsed dolphins, with five crosses in the field – carved by Donatello. They are still discernible in the tondo shown opposite, by Della Robbia, even after defacement by supporters of the house of Medici.

"In this same year, after Sunday was passed, on Monday, the 14th day of April, at the hour of dinner, Iacomo da Ronco says that he left Checco and Lodovico Pansecco and went into the palace, where he found his nephew Guasparino, son of Matío da Ronco, brother of the said Iacomo, and this Guasparino was page, valet and footman of count Gerolimo. The same Iacomo says that he called the said Guasparino, his nephew, and told him: 'Guasparino, you know we have long wished to speak to the count of our deeds, and we have never been able to talk to him in private. At what hour can we speak to the count, without anyone else present, in order to state our case?'

"Now, this Guasparino was chief valet and footman to the count. Iacomo da Ronco says that this Guasparino, his nephew, replied: 'This evening, when the count has dined, he will be alone, and all his family and squires will be at dinner: and I shall be on guard at the bedchamber. So today you may come and talk to the count at your pleasure and tell him your news.' Iacomo da Ronco said: 'Good, and how will I know the hour to come?' He says that Guasparino replied: 'When the time is come I will give you a signal. Be in the square.' Iacomo says that he now felt certain of achieving his purpose; and at once went to find Checco de l'Urso and Lodovico Pansecco who were awaiting him. The same Iacomo says that he raised all their spirits, saying 'Now is the time to be brave.' And he told them of all that had to be done.

"They then called Misser Lodovico de l'Urso and told him everything, and prepared themselves. Iacomo da Ronco says that Checco, Lodovico Pansecco and himself all put on their breastplates and armed themselves with a knife and a dagger and then went arm in arm to the square. And so, at the appointed hour, count Gerolimo went in to dine; and, after he had dined, the said Guasparino went to the windows and saw the men strolling in the square; he took off his cap and signalled for them to come up. They all immediately went up to the hall, then into the audience chamber. And things being thus, Checco de l'Urso entered the bedchamber, where he found the count leaning on his elbow at the window. According to him, the count said: 'Welcome, Checco. How are you?' Checco replied: 'I am well. I wish to show you a letter from a friend of mine; he wants to repay Your Lordship the money he borrowed.'

"At this, Iacomo da Ronco, or it may have been Lodovico Pansecco, entered. The count turned round and, suspecting something was amiss, tried to flee. Checco seized him and delivered a dagger thrust to the stomach. At that point either Lodovico Pansecco or Iacomo

KNIGHTS IN ARMOUR

The shrine of the Madonna delle Grazie, at Curtatone near Mantua, was built between the end of the fourteenth and the beginning of the fifteenth century. At some time in the early sixteenth century one of the monks constructed a wooden structure inside the church in which were placed coloured figures in wood, papier-mâché and metal, representing great leaders and warriors – seventeen of the latter dressed in authentic suits of armour. These suits, restored in the present century, proved to be rare and valuable examples of the armourer's art, dating from the second half of the fifteenth century. One, made in northern Italy between 1450 and 1460, is illustrated in fig 1.

A suit of armour, is defined as "an articulated system of plates and sheets of metal, protecting the mounted combatant from head to foot," or "at every point," as the saying goes. The suit of armour first came to be used in the fourteenth century, replacing the coat of mail. By the mid 1650s it had been rendered obsolete by the invention of firearms, portable and otherwise.

In its essentials it was in use from the 1420s, though continual refinements, variants – fashions, even – would be seen as time went on.

The best armourers were to be found in the workshops of Italy and Germany, masters of their trade. Italy boasted the Milanese masters, Germany the armourers of Nuremberg, Landshut, Innsbruck and Augsberg, and the two styles – the Italian with its smooth, curved surfaces, the German with angles, points and grooving – were mutually influential. The Germans adopted the more flowing Italian forms, the Italians the parallel grooving characteristic of the "Maximilian" style, said to have been introduced by the Emperor Maximilian I.

Italian jousting armour merits separate consideration. In the joust, pairs of horsemen charged together, lances in rest, from opposite ends of and across a low barrier which ran the length of the lists. Jousting armour was reinforced on the left side, that exposed to the opponent's attack.

The heavy steel harness consisted of many pieces, each with its correct technical name (2 and 3). Its dual purpose was to furnish total protection, with no "dead" or vulnerable points and by means of articulation – adequate mobility.

2 3

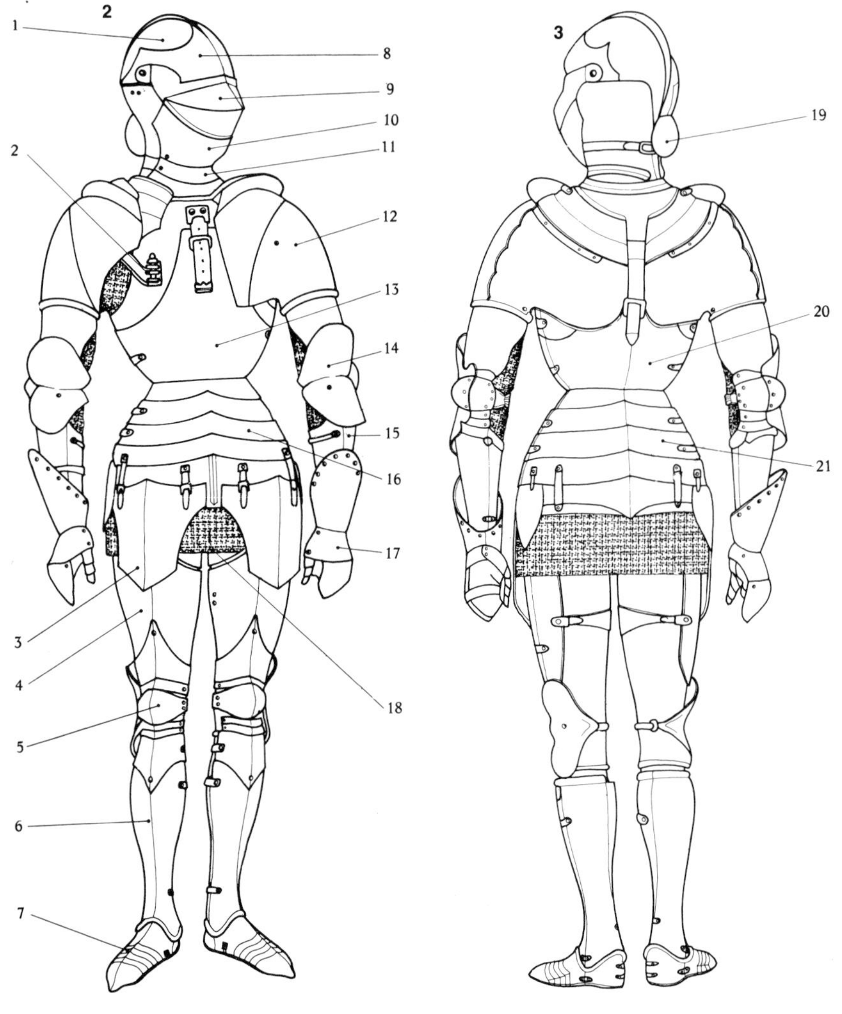

Breakdown of a suit of armour. 1. skull; 2. rest; 3. tasset; 4. cuisse; 5. poleyn; 6. greave; 7. sabaton; 8. brow reinforce; 9. upper bevor; 10. lower bevor; 11. gorget plate; 12. pauldron; 13. breastplate and lower breastplate; 14. cowter; 15. lower cannon of vambrace; 16. skirt; 17. gauntlet; 18. mail shirt; 19. roundel on helmet; 20. backplate, with lower backplate; 21. rump guard.

1

The most beautiful armour, on which craftsmen gave full expression to their consummate skills, was not for use in battle, but on ceremonial occasions. The light helmet, of the type known as *borgognotta* and the *rotella*, or buckler, in illustrations 6 and 7, belonged to one of the most celebrated captains of the sixteenth century, Alessandro Farnese, great-grandson of Paul III. As Duke of Parma he had fought bravely at Lepanto; as governor of the Low Countries he fought for Philip II, with courage and diplomacy, against the rebellious Dutch; he crossed swords successfully with Henri IV of France; and when he died, in a camp

4

5

6

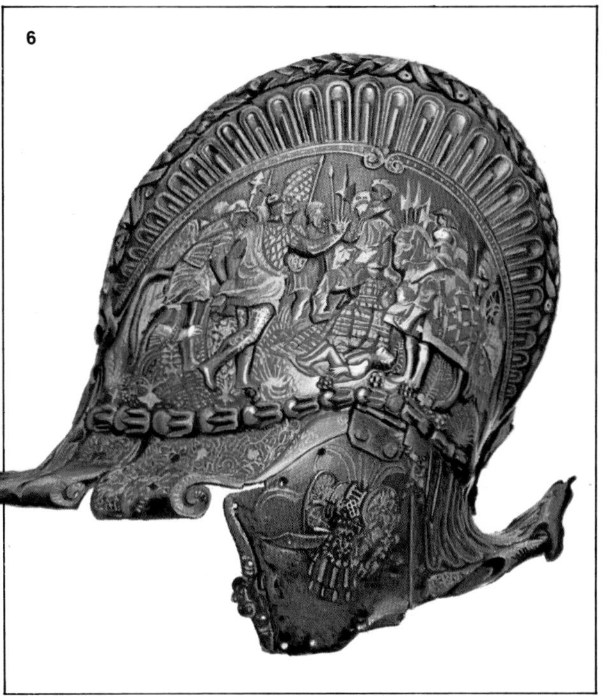

7

near Arras, the king he had so brilliantly served was about to deprive him of command. The two magnificent pieces illustrated are of Italian manufacture, c. 1563–65.

The *borgognotta* was a type of cavalry helmet of the sixteenth century, but the *rotella* or small shield, or buckler, was more often an item of parade armour. Some types, incorporating lanterns, were extremely effective in nocturnal military pageants.

The bill or halberd (8) was an infantry weapon, and could be used with deadly effect against mounted knights. It, too, was relegated to parade use after the introduction of firearms, carried by ceremonial guards at court for many years.

Maces (fig 9 shows an Italian example from the first half of the sixteenth century) and war hammers (fig 10, is a north Italian type – c. 1510), were weapons for both infantry and cavalry, rudimentary, perhaps, but against which only a complete armour carapace was the answer.

Warfare in Italy, at the period when mercenaries were extensively employed, could be relatively mild and bloodless. Machiavelli claims that in the battle of Anghiari, "a fray which continued for 20 or 24 hours, a single man was killed, and that not from wounds or any honourable cause, but by falling from his horse and being trampled. Men fought in such security, all mounted, encased in armour and safe from death on surrender, that there was no reason to be killed; their armour protected them while they fought and they surrendered when they could fight no more." A mode of warfare that was to change utterly in the sixteenth century, when Italy was ravaged by French, Spanish, Swiss and German invaders.

Weapons more reminiscent of the court than of the battlefield are the two folding Italian daggers (4 and 5) of the mid sixteenth century, for hunting boar and stag. The guards could be folded flat to the hilt, the hilt to the blade, and the blade itself folded in two or three. These daggers were small, portable and, because of the hingeing, very expensive; not too reliable under pressure, but fashionable, and, therefore, the choice of fashionable noblemen and princes.

When he ceased to wear armour, the gentleman carried a *striscia*, or long, narrow sidearm with pointed blade (11, an Italian example, with gilded decoration, c. 1600). This was the usual sidearm from the sixteenth century onwards, and became the accepted weapon for the duel.

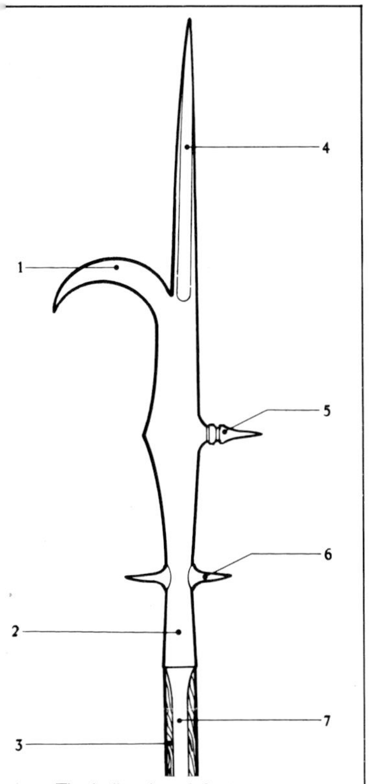

The halberd, an infantry weapon, in use up to the mid sixteenth century. 1. fluke; 2. socket; 3. shaft; 4. spike; 5. peen; 6. lugs (cross guard); 7. langet.

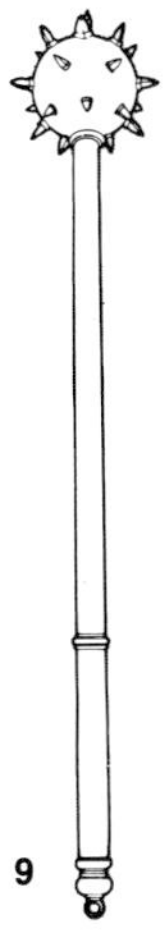

9

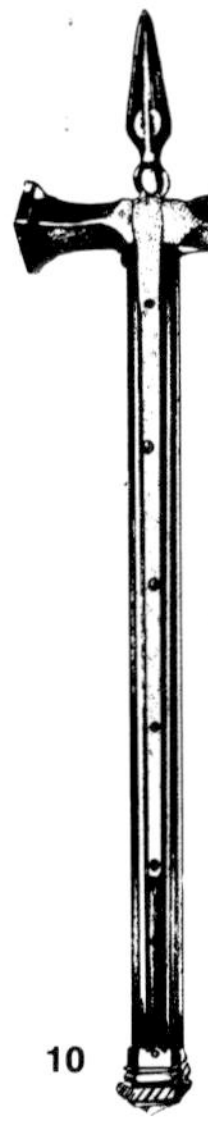

10

11

The preceding pages show photographs of arms and armour from the second half of the fifteenth century, discovered in the sanctuary of Santa Maria delle Grazie near Mantua. In one room of the Corte Vecchia *(the oldest part of the ducal palace of the Gonzaga at Mantua) are decorative frescoes by Pisanello that were still uncompleted at the time of the artist's death in 1455. The "chivalric" treatment, with heroic knights in armour and caparisoned horses, was already a little out of date.*

da Ronco entered. Count Gerolimo, realizing he was wounded, ran to the door at the back of the room, but Lodovico Pansecco and Iacomo da Ronco seized him round the ankles and forced him to the ground, inflicting a great wound to his head, giving him four or five stab wounds in all, and killed him. Then Misser Coradino, son of Misser Giolian Feo, the count's cousin, who at that time was in the closet, heard the noise and came out. He was first to see the count dead. He started to shout: 'Help, the count has been murdered.' Instantly one of the count's footmen, Nicolò da Cremona, came running, together with a secretary and footman of the count called Misser Andrea, son of Misser Dominico Rizo, and a certain Biaso from Casa Figara, a town near Forlí, and the count's jester, called el Greco, who was armed. They began to fight with Checco and Iacomo da Ronco and Lodovico Pansecco. By then, Checco's son Agaminonne, and Dedo de l'Urso and Batista, son of Misser Lodovico de l'Urso, and Matío de Gelasso were at the top of the stairs that lead to the loggia and the lord's chamber. Hearing the uproar, they burst into the chamber, where there was a great struggle going on, although those armed were having the worst of it. The noise was beyond description. Misser Lodovico suddenly appeared with a crowd of supporters, shouting: 'Liberty, liberty!'

"Then the guests and men at arms flocked in, together with all the count's family. And in the fracas, Agaminonne, the son of Checco de l'Urso, was fatally wounded. The hubbub spread down into the streets, and before long the whole population was roused. Then Misser Lodovico de l'Urso began shouting: 'Long live the people and liberty!' and they all responded: 'Long live the people and liberty!' At this point, wishing to see and hear what was happening, I quickly snatched up a heavy club and ran to the square, which was filled with townspeople. I entered the gate of the lord's palace; I saw Checco de l'Urso with a breastplate on and a halberd in his hand. Behind him were Matío de Galasso, the son of Misser Lodovico de l'Urso, and Dedo de l'Urso, and many workmen and pikemen. I then saw my lady the countess, wife of count Gerolimo, weeping at the window with her ladies, and calling out; and the whole household was running hither and thither.

"I stayed in the corner of the loggia, near the well, at the foot of the stairs leading up to the great hall in order to see what was happening. And at that moment I saw Misser Antonio da Montechie, the *bargello* [commander of the guard] come running through the courtyard with men in pursuit. At once he was seen by Checco and Matío de Galasso and their followers; They caught up with him as he reached the staircase leading to the green apartments, the loggia and his lordship's chamber. He was within three steps of the door of the prison in the clock tower when I saw him dragged to the ground and hacked to pieces by more than a hundred halberds, billhooks, pikes and swords.

Above: detail of the sinopia or preliminary mural drawing, and (opposite) of Pisanello's recently discovered fresco decoration at Mantua. First summoned to Mantua by the Marchese Gianfrancesco Gonzaga, possibly in 1415, Pisanello began work on this huge Arthurian fresco in 1447 for the Marchese Ludovico III, *"il Turco." The subject may be the bloody, three-day-long tournament held at* Louverzep *castle, in which Tristan triumphed under the gaze of Iseult.*

I saw it all happen before my eyes. My lady was screaming, 'No, no, do not kill him!' She was at the window above the stair, opposite the tower door – the window of my Lord's room.

"Then I saw what looked like workmen and peasants who dragged him by the feet to where I was, at the well. They brought fire, and lit it beneath his long hair. One stripped off his shoes and hose, one his other garments, another his shirt, and left him naked. Immediately some peasants – I think they were peasants, I was so shocked and confused – came to look at him lying there dead. Then I saw Checco de l'Urso, with Matío de Galasso and the rabble climb the steps and enter the chamber of my Lady the countess, wife of the count Gerolimo; and they took her prisoner, with her children, and brought them to the house of Misser Lodovico de l'Urso.

"I then saw the entire palace sacked from top to bottom, everything portable being carried away by the mob. As I stood there, I heard a great noise and ran out to see. The lord count Gerolimo was lifeless on the ground, thrown from the window of the room where he had been killed. And then they threw down three men-at-arms who had been dear to him – Marco Scoziacarro of Forlí, Carlo of Imola, whose wife Magoncina is a native of this town, and Ciccolino, to whom the lord count Gerolimo had awarded a wife against the wishes of her family and friends.

FERDINAND · CONZAGA SEN PROREX · SICILIÆ PRODVX INSVBR
Trinacriæ Prorex, Produx FERNANDE fuisti,
GONSAGA, Insubrium, pace, Sagòque probus.

Opposite: execution of participants in the 1506 conspiracy against Alfonso I d'Este, Duke of Ferrara, and his brother Cardinal Ippolito (from the Libro dei Giustiziati, *Ferrara, Biblioteca Comunale Ariostea). The main instigators of the conspiracy were a brother and an illegitimate half-brother of the intended victims: the illegitimate Giulio d'Este, whom Ippolito had tried to have blinded by his servants for offenses against women (Giulio lost an eye on that occasion), and Ferrante d'Este, younger brother of Alfonso and elder brother of Ippolito. The two conspirators were never executed, but confined to prison for life. Right: Ferrante (Ferdinando) I Gonzaga, governor of Milan on behalf of Charles V, and Count of Guastalla; with the agreement of the emperor he organized the conspiracy which resulted in the killing (Piacenza, 10 September 1547) of Pier Luigi Farnese, son of Pope Paul III and Duke of Parma and Piacenza.*

"I then saw Simone dei Fiorini come forward with a halberd; some say that with this weapon he inflicted a wound on the count, who was already dead and lifeless: I did not see it because of the great crowd of people around him. Standing there I saw Pagliarino, nephew of the said Iacomo da Ronco, pulling and dragging count Gerolimo by the feet; people shouted and he left the body alone. Soon some bearers arrived with a stretcher and took him away, completely naked, spouting blood."

Once revenge had been taken, it was the Orsi themselves who informed Lorenzo de' Medici: "Magnificent and most noble Lord. We are certain that Your Magnificence will already have been advised of the death of this evil and accursed man, whom we do not wish to call Lord because he was not worthy of that honour. However, in order to partly satisfy our debt to you, although it was not possible earlier, it seemed to us, in view of his arrogant presumption and brutishness, who so desired to stain his hands with the blood of your Magnificent and Most Excellent house, to inform you of the deservedly cruel death that we have inflicted on him." And so the vendetta was completed.

Threat to property

When, in 1545, the Farnese pope Paul III invested his son Pier Luigi with the dukedom of Parma and Piacenza, he was violently intruding into a feudal situation whose complexities dated at least from the period of the mid fourteenth to mid fifteenth century, when the dominant Visconti made their *pacta* and *conventiones* with the local nobility. The new state robbed Milan of physically and strategically valuable territory, and drove a wedge between the Gonzaga domains of Mantua and Monferrato south of the Po. The rivalry of Gonzaga and Farnese was born with Alessandro Farnese's elevation to the papacy in 1534, and the chief antagonists for 13 years had been Pier Luigi and don Ferrante Gonzaga. The former, Duke of Castro since 1537, was now Duke of Parma; the latter governed Milan for the Holy Roman Emperor. Behind them, however, were other more important rivals: the pope and Charles V.

"Don Ferrante," says Giuliano Gosellini, the chronicler of this conspiracy, "being informed that the count Giovanni Anguisola Gonzaga of Castel Giusfrè was the man of most authority in that city, the bravest and with the strongest party, and that, as a good citizen, he constantly bewailed the wrongs his homeland suffered from Pier Luigi, who greedily and continually attempted to deprive him and his fellow feudal lords of their ancient and noble privileges, judged him the perfect instrument in his design for getting rid of his rival."

The plot was supported by Charles V, with the active participation of the local nobility: the count Giovanni Anguissola Gonzaga and his brother-in-law Luigi, the marchese Camillo Pallavicino and his brothers Girolamo and Alessandro, the count Agostino Lanti, Giovan Luigi Confalonieri and his brother-in-law the count Scotti. But let us hear for a moment the account of another eyewitness, a *credenziero* at Piacenza, devoted to his master's memory.

"I, a butler of Piasenza, speaking in fond

30 LIBRO

GALEAZZO MARIA figliuolo di Francesco Sforza per memoria della paterna virtù, & per propria liberalità, accompagnato da rara bellezza di corpo, che nella sua florida età lo rendeua molto amabile, si godeua pacificamente lo Stato paterno, con nome di ottimo Prencipe, se da sfrenata lussuria non s'hauesse lasciato vincere, la quale gli apportò anco la morte, per congiura di Girolamo Olgiato, d'Andrea Lampugnano, & di Carlo Visconte, à cui haueua il Duca (come vogliono alcuni) violata vna Sorella, & dopò sottopostola anco ad alcuni suoi famigliari. Vogliono altri che ciò facessero solo per desio di gloria, incitati à ciò da vn loro Pedante Salernitano. Sia come si voglia l'ammazzarono in Milano nella Chiesa di S. Stefano, nel mezo della sua guardia mentre era per vdir Messa. Non è da tacersi l'animo intrepido dell'Olgiato, ilquale essendo prigione con certezza d'hauere à morire crudelmente, compose alcuni versi latini sopra GALEAZZO morto, conchiudendo, che à Tiranni non è cosa alcuna sicura; e posto nelle mani del Carnefice ne' più attroci cruciati, confortaua se stesso, dicendo, rincorati Girolamo, che benche la morte sia acerba, haurai però fama perpetua. Fù GALEAZZO fautore de virtuosi, & di Signorile splendore, che si poteua pareggiare à Rè grandissimi. Haueua ordinariamente vna banda di più di due mila huomini d'arme di tutta la nobiltà Italiana. Morì egli di XXXIII anni, hauendone dominato dieci, lasciando Gio: Galeazzo, & Hermete suoi figliuoli, & due femine hauute da Bona sua moglie.

E' cauata questa effigie da vna tauola che è dipinta nel Duomo di Milano.

BONA

Another princely victim of conspiracy: Galeazzo Maria Sforza, killed on Christmas Day, 1476. He is described in the print above as a man "of rare physical beauty," who "lived in peaceful enjoyment of his patrimony."

remembrance of the duke [Pier Luigi], report that I was ill during September of the year 1547, and that one day, a Saturday, at about the fourteenth hour, having eaten and retired to bed, I heard a tumult in the old citadel where the duke was lodged. I arose and went to the window of my bedchamber that looks out over the square within the citadel, and there I saw Agostino de Lando, the lame de Scipione, the *signore* Alexandro de Scipione, Gio. Aluisio Confalonero and Giovanni Anguisciola and the cavalier Panaro, all of them armed, with coats of mail and halberds and arquebuses and different types of weapon, with many people behind them; also present was a certain Iosepho del Pozzo and Cesare Marchone. And as the men came inside they formed two groups; one, led by Gio. Anguisola, went up to the hall where the duke of blessed memory was with his entourage, while the other remained down below at the gate to the citadel, and when the men in the group above had arrived they began to attack the duke's guards, who were Germans, while those below attacked at the same time. Soon the said Giovan Anguisola, Franceschino Malvicino and a Spaniard broke into the duke's chamber, killing him at once with hunting knives, inflicting seven or eight wounds, which I myself saw after he was dead. When they had slain the duke, they put him in a window of the citadel facing the city and Gio. Anguisola, Gio. Aluisio Confaloniero and Franceschino Malvicino began shouting 'Liberty, liberty!' and other words. After a while they flung him into the ditch of the citadel, then the rest of the corpses, fourteen there were, stripped naked, except for the duke, who was wearing an undershirt. Having done this, they came down and raised the bridge, locking themselves in the citadel, and fired three cannon shots towards the Po as a signal for don Ferrante's men to advance, and within two or three hours they were in the city. . . ."

This succinct and informative testimony of Giovan Francesco Cesi dal Monte, butler to Pier Luigi, was given on 6 July 1549.

Threat to honour

"On the 22nd day, the feast of St Mary Magdalen, at one o'clock in the morning, certain men of Urbino entered the palace of the count of Urbino and slew him in his chamber. And with him were slain Messer Manfredi da Carpi, the protonotary, and Tomaxo, son of Messer

LAMENTO DEL DVCA
GALEAZO MARIA, DVCA
DI MILANO.
Quando fu morto nella Chieſa di Santo Stefano
da Giouan'Andrea da Lampognano,
Sacra & ſenza macula Maria
madre del buõ Gieſu figliuola e ſpo-
te di charita humile & pia (ſa
gine bella e miſericordioſa
ugio de gli afflitti albergo & pace
endor del Sole e Stella luminoſa
ga per me il tuo figlio ſel ti piace
a ſe raccolga queſt'alma tapina
laſſa il mondo miſero & fallace
O coronata al ciel alta Regina
ſoccorrimi all'eſtremo di mia guerra
ſi ch'io non uada all'infernal fucina
E uoi chel corpo mio uedete in terra
& l'altrui ferro nel mio ſangue tinto
dirouui il nome mio che tanto erra
Galeazzo Maria ſon Duca quinto
di Milan hor udite i dolor miei
con gliocchi uoſtri di lachrime tinti

The death of Galeazzo Maria Sforza recorded in a popular print. The poem beneath includes the lines: "High Queen of heaven, save me at the end of this my struggle, from the fires of Hell."

Giudicino d'Arimino. It was said that he was killed because of his dishonourable habits and his cruelty to the people of Urbino. May his soul rest in peace. Amen."

Thus, in Rimini, the compiler of the *Cronaca malatestiana* recorded the news of the slaying of Oddantonio da Montefeltro, which occurred on the night of 21 – 22 July 1444. In Forlí, the *Annales Foroliviensés* tell the same tale: *Die XXII iulii. Otto comes duxque Urbini, ob violatam pudicitiam feminarum, a popularibus nocte trucidatur (The 22nd day of July*, by night. Otto, count and lord of Urbino, for having violated the chastity of women, was murdered by the people).

At his accession Oddantonio was barely seventeen years old, a hot-blooded young man, whose misfortune it was to have become involved with two unbridled libertines, the same protonotary, Manfredi da Carpi, and Tommaso dell' Agnello, a native of Rimini, both of whom dynastic historians such as Bernardino Baldi (1553–1616) are quick to accuse of every sort of evil: Manfredi for having seduced the wife of the doctor Serafino Serafini, a member of a powerful family in the city; Tommaso for having violated the wife of one of the Ricciarelli, a feudal family of the county. Serafino is said to have organized the conspiracy, whose aim was to eliminate the two counsellors together with their protector.

That night, the humanist Agostino Dati, who was also staying at the palace, only escaped with his life by fleeing naked to a nearby church. Agostino is the only eyewitness to have left a direct account of the slaughter. Following the conspirators' success, the palace was subjected to plunder, and the corpses of the duke and his counsellors thrown to the mob.

The "Catiline Conspiracy"

During the Christmas Mass of 1476 Giovann' Andrea Lampugnani, Carlo Visconti and Girolamo Olgiati attacked and killed the duke of Milan, Galeazzo Sforza. "In the middle of the church," as Orfeo da Ricavo wrote a day or two later to Sforza Bettini in Florence, "these three suddenly revealed themselves, dressed alike, and in a trice that traitorous Giovanni Andrea plunged his dagger into the duke's body, up to the hilt. The poor Signore raised his hands and said: 'I am dead!' At that very moment he was dealt another blow in the stomach and four dagger thrusts from the other two: on the left side of head and throat, above the temple and in the right rib. It all happened in the twinkling of an eye. He fell backwards, almost hitting me on the chest, but I was not quick enough to hold him and he fell to the floor. Even then two of those traitors would not leave him alone. Then they ran."

Visconti and Olgiati made good their escape for the moment, but their companion, having ended up in the midst of the women attending Mass, "stumbled and fell. The attendants, who came running at the commotion, saw him on the ground with the blade in his hand and he was badly wounded in the scuffle . . . That traitorous Giovanni Andrea was dragged through the streets by the populace, children included, and finally the pigs ate him. His right hand was burned and nailed to a pillar . . . ."

The other two conspirators were later captured, and Girolamo Olgiati accused his master, the Bolognese humanist Cola Montano, who had been teaching in Milan since 1462, of having incited him to tyrannicide; and he had told him stories of the imperishable memory and eternal glory of those Athenians, Carthaginians and Romans who had conspired against tyrants. They were much influenced by the Catiline Conspiracy [64–63 BC]. Their sole idea was to imitate those ancient Romans and become the liberators of their fatherland.

The same eagerness to ascribe the plot to isolated fanatics is echoed by Duchess Bona in her official communiqué to the pope: *unus hominis scelere et perfidia* (a few men acting criminally and perfidiously). At a time when the exiled brothers of the duke had been received in France by Louis XI and when the French king himself, on hearing the news of the death of both Galeazzo and Charles the Bold, ordered *festes solempnelles* in his kingdom to mark the disappearance of *noz anciens ennemis*, we can understand why the duchess was concerned to minimize the importance of the conspiracy. In truth, more than a little justification and grounds for conspiracy could be laid at the door of the late duke. The portrait painted of him by Bernardino Corio (1459–1512) in his *Storia di Milan*, presents an unattractive individual.

The appeal to classical tyrannicides was thus both possible and probable, and we may note that it occurs in official versions of the origins of the conspiracy. We, therefore, find the figure of the tyrant, recognizable in its essential characteristics, as well as the phenomenon of universal discontent; in addition, there was widespread familiarity at the time with the writings of classical Latin authors, which made it easy for people to draw contemporary parallels.

Blood, property, honour: the three factors that cause conspiracies, according to Machiavellian theory, are exemplified by these episodes chosen from the many bloody incidents that punctuate the history of the Italian courts from the Middle Ages to the Renaissance. Although they differed in outcome, the ritual was always the same. In dethronement, as in enthronement, the populace was always called upon to assume an unique and vital role. Their acclamation of a prince is one side of the coin, the mangling of his corpse the other. Nor does it matter if the dismembered corpse is that of the assailant, since he too represents power.

The cutting up of the body, in fact, obeyed a ritual as cruel as it was formalized: a ritual that in no way represents – the subjection of those in power to the same hanging, drawing and quartering which they themselves inflicted on the lower orders.

Despite what has been all too often arbitrarily repeated in the past, this is not a conscious inversion of the "high-low" social system, but a symbolic divestment of the symbols of power. It is noticeable that the very first act performed on the corpse was the removal of all clothing. This was an essential preliminary, which corresponds to the ceremonial investiture that takes place at the moment of enthronement. The next step was dissection, the prime purpose of which was to remove all the physical attributes of power: the head (or the eyes, as symbols of the whole), the right hand and the male member. The dragging of the corpse through the streets of the city, an act which marked the end of the ritual, represents a reversal of the triumphal procession held at the moment of enthronement.

Even at moments of the greatest savagery, therefore, the populace of medieval and Renaissance cities revealed not only a life immersed in ritual, but also an inability to live beyond the bounds of sacred ceremony.

Chronology, family trees, bibliography

The states of Italy after the Treaty of Chateau-Cambrésis, 1559

1 *Duchy of Savoy*
2 *Marquisate of Saluzzo*
3 *Countship of Tenda*
4 *Principality of Monaco*
5 *Principality of Masserano*
6 *Marquisate of Monferrato*
7 *Republic of Genoa*
8 *Marquisate of Finale*
9 *Duchy of Milan*
10 *Duchy of Parma*
11 *Principality of Massa*
12 *Principality of Trent*
13 *Republic of Venice*
14 *Duchy of Mantua*
15 *Duchy of Modena and Reggio*
16 *Republic of Lucca*
17 *Duchy of Ferrara*
18 *Papal States*
19 *Republic of San Marino*
20 *Duchy of Urbino*
21 *Duchy of Florence*
22 *Countship of Santa Fiora*
23 *State of the Presidi of Tuscany*
24 *Duchy of Castro*
25 *Kingdom of Naples*
26 *Republic of Ragusa*
27 *Kingdom of Sicily*
28 *Kingdom of Sardinia*
29 *Corsica*

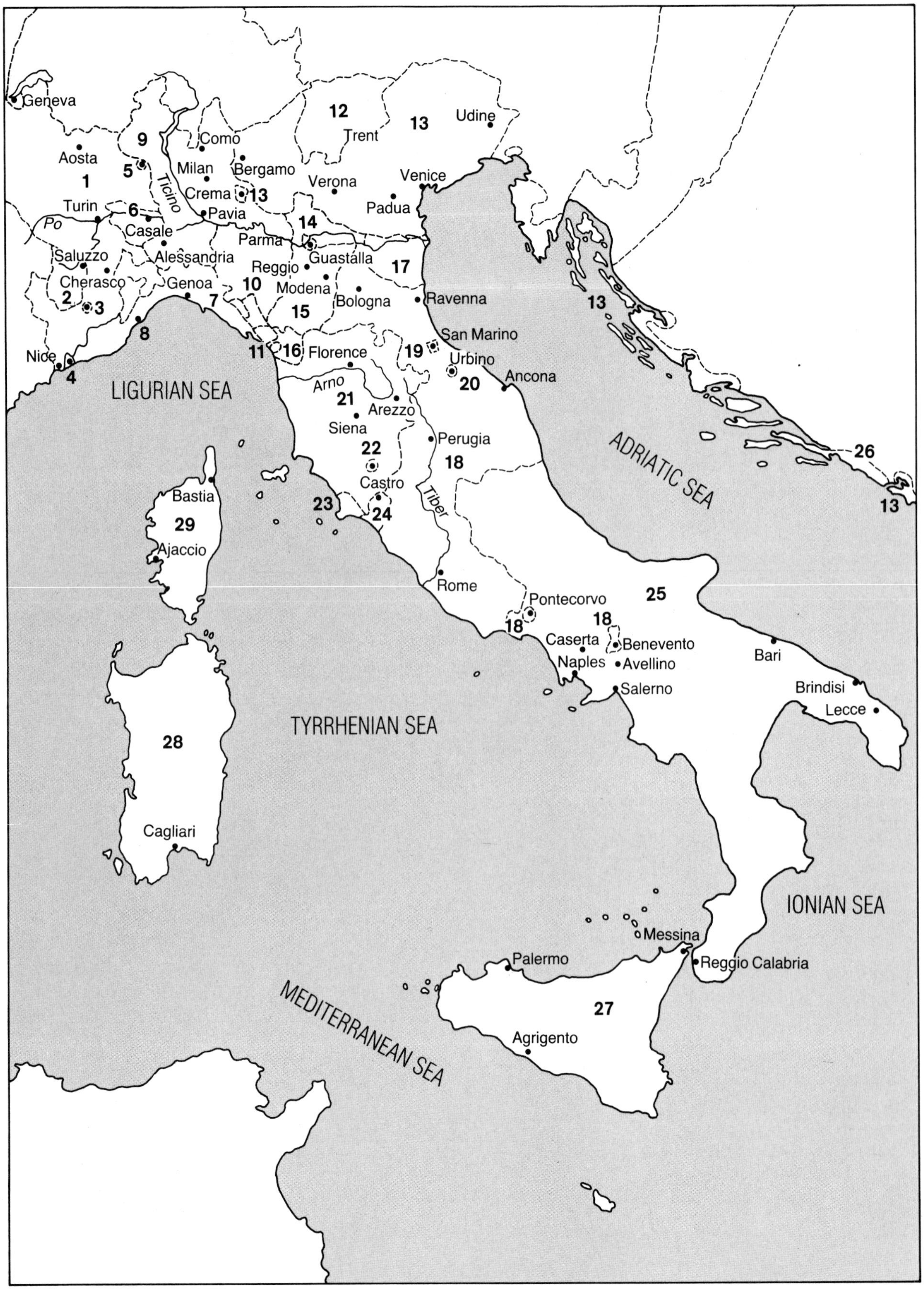

The history of a dynasty

Rise and fall of the Gonzaga of Mantua

1271
Fiordalice dei Bonacolsi, sister of Pinamonte dei Bonacolsi, buys a house in the *contrada* of S. Croce in Mantua, the city that was on the way to becoming the fiefdom of the Gonzaga family.

1273
Pinamonte dei Bonacolsi becomes overlord of Mantua.

1288
Tagino dei Bonacolsi, son of Pinamonte, has a palazzo close to the house of his aunt Fiordalice.

1291
Bardellone, another son of Pinamonte, lives in a palazzo in the same area. He seizes power from his father.

1295
Guido dei Bonacolsi, known as Botesella, nephew of Tagino and Bardellone, owns the Magna Domus in the *contrada* of S. Croce.

1299
Guido, in turn, seizes power from his uncle Bardellone.

1300
Botesella builds his Palazzo del Capitano in the *contrada* of S. Alessandro, adjoining the *contrada* of S. Croce, thus forming a vast complex of Bonacolsi property, situated on the two sides of the road separating the two *contrade*.

1303
First extension of the Piazza di S. Pietro (now Piazza Sordello) to approximately half its present size.

1310
By the simple maneuver of banning the boundary road between the two *contrade* to the public, the Bonacolsi ensure they now have an area of Mantua exclusively to themselves.

1322
The brothers Guido, Filippino and Feltrino, sons of Luigi Gonzaga, occupy a palazzo in the *contrada* degli Scaglioni di S. Alessandro (behind the *contrade* of S. Alessandro and S. Croce, towards the lake).

1328
Meanwhile, power has shifted from the Bonacolsi to the Gonzaga.

1330
The palazzo in the *contrada* degli Scaglioni is well on the way to becoming a showpiece, while the acquisition of nearby property extends the Gonzaga holdings as far as the church of S. Croce.

1355
The Gonzaga buy up all the Bonacolsi property in Mantua, including the Palazzo del Capitano, and the Magna Domus.

1370
Under the aegis of Luigi II, further urbanization takes place, with the creation of the Corte complex, enclosing all the historical Bonacolsi and Gonzagan palazzi.

1388
Francesco I is proclaimed lord of Mantua. He puts work in hand on the Casa Zoiosa (Maison Joyeuse).

1395
Work on the Castello is begun, to plans by Bartolino da Novara.

1396
Second extension of the Piazza di S. Pietro to its modern size (Piazza Sordella).

1400
Completion of the Castello.

1407
Death of Francesco I; succeeded by his son Gianfrancesco, a minor.

1415
Gianfrancesco comes of age. Improvements to the Palazzo del Capitano and Magna Domus include the adoption of mullioned windows, replacing the earlier, round-arched, pattern.

1423
Vittorino da Feltre establishes his school in the Casa Zoiosa.

1423
Three *palazzetti* added to the Corte complex.

1433
The Emperor Sigismund confers on Gianfrancesco the title of first Marquis of Mantua.

1442
Alterations to one of the *palazzetti*, in a room of which Pisanello is working on a fresco (uncompleted at his death).

1443
Rebuilding of the church of S. Croce.

1444
Death of Gianfrancesco; succeeded by his son Ludovico, or Luigi III il Turco (second marquis).

1458
Luca Fancelli starts work on the adaptation of the Castello as a residence.

1459
The first chapel of the Castello is built (to the design of Andrea Mantegna), and the adaptation programme completed; Luigi III moves from the Corte to the Castello.

1465
Mantegna begins work on the decoration of the Camera degli Sposi.

1472
Construction of Mantegna's new loggia for the courtyard of the Castello.

1474
Completion of Mantegna's murals for the Camera degli Sposi.

1478
Death of Luigi III; succeeded by his son Federico I. Renovations carried out to parts of the Corte, near the church of S. Croce.

1479
Federico I creates a small lakeside building at the Castello, with a *porto*, its own *porticello*, and a labyrinth.

1480
The old Scaglione palazzo in the Corte is demolished, and Fancelli begins construction of the Domus Nova.

1483
A new *studio* in the Castello.

1484
Death of Federico I; succeeded by his son Francesco II. Work is suspended on the Domus Nova.

1490
Isabella d'Este comes to Mantua as bride of Francesco II.

1491
Isabella converts a room of the Castello into her *studiolo*.

1496
Renovation undertaken of Isabella's *studiolo*, for which a series of allegorical pictures is planned.

1498
Isabella decides to assemble her collection of paintings, *objets d'art*, etc. in the so-called *grotta*, a room beneath the *studiolo*.

1500
The Corte begins to be known as the Corte Vecchia.

1502
Isabella receives Michelangelo's *Cupid* as a gift from Cesare Borgia.

1502
Work begins on the Palazzo di S. Sebastiano, near the Porta Pusterla.

1507
Isabella's *grotta* refurbished.

1511
Completion of the five allegorical pictures – by Mantegna, Perugino and Lorenzo Costa – for Isabella's *studiolo*.

1515
Isabella wishing to move from the Castello into the Corte Vecchia, has ground-floor rooms prepared near the church of S. Croce. Work is finally completed on the Palazzo di S. Sebastiano.

1519
Death of Francesco II; succeeded by his son Federico II.

1520
New apartment built for Isabella by Battista da Coro, in a new wing, close to her S. Croce rooms. As in the Castello, her suite includes a *studiolo* and *grotta*.

1522
Inscription in the private courtyard marks the completion of Isabella's dowager apartment in the Corte Vecchia to which she moves from the Castello.

1525
Giulio Romano begins work on the Palazzo del Te, beyond the Porta Pusterla, for Federico II.

1530
The emperor Charles V confers a dukedom on Federico II.

1531
Giulio Romano renovates part of the Castello, and creates the Palazzina Paleologa for the new Duchess, Margherita Paleologa of Monferrato.

1532
Two allegories by Correggio added to the adornment of Isabella's *studiolo*.

1535
Completion of the Palazzo del Te.

1536
Giulio Romano begins work on the rooms known as the Corte Nuova, in the Castello; a series of paintings depicting the Twelve Caesars, for one of the rooms, is commissioned from Titian.

1538
Titian finishes work on the Twelve Caesars. Giulio Romano builds the *Rustica*, or rusticated short southern side of the Cortile della Mostra, opposite the Corte Nuova.

1539
Giulio Romano finishes the Corte Nuova.

1540
Death of Federico II; succeeded by his son Francesco III, a minor.

1549
Giovan Battista Bertani begins his extensions to the Corte Nuova, enclosing the *cortile pensile* with other buildings, and surrounding the *prato* of the Castello with arcades, besides constructing a theater – the first permanent theater under Gonzagan rule. Francesco III settles into Giulio Romano's apartments in the Corte Nuova.

1550
Death of Francesco III; succeeded by his brother Guglielmo, a minor.

1556
Guglielmo comes of age. Bertani resumes work on the extension of the Corte Nuova, enlarging the *Rustica* and beginning the final layout of the Cortile della Mostra.

1557
Internal decoration of the *Rustica* begun under Bertani's direction.

1561
Work on the *Rustica* completed. Bertani builds a small church between the *prato* and the *Cortile della Mostra*.

1565
This small church is demolished and a larger one, to be dedicated to St. Barbara, begun, to Bertani's designs. A new chapel built in the Castello.

1565
The collegiate church of S. Barbara completed.

1565
Work begins on the bell tower of S. Barbara. Duke Guglielmo decides to remove to the Corte Vecchia, leaving the Corte Nuova to his son and heir, Vincenzo.

1566
Work begins on modernizing part of the Corte Vecchia, following possession by Duke Guglielmo.

1567
Completion of the bell tower of S. Barbara.

1568
Extensions begun to the church of S. Barbara.

1570
Completion of the enlargement of S. Barbara.

1572
Work begun on what was later known as the *bastione del Giardino*, behind the Corte Nuova, overlooking the lake.

1574
Guglielmo moves into the Corte Vecchia. In Bertani's part of the Corte Nuova an anonymous artist decorates the *Sala di Manto* (where frescoes illustrate the tale of the Theban Manto, priestess of Apollo and mother of the legendary founder of the city), and the *Sala dei Capitani*.

1575
Pompeo Pedemonte submits designs for a new rectory for the church of S. Barbara; his plans were never carried out.

1576
Completion of the *bastione del Giardino* project. Decoration continues of the Corte Nuova, and of the Corte Vecchia.

1579
Work commences on the hanging garden in the Corte Vecchia. In Venice, Tintoretto is at work on his series of paintings of the Glories of the Gonzaga for the *Sala dei Marchesi* and *Sala dei Duchi* in Bertani's Corte Nuova extension.

1581
Construction of a wide connecting passageway between the Corte Vecchia and Corte Nuova, along the left-hand side of S. Barbara. Remodelling of the piazzetta in front of the church.

1582
Building of new stables on the road by the lake.

1586
Tintoretto finishes his series of paintings on the glories of the Gonzaga; the hanging garden completed; and the creation of the *Cortile delle Otto facce*.

1586
Pedemonte submits a new design for the rectory of S. Barbara.

1587
Work begins on Pedemonte's rectory. Death of Duke Guglielmo; succeeded by his son Vincenzo I.

1588
Work on the S. Barbara rectory suspended. Fire destroys Bertani's theater and seriously damages the adjacent armoury.

1591
A new theater built, designed by Ippolito Andreasi, otherwise known as "l'Andreasino."

1592
Work begins on the *Galleria della Mostra* on the long western side of the courtyard.

1595
Antonio Maria Viani begins preliminary work on the creation of the "green" apartment in the Corte Vecchia, besides other renovations elsewhere in the palace complex. A "public" theater built in the vicinity of the new stables.

1596
New armoury installed on upper floor of the Palazzo del Capitano.

1600
Two Flemish painters appointed to the court: Rubens and Frans Bonrhus the Younger.

1601
Viani's plans for a more elaborate ducal apartment, for Vincenzo I, put into operation.

1602
As part of Viani's design, two sides of the *cortile d'onore*, with galleries leading to the duke's new apartment, are completed.

1605
Completion of *Galleria della Mostra*, together with the decoration of *Corridoio dei Mori*.

1608
Completion of Viani's large theater (for the performance of *melodrammi*), and of an entrance arch to the *prato* of the Castello.

1612
Death of Vincenzo I; succeeded by his brother Ferdinando.

1614
Work begins on the villa La Favorita, designed by Nicolò Sebregondi by the lake shore.

1616
Decoration of the *Salone degli Arcieri*, the *Stanze delle Città* and *Stanze delle Metamorfosi*.

1624
Completion of the villa La Favorita.

1626
Death of Duke Ferdinando; succeeded by his brother Vincenzo II.

1627
Completion of the *appartamento dei Nani* (apartment of the court dwarfs). First sale of pictures from the ducal collection. Death of Duke Vincenzo II, with whom the direct Gonzaga line ends.

1628
Carlo I Gonzaga, Vincenzo's cousin, of the junior Nevers line, claims the dukedom, but Imperial investiture is refused. Second sale of a large quantity of sculpture.

1630
Capture and sack of Mantua by Imperial troops.

Some of the Ruling Families of Renaissance Italy

Ercole I d'Este, Duke of Ferrara, Modena and Reggio; a fifteenth-century miniature.

Ferrara: the House of Este

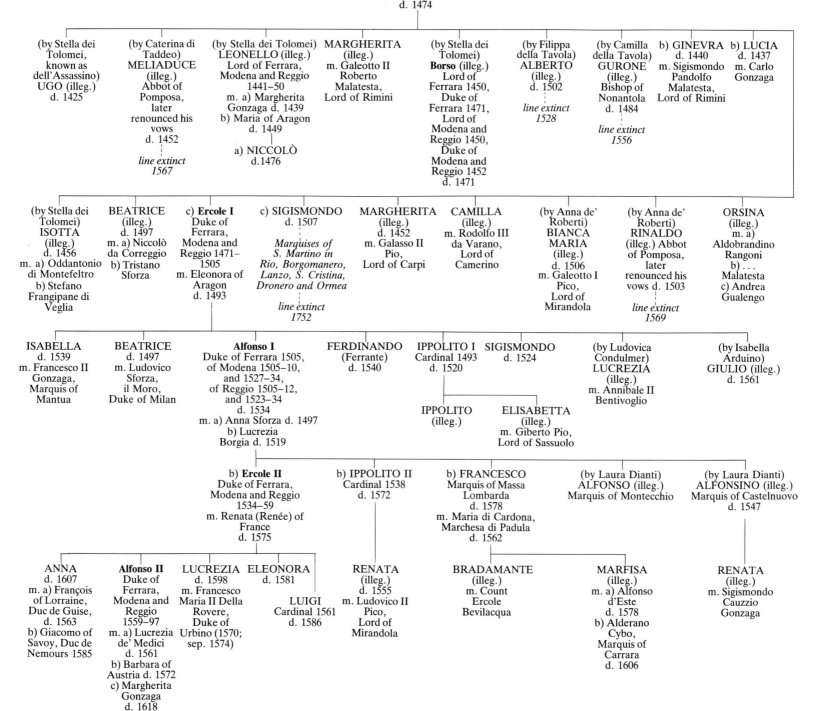

NICCOLÒ III
Lord of Ferrara and Modena 1393, of Reggio 1409, and of Parma 1409–20
d. 1441
m. a) Gigliola da Carrara d. 1416
b) Parisina Malatesta d. 1425
c) Ricciarda di Saluzzo d. 1474

(by Stella dei Tolomei, known as dell'Assassino) UGO (illeg.) d. 1425

(by Caterina di Taddeo) MELIADUCE (illeg.) Abbot of Pomposa, later renounced his vows d. 1452 — *line extinct 1567*

(by Stella dei Tolomei) LEONELLO (illeg.) Lord of Ferrara, Modena and Reggio 1441–50 m. a) Margherita Gonzaga d. 1439 b) Maria of Aragon d. 1449
- a) NICCOLÒ d.1476

MARGHERITA (illeg.) m. Galeotto II Roberto Malatesta, Lord of Rimini

(by Stella dei Tolomei) **Borso** (illeg.) Lord of Ferrara 1450, Duke of Ferrara 1471, Lord of Modena and Reggio 1450, Duke of Modena and Reggio 1452 d. 1471

(by Filippa della Tavola) ALBERTO (illeg.) d. 1502 — *line extinct 1528*

(by Camilla della Tavola) GURONE (illeg.) Bishop of Nonantola d. 1484 — *line extinct 1556*

b) GINEVRA d. 1440 m. Sigismondo Pandolfo Malatesta, Lord of Rimini

b) LUCIA d. 1437 m. Carlo Gonzaga

(by Stella dei Tolomei) ISOTTA (illeg.) d. 1456 m. a) Oddantonio di Montefeltro b) Stefano Frangipane di Veglia

BEATRICE (illeg.) d. 1497 m. a) Niccolò da Correggio b) Tristano Sforza

c) **Ercole I** Duke of Ferrara, Modena and Reggio 1471–1505 m. Eleonora of Aragon d. 1493

c) SIGISMONDO d. 1507 — *Marquises of S. Martino in Rio, Borgomanero, Lanzo, S. Cristina, Dronero and Ormea* — *line extinct 1752*

MARGHERITA (illeg.) d. 1452 m. Galasso II Pio, Lord of Carpi

CAMILLA (illeg.) m. Rodolfo III da Varano, Lord of Camerino

(by Anna de' Roberti) BIANCA MARIA (illeg.) d. 1506 m. Galeotto I Pico, Lord of Mirandola

(by Anna de' Roberti) RINALDO (illeg.) Abbot of Pomposa, later renounced his vows d. 1503 — *line extinct 1569*

ORSINA (illeg.) m. a) Aldobrandino Rangoni b) . . . Malatesta c) Andrea Gualengo

---

Children of Ercole I:

ISABELLA d. 1539 m. Francesco II Gonzaga, Marquis of Mantua

BEATRICE d. 1497 m. Ludovico Sforza, il Moro, Duke of Milan

Alfonso I Duke of Ferrara 1505, of Modena 1505–10, and 1527–34, of Reggio 1505–12, and 1523–34 d. 1534 m. a) Anna Sforza d. 1497 b) Lucrezia Borgia d. 1519

FERDINANDO (Ferrante) d. 1540

IPPOLITO I Cardinal 1493 d. 1520
- IPPOLITO (illeg.)
- ELISABETTA (illeg.) m. Giberto Pio, Lord of Sassuolo

SIGISMONDO d. 1524

(by Ludovica Condulmer) LUCREZIA (illeg.) m. Annibale II Bentivoglio

(by Isabella Arduino) GIULIO (illeg.) d. 1561

Children of Alfonso I:

b) **Ercole II** Duke of Ferrara, Modena and Reggio 1534–59 m. Renata (Renée) of France d. 1575

b) IPPOLITO II Cardinal 1538 d. 1572
- RENATA (illeg.) d. 1555 m. Ludovico II Pico, Lord of Mirandola

b) FRANCESCO Marquis of Massa Lombarda d. 1578 m. Maria di Cardona, Marchesa di Padula d. 1562
- BRADAMANTE (illeg.) m. Count Ercole Bevilacqua
- MARFISA (illeg.) m. a) Alfonso d'Este d. 1578 b) Alderano Cybo, Marquis of Carrara d. 1606

(by Laura Dianti) ALFONSO (illeg.) Marquis of Montecchio

(by Laura Dianti) ALFONSINO (illeg.) Marquis of Castelnuovo d. 1547
- RENATA (illeg.) m. Sigismondo Cauzzio Gonzaga

Children of Ercole II:

ANNA d. 1607 m. a) François of Lorraine, Duc de Guise, d. 1563 b) Giacomo of Savoy, Duc de Nemours 1585

Alfonso II Duke of Ferrara, Modena and Reggio 1559–97 m. a) Lucrezia de' Medici d. 1561 b) Barbara of Austria d. 1572 c) Margherita Gonzaga d. 1618

LUCREZIA d. 1598 m. Francesco Maria II Della Rovere, Duke of Urbino (1570; sep. 1574)

ELEONORA d. 1581

LUIGI Cardinal 1561 d. 1586

Florence: the House of Medici

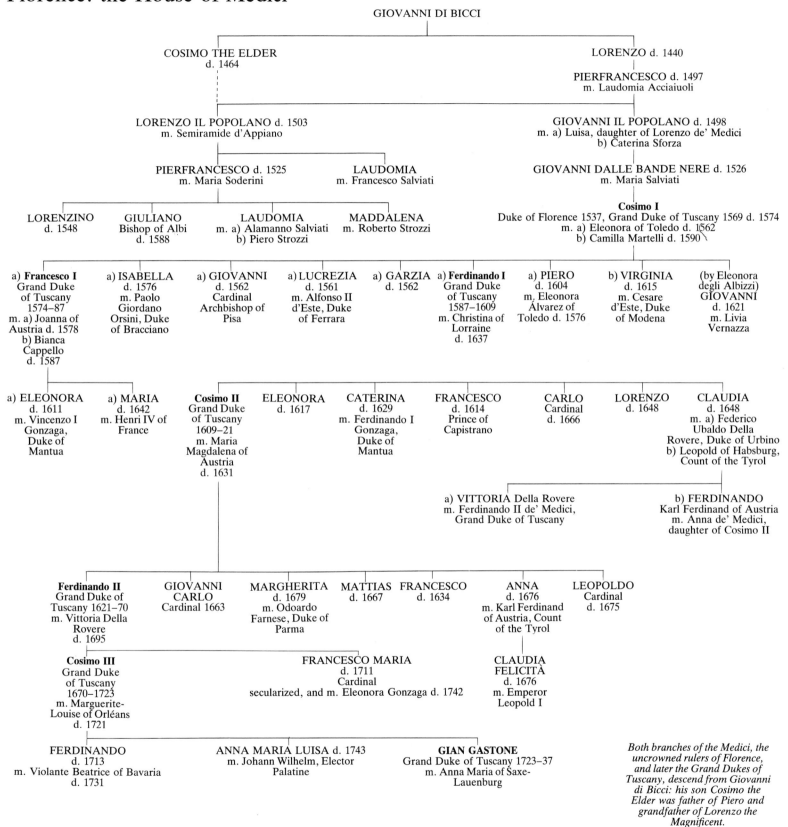

- GIOVANNI DI BICCI
  - COSIMO THE ELDER d. 1464
    - LORENZO IL POPOLANO d. 1503, m. Semiramide d'Appiano
      - PIERFRANCESCO d. 1525, m. Maria Soderini
        - LORENZINO d. 1548
        - GIULIANO, Bishop of Albi, d. 1588
        - LAUDOMIA, m. a) Alamanno Salviati b) Piero Strozzi
        - MADDALENA, m. Roberto Strozzi
      - LAUDOMIA, m. Francesco Salviati
  - LORENZO d. 1440
    - PIERFRANCESCO d. 1497, m. Laudomia Acciaiuoli
      - GIOVANNI IL POPOLANO d. 1498, m. a) Luisa, daughter of Lorenzo de' Medici b) Caterina Sforza
        - GIOVANNI DALLE BANDE NERE d. 1526, m. Maria Salviati
          - **Cosimo I**, Duke of Florence 1537, Grand Duke of Tuscany 1569 d. 1574, m. a) Eleonora of Toledo d. 1562 b) Camilla Martelli d. 1590
            - a) **Francesco I**, Grand Duke of Tuscany 1574–87, m. a) Joanna of Austria d. 1578 b) Bianca Cappello d. 1587
              - a) ELEONORA d. 1611, m. Vincenzo I Gonzaga, Duke of Mantua
              - a) MARIA d. 1642, m. Henri IV of France
            - a) ISABELLA d. 1576, m. Paolo Giordano Orsini, Duke of Bracciano
            - a) GIOVANNI d. 1562, Cardinal Archbishop of Pisa
            - a) LUCREZIA d. 1561, m. Alfonso II d'Este, Duke of Ferrara
            - a) GARZIA d. 1562
            - a) **Ferdinando I**, Grand Duke of Tuscany 1587–1609, m. Christina of Lorraine d. 1637
              - **Cosimo II**, Grand Duke of Tuscany 1609–21, m. Maria Magdalena of Austria d. 1631
                - **Ferdinando II**, Grand Duke of Tuscany 1621–70, m. Vittoria Della Rovere d. 1695
                  - **Cosimo III**, Grand Duke of Tuscany 1670–1723, m. Marguerite-Louise of Orléans d. 1721
                    - FERDINANDO d. 1713, m. Violante Beatrice of Bavaria d. 1731
                    - ANNA MARIA LUISA d. 1743, m. Johann Wilhelm, Elector Palatine
                    - **GIAN GASTONE**, Grand Duke of Tuscany 1723–37, m. Anna Maria of Saxe-Lauenburg
                  - FRANCESCO MARIA d. 1711, Cardinal, secularized, and m. Eleonora Gonzaga d. 1742
                - GIOVANNI CARLO, Cardinal 1663
                - MARGHERITA d. 1679, m. Odoardo Farnese, Duke of Parma
                - MATTIAS d. 1667
                - FRANCESCO d. 1634
                - ANNA d. 1676, m. Karl Ferdinand of Austria, Count of the Tyrol
                  - CLAUDIA FELICITÀ d. 1676, m. Emperor Leopold I
                - LEOPOLDO, Cardinal, d. 1675
              - ELEONORA d. 1617
              - CATERINA d. 1629, m. Ferdinando I Gonzaga, Duke of Mantua
              - FRANCESCO d. 1614, Prince of Capistrano
              - CARLO, Cardinal, d. 1666
              - LORENZO d. 1648
              - CLAUDIA d. 1648, m. a) Federico Ubaldo Della Rovere, Duke of Urbino b) Leopold of Habsburg, Count of the Tyrol
                - a) VITTORIA Della Rovere, m. Ferdinando II de' Medici, Grand Duke of Tuscany
                - b) FERDINANDO, Karl Ferdinand of Austria, m. Anna de' Medici, daughter of Cosimo II
            - a) PIERO d. 1604, m. Eleonora Álvarez of Toledo d. 1576
            - b) VIRGINIA d. 1615, m. Cesare d'Este, Duke of Modena
            - (by Eleonora degli Albizzi) GIOVANNI d. 1621, m. Livia Vernazza

Both branches of the Medici, the uncrowned rulers of Florence, and later the Grand Dukes of Tuscany, descend from Giovanni di Bicci: his son Cosimo the Elder was father of Piero and grandfather of Lorenzo the Magnificent.

Mantua: the House of Gonzaga

Left: Gianfrancesco Gonzaga, first Marquis of Mantua, on a fifteenth-century medal. Right: seventeenth-century engraving of Luigi II Gonzaga, and Gianfrancesco Gonzaga, brother of Federico I, as portrayed by Mantegna.

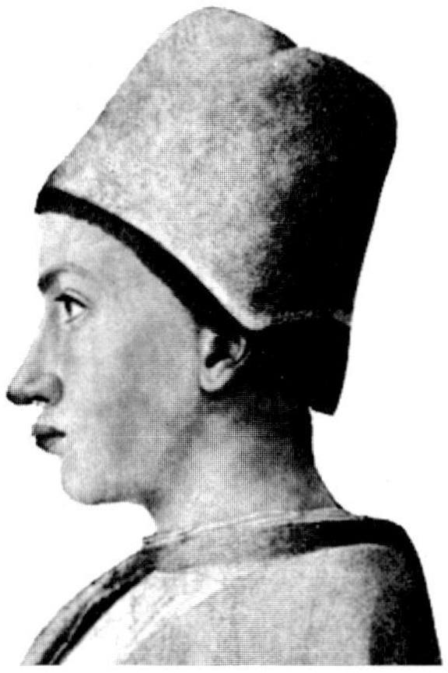

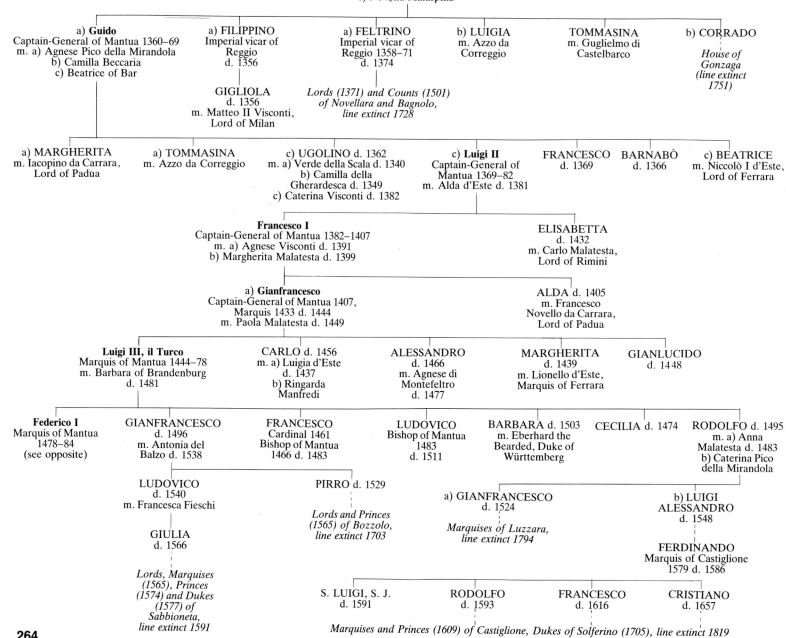

Luigi I
Captain-General of Mantua 1328–60
m. a) Richilda Ramberti d. 1319
b) Caterina Malatesta
c) Novella Malaspina

- a) **Guido** — Captain-General of Mantua 1360–69; m. a) Agnese Pico della Mirandola, b) Camilla Beccaria, c) Beatrice of Bar
  - a) MARGHERITA — m. Iacopino da Carrara, Lord of Padua
  - a) TOMMASINA — m. Azzo da Correggio
  - c) UGOLINO d. 1362 — m. a) Verde della Scala d. 1340, b) Camilla della Gherardesca d. 1349, c) Caterina Visconti d. 1382
  - c) **Luigi II** — Captain-General of Mantua 1369–82; m. Alda d'Este d. 1381
    - **Francesco I** — Captain-General of Mantua 1382–1407; m. a) Agnese Visconti d. 1391, b) Margherita Malatesta d. 1399
      - a) **Gianfrancesco** — Captain-General of Mantua 1407, Marquis 1433 d. 1444; m. Paola Malatesta d. 1449
        - **Luigi III, il Turco** — Marquis of Mantua 1444–78; m. Barbara of Brandenburg d. 1481
          - **Federico I** — Marquis of Mantua 1478–84 (see opposite)
          - GIANFRANCESCO d. 1496 — m. Antonia del Balzo d. 1538
            - LUDOVICO d. 1540 — m. Francesca Fieschi
              - GIULIA d. 1566
                - *Lords, Marquises (1565), Princes (1574) and Dukes (1577) of Sabbioneta, line extinct 1591*
            - PIRRO d. 1529
              - *Lords and Princes (1565) of Bozzolo, line extinct 1703*
          - FRANCESCO — Cardinal 1461, Bishop of Mantua 1466 d. 1483
          - LUDOVICO — Bishop of Mantua 1483 d. 1511
          - BARBARA d. 1503 — m. Eberhard the Bearded, Duke of Württemberg
          - CECILIA d. 1474
          - RODOLFO d. 1495 — m. a) Anna Malatesta d. 1483, b) Caterina Pico della Mirandola
            - a) GIANFRANCESCO d. 1524
              - *Marquises of Luzzara, line extinct 1794*
            - b) LUIGI ALESSANDRO d. 1548
              - FERDINANDO — Marquis of Castiglione 1579 d. 1586
                - S. LUIGI, S. J. d. 1591
                - RODOLFO d. 1593
                - FRANCESCO d. 1616
                - CRISTIANO d. 1657
                - *Marquises and Princes (1609) of Castiglione, Dukes of Solferino (1705), line extinct 1819*
        - CARLO d. 1456 — m. a) Luigia d'Este d. 1437, b) Ringarda Manfredi
        - ALESSANDRO d. 1466 — m. Agnese di Montefeltro d. 1477
        - MARGHERITA d. 1439 — m. Lionello d'Este, Marquis of Ferrara
        - GIANLUCIDO d. 1448
      - ALDA d. 1405 — m. Francesco Novello da Carrara, Lord of Padua
    - ELISABETTA d. 1432 — m. Carlo Malatesta, Lord of Rimini
  - FRANCESCO d. 1369
  - BARNABÒ d. 1366
  - c) BEATRICE — m. Niccolò I d'Este, Lord of Ferrara
- a) FILIPPINO — Imperial vicar of Reggio d. 1356
  - GIGLIOLA d. 1356 — m. Matteo II Visconti, Lord of Milan
- a) FELTRINO — Imperial vicar of Reggio 1358–71 d. 1374
  - *Lords (1371) and Counts (1501) of Novellara and Bagnolo, line extinct 1728*
- b) LUIGIA — m. Azzo da Correggio
- TOMMASINA — m. Guglielmo di Castelbarco
- b) CORRADO
  - *House of Gonzaga (line extinct 1751)*

Federico I
Marquis of Mantua 1478–84
m. Margaret of Bavaria
d. 1479

Francesco II
Marquis of Mantua
1484–1519
m. Isabella d'Este
d. 1539

SIGISMONDO
Cardinal 1505
Bishop of Mantua 1511
d. 1525

GIOVANNI
Marquis of Vescovado
1474 d. 1525
m. Laura Bentivoglio
d. 1523

Marquises of Vescovado Princes of Holy Roman Empire 1593

CHIARA d. 1503
m. Gilbert de Bourbon,
Comte de Montpensier

MADDALENA d. 1490
m. Giovanni Sforza,
Lord of Pesaro

ELISABETTA d. 1526
m. Guidobaldo di
Montefeltro, Duke of
Urbino

Federico II
Marquis of Mantua 1519, Duke 1530
Marquis of Monferrato 1536 d. 1540
m. Margherita Paleologa di
Monferrato
d. 1566

ERCOLE
Bishop of Mantua 1521
Cardinal 1527
d. 1563

FERRANTE
Count of Guastalla 1539 d. 1557
m. Isabella di Capua d. 1559

Counts and Dukes of Guastalla 1621, line extinct 1746

ELEONORA d. 1550
m. Francesco Maria I
Della Rovere, Duke of
Urbino

Francesco III
Duke of Mantua and
Marquis of Monferrato
1540–50
m. Catherine of Austria
d. 1572

ISABELLA d. 1579
m. Ferdinando
Francesco II d'Avalos,
Marquis of Pescara and
Vasto

Guglielmo
Duke of Mantua 1550, Marquis (1550)
and Duke of Monferrato (1574)
d. 1587 m. Eleonora of Austria d. 1594

FEDERICO
Bishop of Mantua
Cardinal 1563
d. 1565

LUIGI, Duc de Nevers
et de Rethel 1565
d. 1595
m. Henriette de Clèves
d. 1601

Vincenzo I
Duke of Mantua and Monferrato 1587–1612
m. a) Margherita Farnese (marriage annulled 1583)
b) Eleonora de' Medici d. 1611

MARGHERITA d. 1579
m. Alfonso II d'Este, Duke of Ferrara

ANNA CATERINA
d. 1621
m. Archduke Ferdinand
of Austria, Count of the
Tyrol

CATERINA d. 1629
m. Henri d'Orléans,
Duc de Longueville

MARIA d. 1601
m. Henri de Lorraine,
Duc de Mayenne

Carlo I
Duc de Nevers et de
Rethel 1595
Duke of Mantua and
Monferrato 1627–37
m. Cathérine de
Lorraine
d. 1618

b) **Francesco IV**
Duke of Mantua and
Monferrato 1612
m. Margherita of Savoy
d. 1655

MARIA d. 1660
m. Carlo Gonzaga-
Nevers, Duc de Nevers
et de Rethel

b) **Ferdinando**
Cardinal 1607–15 Duke of Mantua and
Monferrato 1612–26
m. a) Camilla Faà di Bruno
(marriage annulled 1622)
d. 1662 b) Caterina de' Medici d. 1629

b) MARGHERITA
d. 1632
m. Henri de
Vaudemont, Duc de
Lorraine

b) **Vincenzo II**
Cardinal 1615–16
Duke of Mantua and
Monferrato 1626–27
m. Isabella Gonzaga-
Novellara

b) ELEONORA
d. 1655
m. Emperor Ferdinand
II

CARLO
Duc de Nevers et de
Rethel
d. 1631
m. Maria Gonzaga
d. 1660

LUDOVICA MARIA (Maria Luisa)
d. 1667
m. a) Ladislas Vasa, King of Poland
b) John Casimir Vasa, King of Poland

ANNA d. 1684
m. Edward of
Wittelsbach-Simmern

Carlo II
Duke of Mantua and Monferrato 1637–65
Duc de Nevers et de Rethel 1637–59
m. Isabella Clara of Austria d. 1685

Ferdinando Carlo
Duke of Mantua and Monferrato
1665–1708
m. a) Anna Isabella Gonzaga-Guastalla
d. 1703
b) Suzanne-Henriette de Lorraine Elbeuf
d. 1710

ELEONORA
d. 1687
m. Emperor Ferdinand
III

Titian's portrait of Federico II, first Duke of Mantua (detail); and his father Francesco II, Marquis of Mantua, in a sculpture attributed to Mantegna.

Milan: the House of Visconti

STEFANO
Lord of Arona 1325
d. 1327
m. Valentina, daughter of Bernabò Doria

MATTEO II
Lord of Milan 1354
d. 1355
m. Gigliola, daughter of Filippino Gonzaga
d. 1356

GALEAZZO II
Lord of Milan 1354
d. 1378
m. Bianca of Savoy
d. 1387

BERNABÒ
Lord of Milan 1354–85
d. 1385
m. Regina Della Scala
d. 1384

CATERINA
d. 1382
m. Ugolino Gonzaga

VIOLANTE
d. 1376
m. a) Lionel of Antwerp, Duke of Clarence d. 1361
b) Secondollo Paleologo, Marquis of Monferrato d. 1378
c) Ludovico, son of Bernabò Visconti
d. 1404

Gian Galeazzo
Count of Virtù 1361, Lord of Milan 1378
Duke of Milan 1395–1402
m. a) Isabelle de Valois d. 1372
b) Caterina, daughter of Bernabò Visconti
d. 1404

a) VALENTINA
d. 1408
m. Louis de Valois, Duc d'Orléans
d. 1407

a) AZZONE

a) CARLO

b) **Giovanni Maria**
Duke of Milan 1402–12
m. Antonia Malatesta

b) **Filippo Maria**
Duke of Milan 1412–27
m. a) Beatrice Balbo Lascaris, Countess of Tenda d. 1418
b) Maria of Savoy
d. pre-1469

(by Agnese del Maino)
BIANCA MARIA
(illeg.)
m. **Francesco Sforza**
Duke of Milan 1450–66

(by Agnese Mantegazza)
GABRIELE MARIA
(illeg.)
Lord of Pisa 1402–05
d. 1408

MARCO
d. 1382
m. Elizabeth of Bavaria
d. 1382

RODOLFO
d. 1389

LODOVICO
d. 1404
m. Violante, daughter of Galeazzo II Visconti

CARLO
d. 1404
m. Beatrice d'Armagnac

GIAN CARLO d. 1418

GIANMASTINO
d. 1405

VALENTINA
m. Antonio Gentile Visconti
Lord of Belgioioso

TADDEA
d. 1381
m. Stephen III, Duke of Bavaria-Ingolstadt

VALENZA
d. 1393
m. Pierre I de Lusignan, King of Cyprus

VERDE
d. 1403
m. Leopold III of Habsburg, Count of the Tyrol

AGNESE
d. 1391
m. Francesco Gonzaga

ANTONIA
m. Eberhard III, Count of Württemberg

CATERINA
d. 1404
m. Gian Galeazzo Visconti, Duke of Milan

MADDALENA
d. 1404
m. Frederick, Duke of Bavaria-Landshut

LUCIA
d. 1427
m. a) Frederick, Landgrave of Thuringia and Margrave of Misnia
b) Edmund Holland, 3rd Earl of Kent

ELISABETTA
della Piccinina
m. Ernst, Duke of Bavaria

(by Montanina Lazzari)
SAGROMORO (illeg.)
d. 1385
m. a) Elizabeth of Bavaria d. 1382
b) Achilletta Marliani

Lords of Brignano and Counts of Saliceto (line extinct 1716); Marquises of Borgoratto and of S. Giorgio

(by Beltramola Grassi)
AMBROGIO (illeg.)
d. 1373

ASTORRE (illeg.)
d. 1413

line extinct 1782

ELISABETTA (illeg.)
m. Lutz Wirtinger von Landau (Lucio Lando)

ISOTTA (illeg.)
m. Carlo Fogliani

DONNINA (illeg.)
m. John Hawkwood (Giovanni Acuto)

From left: verso of a medal struck by Pisanello for Filippo Maria Visconti (1440); a golden florin of Gian Galeazzo Visconti (1400); and a portrait, attributed to Pisanello, of Gian Galeazzo.

Milan: the House of Sforza

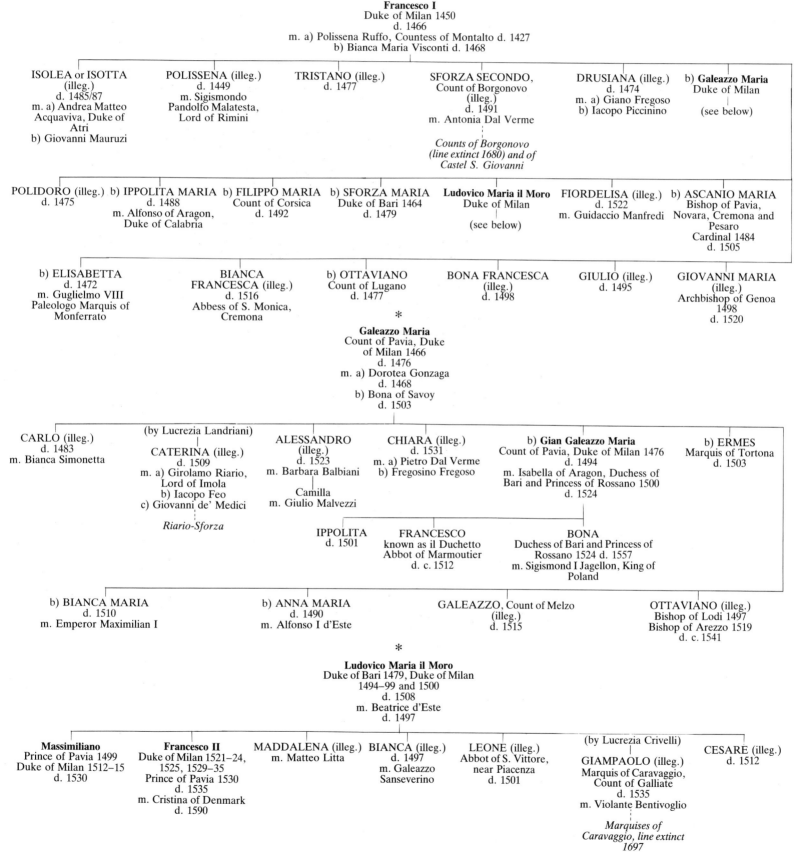

Francesco I
Duke of Milan 1450
d. 1466
m. a) Polissena Ruffo, Countess of Montalto d. 1427
b) Bianca Maria Visconti d. 1468

- ISOLEA or ISOTTA (illeg.) d. 1485/87 m. a) Andrea Matteo Acquaviva, Duke of Atri b) Giovanni Mauruzi
- POLISSENA (illeg.) d. 1449 m. Sigismondo Pandolfo Malatesta, Lord of Rimini
- TRISTANO (illeg.) d. 1477
- SFORZA SECONDO, Count of Borgonovo (illeg.) d. 1491 m. Antonia Dal Verme
  - *Counts of Borgonovo (line extinct 1680) and of Castel S. Giovanni*
- DRUSIANA (illeg.) d. 1474 m. a) Giano Fregoso b) Iacopo Piccinino
- b) **Galeazzo Maria** Duke of Milan (see below)
- POLIDORO (illeg.) d. 1475
- b) IPPOLITA MARIA d. 1488 m. Alfonso of Aragon, Duke of Calabria
- b) FILIPPO MARIA Count of Corsica d. 1492
- b) SFORZA MARIA Duke of Bari 1464 d. 1479
- **Ludovico Maria il Moro** Duke of Milan (see below)
- FIORDELISA (illeg.) d. 1522 m. Guidaccio Manfredi
- b) ASCANIO MARIA Bishop of Pavia, Novara, Cremona and Pesaro Cardinal 1484 d. 1505
- b) ELISABETTA d. 1472 m. Guglielmo VIII Paleologo Marquis of Monferrato
- BIANCA FRANCESCA (illeg.) d. 1516 Abbess of S. Monica, Cremona
- b) OTTAVIANO Count of Lugano d. 1477
- BONA FRANCESCA (illeg.) d. 1498
- GIULIO (illeg.) d. 1495
- GIOVANNI MARIA (illeg.) Archbishop of Genoa 1498 d. 1520

*

Galeazzo Maria
Count of Pavia, Duke of Milan 1466
d. 1476
m. a) Dorotea Gonzaga d. 1468
b) Bona of Savoy d. 1503

- CARLO (illeg.) d. 1483 m. Bianca Simonetta
- (by Lucrezia Landriani) CATERINA (illeg.) d. 1509 m. a) Girolamo Riario, Lord of Imola b) Iacopo Feo c) Giovanni de' Medici
  - *Riario-Sforza*
- ALESSANDRO (illeg.) d. 1523 m. Barbara Balbiani
  - Camilla m. Giulio Malvezzi
- CHIARA (illeg.) d. 1531 m. a) Pietro Dal Verme b) Fregosino Fregoso
- b) **Gian Galeazzo Maria** Count of Pavia, Duke of Milan 1476 d. 1494 m. Isabella of Aragon, Duchess of Bari and Princess of Rossano 1500 d. 1524
  - IPPOLITA d. 1501
  - FRANCESCO known as il Duchetto Abbot of Marmoutier d. c. 1512
  - BONA Duchess of Bari and Princess of Rossano 1524 d. 1557 m. Sigismond I Jagellon, King of Poland
- b) ERMES Marquis of Tortona d. 1503
- b) BIANCA MARIA d. 1510 m. Emperor Maximilian I
- b) ANNA MARIA d. 1490 m. Alfonso I d'Este
- GALEAZZO, Count of Melzo (illeg.) d. 1515
- OTTAVIANO (illeg.) Bishop of Lodi 1497 Bishop of Arezzo 1519 d. c. 1541

*

Ludovico Maria il Moro
Duke of Bari 1479, Duke of Milan 1494–99 and 1500
d. 1508
m. Beatrice d'Este d. 1497

- **Massimiliano** Prince of Pavia 1499 Duke of Milan 1512–15 d. 1530
- **Francesco II** Duke of Milan 1521–24, 1525, 1529–35 Prince of Pavia 1530 d. 1535 m. Cristina of Denmark d. 1590
- MADDALENA (illeg.) m. Matteo Litta
- BIANCA (illeg.) d. 1497 m. Galeazzo Sanseverino
- LEONE (illeg.) Abbot of S. Vittore, near Piacenza d. 1501
- (by Lucrezia Crivelli) GIAMPAOLO (illeg.) Marquis of Caravaggio, Count of Galliate d. 1535 m. Violante Bentivoglio
  - *Marquises of Caravaggio, line extinct 1697*
- CESARE (illeg.) d. 1512

Naples: the House of Aragon

Alfonso the Magnanimous
King of Aragon (V), Catalonia (IV),
Sicily and Sardinia 1416, and Naples (I) 1442–58
m. Maria of Castille

(by Giraldonna Carlino)
Ferdinando I (Ferrante)
Duke of Calabria
King of Naples 1458–94
m. a) Isabella di Chiaromonte d. 1465
b) Giovanna of Aragon, daughter of John II, King of Aragon

ELEONORA (illeg.)
Duchess of Amalfi
m. a) Raimondo Orsini del Balzo, Duke of Gravina
b) Marino Marzano, Duke of Sessa

MARIA (illeg.)
d. 1449
m. Leonello d'Este, Marquis of Ferrara

a) **Alfonso II**
Duke of Calabria
King of Naples 1494, abd. 1495
d. 1495
m. Ippolita Maria Sforza
d. 1488

a) **Federico**
(Prince of Altamura and of Squillace)
King of Naples 1496, abd. 1501
d. 1504
m. a) Anna of Savoy
d. 1480
b) Isabella del Balzo
d. 1533

a) ELEONORA
d. 1493
m. Ercole I d'Este, Duke of Ferrara

a) BEATRICE
d. 1508
m. Matthias Corvinus, King of Hungary

a) GIOVANNI
d. 1485
Cardinal

a) FRANCESCO
Duke of S. Angelo

b) GIOVANNA
m. a) Leonardo Della Rovere, Duke of Sora
b) Ferdinando II, King of Naples

b) FERDINANDO
(Prince of Taranto, Duke of Calabria)
d. 1550
m. a) Germaine de Foix d. 1538
b) Mencía di Mendoza

a) CARLOTTA
m. Guy XVI de Laval

a) GIULIA
d. 1542
m. Gian Giorgio Paleologo, Marquis of Monferrato

MARIA (illeg.)
d. 1460
m. Antonio Piccolomini Todeschini, Duke of Amalfi

FERDINANDO (illeg.)
Duke of Montalto

ENRICO (illeg.)
Marquis of Gerace
d. 1478
m. Polissena Centegli

Ferdinando II
(Ferrandino)
(Prince of Capua, Duke of Calabria)
King of Naples 1495–96
m. Giovanna of Aragon, daughter of Ferdinando I

ISABELLA
d. 1524
m. Gian Galeazzo Maria Sforza, Duke of Milan

(by Trusia Gazzella)

ALFONSO (illeg.)
Duke of Bisceglie
d. 1500
m. Lucrezia Borgia

SANCIA (illeg.)
Princess of Squillace
m. Giuffrè Borgia

ANTONIO I
Duke of Montalto

MARIA
d. 1568
m. Alfonso d'Avalos, Marquis of Vasto and Pescara

LUIGI
Marquis of Gerace
m. Battistina Cibo
Cardinal 1494
d. 1519

CARLO
Marquis of Gerace
m. Ippolita d'Avalos

GIOVANNA
m. Alfonso Piccolomini Todeschini, Duke of Amalfi

CATERINA
m. Gentile Orsini, Count of Nola

(by Giulia Campana)
TULLIA (illeg.)
d. 1556

Giovanna of Aragon (portrait attributed to Leonardo da Vinci), and her husband Ferdinando I, King of Naples (bronze by Guido Mazzoni).

Parma: the House of Farnese

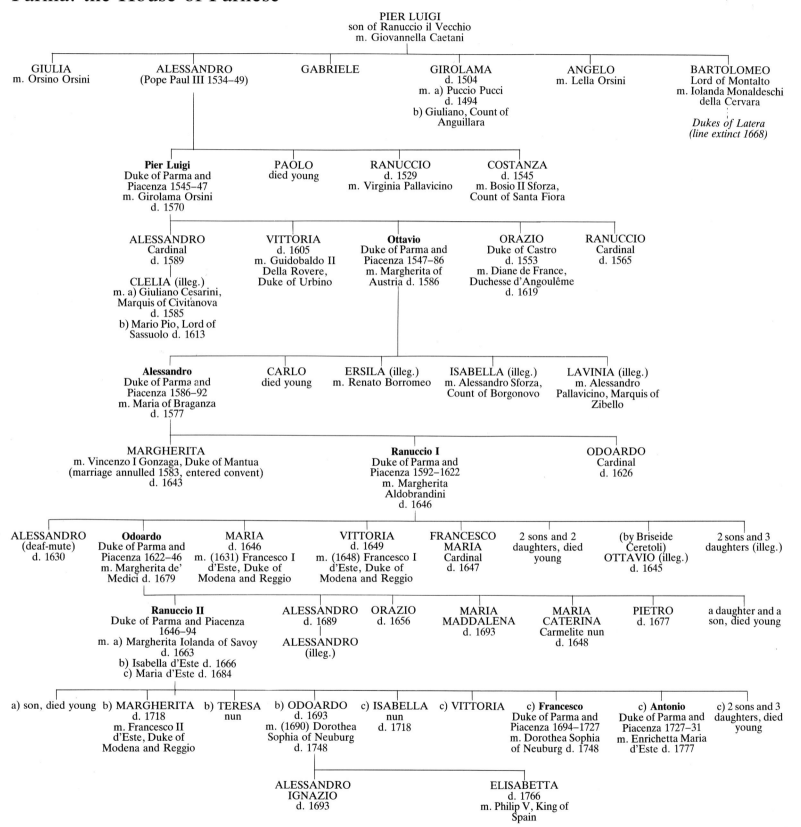

- PIER LUIGI, son of Ranuccio il Vecchio, m. Giovannella Caetani
  - GIULIA, m. Orsino Orsini
  - ALESSANDRO (Pope Paul III 1534–49)
    - **Pier Luigi**, Duke of Parma and Piacenza 1545–47, m. Girolama Orsini d. 1570
      - ALESSANDRO, Cardinal, d. 1589
        - CLELIA (illeg.), m. a) Giuliano Cesarini, Marquis of Civitanova d. 1585 b) Mario Pio, Lord of Sassuolo d. 1613
      - VITTORIA, d. 1605, m. Guidobaldo II Della Rovere, Duke of Urbino
      - **Ottavio**, Duke of Parma and Piacenza 1547–86, m. Margherita of Austria d. 1586
        - **Alessandro**, Duke of Parma and Piacenza 1586–92, m. Maria of Braganza d. 1577
          - MARGHERITA, m. Vincenzo I Gonzaga, Duke of Mantua (marriage annulled 1583, entered convent) d. 1643
          - **Ranuccio I**, Duke of Parma and Piacenza 1592–1622, m. Margherita Aldobrandini d. 1646
            - ALESSANDRO (deaf-mute) d. 1630
            - **Odoardo**, Duke of Parma and Piacenza 1622–46, m. Margherita de' Medici d. 1679
              - **Ranuccio II**, Duke of Parma and Piacenza 1646–94, m. a) Margherita Iolanda of Savoy d. 1663 b) Isabella d'Este d. 1666 c) Maria d'Este d. 1684
                - a) son, died young
                - b) MARGHERITA, d. 1718, m. Francesco II d'Este, Duke of Modena and Reggio
                - b) TERESA, nun
                - b) ODOARDO, d. 1693, m. (1690) Dorothea Sophia of Neuburg d. 1748
                  - ALESSANDRO IGNAZIO, d. 1693
                  - ELISABETTA, d. 1766, m. Philip V, King of Spain
                - c) ISABELLA, nun, d. 1718
                - c) VITTORIA
                - c) **Francesco**, Duke of Parma and Piacenza 1694–1727, m. Dorothea Sophia of Neuburg d. 1748
                - c) **Antonio**, Duke of Parma and Piacenza 1727–31, m. Enrichetta Maria d'Este d. 1777
                - c) 2 sons and 3 daughters, died young
              - ALESSANDRO, d. 1689
                - ALESSANDRO (illeg.)
              - ORAZIO, d. 1656
              - MARIA MADDALENA, d. 1693
              - MARIA CATERINA, Carmelite nun, d. 1648
              - PIETRO, d. 1677
              - a daughter and a son, died young
            - MARIA, d. 1646, m. (1631) Francesco I d'Este, Duke of Modena and Reggio
            - VITTORIA, d. 1649, m. (1648) Francesco I d'Este, Duke of Modena and Reggio
            - FRANCESCO MARIA, Cardinal, d. 1647
            - 2 sons and 2 daughters, died young
            - (by Briseide Ceretoli) OTTAVIO (illeg.) d. 1645
            - 2 sons and 3 daughters (illeg.)
          - ODOARDO, Cardinal, d. 1626
        - CARLO, died young
        - ERSILA (illeg.), m. Renato Borromeo
        - ISABELLA (illeg.), m. Alessandro Sforza, Count of Borgonovo
        - LAVINIA (illeg.), m. Alessandro Pallavicino, Marquis of Zibello
      - ORAZIO, Duke of Castro, d. 1553, m. Diane de France, Duchesse d'Angoulême d. 1619
      - RANUCCIO, Cardinal, d. 1565
    - PAOLO, died young
    - RANUCCIO, d. 1529, m. Virginia Pallavicino
    - COSTANZA, d. 1545, m. Bosio II Sforza, Count of Santa Fiora
  - GABRIELE
  - GIROLAMA, d. 1504, m. a) Puccio Pucci d. 1494 b) Giuliano, Count of Anguillara
  - ANGELO, m. Lella Orsini
  - BARTOLOMEO, Lord of Montalto, m. Iolanda Monaldeschi della Cervara
    - *Dukes of Latera (line extinct 1668)*

Verona: House of the Scaligeri

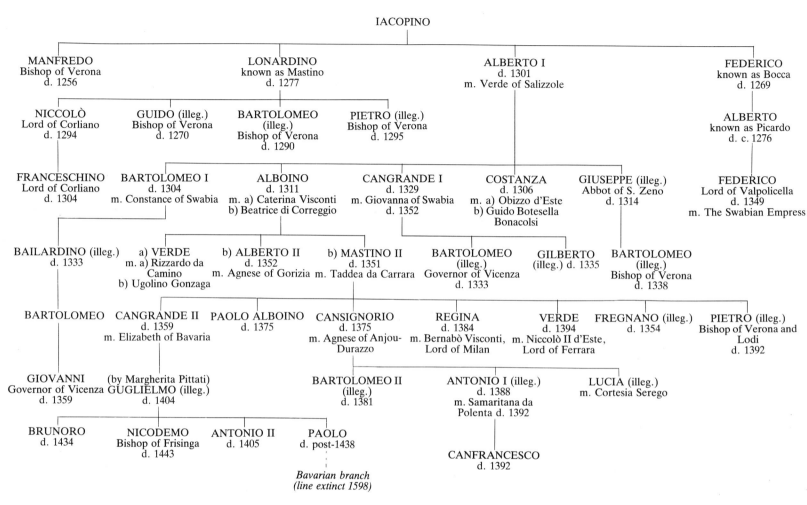

- IACOPINO
  - MANFREDO, Bishop of Verona, d. 1256
  - LONARDINO, known as Mastino, d. 1277
    - NICCOLÒ, Lord of Corliano, d. 1294
      - FRANCESCHINO, Lord of Corliano, d. 1304
    - GUIDO (illeg.), Bishop of Verona, d. 1270
    - BARTOLOMEO (illeg.), Bishop of Verona, d. 1290
    - PIETRO (illeg.), Bishop of Verona, d. 1295
  - ALBERTO I, d. 1301, m. Verde of Salizzole
    - BARTOLOMEO I, d. 1304, m. Constance of Swabia
      - BAILARDINO (illeg.), d. 1333
        - BARTOLOMEO
          - GIOVANNI, Governor of Vicenza, d. 1359
    - ALBOINO, d. 1311, m. a) Caterina Visconti, b) Beatrice di Correggio
      - a) VERDE, m. a) Rizzardo da Camino, b) Ugolino Gonzaga
      - b) ALBERTO II, d. 1352, m. Agnese of Gorizia
      - b) MASTINO II, d. 1351, m. Taddea da Carrara
        - CANGRANDE II, d. 1359, m. Elizabeth of Bavaria
          - (by Margherita Pittati) GUGLIELMO (illeg.), d. 1404
            - BRUNORO, d. 1434
            - NICODEMO, Bishop of Frisinga, d. 1443
            - ANTONIO II, d. 1405
            - PAOLO, d. post-1438
              - *Bavarian branch (line extinct 1598)*
        - PAOLO ALBOINO, d. 1375
        - CANSIGNORIO, d. 1375, m. Agnese of Anjou-Durazzo
          - BARTOLOMEO II (illeg.), d. 1381
          - ANTONIO I (illeg.), d. 1388, m. Samaritana da Polenta d. 1392
            - CANFRANCESCO, d. 1392
          - LUCIA (illeg.), m. Cortesia Serego
        - REGINA, d. 1384, m. Bernabò Visconti, Lord of Milan
        - VERDE, d. 1394, m. Niccolò II d'Este, Lord of Ferrara
        - FREGNANO (illeg.), d. 1354
        - PIETRO (illeg.), Bishop of Verona and Lodi, d. 1392
    - CANGRANDE I, d. 1329, m. Giovanna of Swabia d. 1352
      - BARTOLOMEO (illeg.), Governor of Vicenza, d. 1333
      - GILBERTO (illeg.), d. 1335
    - COSTANZA, d. 1306, m. a) Obizzo d'Este, b) Guido Botesella Bonacolsi
    - GIUSEPPE (illeg.), Abbot of S. Zeno, d. 1314
      - BARTOLOMEO (illeg.), Bishop of Verona, d. 1338
  - FEDERICO, known as Bocca, d. 1269
    - ALBERTO, known as Picardo, d. c. 1276
      - FEDERICO, Lord of Valpolicella, d. 1349, m. The Swabian Empress

Cansignorio and Cangrande Della Scala: equestrian statues on the Scaligeri tombs, Verona.

Bibliography

The court and the prince

Garati da Lodi *Il Tractatus de principibus di Martino Garati da Lodi* (fifteenth century), G. Rondinini Soldi ed., Milano-Varese 1968
1510 P. Cortesi, *De cardinalatu*, S.N. Nardi, in Castro Cortesio
1539 A. de Guevara, *Libro llmado: Menosprecio de corte y albança de aldea*, Valladolid
1543 F. Priscianese, *Del governo della corte d'un Signore in Roma*, F. Priscianese fiorentino, Rome
1609 P.A. Canoniero, *Il perfetto cortegiano et dell'ufizio del principe verso 'l cortegiano*, B. Zanetti, Rome
1642 G. Lunadoro, *Relatione della corte di Roma e de'riti da osservarsi in essa*, O. Scardutii, Viterbo
1656 E. Du Refuge, *Traicté de la Cour ou Instruction des courtisans*, Elzevires, Amsterdam
1977 A.G. Dickens ed., *The Courts of Europe. Politics, Patronage and Royalty*, 1400-1800, London
1980 N. Elias, *La civiltà di corte*, Bologna
1980 C. Tardits, *Le royaume bamoum*, Paris
1980 C. Vasoli, *La cultura delle corti*, Bologna
1982 G. Papagno – A. Quondam eds., *La corte e lo spazio: Ferrara estense*, Rome
1983 M. Cattini – M.A. Romani eds., *La Corte in Europa. Fedeltà, favori, pratiche di governo*, Brescia
1984 C. Ossola – A. Prosperi eds., *La corte e il 'Cortegiano'*, Rome
1984 G. Olmi – C. Mozzarelli eds., *La corte nella cultura e nella storiografia. Immagini e posizioni fra Otto e Novecento*, Rome
1984 A. Ferrajoli, *Il ruolo della corte di Leone X*, Rome
1984 B. Basile ed., *'Bentivoliorum magnificentia': Cultura e potere nella Bologna del Rinascimento*, Rome
1985 S. Bertelli – G. Crifò eds., *Rituale, Cerimoniale, Etichetta*, Milan

Love and the court

1309 Francesco da Barberino, *Il trattato d'amore*, Rome 1898
1525 M. Equicola, *Libro de natura de amore*, L. Lorio, Venice
1576 M. Calvi, *Del tractado de la hermosura*, P. Sotardo Boncio, Milan
1889 M. Rossi, *Saggio sui trattati d'amore del Cinquecento*, Recanati
1890 P. Rajna, *Le corti d'amore*, Milan
1908 P. Rousselot, *Pour l'histoire du problème de l'amour au Moyen Age*, Münster

The cult of good manners

1528 B. Castiglione, *La seconda edizione del 'Cortegiano'*, G. Ghinassi ed., Florence 1968
1530 Erasmus, *De civilitate morum puerilium ... libellus*, Ch. Wechel, Paris
1551 G. Della Casa, *Galateo*, in *Prose di Giovanni*
/54 *Della Casa*, A. di Bendetto ed., Turin 1970
G. Della Casa, *Trattato degli uffici comuni fra gli amici superiori e inferiori*, ibid.
1574 S. Guazzo, *La civil conversatione*, T. Bozzola, Brescia
1631 V. Nolfi, *Ginipedia, ovvero Avvertimenti civili per donna nobile*, in A. D'Ancona, *La gentildonna del secolo XVII a convito*, Pisa 1898
1908 A. Franklin, *La civilité, l'etiquette, le bon ton du XIIIe au XIXe siècle*, Paris
1971 C. Levi-Strauss, *The origin of table manners*, vol. 3 of *Science of Mythology*, London 1978
1982 N. Elias, *La civiltà delle buone maniere*, Bologna

Household offices:

the Midwife

1607 L. Bourgeois, *Recit veritable de la naissance des Meissegneurs et Dames des Enfans de France*, H. Ruffin, Paris

mastro di casa

1598 C. Evitascandolo, *Dialogo del Maestro di casa*, S. Mancini, Rome
1636 A. Adami, *Il novitiato del Maestro di casa*, P.A. Faccioti, Rome
1668 F. Liberati, *Il perfetto Maestro di casa, distinto in tre libri*, M. Hercole, Rome

steward

1609 C. Evitascandolo, *Libro dello scalco, quale insegna questo honesto servitio*, C. Vulietti, Rome
1631 A. Frugoli, *Practica e scalcaria*, F. Cavalli, Rome
1647 G.F. Vasselli, *L'apicio, overo il maestro dei conviti*, Bologna
1660 D. Romoli, *La singolare dottrina ... dell'offitio dello Scalco*, M. Tramezzino, Venice
1669 V. Mattei, *Tratto nobilissimo di scalcheria*, G. Dragoncelli, Rome
1683 G.B. Rossetti, *Dello Scalco*, D. Mammarella, Ferrara

secretary

1565 F. Sansovino, *Del Segretario, libri quattro*, F. Rampazetto, Venice
1587 T. Tasso, *Il Secretario*, V. Baldini, Ferrara
1594 B. Guarini, *Il Segretario*, B. Magiotti, Venice
1594 A. Ingegneri, *Del buon segretario libri tre*, G. Falcotti, Rome
1620 V. Gramigna, *Il Segretario*, Cecconelli, Florence
1635 V. Malvezzi, *Ritratto del privato politico christiano*, G. Monti and C. Zenero, Bologna

servants

1575 I. Bonaccossa, *De servis vel famulis tractatus*, D. Zenaro, Venice

carver

1593 V. Cervio, *Il Trinciante*, heredi F. Tramezini, Venice
1609 C. Evitascandolo, *Dialogo del Trenciante*, C. Vullietti, Rome
1639 M. Gieger, *Li tre trattati*, P. Frambotto, Padua

Ceremony

Constantinus VII Porphyrogenitus, *Livre des cérémonies* (tenth century), edited and translated by A. Vogt, Paris 1935-40
1511 Patrizi Piccolomini, *M. Dykmans ed., L'œuvre de Patrizi Piccolomini ou le Cérimonial papal de la première Renaissance*, Vatican City 1980-82
1564 Paride Grassi, *De ceremoniis cardinalium et episcoporum*, Blado, Rome
1736 G. De Giovanni, *De divinis Siculorum officiis tractatus*, officina Collegii borbonici nobilium, Panormi
1920 L. Brehier – R. Battifol, *Les survivances du culte impérial romain*, Paris
1946 C. Kantorowicz, *Laudes regiae. A Study in Liturgical Acclamations and Medieval Rule Worship*, Berkeley
1973 B. Schimmelpfennig, *Die Zerimonienbrücher der Römischen Kurie im Mittelalter*, Tübingen

Princely and signorial families

1829 P. Litta, *Famiglie celebri italiane*
-46

Angioini

1954 E.G. Leonard, *Gli Angioini di Napoli*, Varese

Aragona

1922 L. Montalto, *La corte di Alfonso I d'Aragona: vesti e gale*, Naples
1976 A. Ryder, *The Kingdom of Naples under Alfonso the Magnanimous. The Making of a Modern State*, Oxford

Bentivoglio

1937 C.M. Ady, *The Bentivoglio*, London

Este

1891 A. Solerti, *Ferrara e la corte estense nella seconda metà del secolo decimosesto. I discorsi di Annibale Romei*, Città di Castello
1909 G. Bertoni – E.P. Vicini, *Il castello di Ferrara ai tempi di Niccolò III*, Bologna
1970 L. Chiappini, *Gli Estensi*, Varese
1973 W. Gundersheimer, *Ferrara. The Style of a Renaissance Despotism*, Princeton NJ

Farnese

1954 G. Drei, *I Farnese: grandezza e decadenza d'una dinastia italiana*, Rome
1969 E. Nasalli – Rocca, *I Farnese*, Varese
1984 M.A. Romani – A. Quondam eds., *Le corti farnesiane di Parma e Piacenza (1545-1622)*, Rome

Gonzaga

1967 G. Coniglio, *I Gonzaga*, Varese
1975 G. Amadei, *I Gonzaga a Mantova*, Cassa di Risp. delle PP. Lombarde
1977 *Mantova e i Gonzaga nella civiltà del Rinascimento*, Atti del Convegno, Accademia Naz. dei Lincei e Acc. Virgiliana, Milan

Malatesta

1974 P. J. Jones, *The Malatesta of Rimini and the Papal State. A Political History*, Cambridge

Medici

1947 E. Pieraccini, *La stirpe dei Medici di Cafaggiolo*, Florence
1977 J.R. Hale, *Florence and the Medici: The Pattern of Control*, London
1981 K. Langedijk, *The Portraits of the Medici – 15th-*
-83 *18th Centuries*, Florence

Montelfeltro

1859 F. Ugolini, *Storia dei conti e duchi d'Urbino*, Florence

1893 A. Luzio – R. Renier, *Mantova e Urbino. Isabella d'Este ed Elisabetta Gonzaga nelle relazioni famigliari e nelle vicende politiche*, Turin-Rome

Orsini

1565 F. Sansovino, *De gli huomini illustri della casa Orsina*, Stagnini, Venice

1955 G. Brigante Colonna, *Gli Orsini*, Milan

1981 *Bracciano e gli Orsini nel '400.* Catalogue edited by A. Cavallaro, A. Mignoni Tantillo, R. Siligato, Rome

Pallavicino

1969 E. Nasalli Rocca, *La posizione politica dei Pallavicino dall'età dei Comuni a quella delle Signorie*, "Archivio Storico per le PP. Parmensi", s.IV, XX: 65-113

Paleologhi

1780 Benvenuto Di Sangiorgio, *Cronaca*, G. Vernazza ed., Turin

1835 Sancio, *Cenno storico intorno ai Marchesi del Monferrato di stirpe Palaeologa, Casale*

Parma

1846-1858 L. Scarabelli, *Istoria civile dei ducati di Parma, Piacenza e Guastalla*, Lugano (?)

1981 R. Greci-M. Di Giovanni Madruzza-G. Molazzini, *Corti del Rinascimento nella provincia di Parma*, Turin

Romagna

1972 J. Larner, *Signorie di Romagna. La società romagnola e l'origine delle Signorie*, Bologna

Rossi

1911 N. Pellicelli, *Pier Maria Rossi e i suoi castelli*, Parma

1969 E. Nasalli-Rocca, *Le origini e la posizione politica dei Rossi di San Secondo dall'età del Comune a quella della Signoria*, "Arch. st. per le PP. Parmensi", s.IV, XXI: 83-103

Scaligeri

1959 G.L. Mellini, *La 'sala grande' di Altichiero e Jacopo d'Avanzo ed i palazzi scaligeri di Verona*, "Critica d'arte", VI, 35: 313-333

1966 M. Carrara, *Gli Scaligeri*, Varese

Sforza

1913-1929 F. Malaguzzi-Valeri, *La corte di Ludovico il Moro*, Milan

1968 C. Santoro, *Gli Sforza*, Varese

Sforza-Riario

1983 F. Pasolini, *Caterina Sforza*, Rome

Svevi

1981 E. Horst, *Federico II di Svevia*, Milan

Gifts

1906 G. Imbert, *La vita fiorentina nel Seicento. Secondo memorie sincrone 1644-1670*, Florence

1965 M. Mauss, *Saggio sul dono. Forma e motivo dello scambio nelle società arcaiche* (1923) in *Teoria generale della magia*, Turin

1973 C. Zaccagnini, *Lo scambio dei doni nel Vicino Oriente*, Rome

1978 B. Malinowski, *Argonauti del Pacifico Occidentale. Riti magici e vita quotidiana nella società primitiva*, Perugia

1980 M. Sahlins, *La sociologia dello scambio primitivo*, in *L'economia dell'età della pietra*, Milan, pp. 189-271

1983 K. Polanyi, *La sussistenza dell'uomo*, Turin

Hospitality

1685 G. Leti, *Il Ceremoniale historico, e politico*, Amsterdam

1962 M. I. Finley, *The World of Odysseus*, London 1972

1967 D. Queller, *The Office of Ambassador in the Middle Ages*, Princeton, NJ

1973 G. Caligaris, *Doni e ospiti stranieri alla corte sabauda nel XVII secolo*, Turin

1975 G. Caligaris, *Viaggiatori illustri ed ambasciatori stranieri alla corte sabauda nella prima metà del Seicento: ospitalità e regali*, in Studi piemontesi, pp. 151-171

1983 A. Gourvitch, *Les catégories de la culture médiévale*, Paris

Travel

1976 M. Guglielminetti (ed.), *Viaggiatori del Seicento*, Turin

1980 G. Nori, *La Corte itinerante. Il pellegrinaggio di Niccolò III in Terrasanta*, in *La corte e lo spazio: Ferrara estense* (various authors), Rome, pp. 233-246

Feasting

Celebrino Eustachi da Udine, *Opera nuova che insegna apparecchiare una mensa a un convito et etiam tagliare a tavola* (sixteenth century)

1549 C. Messibugo (Cristofaro di Messi detto Sbugo), *Banchetti, composizioni di vivande et apparecchio generale*, G. de Bughet e A. Hucher, Ferrara

1639 M. Giegher, *Trattato sul modo di piegare ogni sorta di panni lini: cioè salviette e tovaglie e d'apparecchiare una tavola*, P. Frambotto, Padua

1641 Il ripieno (Benedetto Buonmattei), *Descrizione dello stravizzo dell'Accademia della Crusca del 14 luglio 1641*, in F. Redi, *Lettere*, Florence 1825

1927 C. Hibbard Loomis, *The Table of the Last Supper in Religious and Secular Iconography*, "Art Studies" V: 71-8

1981 C. Grottanelli, *L'ideologia del banchetto e l'ospite ambiguo*, "Dialoghi di archeologia", 3: 122-154

1983 A. Veca, *Simposio, cerimonie e apparati*, Galleria Lorenzelli, Bergamo

1983 G. Calvi-S. Bertelli, *La bocca del Signore: commensalità e gerarchie sociali fra Cinque-Seicento*, "Metamorfosi", 7: 197-218

Science and the mania for collecting

1934 F. Saxl, *La fede astrologica di Agostino Chigi*, Rome

1960 A. Rotondò, *Pellegrino Prisciani, 1435-1518*, "Rinascimento", IX: 69-110

1967 L. Berti, *Il Principe dello Studiolo*, Florence

1974 J. von Schlosser, *Raccolte d'arte e di meraviglie del tardo Rinascimento*, Florence

1974 A. Grote, *Il tesoro di Lorenzo il Magnifico*, Florence

1976 J. Evans, *Magical Jewels of the Middle Ages and the Renaissance*, New York

1978 G. Lensi Orlandi, *Cosimo e Francesco de' Medici alchimisti*, Florence

1980 M. Dezzi Baldeschi, *Lo stanzino del principe in Palazzo Vecchio*, Florence

Symbols and emblems

1555 P. Giovio, *Ragionamento sopra motti e disegni d'arte e d'amore che comunemente chiamiamo imprese*, Rome

1571 G. De Mentenay, *Emblèmes ou devises chréstiennes*, Marcorelle, Lyons

1923 L. Volkmann, *Bilderschriften der Renaissance: Hieroglyphik und Emblematik in ihren Beziehungen und Fortwirkungen*, Leipzig

1928 J. Gelli, *Divise, motti, imprese di famiglie e personaggi italiani*, Milan

1950 G. Boas ed., *The Hieroglyphics of Horapollo*, New York

1950 F. Hartt, *The Gonzaga symbols in the 'Palazzo del Te'*, "Journal of the Warburg and Courtauld Institutes", XIII: 151-188

1967 A. Schöne – A. Henkel, *Emblemata: Handbuch zur Sinnbildkunst des XVI. und XVII. Jahrhunderts*, Stuttgart

1975 E. Panofsky, *Studi di iconologia*, Turin

1981 G. Innocenti, *L'immagine significante: studio sell'emblematica cinquecentesca*, Padua

1984 M.A. De Angelis, *Gli emblemi di Andrea Alciato nella edizione Stayner del 1531. Fonti e simbologia*, Rome

The palace

1450 L.B. Alberti, *De re aedificatoria*, G. Orlandi e P. Portoghesi eds., Milan 1966

1544 P. Cataneo, *I quattro primi libri di architettura*, Figliuoli di Aldo, Venice

1937 R. Pane, *Architettura del Rinascimento a Napoli*, Naples

1960 B. Zevi, *Biagio Rossetti, architetto ferrarese, il primo urbanista moderna*, Turin

1973 C.L. Frommel, *Die römische Palastbau der Hochrenaissance*, Tübingen

1973 L. Benevolo, *Storia dell'architettura del Rinascimento*, Bari

1975 G. Cuppini-C. Perogalli, *Il palazzo italano*, Milan

The villa

1951 J.S. Ackerman, *The Belvedere as a Classical villa*, "Journal of the Warburg and Courtauld Institutes", XIV: 70-91

1953 U. Tarchi, *La villa detta 'La Simonetta' nel suburbio di Milano*, Accademia Naz. dei Lincei, Rome

1960 D.R. Coffin, *The Villa d'Este at Tivoli*, Princeton NJ

1969 *Colorno, la Versailles dei duchi di Parma*, Dep. di SP per le PP. Parmensi, Parma

1969 U. Bellocchi, *'Le ville' di A.F. Coni*, Modena

1970 I. Belli Barsali, *Ville di Roma*, Milan

1976 D.R.E. Wright, *The Medici villa at Olmo at Castello*, Princeton NJ

1979 D.R. Coffin, *The Villa in the Life of Renaissance Rome*, Princeton NJ

1980 D. Mignani, *Le ville medicee di Giusto Utens*, Florence

Furniture and dress

1601 B. Baldi, *Di Herone Alessandrino, degli Automati overo machine semoventi libri due*, translated from the Greek, G.B. Bortoni, Venice

1627 G. Bragaccia, *L'ambasciatore*, F. Bolzetta, Padua

1896 A. Luzio-R. Renier, *Il lusso di Isabella d'Este marchesa di Mantova:* I. Il guardaroba; II. III. Gioielli e gemme; IV. V. VI: Gli arredi degli

appartamenti; VII. VIII.: Accessori e segreti della "'toilette', Nuova antologia", LXIII, XI: 441-470; LXIV, XIV: 295-325; LXV, XVIII: 261-287; LXIX, XX: 666-689
1903 L. Beltrame, *La guardaroba di Lucrezia Borgia*, Milan
1952 M. Rocamora, *La mode en Espagne au XVI*^{e} *siècle*, "Actes du Ier Congrès International d'Histoire du Costume", Venice: 68-76
1965 F. Boucher, *Histoire du costume en Occident*, Paris
1981 A. Lurie, *The Language of Clothes*, New York

The garden

1971 L. Bek, *Ut ars natura – Ut natura ars. Le ville di Plinio e il concetto del giardino nel Rinascimento*, "Abalecta Romana Instituti Danici", VII: 109-156
1973 J. Theurillat, *Les Mystères de Bomarzo et les jardins symboliques de la Renaissance*, Geneva
1976 E. Kretzulescu-Quaranta, *Les jardins su songe*, Paris
1977 M. Levi D'Ancona, *The garden of the Renaissance. Botanical Symbolism in Italian Painting*, Florence
1978 T. Comito, *The Idea of the garden in the Renaissance*, Brunswick NJ
1979 G. Venturi, *Le scene dell'Eden*, Ferrara
1979 L. Zancheri, *Pratolini il giardino delle meraviglie*, Florence
1980 M. Calvesi, *Il sogno di Polifilo prenestino*, Rome
1980 M. Fagiolo ed., *La città effimera e l'universo artificiale del giardino. La Firenze dei Medici el'Italia*, Rome
1982 B. Basile, *Giardini e alberi della cultura*, "Intersezioni", II, 347-369

Theater

1938-54 M. Apollonio, *Storia del teatro italiano*, Florence
1966 P. Bjurström, *Feast and Theatre in Queen Christina's Rome*, Stockholm
1972 C. Molinari, *Teatro*, Milan
1974 P. Fabbri, *Gusto scenico a Mantova nel tardo Rinascimento*, Padua
1975 P. Carpeggiani, *Teatri e Apparati scenici alla corte dei Gonzaga tra Cinque e Seicento*, "Boll. del Centro Int. di Studi di Architettura A. Palladio", XVII: 101-118
1975 L. Zorzi ed., *Il luogo teatrale a Firenze. Spettacolo e Musica nella Firenze medicea*, catalogo della mostra, Milan
1980 S. Romagnoli-E. Garbero eds., *Teatro a Reggio Emilia*, Florence
1980 L. Zorzi ed., *La scena del Principe. Firenze e la Toscana dei Medici nell'Europa del Cinquecento*, exhibition catalogue, Florence
1980 L. Zorzi, *Il teatro e la città*, Turin
1983 F. Cruciani, *Teatro del Rinascimento*. Rome, 1450-1550
1983 M. Pieri, *La scena boschereccia nel Rinascimento Italiano*, Padua
1983 F. Ruffini, *I teatri prima del teatro. Visioni dell'edificio e della scena tra Umanesimo e Rinascimento*, Rome

Festivals

1608 C. Rinuccini, *Descrittione delle feste fatte nelle nozze de' Ser.mi Principi di Toscana Cosimo de' Medici e Maria Maddalena d'Austria*, Eredi G. Rossi, Bologna
1956-75 J. Jacquot ed., *Les Fêtes de la Renaissance*, Paris
1961 E.D. James, *Seasonal Feasts and Festivals*, New York
1964 K. Thomas, *Work and Leisure in Pre-Industrial Society*, "Past and Present", 29: 50-62
1969 G. Gaeta Bertelà – A. Petrioli Tofani eds., *Feste e apparati medicei da Cosimo I a Cosimo II*, exhibition catalogue, Florence
1971 J. Heers, *Fêtes, jeux et joutes dans les societés d'Occident à la fin du moyen âge*, Montreal
1977 M. Fagiolo Dell'Arco-S. Carandini, *L'effimero barocco. Strutture delle festa nella Roma del'600*, Rome

Jousting and hunting

1946 M. Tosi, *Il torneo di Belvedere in Vaticano e i tornei in Italia nel Cinquecento*, Rome
1960 G. Boccia ed., *La caccia e le arti*, Florence
1965 G. Innamorati ed., *Arte della caccia*, Milan
1967 L.G. Boccia – E.T. Coelho, *L'arte dell'Armatura in Italia*, Milan
1967 L.G. Boccia, *Nove secoli di armi da caccia*, Florence
1975 L.G. Boccia-E.T. Coelho, *Armi bianche italiane*, Milan

Funerals

1899 P. Caffaro, *Tombe e funerali di principe di Savoia e di Savoia-Acaia in Piemonte*, Pinerolo
1960 R.E. Giesey, *The Royal Funeral Ceremony in Renaissance France*, Geneva

Saints and the court

1777 Anon., *Vita della beata Beatrice seconda d'Este*, Ferrara
1903 G. Parpagnoli, *Ribelle di Dio: san Luigi Gonzaga*, Milan
1949 A. Magnaguti, *La beata Osanna degli Andreasi*, Padua
1981 C. Corradini-W. Pratissoli, *Correggio e san Quirino: un culto tra storia e letteratura*, Modena
1984 G. Calvi, *Storie di un anno di peste* (P.II: Domenica da Paradiso), Milan

Astrology and religious syncretism

1958 S. Samek Ludovici, *Il 'De sphaera' estense e l'iconografia astrologica*, Milan
1961 E. Garin, *La cultura filosofica del Rinascimento italiano*, Florence
1971 E. Wind, *Misteri pagani del Rinascimento*, Milan
1979 A. Parronchi, *Il cielo notturno della Sacrestia vecchia di San Lorenzo*, Florence
1981 J. Seznec, *La sopravvivenza degli antichi dèi*, Turin

Conspiracies

L. Cobelli, *Cronache forlivesi dalla fondazione della città all'anno 1498*, in *Monumenti storici pertinenti alle PP della Romagna* (fifteenth century) G. Carducci-E. Fati eds., I, Bologna 1874
Giovanni di Messer Pedrino dipintore, *Cronaca* (fifteenth century) L. Borghesi-M. Vattusso eds., Vatican City 1934
Poliziano, *De coniuratione pactiana commentarii (Della congiura dei Pazzi)*, (fifteenth century) ed. Padova 1958
G. Gosellini, *Congiura di Piacenza contro Pier Luigi Farnese* (sixteenth century), Florence 1864
1503 B. Corio, *Patria historia* Apud A. Minutianum, Mediolani (*Storia di Milano*, A. Morisi Guerra ed., Turin 1978)
1503 A. Dati, *Opere*, Nardi, Siena
1531 N. Machiavelli, *Discorsi sopra la prima deca di Tito Livio*, Blado, Rome
1544 G. Simonetta, *Istoria di Francesco Sforza*, Bartolomeo detto l'Imperador, Vinegia
1565 C. Porzio, *La congiura dei baroni*, Manuzio, Rome
1864 F. Odorici, *Pier Luigi Farnese e la congiura piacentina del 1547*, Milan
1864 A. Cappelli, *La congiura dei Pio signori di Carpi contro Borso d'Este*, "Atti e Mem. della Dep. di SP, Modena", II: 367-416
1878 A. Bertolotti, *La morte di Pier Luigi Farnese. Processo e lettere inedite*, "Atti e Mem. della R. Dep. di SP per le PP dell'Emilia", n.s., III,1:25-53
1894 G. Capasso, *"Lamento" per la morte di Pier Luigi Farnese*, Parma (attr. to Marquis Camillo Fogliani Sforza)
1899 G. Curti, *La congiura contro Pier Luigi Farnese*, Milan
1899 E. Casanova, *L'uccisione di Galeazzo Maria Sforza e alcuni documenti fiorentini*, "Arch. st. lombardo", XXVI, 12:299-332
1926 E. Perito, *La congiura dei baroni e il conte di Policastro, con l'edizione completa e critica dei sonetti di G.A. de Petruccis*, Bari
1977 E. Pontieri, *La politica mediceo-fiorentina nella congiura dei baroni napoletani contro Ferrante d'Aragona, 1485-1492. Documenti inediti*, Naples
1980 R. Villari, *La rivolta antispagnola di Napoli. Le origini, 1585-1647*, Rome-Bari
1981 O. Ranum, *The French Ritual of Tyrannicide in the late Sixteenth Century*, "The Sixteenth Century Journal", XI:63-81

Index

Picture sources

The abbreviations a, b, c, r, l, refer to the position of the illustration on the page (above, below, center, right, left).

Photographers and agencies

Jörg P. Anders, 171bl
Federico Arborio Mella, Milan, 52ar, 130, 140ar, 140cr, 140br, 142
Artothek, (Joachin Blauel), 171ar
Raffaello Bencini, Florence, 128ar, 129b, 138bl, 139
Giorgio Calzolari, Mantua, 17b
Angelo Ceresa, Parma, 2, 25b, 72, 73, 89a
Giancarlo Costa, Milan, 19, 44ar, 70, 74, 109al, 116, 121bl, 124, 161, 172, 174, 175, 180-181, 192a, 193, 233
Paolo Dalmasso, Florence, 6, 12b, 13c, 32b, 40a, 53ar, 53br, 58, 59, 63, 71al, 71ar, 102, 120cl, 120bl, 190b
Deltaprint, Verona, 38, 80a
Di Marzo, Milan, 236
Fotocielo, Rome, 225a
Fototeca Storica Nazionale, Milan, 110a, 120br, 191, 192b, 218a, 221, 238
Fratelli Fabbri Editori, Milan, 115, 244a, 245
Nicola Ghini, Florence, 80b
Giovetti, Mantua, 89b, 92, 93, 137a, 171al, 215, 217, 239
Photographie Giraudon, Paris, 87b, 90
Glam 2003, Bergamo, 173
Grassi, 71br
Lucchetti, Bergamo, 9
McGraw-Hill, archives, 110b (B.B. Heim), 111
Foto Moderna, Urbino, 86, 87al, 87ar
N.Y. Historical Society, 163a
Ottfried Neubecker, 112cd
Toni Niccolini, Milan, 15, 24, 25a, 53al, 60, 61, 64, 66, 67, 81, 82, 83, 84, 85, 104c, 104b, 105, 112a, 112bl, 247
Nimatallah, 103
Piero Orlandi, Milan, 57
Mario Paltrinieri, Milan, 240, 241
Rocco Pedicini, Naples, 51
Donato Pineider, Florence, 146, 147
Giovan Battista Pineider, Florence, 131
Publifoto, Palermo, 47cl
Luisa Ricciarini, photographic agency, Milan, 31, 76, 95, 106, 107, 114a, 118b, 119, 125, 170, 179, 180b, 188, 200al, 206, 207, 208, 209, 210, 211a, 220a
Guido Sansoni, Florence, 100ar, 100cr, 100br, 101bl, 108, 109ar, 109b, 134a, 135a, 136, 140l, 149, 150, 152, 153, 154, 155, 160, 163b, 169a, 182, 183, 198a
Scala, Istituto Fotografico Editoriale, Florence, 21, 28, 42, 43a, 44al, 69br, 78, 88, 99, 118a, 122, 216, 228, 232
Enrico Valeriani, Rome, 43b, 45b
Vallecchi Editore, 13ar
Augusto Viggiano, Bologna, 22a
Foto Villani, 205
Photographic archives Arnoldo Mondadori Editore, 8, 13al, 14 (Del Grande), 16, 17a (W. Mori), 22b, 23, 32a (W. Mori), 33, 34, 36b, 37b, 40b, 44b, 45a, 48a, 49ar, 49br (Monti), 50a (Panicucci), 50b (Alinar), 52al, 52bl, 52br (Alinari), 53bl (Alinari), 55, 56a (Saporetti, 56b, 57a (M. De Biasi), 62a (Panicucci), 62b (Mongini), 65 (Arte e Colore), 75 (Alinari), 79, 97, 98, 100al, 100bl, 101al, 120a, 121ar, 121br, 126 (Savio), 138r, 157 (M. De Biasi), 158, 164-165, 168 (Rampazzi), 176bc, 176br, 177al, 177bc (Alinari), 177ar (Alinari), 177br, 186, 187, 190a, 194, 195, 198b, 200b, 201 (Lucchetti), 204c, 204b, 205al, 212b (Lunel), 213b (Lunel), 220b (Alinari), 222al, 222ar, 222bl, 222br, 223, 224a (M. De Biasi), 224b, 225b (Cianetti), 226 (Chomon-Perino), 227 (Alinari), 231, 234l (Alinari), 234r, 237, 242, 244b (Alinari), 246a, 246b (Alinari), 248, 249, 250 (W. Mori), 251 (W. Mori), 252, 253, 254, 255, 264l (Alinari), 264r (Alinari), 264c (Dani), 265r (Alinari), 266l, 266c, 268l (Alinari), 268r (Anderson), 270r (Gentilini), 270l (Lunel)

Museums, libraries and collections

Accademia Carrara, Bergamo, 11b, 34a, 94, 264r
Alte Pinakothek, Munich, 171ar
Amministrazione Provinciale di Firenze, 128, 129b, 138bl, 141, 184, 185
Archivio Fotografico del Castello Sforzesco, Milan, 129a, 177ac
Archivio di Stato, Milan, 116
Archivio di Stato, Naples, 115a
Archivio di Stato, Parma, 134b, 144, 145b
Archivio di Stato, Siena, 176a
Attingham Park, Courtesy of the National Trust, 11a
Biblioteca Ambrosiana, Milan, 178
Biblioteca Comunale Ariostea, Ferrara, 166, 167, 252
Biblioteca Capitolare del Duomo, Milan, 195b
Biblioteca Civica, Bergamo, 173
Biblioteca Civica, Ferrara, 135b, 148
Biblioteca Comunale, Mantua, 137a
Biblioteca Estense, Modena, 35, 96, 180-181, 242, 262
Biblioteca Marucelliana, Florence, 149
Biblioteca Medicea Laurenziana, Florence, 200ar
Biblioteca Moreniana, Florence, 146, 147, 152, 198a
Biblioteca Nazionale Braidense, Milan, 140ar, 140cr, 140br
Biblioteca Nazionale Centrale, Florence, 48b, 49ar, 104a, 119r, 155, 162, 180b, 183a
Biblioteca Palatina, Parma, 145a
Biblioteca Piccolomini, Siena, 76
Biblioteca S. Ambrogio, Milan, 19a
Staatsbibliothek, Munich, Milan, 47a
Biblioteca Trivulziana, Milan, 161, 177al, 186, 192b, 236, 255, 264c
Bibliothèque Nationale, Paris, 10, 20, 26, 114b
British Museum, London, 115b
Caisse Nationale des Monuments Historiques et des Sites, Paris, 41
Civica Raccolte Stampe Bertarelli, Milan, 13b, 36a, 37a, 101cr, 101br, 132cr, 133cl, 137b, 151, 214
Collegio Borromeo, Pavia, 233
Collezione Thyssen Bornemisza, 117
Collezione Scotti-Casanova, Rome, 95
Collezione Trivulzio, Milan, 121bl
Comune di Ferrara, 235
Gabinetto Disegni e Stampe degli Uffizi, Florence, 136, 138al, 140al, 143, 150, 153, 154, 156, 163b, 169a, 182, 183b
Gabinetto Fotografico Soprintendenza Beni Artistici e Storici di Firenze, 18, 176bl, 230
Galleria dell'Accademia, Florence, 250
Istituto di Belle Arti, Siena, 142
Kunsthistorisches Museum, Vienna, 46, 47b
Metropolitan Museum of Art, New York, 196
Musée Condé, Chantilly, 179
Musée National du Louvre, Cabinet des dessins, Paris, 125
Musée National du Louvre, Paris, 17a, 34b, 90
Museo degli Argenti, Florence, 28, 29, 170, 209, 212a, 212c, 213a
Museo Capodimonte, Naples, 31
Museo del Castello Sforzesco, Milan, 33, 206b
Museo Firenze com'era, Florence, 218b
Museo Mediceo, Florence, 219
Museo Nazionale del Bargello, Florence, 120cl, 120bl, 160, 207, 244a, 245, 264l
Museo delle Pietre Dure, 210
Museo Poldi Pezzoli, Milan, 211b
Museo del Prado, Madrid, 103
Museo di San Marco, Florence, 232
Museo S. Martino, Naples, 54-55
Museo di Storia della Scienza, Florence, 118b, 119l
Nationalmuseum, Stockholm, 199, 204a
Oesterreichische Nationalbibliothek, Vienna, 133
Palazzo Borromeo, Milan, 197
Palazzo Braschi, Rome, 169b
Pierpont Morgan Library, New York, 71bl
Pinacoteca Ambrosiana, Milan, 176br
Pinacoteca di Brera, Milan, 16, 177bl
Pinacoteca Vaticana, Rome, 244b
Réunion des Musées Nationaux, Paris, 91, 123, 222cl, 226r
Soprintendenza ai Monumenti e alle Gallerie, Bari, 49cl, 49bl
Staatliche Museen Preussischer Kulturbesitz, Berlin, 171bl
Vatican, Rome, 42, 43, 44, 45, 122, 228